"The penetrating essays in this book analyze Bultmann's theology, applauding its strengths while also criticizing its weaknesses. This is a richly rewarding volume that newly assesses the ongoing significance of Bultmann for contemporary New Testament theology."

—Donald A. Hagner, *George Eldon Ladd Professor Emeritus of New Testament, Fuller Theological Seminary*

"In *Beyond Bultmann*, leading New Testament scholars are trenchant in their criticisms of Bultmann's theological interpretation of the New Testament, but succeed brilliantly in clarifying Bultmann's aims and achievements. *Beyond Bultmann* shows the possibilities and pitfalls of a traditional discipline now capable of addressing a more secular audience."

—Rev. Robert Morgan, *Fellow of Linacre College, University of Oxford*

"*Beyond Bultmann* points out the continuing importance of engaging and evaluating Bultmann as interpreter of the New Testament—in all of his historical, exegetical, and theological strengths and weaknesses. There is no better resource for this task than this critical and constructive study."

—Michael J. Gorman, *Raymond E. Brown Professor of Biblical Studies and Theology, St. Mary's Seminary & University, Baltimore*

Beyond Bultmann

Reckoning a
New Testament Theology

Bruce W. Longenecker
Mikeal C. Parsons
Editors

BAYLOR UNIVERSITY PRESS

© 2014 by Baylor University Press
Waco, Texas 76798-7363

Cover design by Hollis Duncan
Cover image: Codex Sinaiticus © The British Library Board, All Rights Reserved, ADD.43725 f257v

Library of Congress Cataloging-in-Publication Data

Beyond Bultmann : reckoning a New Testament theology / Bruce W. Longenecker and Mikeal C. Parsons, editors.
  382 pages cm
  Includes bibliographical references and index.
  ISBN 978-1-4813-0041-4 (pbk. : alk. paper)
  1. Bultmann, Rudolf, 1884–1976. Theologie des Neuen Testaments. 2. Bible. New Testament—Theology. I. Longenecker, Bruce W., editor of compilation.
  BS2397.B49 2014
  230'.0415--dc23

                                2013050294

CONTENTS

EDITORS' PREFACE

Rudolf Bultmann was a very lucky man. In the early second century, Pliny the Younger defined "lucky people" as "those with the divinely-given gift either of doing something worth writing about or writing something worth reading." To this, he then added the following note: "Luckiest of all are those who have done both" (*Letters* 6.16.3). If it is acceptable to articulate the importance of a person in terms of "luck," then clearly Rudolf Bultmann should be included among the category of people whom Pliny calls the "luckiest of all," since even today his publications are both worth reading and worth writing about.

Perhaps it is preferable to abandon the category of luck altogether, in which case the words of Ernst Käsemann make much the same point. Rudolf Bultmann, he said, will continue to "be studied and have influence when even the names of Bultmann's contemporary opponents are scarcely remembered."[1] This may be particularly true with regard to Bultmann's monumental *Theology of the New Testament*, with its many contributions to the study of the New Testament and early Christian origins, to theological hermeneutics, and to biblical theology. Seven decades after its publication, Bultmann's *Theology of the New Testament* may have waned in comparison to its initial influence back in the mid-twentieth century, but it is still selling more copies per year than many books hot off the press.

The book is, of course, such a tour de force, so powerful in its thesis and so demanding in its challenge, that engaging with it requires insight and awareness about what we are getting into when we open its covers. The rabbis of old warned that studying the mysteries of the divine throne room was both important and dangerous, and that only people with maturity of years and character should explore those perilous mysteries. Something similarly might be said to a lesser degree of the study of Bultmann. He cannot simply be left behind; he is too much of a theological and exegetical giant to relegate him to the past. But to what extent can we move forward in relation to the powerful influences he has exerted within New Testament studies?

That is, in essence, what this book explores. Writing about Bultmann's *Theology of the New Testament* is the assignment undertaken by the scholars who have kindly agreed to contribute to this book despite their own busy schedules – each one a leading New Testament scholar with the gravitas to engage with someone of Bultmann's stature and with a sterling command of the field in which he or she has been asked to contribute.

Most of the contributors were asked to engage with a single chapter of Bultmann's *Theology of the New Testament* (although in the case of Bultmann's chapters on Johannine theology, two contributors engage with selected themes from those chapters). Their task was not to assemble an overview of publications that have appeared since Bultmann's day, but to reflect on the viability of Bultmann's contribution in light of developments within New Testament studies since that time. They were not asked to shape their reflections in relation to a structural template, nor to conform to a single interpretation of Bultmann and comply with specified percentages of commendation or criticism when analyzing his case. As reflected in the essays of this book, each contributor has his or her own view of Bultmann's strengths and weaknesses at any particular point in Bultmann's argument. What unites them all, beyond their obvious reputation as leading voices in New Testament scholarship, is not an enforced uniformity of voice but an interest in engaging with Bultmann afresh in relation to their own perception of the issues covered in his *Theology of the New Testament*.

This book comprises, then, thirteen essays. The eleven essays of part 1 ("Bultmann by the Book") follow the sequence of Bultmann's *Theology of the New Testament* and address issues that lie at the heart of his presentation. The two essays included in part 2 ("Bultmann in History and Theology") help to put Bultmann in context. The first of these two final essays outlines the historical context in which Bultmann wrote his *Theology of the New Testament* and assesses the extent to which historical issues of his day fed into his presentation of issues. The second offers an overview of Bultmann's theological project as it pertains to his *Theology of the New Testament.* We have placed these excellent essays at the back of the book, where they play more of a synthetic role in bringing together various points discussed along the way in the chapter-by-chapter analyses. Some readers, however, might prefer to begin their reading with those two essays, which can serve more as an introduction to the volume since they paint broad canvases against which the individual chapters of the book can be read.

In the immediate aftermath of the publication of Bultmann's *Theology of the New Testament,* John Reumann estimated that "while Bultmann may not be giving all the right answers, he is certainly asking significant questions."[2] What we have in this collection of essays is a group of first-rate veteran scholars who offer their own reflections on the questions Bultmann was exploring, on the answers that he gave, and on the way ahead in relation to both. What Bultmann once said of many of his critics cannot be said of the scholars who are included in this volume: "It is incredible how many people pass judgment on my work without having read a word of it. . . . I have sometimes asked the grounds for a writer's verdict, and which of my writings he has read. The answer has regularly been, without exception, that he has not read any of my writings."[3] Readers of *Beyond Bultmann* will find a collection of essays by scholars who have, in fact, read Bultmann, who have read him closely, carefully, and critically, and who have important things to say about Bultmann's weighty contributions. Bultmann's *Theology of the New Testament* does not deserve to become a treasure trove to be raided for the odd quotation here or there. Instead, it deserves to be read carefully and for profit within the guild of New Testament scholarship. But if it is something worth reading and worth writing about, we must do so with a critical eye. It is the hope of the editors and contributors of this volume that Bultmann's *Theology of the New Testament* will continue to be read, not raided, but that the reading of his important book will be enhanced by a critical and informed engagement with it.

* * *

Several further points require brief mention. First, among the contributors and editors of this book, no one is receiving royalties or payment for his or her efforts. Instead, all the proceeds from sales of this book are being donated to a worthy charity titled "Toilet Twinning." In the Babylonian Talmud, a Jew enamored with the teaching of Jesus advised that, from what he knew of Jesus, it would be acceptable to Jesus for a prostitute's tainted money to be accepted by Temple functionaries and used to do good by purchasing a toilet for the High Priest ('Abodah Zarah 17a). Although the analogy is not precise, all proceeds from sales of this book will be used to do good by purchasing much needed toilets for people who are financially disadvantaged in economically developing countries. For more information about the charity, see ToiletTwinning.org.

Second, the editors wish to thank the following people for their contributions to this volume: our assistant Peter Rice for his stellar editorial work, and Mark Biddle (the Russell T. Cherry Professor of Old Testament at the Baptist Theological Seminary at Richmond) for his translations (from German to English) of the essays by Jörg Frey, Udo Schnelle, and Angela Standhartinger. Since this work was supported in part by funds from the Department of Religion and the Office of the Vice Provost for Research at Baylor University, we express our gratitude for the strong support that we both enjoy from our home institution.

Third, the editors would like to dedicate this volume to N. T. (Tom) Wright and Beverly Roberts Gaventa, who, even in their differences, have written much that is "worth reading" and "worth writing about."

PART I

BULTMANN BY THE BOOK

Chapter 1

THE MESSAGE OF JESUS

Samuel Byrskog

Bultmann's Two Studies of the Historical Jesus

Rudolf Bultmann published two studies of the historical Jesus, namely, the book *Jesus* in 1926 and the first chapter of his *Theology of the New Testament* in 1953.[1] Both of them focus on Jesus' message, not his person.

The *Jesus* book has four chapters. The first, "Der zeitgeschichtliche Rahmen des Auftretens Jesu" ("The Historical Context of the Ministry of Jesus"), examines Jewish religion, messianic movements, and John the Baptist. Central to Jewish religion was belief in election; this belief fed apocalyptic hopes and was, according to Bultmann, coupled with obedience, sometimes to the extent that scribal Judaism stressed obedience at the cost of apocalyptic. After being a disciple of John the Baptist, Jesus became known as a messianic prophet and was, like the Baptist, executed as such.

The second chapter, "Jesu Verkündigung: Das Kommen der Gottesherrschaft" ("Jesus' Proclamation: The Coming of the Kingdom"), has sections on the call to salvation and repentance, on the kingdom of God, on universalism and individualism and dualism and pessimism, and on the future and the present time of decision. Bultmann stresses here the eschatological dimension of Jesus' message and suggests that Jesus and his followers went to Jerusalem to welcome the kingdom. The future was at hand and forced people to decision. Jesus' activity

3

was a sign of its coming and his message a call for decision to make repentance. This salvation was mainly for the Jewish people of God.

The third chapter focuses on Jesus as teacher under the rubric "Jesu Verkündigung: Der Wille Gottes" ("Jesus' Proclamation: The Will of God"). It discusses Jesus as rabbi, the authority that he attributed to Scripture, the Jewish ethic of obedience, Jesus' demand for obedience, the possibility to comprehend that demand fully, ascetics and worldview, the love command, and the will of God and the coming of his kingdom. Although Jesus associated with people outside the scribal circles, he appeared as a Jewish rabbi, acknowledged the authority of Old Testament law, and affirmed genuine Jewish practices. His instruction differed from other Jewish teaching in that he did not assert the formal authority of the law and the obedience of each commandment but sought, like some rabbis, to restore its original intention and its central concern of true obedience to God's will as it becomes evident for each person at the moment he or she stands before God in a situation of decision. Rather than insisting on ascetic behavior, Jesus taught the willingness to sacrifice in view of God's demands. The love commandment, which Bultmann believed played a minor role in Jesus' teaching, is the power to overcome one's own will, not an ethical program. In its double form it makes real the bond between humans on the basis of their obedience to God. That obedience is related to the eschatological situation of God's kingdom and expresses itself as readiness for the kingdom and acceptance of God's demands at the moment of decision.

In the final chapter, "Jesu Verkündigung: Der ferne und der nahe Gott" ("Jesus' Proclamation: The Remote and Near God"), Bultmann treats the Jewish concept of God, the eschatological future, God's providence, theodicy, miracles, prayer, faith, God as father, the remoteness and nearness of God, and sin and forgiveness. Like other Jews, Jesus believed in God the Creator who is both remote and close (just as he is, in a paradoxical sense, the God of both the future and the present), and in him who cares for his people, regardless of the laws of nature and in the face of human suffering. This paradoxical belief became evident in Jesus' conviction that miraculous events are linked to divine (or demonic) causality, and he himself performed miracles as a sign of the coming of God's kingdom and the presence of the remote God in the world. This belief was also evident in the idea that prayer influences the almighty God. Jesus called his conviction about miracles and prayer "faith," and he approached God, as did other Jews of his day, as father. According to Bultmann, the paradox of the remote and near God was manifest in Jesus' teaching on divine forgiveness, because here the distant Creator forgoes his rightful claims on the things that belong to him and instead becomes existentially close to the person who recognizes and hears the call to decision based on these claims. Jesus brought this mystery to human beings, not through his death and resurrection, but through his word.

More than two decades later Bultmann addressed again the problem of the historical Jesus in the first chapter of his *Theology*. This time he did not call his study *Jesus*, not even within quotation marks as he occasionally did earlier, but "Die Verkündigung Jesu" ("The Proclamation of Jesus"), immediately indicating that he did not intend to discuss Jesus' person.

Also, this time Bultmann divides his discussion into four sections, but with some differences in content and emphasis. After a few remarks about Jesus' message as a presupposition for the theology of the New Testament and about the Synoptic Gospels as sources, presupposing the two-source hypothesis and building on his revised study of the history of the synoptic tradition,[2] he turns to what he labels "Die eschatologische Verkündigung" ("The Eschatological Proclamation"), leaving out a separate discussion of the Jewish background of Jesus' message. This section is similar to the second chapter of his book *Jesus*, although much briefer. Bultmann stresses here the influence of Jewish apocalyptic hopes on the dominant concepts of Jesus' proclamation of the impending, miraculous coming of God's eschatological kingdom. Jesus' words and deeds were signs of its dawning, and his entire activity was a call to decision for or against it, to the extent that his person, while not the object of faith, signified this call.

The second section is titled "Die Auslegung der Forderung Gottes" ("The Interpretation of the Demand of God") and corresponds to the third chapter of his earlier book. Now somewhat more reserved regarding the notion that Jesus appeared as a Jewish rabbi, Bultmann emphasizes that Jesus' interpretation of the demand of God was a protest against Jewish legalism—much like the Old Testament prophets reacted against formalized cultic worship but with the difference that Jesus reacted against formal obedience to the law and abolished cultic and ritual regulations in order to set human beings free for a true relationship to God. According to Bultmann, Jesus never denied the legitimacy of the Old Testament and Jewish practices. He differed from the scribes only in his interpretation of Scripture, leaving aside its cultic and ritual prescriptions and protesting against practices reflecting personal vanity and legalistic ritualism. The demand to love neighbor and God surpassed all other requirements and made human beings responsible to God. The unity of this ethical teaching and the message about God's kingdom became evident in the notion of the fulfillment of God's will in terms of readiness for the kingdom and as a condition for participation in salvation. For this reason Jesus' message was, according to Bultmann, a cry to the Jewish people of woe and repentance.

The third section, "Der Gottesgedanke Jesu" ("Jesus' Concept of God"), focuses on Jesus' prophetic consciousness of living at the end time and also on the idea of God as the Creator who is at hand with judgment and forgiveness. Jesus believed (in distinction to the prophets) that this divine presence had to do with individuals to the extent that the relationship between God and humans was released from its ties to history (*entgeschichtlicht*) and that God and individuals were freed from the world (*entweltlicht*). This "dehistorization" and "desecularization" constituted the paradox that the God who is distant has come close to each person.

The final section, "Die Frage nach dem messianischen Selbstbewusstsein Jesu" ("The Issue of Jesus' Self-Understanding"), has no counterpart in Bultmann's earlier book. In that book Bultmann dealt, as we saw, with messianic movements and concluded that Jesus died as a messianic prophet.[3] Now, in a chapter dealing with the message of Jesus, Bultmann enters into a debate about Jesus' self-consciousness and makes a negative case, arguing that Jesus' life and work were not messianic in the traditional sense, that Jesus did not reinterpret the traditional concept of the Messiah, and that he was not conscious of his destiny as the future Messiah or the Suffering Servant. William Wrede had conclusively shown, according to Bultmann, that the notion of the messianic secret was created at a time when early Christians no longer found Jesus' unmessianic life conceivable.[4]

Scholarly Reactions

This brings us up to speed on the message of Jesus according to Bult-mann. Although different, his two studies show a basic continuity that points to the core of his convictions about the historical Jesus.

His proposals have been widely discussed, endorsed, and rejected, sometimes in direct exchange with him, sometimes indirectly. To some extent the debate concerns how we evaluate the synoptic tradition. Bultmann had studied it thoroughly and partly built on his previous results.[5] If those results are challenged, a different picture of the historical Jesus may emerge.[6] It is, for instance, curious that while Bultmann in his work on the historical Jesus and elsewhere paid much attention to human existence as experienced from the perspective of individuals, in his study of the synoptic tradition he stressed the creative force of the community and neglected to account for what eye-witnesses and other individuals experienced in their direct or indirect encounter with Jesus. Generally speaking, his form-critical program has today lost its grip, and new ways of handling the synoptic tradition and assessing the historicity of the Jesus tradition are emerging.[7]

Rather than rehearsing the debate regarding the so-called second quest of the historical Jesus, I will select a few aspects of that debate to indicate some reactions to Bultmann's account of Jesus' message in contemporary scholarship. One basic feature that has been largely endorsed is his idea of the eschatological and prophetic character of Jesus' message. Bultmann combined a view of Jesus that regarded him as both prophet and teacher (putting primary emphasis on the former) and synthesized two aspects of him that had been held separate and formed the basis of controversy in Jesus research at the beginning of the last century. Today's scholarship does not contest the eschatological dimension of Jesus' message.[8]

Another major aspect of his study has been rejected, however—namely, his sketch of Jewish legalism and Jesus' stance toward it. Although Bultmann was cautious to place Jesus within the tradition of the Old Testament prophets and regarded him as fully Jewish, never giving in to attempts to distance him from his Jewishness,[9] he imposed a development on ancient Israelite religion that implied that it moved toward an increasing legalism, and he distanced the core of Jesus' innovative message from typical Jewish beliefs and practices.

Bultmann's views were not unusual at the time, but they have been decisively questioned through the appreciation of the covenantal ramifications of common Judaism, which places the observance of the law within a context of God's merciful election, as well as of the pluralism of Jewish piety and practices, including the complex ethnic character of lower Galilee.[10]

Other ideas in Bultmann's account recur in modified forms. His argument that Jesus proclaimed a call for decision has lost its existential dimension, and scholars avoid his terminology for the individual's response to the eschatological situation. Yet the notion of repentance is still central. Although many recognize that the sources do not abound in references to repentance,[11] and that the accounts in the double tradition that do mention it deal with the repentance of towns rather than individuals (Matt 11:21/Luke 10:13; Matt 12:41/Luke 11:32), they also realize that several parables illustrate how Jesus called fellow Jews to return to the Lord. Just as scholars hold on to the view that Jesus required national and individual repentance in view of the impending kingdom, Bultmann was convinced that he called people to decision for or against it.

Bultmann's early conviction that Jesus was a rabbi is today expressed with caution, because we have realized that the term "rabbi" and its equivalents in the Gospels cannot refer back to a trained Torah teacher before 70 C.E.[12] Yet Greek didactic designations are applied to Jesus and his activity in the Gospels and make it reasonable to believe that he appeared as a Torah teacher without formal education. The pertinent question concerns what kind of Torah teacher he was. Bultmann's focus on the love command as the only real requirement before God is now questioned in view of Jesus' thorough Jewishness, which would have required appreciation of the Torah in its entirety.[13] Most scholars agree, however, that it was Jesus' own teaching that resulted in the importance attached to the love command in the Jesus tradition and earliest Christianity.

The proposal that Jesus was never the object of faith is today taken for granted. Scholars recognize with Bultmann that the faith that Jesus asked for was trust in his miraculous powers and in God. To that effect, Jesus is mostly seen as the medium of God's power to those who have confidence in God. However, although Bultmann refrained from making Jesus' person central for the coming of the kingdom, he did regard him as an "eschatological phenomenon" and thus implicitly admitted that he claimed an eschatological empowering for his mission. Bultmann's position on this question has today been modified by scholars who consider it likely that Jesus regarded his own person as more instrumental for the coming of the kingdom.

In particular, two aspects of Bultmann's study suggest a greater appreciation for Jesus' person than he admitted—namely, his discussion of God as father and (somewhat paradoxically) Jesus' nonmessianic claims and references to another Son of Man. Bultmann's argument that Jesus thought of God as a loving and caring father has received clearer contours. It is not without reason that Jesus' practice of addressing God as *abba* has been seen as one of the clear results of modern scholarship.[14] We might differ in our understanding of its implications, but the term *abba* seems to have suggested a special relationship to God and sense of authority to proclaim his kingdom.

It might be possible even to propose that Jesus looked forward to a divine vindication of himself. The question concerning Jesus' messianic consciousness has not been resolved, despite Bultmann's admiration for Wrede's study. The present debate has become more subtle due to the fact that anointing was a diversified practice relevant for kings, priests, and prophets alike and the argument that Jesus was executed as a messianic prophet on the basis of what he said and did,[15] as Bultmann had noted.

However, in his *Theology* Bultmann links the negative argument about Jesus' messianic consciousness to the expression Son of Man. Virtually no one today would endorse Bultmann's idea that Jesus spoke of another, future Son of Man and that Jesus for that reason did not think of himself as a Messiah. Although the debate continues,[16] scholarship has realized that the expression "Son of Man" was in some sense Jesus' self-designation. We might, somewhat surprisingly, detect a remote echo of Bultmann when scholars today combine the general and the self-referential uses of the underlying Aramaic idiom and argue that Jesus used it to refer to "a man like me." If we also recognize the importance of the tradition emerging from Dan 7:13, as is often done, it is possible to assume that Jesus applied the hopes of vindication to his own fate.[17] To be sure, this expression is kept separate from the motif of God's kingdom, and the prominence of it on Jesus' lips does not give direct evidence of his role in the eschatological drama.

Nevertheless, its relation to Dan 7:13 might indicate a vindication in connection with dominion and kingship.

Bultmann denied that Jesus considered his suffering and death as instrumental for the coming of the kingdom, and scholarship is still divided on this issue. The vindication that might be implied in Jesus' use of the expression "Son of Man" does not necessarily suggest a special significance attached to suffering and death but only that Jesus thought they would lead to a better time. Most scholars realize that Jesus did not die because of his disagreements with the Pharisees, seeing his provocative actions toward the Jewish leadership in the temple (coupled with the threat felt from the Roman authorities to their hold over Israel) to be the immediate reason for his execution.[18] To that extent, his death had no deeper meaning connected to his preaching and person.

Yet scholars also consider it likely that Jesus did not go up to Jerusalem only to celebrate Passover but, as Bultmann pointed out, also to welcome the kingdom. His awareness of standing in the tradition of Israel's prophets, as Bultmann also believed he did, might have included a growing consciousness of his martyrdom during the feast.[19] The journey to Jerusalem and the idea of suffering as a prophet indicate that his death was not unforeseen by Jesus himself.

That Jesus, in addition, gave soteriological meaning to his anticipated suffering and death is uncertain. All that can be said with some confidence (and this might be seen as a development of Bultmann's prophetic and eschatological understanding of Jesus' message) is that if he entertained the idea of suffering the death of a martyr, he might have attached a significance to it that meant that it contributed to the ending of Israel's pain. Indications of Jesus' interpretation of his suffering and death as a sacrifice on behalf of others are remote. The two main traditions of the Last Supper agree merely in suggesting that Jesus alluded to his body and to his covenantal blood and looked forward to the eschatological future. The sacrificial interpretation once advocated is no longer secure,[20] only the idea that the supper indicated an eschatological belief in something beyond Jesus' death. Other concepts such as the Suffering Servant could add a dimension indicating that Jesus saw his death as vicarious suffering. On this point, however, the evidence is ambiguous.[21] So, although Bultmann's conviction that Jesus did not attach special significance to his suffering and death has been modified and scholarship today maintains that he saw them as instrumental for the coming of the kingdom, the present state of research confirms the difficulties Bultmann sensed in attributing to Jesus a further, more precise sacrificial and vicarious interpretation of his fatal destiny.

Finally, we should note Bultmann's depiction of the God of Jesus. His conviction that Jesus thought of God as both remote and close to each individual might today be considered as too tightly attached to kerygmatic theology and existential philosophy. The theological and philosophical foundation of Bultmann's interpretation is no longer central, and concepts that more adequately describe the God whom Jesus confessed are preferred. The idea that he believed in an elevated and remote God lives on in the significance scholars attach to Jesus' notion of divine judgment. Similarly, the idea of a God who is close to each person is reinforced through the notion that Jesus trusted in God as a caring father and was convinced of the nearness of God's kingdom and his salvific reign.

Bultmann's Jesus and the So-Called *Historismus*

Bultmann's main purpose for giving his account of the message of the historical Jesus was never purely historical. Discussing the proposals of Bultmann, we often forget that historical reconstruction was not his first priority. He knew how to play by the rules of form criticism and used them to answer questions of historicity. Biblical scholars favoring the historical-critical paradigm like to discuss them (since the way scholars apply those rules is certainly open to criticism), but these proposals were not his most enduring contribution to understanding the message of Jesus.

His first statement in *Theology of the New Testament* is classical: "*The message of Jesus* is a presupposition for the theology of the New Testament rather than a part of that theology itself" (1.3).[22] Several New Testament scholars have here detected a disregard for the historical Jesus and his message due to Bultmann's project of demythologizing the New Testament and his emphasis on the existential encounter with the kerygma and the call to decision. To that effect, his statement and entire theology represent a flight from history.[23]

However, in order to comprehend this statement fully, it is necessary to place Bultmann's presentation of Jesus' message against the background that formed his thinking. His two accounts are very different from the paradigm of historical Jesus research that dominated the field of liberal theology during Bultmann's early years, constituting a reaction against its focus on Jesus' inner life and the reconstruction of history. For reasons that might go back to deeply felt experiences during World War I, Bultmann never gave up his struggle to present a feasible theological alternative to the optimism of historical reconstruction and to propagate a view of history that made clear that the message of the historical Jesus is a presupposition rather than a constitutive element of theology. It is his fight against the so-called *Historismus* that gives depth to his two presentations and his statement at the beginning of his *Theology*.[24]

Bultmann grew up at a time when history was both endorsed as an object to be reconstructed and questioned in view of the difficulties involved in such reconstructions. The confident belief in the power of human reason to establish truth was a widespread effect of the Enlightenment. Among historians, Leopold von Ranke (1795–1886), although not interested in method himself,[25] exercised strong influence in ascertaining the possibility of reconstructing the brute facts of the past. Johann Gustav Droysen (1808–1884), von Ranke's more hermeneutically sensitive colleague in Berlin, spoke of history as a spiritual image of what had happened, formed on the basis of its significance ("ein geistiges Gegenbild des Geschehenen nach seiner Bedeutung"),[26] but his ideas were ignored.

The liberal theologians made historical reconstruction an essential part of theology. Adolf von Harnack (1851–1930) was one of Bultmann's teachers in Berlin. He became a powerful representative of liberal Protestantism, which turned its back on the Christ of dogma and claimed to recover the essence of Christianity through reconstruction of the simplicity and freedom of Jesus.[27] Harnack's older colleagues Albrecht Ritschl (1822–1889) and Wilhelm Herrmann (1846–1922) were other prominent exponents of liberal theology. Bultmann studied systematic theology with Herrmann.

Equally important was the increasing appreciation of the problems involved in historical reconstruction. The charge of the 1896 edition of Martin Kähler's (1835–1912) book was that the sources do not yield the kind of historical information about Jesus that liberal theology requires.[28] Against the liberal life-of-Jesus reconstructions, Kähler insisted that the pictures of Jesus in the Gospels are impregnated with interpretation throughout. All we have is Jesus seen in his significance. Kähler's study, though neglected at first, questioned the close link between historical reconstruction and theology.

Ernst Troeltsch (1865–1923) was a representative of the history of religions school and raised questions about the idea that early Christianity was a decisive religious phenomenon. As much philosopher and theologian as historian, he formulated in 1898 the famous methodological agenda of historical study: criticism, analogy, and correlation. Criticism requires that no evidence is immune from being challenged and can provide only probable results; analogy presupposes that there can be no historical understanding without some similarity between the event under investigation and events that we have experienced ourselves; correlation assumes that events in history are interconnected.[29] The effect of the three principles was that history was relativized, so that it became impossible to identify any one expression of religion as absolute for all others.

History and the Historical Jesus Redefined

Such was the scholarly atmosphere when the young Bultmann published his first study of the historical Jesus in 1926.[30] There were other contributors arguing in a similar direction, most notably Johannes Weiss, Wrede, and Albert Schweitzer,[31] with Weiss and Schweitzer adding an eschatological and apocalyptic understanding of Jesus.

Bultmann was involved in this intellectual transition. Already in 1926 he was moving away from the mode of reconstruction evident in his *Lizentiatsarbeit* (an early graduate dissertation, 1910) and *Habilitation* (a postdoctoral dissertation, 1912).[32] While the former work contributed to the study of literary forms in Paul, the latter revealed his interest in church history. Both fit well within the historical paradigm of the time, as do his other studies from this period.

Rather than continuing with the same kind of analysis, he began working with the synoptic tradition and published in 1921 the first edition of *Die Geschichte der synoptischen Tradition*. The manuscript had been finished two years earlier.[33] Although it was strongly influenced by the scholarship of his teacher Hermann Gunkel, the book indicates new sensitivity to the problem of historical reconstruction and the interconnection between the present time of the kerygma and past history. Inspired by Wrede's questioning of Mark as a historical source and Julius Wellhausen's discussion of the influence of the early Christian communities on the synoptic tradition, he abandoned the historicizing mode of studying the Gospels in favor of reading them from the perspective of the kerygma. It is noteworthy that he planned to introduce this book with reflections on David Friedrich Strauss (1808–1874),[34] presumably on Strauss' concept of myth.[35] It is equally noteworthy that he insisted that traditions from and about the past are used to address the present time of the community and are deeply influenced by those concerns. This does not mean that he denied the pastness of history. It was precisely an evolutionary, diachronic *history* of the synoptic tradition he wrote, and this history moves back and forth between the past and the present dimension of tradition and results in a development from oral simplicity to textual complexity. In the first edition he had not yet developed the notion of the *Sitz im Leben*,[36] but his conviction that the forms of the tradition were shaped by folkloristic and oral currencies opened up a more dynamic view of interaction between the past and the present than the one assumed by scholars who worked only with written sources, and it indicated modes of transmission that made the history of the synoptic tradition into a history of the Church's activities.

Bultmann's book *Jesus* was thus composed shortly after he had established his view of the synoptic tradition and indicated the inextricable influence of the present time of the community on its view of the past. Ernst Baasland describes this time as a move away from Bultmann's "late liberal phase" (*spätliberale* phase) between 1917 and 1922 to his "early dialectical phase" (*frühdialektische* phase) between 1923 and 1926.[37] It might at first appear strange that he now devoted significant attention to the message of the historical Jesus rather than the kerygma of the early Christ believers. Karl Barth, his friend and the most articulate proponent of dialectical theology, was skeptical of his book even before it appeared.[38] But for Bultmann this was the logical step to take.

Bultmann wished to go beyond the mere reconstruction of Jesus' message. In a letter to pastor Hans Roth in Ahlhorn dated September 25, 1928 (two years after the publication of his book), Bultmann explained what he had intended to do: "I have described a 'historical Jesus' not in the sense of *Historismus* (at least this was not my intention) that understands Jesus as a phenomenon of the past, to be sure, but as he speaks to the understanding conditioned by history, which allows itself to be addressed through history and does not place itself in an 'observing' position outside history."[39] The letter indicates Bultmann's distance from *and* involvement in history, but on the basis of an understanding of history that was decisively different from those concepts of history that regarded it as equivalent to historical reconstruction and authenticity. Turning to the introduction of his book, we see a more subtle intention that is in line with his sensitivity to what history is. In the very first paragraph he distances himself from the idea that the historical Jesus is an object to be observed in the past, emphasizing that the study of history inevitably takes place from the perspective of someone living within history. While nature can be observed from a distance, history cannot. There is a dialogue between two occurrences *within* history, namely, the inquiring person and the past events. This dialogue does not take place after the past has been reconstructed; it is the very means of discovering and understanding it. The accusation of ending up in a subjective game with the past misunderstands the dialectical relationship between the past and the present in Bultmann's thinking. The dialogue he envisions involves a sincere questioning of the past, where the past is an authoritative voice.

> This dialogue is not a witty subjective game of the observer but a real historical inquiry where the author of history questions precisely his subjectivity and is prepared to listen to history as an authority. . . . All the things that relate to the observer—all the presuppositions that he brings with him from his time and education and his personal opinions—must be given up precisely here, so that history may really speak. But it will not speak when you close your ears, that is, when you claim to be neutral to it, but only when you approach it with questions and want to learn from it.[40]

This view takes history seriously. The person who refers to methods of historical reconstruction, according to Bultmann, while possibly moving beyond the partiality of each individual scholar, is caught within the subjectivity of the method. Historical objectivity is illusionary.

Bultmann's early book on the historical Jesus inevitably reflects his own encounter with the historical Jesus because the study of history is always personal and takes place within the history of human beings. In this sense it is, according to Bultmann, more objective and historical than those reconstructions that claim to have discovered what happened and to have found the essence of history. While they believe history contains something that goes beyond history, Bultmann argues that all history is bound to time. Therefore, and not because of his skepticism toward the historicity of the synoptic tradition, he abstains from claiming that Jesus went beyond his own time and does not explore Jesus' inner life (*Persönlichkeit*); instead, he focuses solely on Jesus' message.

History and the Historical Jesus as Past and Present

These ideas of the young Bultmann were presented to Martin Heidegger (Bultmann claims to have read the introduction to him) and formed the beginning of their long intellectual exchange.[41] The problem of history followed him throughout his career and formed the background of his famous introduction to his *Theology*. While the message of the historical Jesus can be reconstructed, theology is not bound to the pastness of time or the insecurities of historical reconstruction but addresses the encounter with the past in the historical present. The message of the historical Jesus is therefore theologically relevant only in dialogue with the eschatological now.

Although not lingering on the problem of history in his *Theology*, Bultmann had not given up the ideas of his youth. This problem occupied his thinking from the early 1920s and found its most eloquent expression a few years after the publication of his *Theology* in the Gifford Lectures given in Edinburgh in early 1955 and published with minor additions and references two years later under the title *History and Eschatology*.[42]

In these lectures he traced the view of history from the ancient Greek and Roman historians up to his own time and presented his own synthesis, focusing on the shift from the old cyclical interpretation of history to teleological and eschatological alternatives. Developing and confirming what he indicated in 1926, but now with awareness of the philosophical discussions concerning human existence, Bultmann challenges the purely teleological approach and links together history and eschatology in the historical event of Christ. Because history exists in relation to human existence and can be perceived only from the present time of each individual, the eschatological moment that makes history meaningful is always in the present. "Always in your present lies the meaning in history, and you cannot see it as a spectator, but only in your responsible decisions," he ends.[43]

Five years later Bultmann returned to the question of the historical Jesus and addressed the problem of the relationship between the kerygma and the historical Jesus.[44] Ernst Käsemann (1906–1998) had in 1953 reopened this question. Although not suggesting a legitimation for the kerygma in the historical past, he argued that we must for theological reasons find a recognizable continuity between the preaching *about* Jesus and the preaching *of* Jesus, because the Gospels express their theology in the form of historical narrative to the extent that the proclaimed Christ is present in the eschatological words and deeds of the historical Jesus.[45] Bultmann maintains that the Christ of the kerygma cannot be identified with the historical Jesus, but he also acknowledges the continuity between the eschatological message of Jesus and early Christian preaching. Since Jesus was an "eschatological phenomenon," his message involved Christology, he admits, but this is only to be grasped when the historical-critical approach is extended into an existential meeting with history: "History is an address to it [the historical-critical approach], and it is, so to say, manifested in *hearing*, not in distanced *observance*."[46]

In other words, the past message of Jesus is available only from the perspective of the present, for the early Christians as well as for the modern scholar. It was for this reason that Bultmann's study of Jesus' message could not be anything but a dialogue that moved between the past and the present and heard the voice from the past as a message of the eschatological future of God's kingdom. It was also for this reason that the message of the historical Jesus in itself belonged to the presuppositions of New Testament theology.

A Revival of Bultmann's Jesus?

Bultmann died on July 30, 1976. He had established himself as the leading biblical scholar of the century and made an unparalleled impression on New Testament scholarship and theological hermeneutics. His lifelong discussion of the merging of temporal horizons, beginning in 1926 with his small book *Jesus* and continuing with studies of the message of Jesus and the problem of history, has in unexpected ways recurred in historiographical discussions concerning the hermeneutical negotiations between the past and the present that take place in each encounter with history. Hans-Georg Gadamer attended Bultmann's seminars in Marburg and made the idea of the merging of horizons widely known.[47] Hermeneutically informed scholars realize today that historical facts do not exist in abstraction from interpretation but are available as language-bound perceptions of reality and that the historian participates in the same structure of being as the persons who lived in the past. Influenced by Gadamer, scholars of historiography might speak of history as a living voice with which the historian interacts.[48]

Some scholars would draw the conclusion that the pastness of history is forever lost in the arena of fiction and subjectivity and that the message of the historical Jesus is irretrievable. This was not Bultmann's position. He held, rather, that history is constituted not by facts of the past but by the inquirer's dialogue with them on the basis of certain data and his or her experiences. This view does not deny the possibility of knowing that something existed. It seeks to avoid the epistemological naïveté of historical positivism and argues that the reality of the thing known about the past is something different from the knower but also that the access to it lies along the path of a dialogue between the experience and belief of the scholar and various kinds of data about the past. We might see in Bultmann's thinking an early form of what is today known as "critical realism."[49]

Granting that Bultmann never denied the "historicity of history," we might ponder briefly on the recurrence of similar ways of thinking in recent Jesus research. One of the critiques against Bultmann has been his failure to take into account the role of memory when moving from the Synoptic Gospels back to the message of Jesus and when discussing how the present time interacts with the past in the construction of history. This critique might focus on his silence concerning the memories of eyewitnesses or on his disregard for a theoretically coherent picture of how oral forms were carried from one person or group to another.

Considering Bultmann's emphasis on folkloristic orality and on the collective force of the community as well as on the dialogue between the past and the present, it is surprising that he did not include any discussion of the theories of social or collective memory. These are not recent inventions. The influential sociologists Émile Durkheim (1858–1917) and Maurice Halbwachs (1877–1945) were active during Bultmann's formative years. They had a functionalist perspective on society, which could have helped define the purpose of collective tradition. Durkheim had studied in Germany, including Marburg, and was teaching sociology at Sorbonne from 1902 until his death. Halbwachs, who had also studied in Germany, worked with Durkheim and became professor of sociology at Strasbourg and later (from 1935) at Sorbonne. With the publication of *Les cadres sociaux de la mémoire* in 1925,[50] Halbwachs initiated a line of thought that stressed the collective memory of societies and groups, insisting that all memory, even individual memory, depends upon the "social frameworks" (*cadres sociaux*) within which it is situated. Halbwachs died in Buchenwald in 1945. Five years later his sister Jeanne Alexandre published *La mémoire collective* on the basis of manuscripts found among his papers.[51]

Bultmann shows no awareness of Durkheim and Halbwachs but seems to have developed his view of the synoptic tradition as well as of history without taking into account the mnemonic explanation of how the past enters into and is conquered by the present time of the remembering community. The reasons for this are probably that he developed form criticism on the basis of the work of Gunkel and that his interest in history and Jesus' message was related to the debate with German theology and the *Historismus* and—later—to Heidegger's philosophy. French sociology could not at this time compete with German theology and philosophy.

The current discussion of social and collective memory among scholars of the historical Jesus pays little attention to Bultmann.[52] Yet the historiographical underpinnings of his book *Jesus* and of the first chapter of his *Theology* might receive new attention through the hermeneutical implications of the recent debate about "the remembered Jesus" and provide a link to sociologically informed work with tradition and theology. Taking seriously the notion that the remembered Jesus *is* the historical Jesus (as articulated by Anthony Le Donne),[53] we detect unexpected hermeneutical similarities between Bultmann's philosophical and theological view of history and the present state of some historical Jesus research.

Two such similarities are noteworthy. To begin with, the notion of time inherent in Bultmann's focus on the eschatological present is similar to the idea of "mnemonic time." Bultmann, as we saw, regarded himself and all others to be inevitably imprisoned in time. In theories of social and collective memory, it is common to speak of a "mnemonic negotiation." In her book *Theories of Social Remembering*, the sociologist Barbara Misztal includes a chapter titled "The Dynamics of Memory Approach: Memory as a Process of Negotiation" and discusses the active mediation of temporal meanings of the past, locating memory in the space between an imposed ideology of the present and the possibility of an alternative way of understanding the past.[54] This approach, in short, "stresses the presence of the past in the present through psychological, social, linguistic and political processes."[55]

This insight has similarities to ancient notions of memory and time. Augustine discusses time in relation to memory in books 10 and 11 of his *Confessions*. In order to come to terms with the duration of time, he insists that time past and future does not exist externally to the mind and that the present exists only for the moment. Time is an entity in memory because a person is able to sense the duration of an event or the interval of time in memory, while the present exists by attention and the future by expectation (11.26). According to Augustine (who might have been influenced by Aristotle and Plotinus at this point),[56] memory arranges the past according to sequential structures between perceptions of the past and on the basis of a sense of temporal distance *and* interaction between the past and the present. History is, as it was for Bultmann, accessible and understandable through a mental dialogue between two temporal horizons.

The notion of mnemonic time relates to a second point—namely, Bultmann's focus on each individual's existence in relation to his or her position within history. Although Bultmann highlighted the creative community in his study of the synoptic tradition, he paid, as we have seen, much attention to human historical existence as experienced from the perspective of the present time of each person when studying the historical Jesus and his message. This double perspective (taking into account the community as well as the individual) finds a resolution in modern theories of how social and collective memories interact. An idea that is gaining attention in critical discussion with

Halbwachs is that collective memory does not make the individual into an "automaton" who passively obeys the interiorized collective will.[57] The social perspective on memory sometimes makes a distinction between what is social and what is collective and understands social memory as that part of the mental act of remembering of each person that is socially conditioned. This is something different from the collective memory shared by all members of a group. It combines a focus on the individual with a focus on the broader social ramifications.

The notions of mnemonic time and social memory thus provide clues as to how one might have conceived the cognitive aspects involved when individuals living in certain social contexts related their existence in the present to the past and negotiated mnemonically in the search for belonging. This is not far from Bultmann's conviction that the message of the historical Jesus can be reconstructed through a dialogue between the past and the present, the main difference being that Bultmann applied this insight as much to himself and his contemporaries as to early Christianity and its dialogue with the historical Jesus.

Bultmann's Message of Jesus: No Flight from History

According to Bultmann, Jesus the prophet and teacher proclaimed the liberating future present in God's kingdom but did so without regarding himself as part of that future and urged people to a decision for or against it. Bultmann's reconstruction has been endorsed, rejected, and modified in ways that point to its vital influence on biblical scholarship today.

Bultmann related his reconstruction to a particular notion of history. The message of Jesus was historical not only because of its historicity but also, and primarily, because it took place and can be grasped in the context of human beings living in history. His hermeneutical reflections on history recur today in theories of how people mnemonically shape their images of the past. The understanding of the message of Jesus that Bultmann advocated has close links to recent historiographical approaches since it regards history as a subject with which scholars (who are within history themselves) interact. It also links with theories of social memory in that it stresses how early Christians negotiated between the past and the present in order to make sense of their existence.

Bultmann's famous dictum that the message of Jesus belongs to the presuppositions of New Testament theology needs to be seen in relation to this notion of history. He was thinking of the message in terms of its historicity, and he was convinced that theology cannot be bound to the insecurities of historical reconstruction, regardless of his own attempts to master them. Yet the dictum was not a flight from history. Jesus' message was historical in the most profound way and, as such, held importance for the decisive encounter with God's impending kingdom. In different publications Bultmann showed that he took full account of history and of the fact that all human beings, including himself, are delivered over to it, bound to live with the past in the present, and that it is possible to discover and hear Jesus' message from the distant past only with a sense of existential urgency.

Chapter 2

THE KERYGMA OF THE EARLIEST CHURCH

C. Kavin Rowe

With the aging and/or retirement of scholars who knew the power of Bultmann's thought first- or secondhand, we risk losing our habits of grappling seriously with a remarkable theological thinker. This volume is therefore to be welcomed if for no other reason than that it helps to ensure sophistication in reflection upon issues of New Testament interpretation: an educated engagement with Bultmann's *Theology of the New Testament* requires an awareness of a staggeringly wide range of both subtle and complicated issues. If we are to move beyond Bultmann, we will have to display the requisite level of thought needed to engage him. For that, we may well need a whole volume of contributors.

In this essay my focus is primarily restricted to the section of Bultmann's *Theology* titled "The Kerygma of the Early Church."[1] Despite endorsing the need to move "beyond Bultmann," I first identify two features of his thinking in that section that we should continue to make our own. I then discuss three other features that are problematical and require either considerable refinement or wholesale rejection. I conclude with some brief reflections on the significance of the *Theology* as a whole.

Bultmannian Insights

The German original of Bultmann's *Theology* is structured in three parts. Part 1 contains "The Presuppositions" of New Testament theology; part 2 offers an interpretation of Paul and John that forms the material theological center of the work; part 3 traces the development toward the ancient church. "The Kerygma of the Early Church" is the second chapter of part 1 and follows Bultmann's reconstruction of Jesus' preaching and teaching. The location of this chapter makes a significant statement about Bultmann's understanding of its place within New Testament theology. He opens the *Theology* with the well-known statement that "[t]he message of Jesus is a presupposition for the theology of the New Testament rather than a part of that theology itself" (1.3). He continues, "Christian faith did not exist until there was a Christian kerygma; i.e., a kerygma proclaiming Jesus Christ—specifically Jesus Christ the Crucified and Risen One—to be God's eschatological act of salvation. He was first so proclaimed in the kerygma of the earliest Church, not in the message of the historical Jesus. . . . Thus, theological thinking—the theology of the New Testament—begins with the kerygma of the earliest Church and not before" (1.3). Justifying the fact that he reconstructs Jesus' message anyway, Bultmann goes on to say that of course the preaching of the historical Jesus is not irrelevant for discerning the theology of the New Testament, since in fact Jesus' preaching is "among" the historical presuppositions for the rise of ecclesial kerygma. But it should not be mistaken for a part of the kerygma itself. Ecclesial kerygma, for Bultmann, is the beginning of real theology.

By framing things hermeneutically in this way, Bultmann establishes a dialectic that is central to his overall thought: on the one hand, there is a distance between the historical Jesus and the church, and, on the other, there is a trajectory from the historical Jesus to the church's kerygma, an unfolding of the significance of Jesus in historical time.

"The Kerygma of the Early Church," then, presents the first stuff of New Testament theology. It is not simply a theologically elaborate repetition of what the historical Jesus was about, but it nevertheless follows from him as the content of his significance. On the way to delineating the first kerygma about Jesus, Bultmann makes two highly significant points that remain either self-evidently or defensibly true.

(1) First, he famously says that "the proclaimer became the proclaimed" (1.33). By this Bultmann means that the "essential thing

to see" in the earliest period is that "[h]e who formerly had been the bearer of the message was drawn into it and became its essential content" (1.33). The historical Jesus did not, so Bultmann thinks in light of his extensive study of the Synoptic Gospels (HST), arrive on the Galilean scene proclaiming himself as God's Messiah or Savior. He instead announced "the radical demand of God" (1.34). It was the church that shifted the preaching by Jesus to the preaching about Jesus. Recognizing this fact, however, raises the "central" christological question: "in what sense?" (1.33). In what sense, Bultmann asks, did the Proclaimer become the Proclaimed?

Making his way to an answer, Bultmann rejects four options that historically have been important to the way Christians have conceived of the significance of Jesus. First, the movement from Proclaimer to Proclaimed did not happen because the church recognized Jesus as the Messiah in his earthly life. "Earthly Messiah," in Bultmann's view, did not explicate Jesus' significance. Why? Because initially the church did not think that Jesus was Messiah in his earthly life. "It is clear . . . that when Jesus was proclaimed as Messiah it was as the coming Messiah, in other words as the Son of Man. Not his return as Messiah, but his coming as Messiah was expected. That is, his then past activity on earth was not yet considered messianic by the earliest Church" (1.33; cf. 1.28–32). As far as "Messiah" goes, the earliest church thought of Jesus only as the future/coming Messiah.

Second, the movement from Proclaimer to Proclaimed cannot be explained on the basis of Jesus' teaching or prophetic role. Even Jesus' messianic identity "does not rest upon the fact that he was prophet and teacher" (1.34). The reason? "However much [Jesus'] preaching in its radicality is directed against Jewish legalism, still its content is nothing else than true Old Testament-Jewish faith in God radicalized in the direction of the great prophets' teaching" (1.34). Jesus' teaching and prophetic critique, that is, show no fundamental originality. Indeed, Bultmann argues, Jesus' "concepts of God, world, and man, of law and grace, of repentance and forgiveness . . . are not new in comparison with those of the Old Testament and Judaism, however radically they may be understood" (1.34). Even his radical interpretation of the Torah "stands within the scribal discussions about it" (1.35). Because the content of Jesus' message is still altogether Jewish, his significance cannot, so Bultmann thinks, be seen in this light.[2]

Third, the movement from Proclaimer to Proclaimed cannot be explained in terms of the greatness of Jesus' personality, as if what the earliest church saw in him was an "impressive power behind his teaching" or a "numinous figure" (1.35). True, Jesus worked miracles and the like, but the earliest church understood him neither as someone to "imitate" nor as "one who heroically sacrifices himself for his cause" nor, again, as a supernatural "divine man of the Hellenistic world" (1.35). "The personality of Jesus," says Bultmann, "has no importance for the kerygma either of Paul or of John or for the New Testament in general. Indeed the tradition of the earliest Church did not even unconsciously preserve a picture of his personality. Every attempt to reconstruct one remains a play of subjective imagination" (1.35). Jesus' gravitas, his charisma, his ability to call disciples to himself—none of this explains the move from Proclaimer to Proclaimed.

Fourth, the movement from Proclaimer to Proclaimed cannot be explained on the basis of the church's understanding of Jesus' unique place in history, as if the church originally conceived of him as the most significant event to occur in time. Nor was his ministry "understood as a decisive event for Israel's history like the call of Moses, the exodus from Egypt, the giving of the law on Sinai, or God's raising up of kings and prophets" (1.36). The church does not look back to Jesus because his "importance as Messiah-Son-of-Man lies not at all in what he did in the past, but entirely in what is expected of him for the future. And once this expectation is fulfilled by the eschatological drama, that event will never become, like the crossing of the Red Sea, a past to which one could look back thankfully . . . but it will be God's last deed of all, by which he puts history to an end" (1.36). In what, then, does the movement from Proclaimer to Proclaimed consist? In what "sense" does Bultmann think we should understand this transformation?

Bultmann's answer turns on his coordination of implicit claim with explicit understanding (a mirror image, of course, of the movement from Jesus' proclamation to the proclamation about him). By means of its self-understanding as the eschatological congregation, the earliest church implicitly commented upon the significance of Jesus' life: it was the eschatological occurrence. Jesus' proclamation, that is, entailed eschatological existence, and the church's form of life translated this proclamation by focusing it upon the person of Jesus himself and the one who called all things into being. Proclaiming Jesus explicated Jesus' proclamation precisely in its ability to see Jesus as the eschatological event (1.33–37; cf. esp. 1.43). The earliest church was not as clear on this point as was Paul, for example, but it was nevertheless conscious of "being already the called and chosen Congregation of the end of days" (1.42). Focusing on Bultmann's thesis about Jesus and the eschatological event takes us immediately to the second major theme of this section—the church as the eschatological community.

(2) So, second, in "The Kerygma of the Earliest Church" Bultmann argues that the best way to describe "church" is to speak of it as "the eschatological congregation." Both Paul and the synoptic tradition testify to the earliest church's self-understanding as the "vestibule, so to speak, of God's Reign that is shortly to appear" (1.37). The Twelve are not so much a dozen men appointed as apostles as they are "eschatological regents," those who will "rule the tribes of Israel" (1.37).[3] Subsequent to Jesus' resurrection appearances in Galilee, his followers did not stay put but gathered in Jerusalem, thus signifying their understanding of the central city as the focus of God's coming reign (1.37). And, rather tellingly of course, the church referred to itself as the *ekklēsia*, the principal term the Septuagint used to render the Old Testament's theologically pregnant "congregation of Yahweh (קְהַל־יְהוָה)." Its members were "the chosen," "the elect," and "the saints"—all terms that point to a consciousness of eschatological existence (1.37–38).

Moreover, the earliest church engaged in five practices that evidenced the church's eschatological existence. Baptism was an initiation rite that both made people members of the eschatological congregation and purified them from sin. Common meals brought them together with a feeling of joy (ἀγαλλίασις). Speaking prophecies and in tongues testified to the Spirit's presence. Reading (Old Testament) Scripture—especially the prophecies—interpreted the current time as the end, the final fulfillment of God's promises made long ago. And the church's mission reflects its sense that the "immediately impending end" requires a hastening to spread the news of the coming of God's reign (1.39–42). Individually, these practices may or may not be particularly significant vis-à-vis other first-century Jewish groups. But taken together they signify a community that is "distinguished from other sects and trends" by the fact of its eschatological determination (1.42 et passim).

Of course the history of New Testament scholarship has made it somewhat difficult to know what "eschatological" actually means (whether it is the same as or fundamentally different from apocalyptic, for example). Mercifully, however, Bultmann is clear. Applied to the earliest church, eschatological means a community that is living under the expectation of an imminent end and with a substantively different sense of time than that of the normal, everyday running of the world. It means, further and more specifically, a community that roots its own existence in the fact "that Jesus' having come was itself the decisive event" (1.43). For Bultmann, therefore, the eschatological church and the life of Jesus were inextricably bound.

Indeed, it is exactly "Jesus' meaning" to the earliest church that provides the unity in Bultmann's overarching argument in this section of the *Theology*: to the church that proclaimed him, the Proclaimer means that the eschaton is on its way. That is why, after all, the congregation exists at all.

In a broad sense, these two points of Bultmann's *Theology* should, I think, remain central to the way in which we think about New Testament theology. This is not to say that Bultmann is right in the details of his reconstruction or even that he conceptualizes the material theological concerns in a way that we should emulate (see below). But it is to say that he saw something of the fundamental or underlying questions that confront the inquisitive modern reader of the New Testament.

All moderns are aware of the fact that the rise of the "historical Jesus" creates the need to decide whether or not—or to what degree—New Testament theology should deal with scholarly reconstructions of the man from Nazareth. In one sense, Bultmann, too, obviously takes a clear position on this matter, that is, the historically reconstructed Jesus should play no part in a theology of the New Testament.[4] In another sense, however, with his distinction between the Proclaimer and the Proclaimed, Bultmann merely relocates the same crucial question about the distance between Jesus and the New Testament to the New Testament texts themselves. Any reader of the Synoptic Gospels, he suggests, can see that Jesus does not talk about himself as much as he does about other things—the kingdom of God, the seeking of the lost, the coming of the Son of Man, the poor and downtrodden, the last days, and so forth. And any reader of the Gospel of John or the Apostle Paul can see that something has changed. In John's Gospel, Jesus speaks about himself continuously, and in Paul's letters the focus is not upon Jesus' earthly teaching—either that he taught or the things about which he taught—but upon the implications of the profound change from old to new creation effected by Jesus' death and resurrection. Indeed, outside of Matthew, Mark, and Luke, the whole of the New Testament shows little interest in repeating Jesus' message. Bultmann, in short, may well reject the idea that scholarly reconstructions of Jesus should be admitted into New Testament theology proper, but his conception of the division between synoptic tradition and other New Testament witnesses requires him to conceive an answer to the same basic question of distance posed by the historical Jesus.

While recent studies have shown that the Synoptic Gospels are more concerned with articulating the identity of the Proclaimer than Bultmann ever appreciated,[5] his basic point that the inside of the New Testament itself displays a movement from words of Jesus to words about Jesus remains critically important. We may well now disagree with Bultmann about the hermeneutical viability of form criticism, but no theology of the New Testament that attends to the literary surface area of the New Testament itself can fail to account for the shift that takes place as one moves from the Synoptic Gospels into the rest of the New Testament. As Bultmann saw,[6] this shift contains *in nuce* the essential question of the specific connection between Jesus and the church, or, to state it slightly differently, how Christology and ecclesiology are mutually informing and inseparably intertwined. Systematic theologians have thought long and repeatedly about this connection (or lack thereof). But those who would directly engage in New Testament interpretation need to as well. The reason is simple: the question is endemic to the New Testament itself.

It is no accident, therefore, that Bultmann next moved to consider the church as the eschatological congregation. In broad terms, this understanding of the church is exactly what is to be expected if one sees Jesus as the decisive revelation of God. It is true, thankfully, that more current research on the New Testament has shown that the development of a sense of history and the need for ecclesial order—such as we find in the Acts of the Apostles and the Pastoral Epistles, for example—are not inversely related to a sense of the end. But it remains the case that Bultmann has clearly seen the result of the advent of Jesus. The time in which the community of his followers finds itself differs profoundly from that of the steady running of the world, and the community engages in regular practices that mark this difference. We do not have to agree with Bultmann about the early Christians' understanding of Jesus' return as the (first) coming of the Messiah to see the general accuracy of Bultmann's reading of the church as a community whose sense of time has radically changed in direct relation to God's act in Jesus.

But there are significant problems with "The Kerygma of the Early Church." To these we now turn.

Bultmannian Problems

There are, of course, many small matters that would bring disagreement from a variety of scholars, but this is no more significant than the nature of scholarship itself: we do not always agree. But there are at least three more substantive problems with this section of the *Theology* that call for serious criticism.

First, as is the case with much pre-Sanders scholarship, Bultmann's discussion of things Jewish is problematic. Jesus, he says, criticizes "Jewish legalism" (1.54). The early church failed "to achieve freedom from the Law"; indeed, a "retrogression had taken place so that the old scruples and fidelity to the law had gradually gained ground" (1.54). The antinomian conclusions of "the Hellenists" were "terrifying," and led to the creation of fear-stopping, Torah-upholding sayings by Jesus (e.g., Matt 5:17). The church may well have tried to maintain "a critical attitude toward Jewish legalism" and to break "with the Jewish idea of merit," but it could not free itself because it "clung to the Law" as a "characteristic of the Chosen People which it was conscious of embodying" (1.54–55). The growth of the "church concept" in the earliest Christian community was "of course hindered . . . by its ties to the Jewish congregation. The Church as eschatological Congregation had not yet found appropriate expression in a cult of its own, since it had not cut itself loose from the temple cult" (1.57). In short, and to anticipate the chapter on Bultmann's reading of Paul, one of the problems of the early church was that it was too

Jewish. It was Paul who was able to break the mold and to reach for true freedom from merit.

For all the spinning of the wheels in New Testament scholarship, this is one instance in which research really has moved on. Perhaps it is no fault of his own, but it is nevertheless the case that Bultmann is here woefully out of date. First-century Jews were not "legalists," and their faithful adherence to Torah was not "legalism," a style of living before God that attempted to earn "merit" in his eyes. The Torah was a gift, the sign of God's covenant with his beloved people, the pattern of life by which they testified to his steadfast and loving kindness. Where they failed, God had provided ways by which they could be forgiven and restored, ways that were given in the Torah itself. Bultmann did not live to see New Testament scholars' "new perspective" on the Judaism of the time, but for all of us on this side of it, we have to consider it "beyond" him.

As he progresses through the *Theology* (and in much of his other work), it becomes clear, however, that Bultmann's presentation of ancient Judaism is not only a claim to historical understanding. Judaism, for Bultmann, also represents a deficient theological anthropology, namely, the view that the human problem is something that can be overcome by training the will to obey the law(s) of God. Bultmann is correct that this is a naïve and bad anthropology—as Kierkegaard definitively showed in his discussion of the ethical man—but it was not Judaism's anthropology. It cannot, therefore, be used as the historical foil for the Christian understanding of humanity. At this point at least, scholarship on ancient Judaism would move us beyond Bultmann philosophically as well.[7]

Second, as is well known, Bultmann assigns a remarkably important role to the kerygma. Not only does the title of the section in focus (and the following section) already suggest that what is most important to know about the early church is its kerygma, it is also the case that a close reading of this section helps to shape the understanding of kerygma as a whole that will be employed throughout the *Theology*.

And just here is the problem. If in light of the subsection's title one asks the rather simple question that comes naturally to mind, "what is the kerygma of the earliest church?" the answer is surprisingly elusive. It is elusive, first, because Bultmann does not actually thematize "kerygma" to the degree that one might expect but instead simply uses the language throughout the section as a way to talk about what he's getting at, the *telos*, as it were, of his investigations. And, second, the kerygma of the early church is elusive because, *sensu stricto*, Bultmann does not think that kerygma has a specific conceptual content. It is conceptually received and interpreted, to be sure, but the thing itself does not subsist in concepts. To those unfamiliar with his broader theological corpus, this view of kerygma may seem surprising or even strange, but it is a structurally crucial aspect of Bultmann's larger thought.[8]

It is true, of course, that he can speak of "the specifically Christian kerygma" in contrast and connection to Jesus' message (e.g., 1.59). And it is true, more generally, that he talks frequently of "faith in the kerygma" as if faith had a specific content, for example, faith in "God's dealing in the man Jesus of Nazareth" (2.239, et passim). But such statements are misleading if understood to say that the kerygma itself could ever correspond to, for example, the Apostles' Creed, or some earlier creedal-like formulation. As he puts it in the "Epilogue," the kerygma "is just what theology can never seize in definitive form; it can always take hold of it only as something conceptually stated, and that means as something already theologically interpreted" (2.240). Indeed, throughout the Epilogue Bultmann explicitly discusses the kerygma in a way that makes his work in the earlier parts of the book intelligible.

Kerygma, for Bultmann, is "God's word addressing man as a questioning and promising word, a condemning and forgiving word" (2.240). Crucial here is the axis God-word-address; it is this connection that is meant both to negate the idea that the kerygma is something that can arise from within humanity's natural capacities and to affirm the way in which kerygma is free to remain kerygma. The kerygma is from God's side of things and reaches us as an addressing word that calls us to faith—a self-understanding that results from the decision to hear the address. Precisely because it confronts us as decision-requiring-address, the kerygma does not "offer itself to critical thought but speaks into one's concrete existence" (2.240). Kerygma that could be objectified by critical thought, Bultmann holds, would cease to address the hearer and, hence, cease to be the free gift of God's summons to new self-understanding in an authentic life.

Yet, once one has heard the kerygma and responded in faith, conceptual formulation must occur. The new self-understanding that is faith unfolds itself through "theological thoughts." Both "the kerygma and faith's self-understanding always appear in the texts, so far as they are expressed in words and sentences, already interpreted in some particular way—i.e., in theological thoughts" (2.239). Hence the Bultmannian dialectic: the kerygma both is and is not in the New Testament. It is not there because it does not consist in "theological thoughts"; it is there because it is already interpreted by "theological thoughts."

For some, a dialectic; for others, a pickle. In Bultmann's dialectic, the particularities of the New Testament's message are accidental. Christological content is not fundamentally wed to them; indeed, the content itself is not even really all that important. As he says in a statement that summarizes much of his thinking about the early church, "for the Church, as for Jesus himself, the content of his message was not the decisive thing. In his lifetime he had demanded decision for his person as the bearer of the Word; the Church has now made this decision" (1.43). In practice this means that Bultmann will not be able to find what he is seeking, that a great deal of exegetical groping is done after something that in principle cannot be grasped. In short, for all his emphasis upon the "act of existing" and the existential uptake that is the hearing of the kerygma, the kerygma for Bultmann is finally an abstraction.[9]

As Alasdair MacIntyre convincingly argued, however, we cannot know things such as action or word or person in abstraction but only within wider arenas of meaning that make these things intelligible to us.[10] There is no such thing, in other words, as kerygma or event or even the person of Jesus without the content that makes them intelligible.[11] The content of Jesus' message mattered (and matters) if for no other reason than that it cannot be otherwise. Absent such content we literally cannot know who or what "Jesus" is. However much Bultmann may wish to divide Jesus' message from Jesus or the church's teaching from the church's decision, therefore, he simply cannot do it. Bultmann's abstraction "kerygma" is at bottom only the fictitious creature of his intellect.

It is this problem, perhaps more than any other, that prohibits Bultmann from fully grasping the connection between the Proclaimer and the Proclaimed, which is exactly the unity of person/content through time.[12] Insofar as we recognize the Gospels are Gospels, the

Proclaimer is already the Proclaimed. The claim for unity is there in the very existence of the Gospels themselves; in the Gospel form, Jesus' preaching is the proclamation of Jesus. The literary surface difference between the synoptics and much of the rest of the New Testament is simply a matter of theologically shaped history, that is, the claim that the content of the church's proclamation is the same as the person who proclaimed the church into being.[13] New Testament theology would do well to move beyond Bultmann at this point. Bultmann is right to focus on kerygma inasmuch as all Christian language is inescapably kerygmatic. But his focus turns out to be misleading because, in the end, he speaks not of Christian kerygma but of something that does not exist.[14]

Finally, though many of Bultmann's immediate intellectual forebears were considered Radical Critics (Bousset, Wrede, et al.), and though Bultmann himself often received the same laud/opprobrium, much of the textual work that provides the foundation for such judgments is—in hindsight—something more like guesswork or "uncritical" hypothesis making, a way of reasoning about history that lacks the disciplined historian's reserve and sobriety, or a willingness to be boring. To put it slightly differently, the invention of theories about the dynamics of the early church abounds where textual evidence is remarkably scant. It is true that it is better to be philosophically aware and sophisticated in one's views about history and religion than it is to be naïve or simply confused—and, like F. C. Baur well before him, Bultmann was obviously both aware and sophisticated—but it is no less true that philosophical commitments to *Religionsgeschichte* will not (magically) supply what is left unsaid in the primary sources (even if such commitments turn out to be both defensible and correct). One need not deny, in fact, the basic *religionsgeschichtliche* claim that many things in the New Testament have their roots in "Jewish" or "Hellenistic" soil to appreciate the point that we often cannot see these roots.[15] Again and again, however, Bultmann attempts to see where we cannot. He says, for example, that baptism in the name of Christ "probably goes back to the usage of the Hellenistic-Christian congregations," and then continues, "But perhaps very early exorcistic effect (by means of naming 'the name of Jesus Christ' . . .) was already attributed to baptism. From what time the positive effect of endowment with the 'Spirit' was also attributed to it, is uncertain. It probably arose as a Hellenistic-Christian conception" (1.40). Later, he draws from his book on the synoptic tradition and asserts that Jesus' "sending meant doom for Jerusalem is expressed by the saying Lk. 13:34f. par., probably in origin a Jewish prophecy concerning 'Wisdom,' perhaps once quoted by Jesus, but as we now have it, reinterpreted by the church and put back into his mouth: It was he who had desired in vain to gather Jerusalem's 'children' together, so that it now was forsaken" (1.44). Or, to take only one more example from this indelible feature of the *Theology* as a whole, Bultmann argues that Jesus' saying in Matthew 10:5-6 ("go nowhere . . . but to the lost sheep of the house of Israel") "shows that in the earliest church there was at least a party which altogether rejected the mission to the Gentiles" (1.55).[16] To all this sort of thing, we can only shrug our shoulders and reply: well, maybe or maybe not; how could one possibly know?[17]

Drastically oversimplifying this last point, we could say that Bultmann is far quicker to offer speculative historical reconstructions than he is to accept the academic's inevitable limit of knowledge, the epistemic correlation, that is, to our dreaded confession "we just don't know and never will."[18] Much in the *Theology*, therefore, that has passed as rigorous historical work should instead be redescribed by another genre, indeed, by one of Bultmann's own favorites: "tales about the life of the early church."

Arguing that we should move "beyond Bultmann" at these three points is less a disagreement with him about three separate issues than it is a suggestion that we should move beyond Bultmann in a rather complete sense. His understanding of Judaism and its anthropology, his conception of a kerygma that stands beyond our formulations, and his pervasive textual dismantling and speculative positing of trajectories/parties on the meager basis of the leftover textual bits are both cognitively and operatively basic to the *Theology*. Other essays in this volume deal with additional ways in which the fundamental aspects of the *Theology* can no longer be taken as a guide. But even if they did not, these three matters are deeply enough embedded in the *Theology* as a whole that to see their significance is to question the viability of the *Theology* as a hermeneutical enterprise.[19]

Conclusion

In a volume with the title *Beyond Bultmann*, no essay on the *Theology* would be complete without at least some reflection on the significance of the work as a whole. In my judgment, the significance of the work as a whole is primarily twofold. First, the *Theology* is a unified interpretation of the New Testament and continues to stand as a model for those who wish to conceptualize the totality of the New Testament's message. In an area of scholarship in which an almost rabid specialization is the norm, Bultmann actually knows what he thinks the whole New Testament is basically about—and this in connection to particular contemporary currents of thought that profoundly shape reflection's historicity. This is no small feat. The textual problems are unavoidable, the historical questions legion, the theological complexities ubiquitous, the current philosophical landscape difficult, and, yet, for all that, Bultmann conceptualizes the whole of the thing in a single, unified interpretation.

Moreover, in contrast to some of his revered teachers and his contemporaries, his interpretation is not self-deceptively cast as a detached observer's report on the New Testament documents and their history. It is instead the constructive thought of one who aims to think constructively with the theology of the New Testament. And he is clear where others remain opaque or uncommitted: Paul and John matter most. To be sure, Bultmann thinks, we can learn some things worth knowing from other parts of the canon (and Ignatius), but as a whole the rest of it matters little in comparison to these two towering theologians. It is these two who best understand the way in which the *Sache* of the Christian faith is to be thought and lived. The form of the *Theology*, therefore, is exactly its material content. Bultmannian *Sachkritik* places Paul and John at the center of the New Testament's theology.

Second, the *Theology* is an attempt to keep together two patterns of thought that in the early and mid-twentieth century were generally opposed, namely, *religionsgeschichtliche* investigation and theological interpretation for the present. Bultmann inherited this opposition and, rather than opt for one side of it or the other, he tried to think through the opposition to a more complex or tensive unity. The hybrid that resulted was ultimately a failure—but not because he was wrong in the effort to engage the questions of intellectual unity and truth that go with work on the New Testament. Bultmann failed because the *Theology* reproduced the problem to which he sought the solution. Parts 1 and 3 display *religionsgeschichtliche* irrelevance; part 2 is contemporary existential theology. To be sure, parts 1 and 3 have some existentially relevant moments, and part 2 contains many *religionsgeschichtliche* proposals. But taken as a whole, the *Theology* reinstantiates the distance it tried to overcome.[20] Bultmann is finally of two minds.[21]

Of course, in this way he is simply a man of his time. Twentieth-century theology was occupied with many different things, but it would not be much of an overstatement to say that the predominant hermeneutical question asked in relation to the Bible was how to deal with the rise of historical criticism. Nor would it be much of an overstatement to say that the most influential answers given from within biblical scholarship were varieties of two-mind thinking. Precisely because so many New Testament scholars in the twenty-first century are still asking a version of this question and remain of two minds about issues such as "theology *and* history"—as if they were ultimately different things—Bultmann's brilliant failure is almost as good for us as if it were a success. For what is true of him is surely true of lesser mortals: thinking constructively about New Testament theology cannot be done in two minds.

Chapter 3

THE KERYGMA OF THE HELLENISTIC CHURCH ASIDE FROM PAUL

Udo Schnelle

The *Theology of the New Testament* by Rudolf Bultmann resembles a mountain range with two peaks.[1] At first, one has an "easy" climb because the work suppresses the question of the historical Jesus and treats pre- or non-Pauline Christianity only summarily. Then comes a very steep climb; the sections on Paul and John in the *Theology of the New Testament* each constitute a self-contained masterpiece. Paul and John are the only two "true" theologians in the New Testament; they are, to a degree, the "peak" of theological reflection.[2] John stands in substantive proximity to Paul; both find themselves in the realm of a Hellenism colored by Gnosticism and configure their Christologies "after the pattern of the Gnostic Redeemer-myth" (2.6).[3] After these two peaks comes a steep decline, because Bultmann once again presents the post-Johannine development and the path to the ancient Church only very summarily.

Rudolf Bultmann's *Theology* undoubtedly represents on the one hand an impressive overall design and on the other an extravagant abbreviation because the concentration on Paul and John results in the insufficient presentation and evaluation of essential developments within primitive Christianity.[4] The paramount influence of Paul should not obstruct one's view of the fact that, before and alongside Paul, between 30 and 60 C.E., numerous other missionaries were active and, already before Paul, central theological viewpoints had emerged. These views were developed and gained local acceptance.

Consequently, it is insufficient to speak only of kerygma, as Bultmann did, and thus to remain on the level of the history of ideas. Instead, one must consider the historical preconditions and the active individuals/groups in pre- and non-Pauline early Christianity along with theological developments.

Internal and External Presuppositions

There were internal and external conditions for the rise of pre- and non-Pauline Christianity. Fundamentally, Bultmann correctly asserts the following: "The historical presupposition for Paul's theology is not the kerygma of the oldest Church but that of the Hellenistic Church; it was the latter that mediated the former to Paul" (1.63).[5] Nonetheless, the early Jerusalem church plays a definitive role for further development because the tension between the "Hellenists" and the "Hebrews" in the earliest church initiated the development toward Hellenistic Christianity. The Ἑβραῖοι were Aramaic-speaking Jewish followers of Jesus; in contrast, the Ἑλληνισταί were Greek-speaking Jews from the Diaspora who returned to Jerusalem and became followers of Jesus (cf. Acts 2:5).[6] The outstanding theological figure among the "Hellenists" was Stephen;[7] he appears rather abruptly in Acts 6:8-15 as something like the theological spokesperson for the Hellenistic strand of the Jerusalem church. Apparently, the successful proclamation of the crucified Jesus of Nazareth as Israel's Messiah in conjunction with a critical attitude toward the temple[8] led to a first persecution in Jerusalem, which ended in mob justice with the stoning of Stephen (cf. Acts 7:54-60). The activity of the Hellenists and the death of Stephen date to 32/33 C.E. The significance of the Hellenists for the further development of early Christianity cannot be overestimated. Already in Jerusalem and then later in Damascus (cf. Acts 9:2) and in Antioch (cf. Acts 11:19),[9] the Hellenists developed approaches to Christology with a universalist tendency, which then opened the movement of believers in Christ to a mission beyond the borders of Palestine. They were apparently the first to ponder theologically the spontaneous gift of the Holy Spirit even to non-Jews (cf. Acts 2:9-11; 8:17, 39). It was apparently the Hellenists, too, who quite early translated the Jesus tradition into Greek and thereby opened the message of Jesus to the Greek world.

External sociological and cultural factors also nurtured pre- and non-Pauline Christianity:

1. The preexisting communication system of Jewish communities in the Diaspora offered early missionaries (not just Paul and his coworkers) the first opportunity to proclaim the new message.[10] Along with native Jews, the addressees of this proclamation included primarily proselytes and God fearers.

2. The religious plurality and openness of the Roman Empire in the first century C.E. also benefited the spread of Christianity. As a rule, Romans and Greeks did not doubt the existence of foreign gods, a circumstance that enabled the coexistence and fusion of religions. Greco-Roman religion was traditionally suited not for conflict but for integration. It knew no mission and had no duty to convert other people.

3. The early Christian mission did not aim to offer people an additional religion but, combined with the claim to exclusivity, renunciation of all prior religious ties. The goal already of the earliest proclamation was not adhesion to an additional religion but conversion to the one true God (cf. 1 Thess 1:10). It involved a conscious decision with very binding character.

4. The weaknesses of the old tradition also promoted the success of the new.[11] Thus, Plutarch and Pliny complain about the decline of temple culture and the oracle.[12] The official cults were apparently no longer able to satisfy the religious needs of people sufficiently, as the success of the oriental cults already demonstrates.

5. A further ground was monotheism, which already motivated fascination with Judaism in antiquity.[13] The multiplicity and depiction of gods in the Greco-Roman world apparently led to a loss of plausibility. Through the philosophical critique of polytheism,[14] pagan monotheism had already gained in importance[15] and prepared the way for Christian monotheism.

People

While the sociological presuppositions of the origins of early Christianity played no essential role for Bultmann, people before and contemporary with Paul recede entirely into the background for him. This circumstance does not correspond to the textual evidence, for both Acts and the letters of Paul clearly reveal that there were important missionaries before and contemporary with Paul. Who conducted the earliest mission before and contemporary with Paul outside of Jerusalem? The information is sparse, but in the beginning three names move clearly into the foreground: Philip, Peter, and Barnabas.

After Stephen, Philip was evidently an eminent member of the Hellenists; he stands in second place in the list of the "seven" in Acts 6:5. As "Evangelist Philip" (Acts 21:8), he is apparently not to be identified with the Apostle Philip (cf. Acts 1:13). His missionary activity outside Jerusalem may have begun around 33 C.E. His mission fields were Samaria (Acts 8:5ff.) and the Hellenistic cities of the coastal region (cf. Acts 8:26, 40: Ashdod, Gaza, and Caesarea by the Sea). According to Acts 8:5-25, Philip appeared in Samaria as a charismatic wonder-worker (cf. 8:7-8) and thus became a competitor of the local magician, Simon, who may have seen himself as an incarnation of "the great power of God" (Acts 8:10).[16] Behind the legendary adornments to the account, one can discern a conflict that pervaded the early history of missions: the clash of developing Christianity with local cults, magicians, and magical practices (cf. Acts 13:4-12, 8-20; 16:16-24; 19:11-20).[17] According to Acts 8:26-40, Philip also appeared as the first missionary to Gentiles since he converted the finance minister of the Ethiopian queen. The Ethiopian could have been a "God fearer"; as a eunuch, he was in no sense a proselyte (cf. Acts 8:27). Acts 21:8-9 points to a stable missionary establishment founded by Philip. His "four daughters" may have been students acting as prophets;[18] that is, Philip was the leader of a missionary center with a charismatic-pneumatic orientation, as also indicated by the lodging of Paul and his companions.

According to the portrayal in Acts, Peter was not only the first leader of the Jerusalem church but soon also active outside Jerusalem (cf. Acts 9:32). Peter performed wonders in Lydda and Joppa (Acts 9:32-35, 36-43) and later baptized the Roman centurion Cornelius in Caesarea by the sea (Acts 10:1-48). Acts depicts Cornelius as a God-fearing sympathizer with Judaism (cf. Acts 10:2, 22, 35) who initiated contact with Peter (cf. Acts 10:7-8). The length and position of the account within Acts clearly reveals Luke's intention to attribute the programmatic transition to the Gentile mission and its theological justification (Acts 11:1-18) to a prominent figure from the beginnings. As in Acts 8:14-17, the activity of the Spirit is linked to the authority of the apostles in the early period. Only afterward may those unknown Hellenistic missionaries, who probably were the historic founders of the programmatic mission beyond Judaism, appear in Antioch (cf. Acts 11:19-30). Even if Peter cannot be considered the initiator of the universal mission, he may have been active as a missionary in Lydda, Joppa, and Caesarea.[19] The course of his later life, which brought him far beyond Jerusalem to Antioch, Corinth, and Rome, also speaks in favor of this possibility.

A leading figure in the early history of missions from Jerusalem to Antioch was Barnabas (cf. Acts 4:36-37).[20] He, or his family, was from Cyprus. As a Levite (cf. Ezek 44:9-14), he stood firmly in Jewish tradition and had command of fundamental theological and cultic knowledge. Moreover, his Cyprus roots point to his Hellenistic background—in particular, a knowledge of the Greek language and a cultural engagement with Diaspora Judaism. The sale of land shows Barnabas to be a benefactor of the Jerusalem church (Acts 4:37) whose extraordinary act remained in the memory of developing Christianity. In 1 Cor 9:5-6, Paul counts not only himself but also Barnabas among the apostles—that is, Barnabas was a witness to an appearance of the Risen One and thus a legitimate preacher of Jesus Christ. According to Acts 11:20, unknown missionaries from Cyprus and Cyrene founded the church in Antioch and transitioned to the systematic proclamation of the gospel, "even to the Greeks." Around 35 C.E., sometime after the death of Stephen, Barnabas went to Antioch (there is no report of his having experienced persecution) in order to join or, with others, to establish the church there. In any case, from the very beginning, Barnabas was one of the most prominent members of the Antiochene church; he introduced Paul to the church (cf. Acts 11:25), and he, not Paul, led the first missionary journey (Acts 13:1).

An additional important figure before and contemporary with Paul was Apollos, a Diaspora Jew who had already been educated in the scriptures of the Old Testament in Alexandria and there (or later in Asia Minor or Greece) encountered the new movement of believers in Christ (cf. Acts 18:24). Apollos was active before Paul in the early fifties in Ephesus (Acts 18:24), and he was in Corinth during and after Paul's time there (Acts 18:27; 19:1; 1 Cor 3:4ff.). Notably, Paul accepted the (not unproblematic) work of Apollos in "his" churches (cf. the "parties" in 1 Cor 1:10-17)—Apollos was evidently a well-known missionary who apparently had worked previously in other regions and whose theological orientation Paul accepted.[21] Presumably, he was also the founder of the church in Ephesus, which the sequence of Acts 18:24-28 and 19:1ff. presupposes, explaining why Paul accepted him or had to accept him.[22] In Corinth, Apollos had great missionary success (cf. Acts 18:27, 28). This success was evidently related to his Alexandrian origins and education; Apollos was a gifted exegete, rhetorician, pneumatic, and agitator (cf. Acts 18:24-25, 28), whose theological orientation was linked to the concept of wisdom.

Married couples played a central role in the early phase of developing Christianity. In this respect, the couple Andronicus and Junia referenced in Rom 16:7 merit first mention.[23] Junia was a woman, apparently a freed slave; Andronicus may also have been a freed slave.[24] Since they were already apostles before Paul, they must have joined the new movement of believers in Christ around 31/32 C.E. Jerusalem is the only likely location for their conversion—that is, they were Jewish by birth and members of the Jerusalem church. They may have emigrated from Rome (cf. Acts 2:10) and may have been Hellenists who then worked with Paul for a period before they finally returned to Rome. One thing is certain: a woman was an apostle already before Paul—a historical datum that fits best with the elevated status of women in the beginning phase of early Christianity overall and of the Pauline mission in particular.

Prisca and Aquila were independent missionaries who worked with Paul for a time but were also active before, contemporary with, and after him. They were among the first Christians in Rome and perhaps among the founders of a Roman house church. After the expulsion from Rome in 49 C.E., the couple first went to Corinth (Acts 18:2, 3), where they worked for about one and a half years (cf. Acts 18:18). Like Paul himself, Prisca and Aquila were independent tentmakers (σκηνοποιοί) and belonged to the lower middle class. From Corinth, the couple moved to Ephesus, where they worked with Paul again and founded a house church (cf. 1 Cor 16:19). After the repeal of the Edict of Claudius, Prisca and Aquila returned to Rome around 55/56 C.E., where they led a house church again (cf. Rom 16:3-5). Paul's ebullient thanks in Rom 16:4 indicate that Prisca and Aquila not only supported Paul in his missionary activities and provided him a base and a livelihood, but also intervened for him in dangerous (political?) situations.

Locations: Damascus, Antioch, Rome, Alexandria

Acts gives the impression that initially after Easter only the church in Jerusalem existed. From it, the other churches then developed in succession, and thus Christianity came to be.[25] This image may not be historically accurate for, very early on and rapidly, churches formed that acted independently of Jerusalem and were very significant for Christianity before and contemporary with Paul: Damascus, Antioch, and Rome.

In the first century C.E., Damascus was a Hellenistic commercial metropolis with a considerable Jewish population.[26] The beginnings of the community of believers in Christ in Damascus[27] lie in darkness. The new movement arrived there very early on via the trade routes, although the church may have formed by means of the influx of Hellenists fleeing Jerusalem. It may have understood itself as one of the Jewish synagogues. The report about the call of Paul in Acts 9:1-25 is the sole witness offering limited insight into the early history of the church. The risen Jesus Christ appeared to Paul circa 32/33 C.E. in the vicinity of Damascus and provoked a crisis. The very fact that Paul acted against the church in Damascus testifies to its importance as well as its high profile! According to Acts 9:2, Paul acted in Damascus against adherents of the "Way" (cf. Acts 19:23); this designation for believers in Christ, a designation Luke adopted, may have originated in Damascus. Both the location "Straight Street" (Acts 9:11) and the names "Ananias" and "house of Judas" (Acts 9:10-12) imply a house church in the center of the city. Spirit-filled worship services took place there, as the invocation of the "name of the Lord" (Acts 9:14) and the baptism of Paul (Acts 9:18) demonstrate. Damascus was undoubtedly a key church in the beginning, though traces of it also disappear very quickly.

Syrian Antioch on the Orontes was the third largest city in the Roman Empire[28] and, at the end of the first century C.E., counted a total population of three hundred to six hundred thousand people.[29] Josephus assumes a very large Jewish community in Antioch (cf. *J.W.* 7:43-45); it may have included about twenty to thirty thousand people.

For the early Christian mission, Antioch offered the best conditions because there many Greeks sympathized with the Jewish religion.[30] The proselyte Nicolaus, one of Stephen's circle, was from Antioch (Acts 6:5), and according to Acts 11:19, Christians who had to leave Jerusalem in the context of the persecution of Stephen founded the Antiochene church. The establishment of this church may have occurred around 34 C.E. Hellenistic Jewish-Christians from Cyprus and Cyrene then went to Antioch to preach the gospel with success among the Greek population, too (cf. Acts 11:20). Thus the definitive epoch of early Christianity began in Antioch: the programmatic proclamation of the circumcision-free gospel even to Gentiles. According to the portrayal in Acts, Barnabas and Paul did not belong to the Antiochene church from the outset but joined in the work there only after the beginning of the Gentile mission (cf. Acts 11:22, 25). Paul apparently first came into contact with the Hellenists from Jerusalem in Antioch. The mission of the Antiochene church among Jews and, especially, Gentiles must have been successful because, according to Acts 11:26, the term Χριστιανοί ("Christians") as a third-party designation for the predominantly Gentile-Christian adherents of the new doctrine first appeared there. Thus Christians were first perceived as an independent group alongside Jews and pagans in the early forties. From a pagan perspective, they were now considered a non-Jewish movement and must have gained a perceptible theological profile and their own organizational structure.[31] Why was the Christian message so successful in Antioch? For the first time, the gospel was proclaimed extensively in a major city where there were numerous sympathizers with the Jewish faith and ties to the synagogue were apparently not as close as they were in Palestine. House churches formed in which the new stood in the foreground and not an orientation toward the old. The previous religious, social, and national differences lost significance and a pneumatically defined community developed (cf. Gal 3:26-28), a community perceived from the outside as an independent group and a new religion.

In the first century C.E., Rome was beyond doubt the capital of the world, with about one million inhabitants.[32] The origins of Christianity in Rome cannot be understood apart from the history of the Jewish community there. It was first mentioned in 139 B.C.E.[33] Apparently, at the beginning of the forties, Christianity reached Rome via the trade routes, just as Judaism had before. It can hardly be accidental that there were pre-Pauline churches in Puteoli (Acts 28:13) and Rome (Rom 1:7; Acts 28:15). Not only were there two large communities there, but the main trade route between the eastern part of the empire and the city of Rome ran via Puteoli to Rome. Unknown early Christian missionaries, who came to the world capital as slaves, as freed persons, or as those engaged in commerce or a trade, apparently brought the gospel to Rome.[34] Initially, Jewish Christians were the majority in the church. This circumstance changed because of the expulsions following the Edict of Claudius (49 C.E.). When the Letter to the Romans was written in 56 C.E., Gentile Christians already comprised the majority (cf. Rom 1:5, 13-15; 10:1-13; 11:13, 17-32; 15:15, 16, 18).

One can only carefully draw inferences from Rom 16:3-16 concerning the social stratification within the early Roman church. It lists twenty-eight individuals (twenty-six by name). Inscriptional analysis of the names attested in Rom 16:3-16 demonstrates that of thirteen comparable names, four point to the free and nine to the slave origins of the bearer.[35] Many tasks of community living are performed by women, for only they are said to labor (κοπιάω in Rom 16:6, 12; cf. further v. 13b). Of the twenty-six persons mentioned by name in Rom 16:3-16, twelve came to Rome from the east and were personally known to Paul, which permits one to infer a strong influx of Christians from the eastern portion of the empire into the Roman church. Romans 16:3-16 also offers information concerning the organization of the Roman Christians. Apparently, from the very beginning, there was no closed Christian church with a large assembly space; rather, several house churches arose gradually. Paul mentions the house church around Prisca and Aquila (Rom 16:5), and at least Rom 16:14 and 16:15 attest to the existence of several independent house churches in Rome.[36] By means of the influx from the east, Christianity in Rome grew very rapidly. In 56 C.E., Paul expected from these house churches material and personal support for his Spain mission. The persecution of Christians under Nero in 64 C.E. also presupposes house churches that were expanding extraordinarily and were known throughout the city.

Central Theological Topics

Paul is by no means the second and actual founder of Christianity; rather, before and contemporary with him, independent theological and christological conceptions were developed quite early. In this regard, the christological titles, baptism, and the Lord's Supper, ecclesiological self-designations, the production of texts, and the development of new norms were already playing a central role.

Christological Titles

Jesus' status as the Risen One and his function as eschatological savior and liberator were expressed through the christological titles. The central early title is Χριστός or Ἰησοῦς Χριστός.[37] The title "Christ" is linked to the oldest confessional tradition (cf. 1 Cor 15:3b-5; 2 Cor 5:15) and is associated with statements concerning Jesus' death and resurrection that encompass the entire saving event. Statements concerning Jesus' crucifixion (1 Cor 1:21; 2:2; Gal 3:1, 13), death (Rom 5:6, 8; 14:15; 15:3; 1 Cor 8:11; Gal 2:19, 21), resurrection (Rom 6:9; 8:11; 10:7; 1 Cor 15:12-17, 20, 23), preexistence (1 Cor 10:4; 11:3a, b), and earthly existence (Rom 9:5; 2 Cor 5:16) are associated with Χριστός. The use of Χριστός as a matter of course is no accident, for the addressees were able to receive Χριστός out of their cultural backgrounds in the context of ancient anointing rites. The anointing rites distributed throughout the Mediterranean region attest to a widespread ancient parlance according to which "whoever/whatever is anointed is holy, near to God, consigned to God."[38] Both Jewish Christians and Gentile Christians could understand Χριστός as a title indicating Jesus' unique proximity to God and holiness, so that Χριστός (or Ἰησοῦς Χριστός) as a title became the ideal missionary term.

A different perspective is associated with the κύριος title.[39] By designating Jesus as "Lord," believers submit themselves to the authority of the Elevated One present in the community. Psalm 110:1 LXX may have played a key role in the adoption of the *kurios* title in developing Christology.[40] Here, early Christians found the definitive scripture for Jesus' heavenly dignity and function: he is elevated to the right hand of God, participates in God's might and majesty, and thence exercises his lordship. In this context, the first Christians transferred "Lord," the common address for God, to Jesus quite early (cf. the citation of Joel 3:5 LXX in Rom 10:12-13; further 1 Cor 1:31; 2:16; 10:26; 2 Cor 10:17) and thus gave expression to his unique authority in distinction to other claims (e.g., to the imperial cult).[41] In Hellenistic reception, the Jewish background of the *kurios* title[42] often became associated with a critical idea: In the history of early Christian missions, the κύριος Ἰησοῦς Χριστός crossed paths with many masters and mistresses; for this very reason, it was important to ensure that this designation did not become one among many. There is only one God and one Lord, Jesus Christ, as the pre-Pauline tradition in 1 Cor 8:6 accentuates emphatically.[43]

The presence of the Ascended One in the church is an aspect associated with the title "Lord," as is clearly evident in worship acclamations and in the Lord's Supper tradition. By acclamation, the church acknowledges and professes Jesus as "Lord" (cf. 1 Cor 12:3; Phil 2:6-11). κύριος appears in concentration in the Lord's Supper tradition (cf. 1 Cor 11:20-23, 26ff., 32; 16:22). The church assembles in the mighty presence of the Ascended One whose saving, but also chastising, power (cf. 1 Cor 11:30) is active in the celebration of the Lord's Supper. An ethical component joins the liturgical dimension of the title "Lord." The Lord is the decisive authority by which all areas of daily life are considered (cf. Rom 14:8). The power of the Lord encompasses all realms of life; there is no realm without it. The Lord is the authority before whom the concrete life of Christians takes place.

The title υἱὸς (τοῦ) θεοῦ[44] or "Son of God" appears in pre-Pauline traditions (cf. 1 Thess 1:9-10; Rom 1:3b-4a). From the perspective of the history of religion, Old Testament concepts may have predominated in the development of the Son Christology (cf. Ps 2:7; 2 Sam 7:11-12, 14). The Son of God gave himself up for believers (cf. Gal 2:20; Rom 8:32). Gal 4:4 and Rom 8:3 associate the concept of preexistence with the sending of the Son. Gal 4:6 mentions the lasting significance of this saving event; through the presence of the Spirit of the Son, believers may understand themselves to be children. In addition to pre-Pauline tradition and Paul, the pre-Marcan community was the primary medium of the Son title. This is no accident, for this title, too, was acceptable to both Jews and those who practiced Greco-Roman religions.[45] The expression "(my) beloved son" links the account of Jesus' baptism (Mark 1:9-11), the story of the transfiguration (Mark 9:2-9), and the allegory of the vine dresser (Mark 12:1-12) terminologically and makes them guiding texts.[46] They form a line of christological perception since here, through God's voice, heaven and earth convene and, in each case, the title "Son" denotes the fact that Jesus belongs to God.

Baptism and Lord's Supper

Jesus' baptism in the Jordan by John the Baptist (cf. Mark 1:9-11 par.) may explain why, from the very beginning, the early Christian churches considered baptism the normative initiation rite. The ritual baths at Qumran (cf. 1 QS 2:25–3:12; 1 QS 6:16-17; 5:13), the baptism of proselytes (cf. *Sif.Bam* 108; *b.Ker* 9a), and the baths in certain mystery cults (cf. Apuleius, *Metam.* XI 23) exhibit some analogies but cannot be regarded as the historical antecedent and source for early Christian baptism.[47]

After Easter, the viewpoint apparently prevailed that the events involving Jesus of Nazareth fulfilled the Baptist's proclamations in unexpected ways. The most profound reason for the adoption of the practice of baptism in the early Christian churches may lie in this continuity of eschatological novelty. Continuity with John's baptism manifests itself in the characteristic features of early Christian baptismal practice:

1. Early Christian baptism was not self-baptism but was performed by a baptizer (cf. 1 Cor 1:14, 16; Acts 8:38; 10:48).
2. Like the baptism of John, Christian baptism was a one-time act and differed in this way from ritual baths in ancient Judaism and Hellenism.
3. Like John's baptism, early Christian baptism was probably performed by submersion in flowing water (cf. Acts 8:38; *Did.* 7:1-2).
4. Like John's baptism, Christian baptism was for the forgiveness of sins (cf. 1 Cor 6:11; Acts 2:38) and thus had an eschatological and soteriological dimension.

At the same time, the baptism practice of Christian believers differed in three ways from the baptism of John:

1. It understood the Christ event as the saving eschatological event present in baptism "in the name of the Lord Jesus/in the name of Jesus Christ." Several old formulaic expressions attest to a practice of baptism that attached central significance to the "name of Jesus": εἰς τὸ ὄνομα τοῦ κυρίου Ἰησοῦ ("in the name of the Lord Jesus"—Acts 8:16; 19:5; cf. 1 Cor 1:13, 15; Gal 3:27; Rom 6:3; Matt 28:19); ἐν τῷ ὀνόματι Ἰησοῦ Χριστοῦ

("in the name of Jesus Christ" = Acts 10:48; cf. 1 Cor 6:11); ἐπὶ τῷ ὀνόματι Ἰησοῦ Χριστοῦ ("in the name of Jesus Christ"— Acts 2:38). Neither pagan Hellenism nor the Septuagint yields an exact linguistic derivation for these formulaic expressions.[48] Instead, the variability and breadth of content in these formulas indicate that they must be considered early and specifically Christian creations that find their material grounds in the resurrection of Jesus Christ from the dead and attain their significance in their respective literary contexts.

2. Early Christian baptism is linked to the gift of the Spirit. The experience of the Spirit's presence in the baptism event marks not merely a distinction from John's baptism but the center of early Christian baptismal theology (cf. Mark 1:8; Acts 1:5; 8:14-25; 9:17, 18; 11:16; 2 Cor 1:21-22; Gal 5:24, 25; Rom 5:5; John 3:5). The Spirit separates one from the power of sin, confers righteousness (cf. 1 Cor 1:30; 6:11; Rom 3:25), and defines the new life as the effective power of God (cf. Rom 8:1-11).

3. Baptism incorporates one into the eschatological community of salvation. The baptized live henceforth in the unity of the body of Christ (1 Cor 12:13) and already participate in the power of the world to come (cf. 2 Cor 1:22; 5:5; Rom 8:23).

As for baptism, an impulse from the life of Jesus was also definitive for the development of the sacrament of the Lord's Supper.[49] Jesus' last meal with his disciples in Jerusalem immediately before his arrest is historically very likely (cf. 1 Cor 11:23c). This meal received its particular character through Jesus' awareness that he would soon die. Jesus apparently associated his imminent death with the expectation that the kingdom of God would now break in comprehensively (Mark 14:25). After Easter, the last meal became thanksgiving and praise (1 Cor 11:11, 24/Mark 14:22, 23) and a sign of fulfillment and a memorial (1 Cor 11:24, 25/Luke 22:19: "in my memory") of the representative sufferer (Mark 14:24: "shed for the many"/Luke 22:20 "shed for you"). In the power of the Holy Spirit, the Risen One himself is the living and now mighty subject of his memorial; he is the founder of a new covenant (1 Cor 11:25/Luke 22:20) whose saving effect ("my body/my blood") is available to the believing community.

Finally, the κύριος Ἰησοῦς (1 Cor 11:23: "the Lord, Jesus") proves to be the coming Lord of humanity and the world (1 Cor 11:26: "proclaim the death of the Lord until he comes"; cf. Mark 14:25). Despite variations in the formulation, these fundamental ideas shape all the Lord's Supper traditions. The old pre-Pauline tradition in 1 Cor 11:23-26 offers a closer look into the early Christian practice of the Lord's Supper. In Corinth, the sacramental act was associated with a common meal at which the bread and the cup originally were the frame (μετὰ τὸ δειπνῆσαι, "after the meal" in 1 Cor 11:25; cf. also Luke 22:20). The common meal took place as a feast between two specific actions: the gesture with the bread and the saying about the bread introduced the common meal, while the gesture with the cup and the saying about the cup concluded the meal. This initial practice then gave way to the practice of having meals before the actual sacramental act. Here, the differences between wealthy and poor members of the community in Corinth became evident; one group feasted, the other hungered (cf. 1 Cor 11:21-22, 33-34). As at pagan sacrificial meals, table fellowship developed among the affluent to the exclusion of the poor. Paul harshly criticized this development (1 Cor 11:17-22); he pled for the separation of meals from celebrations of the Lord's Supper (1 Cor 11:22).

The significance of baptism and the Lord's Supper for the movement of believers in Christ can hardly be overestimated on the levels of theology, institution, and identity theory. Theologically, the two sacraments testify to the dawn of the *eschaton*; the elevated Jesus Christ is conceived as present in them as they become down payments on the future. Institutionally, baptism and the Lord's Supper contributed decisively to the formation of an independent identity. Admittedly, the Jerusalem church may have understood its baptismal and communion practice in the context of Judaism; at the same time, however, the two sacraments differ significantly from Jewish cleansing and meal practices in terms of their Christocentricity and their soteriological claims. In addition, baptism and the Lord's Supper were celebrated quite early outside Palestine and were freed from their Jewish contexts in the churches of Syria, Asia Minor, and Greece. Accordingly, in terms of social identity theory, these sacraments became the catalysts of a transethnic consciousness and thus decisively nurtured the process toward an independent movement of believers in Christ.

Ecclesiological Self-Designations

Bultmann correctly saw that an essential element of early Christian identity formation was a corporate consciousness.[50] This evidences itself foremost in its ecclesiological self-designations. In ἐκκλεσία ("assembly/community"), Christians adapted a political term[51] to characterize the essence and the local assemblies of the new community. In the Greco-Hellenistic realms, ἐκκλεσία designated the assembly of free men entitled to vote, a usage also present in Acts 19:32, 39. First Thessalonians 2:14, 1 Cor 15:9, Gal 1:13, and Phil 3:6 demonstrate that the designation ἐκκλεσία τοῦ θεοῦ ("assembly of God") may already have emerged for the new movement of believers in Christ in Jerusalem. Believers there may also have associated ἐκκλεσία with קהל (as in the Septuagint)[52] and thereby aligned Christ's community with God's people, Israel. At the same time, however, the failure to adopt συναγωγή ("synagogue"), and the link to a profane political term of Greek self-government (by the term ἐκκλεσία), expressed the earliest communities' self-understanding in a demarcation over against Judaism. The early Christians referred to themselves as "brothers" (a total of 343 instances; cf. 1 Thess 1:4; 2 Cor 1:1; Gal 1:2; Rom 1:13; Phil 1:12; Phlm 1; etc.) and to Jesus Christ as "the firstborn among many brothers" (Rom 8:29). Thus they express their connection to God and Jesus but especially their mutual affection and respect, their solidarity, and their new consciousness as "God's family."[53] Other ecclesiological designations stand in the history of the tradition of Old Testament/Jewish concepts: for example, "the holy ones" (cf. 1 Cor 1:2; 2 Cor 1:1; Rom 1:7; Phil 1:1; etc.) and "the chosen/called" (cf. 1 Thess 1:4; 1 Cor 1:26-27; Gal 1:6; Rom 1:6; 8:29-39; etc.). They denote the eschatological consciousness of the believers, tracing their origin back to God and acknowledging thereby their separation from the world and from evil. In addition to the basic ecclesiological terms, three basic metaphors shaped the earliest statements about the church already before Paul: "in Christ" (ἐν Χριστῷ), "body of Christ" (σῶμα Χριστοῦ), and "people of God" (λαὸς θεοῦ). With their spatial and temporal aspects, they comprehensively describe the new location and the essence of Christian existence in the community of believers.[54] Acts designates the new movement as "the Way" (ἡ ὁδός)—probably a Christian self-designation derived from Isa 40:3 LXX.[55] The term Χριστιανοί ("Christians") apparently appeared in Antioch for the first time as a third-party designation for the predominantly Gentile Christian adherents of the new doctrine (cf. Acts 11:26). Ignatius, who uses it in his letters unself-consciously as a Christian self-designation,[56] confirms the Antiochene origin of this designation. Formally, Χριστιανοί involves a grecized Latinism,[57] which suggests that the Roman provincial government already had an interest in the new movement.[58] In addition, the form of the word reveals that, in Antioch, the title Χριστός had already become a name for the Risen One.

Early Text Production

The production of texts and literature attained a decisive role in determining early Christian identity, as demonstrated especially by pre-Pauline traditions. At issue are well-shaped, formulaic texts that originated before the production of the Pauline letters, therefore between 40 and 50 C.E., in the churches of Syria (e.g., Antioch) and of southeastern Asia Minor. They offer insight into the earliest theological and social development in primarily Hellenistic churches and provide, simultaneously, a storehouse of knowledge about early Christianity.

The likely oldest mythical account and a central witness to early Christology is the pre-Pauline hymn Phil 2:6-11.[59] Already before Paul, christological reflection widened the change of status from postexistence to preexistence. Underlying this process is an idea that defines the Christology of many writings in the New Testament: one cannot become something that one has not always been. Jesus Christ left his divine status (without losing it!) and took upon himself the most crass opposite conceivable (Phil 2:6-7). The hymn depicts and considers this fundamental process in its individual steps. It culminates in boundless praise for the Lord that makes Jesus Christ the unrestricted Lord of the whole world and (consciously or not) places him above the Roman emperor.[60] The pre-Paul tradition in 1 Cor 15:3b-5[61] is another central text for early Christology. Christ is risen from the dead, and the resurrection has lasting effect on the Crucified One. This situation is possible because it is to be understood throughout as the material subject of the event. The sequence "died-buried" and "awakened-appeared" denotes the events in their temporal and material succession. In connection with Old Testament theophanies, the passive ὤφθη ("appeared") in verse 5 emphasizes that the appearances of the Risen One reflect the will of God. An equally ancient pre-Pauline mission tradition appears in 1 Thess 1:9-10.[62] It links turning to the one true God with turning away from polytheism.

Fixed formulations concerning the death and resurrection of Jesus (belief formulas) occur in 1 Thess 4:14; 1 Cor 15:12, 15; 2 Cor 4:14; Gal 1:1; Rom 4:24; 8:34; 10:9b; 14:9. The death formula, which occurs in 1 Thess 5:9-10; 1 Cor 1:13; 8:11; 2 Cor 5:14; Rom 5:6, 8; 14:15, emphasizes the soteriological dimension of the Christ event as "dying for us."[63] The surrender formula formulates God's behavior toward the Son as taking place "for us" (Gal 1:4; 2:20; Rom 4:25; 8:32).[64] The Son formula in Rom 1:3b-4a is noteworthy;[65] it regards Christ in his corporeal existence as son of David but in his pneumatic existence as Son of God. He is Son of God by virtue of his resurrection, which, according to Rom 1:4a, was affected by the πνεῦμα ἁγιωσύνης ("Spirit of Holiness"), that is, by the Spirit of God. Only through the resurrection is Jesus enthroned as Son of God, a notion that does not presuppose the preexistence and sonship of the earthly Jesus. Fixed formulations also describe the sending of the Son (cf. Rom 8:3), which Gal 4:4 associates with the concept of preexistence.

Acclamations that attest to the lordship of Jesus Christ belong in the realm of early Christian liturgy (cf. 1 Cor 12:3; 16:22). The pre-Pauline tradition about God as εἷς ("one") in 1 Cor 8:6 is extraordinarily important.[66] It boldly links God's history with the history of Jesus Christ. The text reflects the relationship between *theo*logy and Christology in the context of monotheism; the predicate of "oneness" pertains to the Father but simultaneously also to the Lord Jesus Christ. This predication does not result in a division of the one God into two gods; rather, it incorporates the one Lord into the realm of the one God. In terms of his origin and nature, Christ belongs entirely on God's side. At the same time, the one Lord remains subordinate to the one God, and not merely in the sequence of the text, for the Creator God is the Father of the Lord Jesus Christ.

New Norms

In order to introduce a separation from previous religious worlds, early churches had to develop and institutionalize new norms. In particular, baptism, the Lord's Supper, and worship services were altogether ritual loci where the new religious experiences were practiced and consolidated.

The pre-Pauline baptismal traditions (1 Cor 1:30; 6:11; 12:13; 2 Cor 1:21-22; Gal 3:26-28; Rom 3:25; 4:25; 6:3-4) reveal the significance of rites and the concepts they convey for the formation of one's own identity and, simultaneously, for detachment from past values systems:

1. Sin is overcome now in baptism "in the name of Jesus" (cf. 1 Cor 6:11; Rom 6:3-4). Purity before God cannot be attained either through repeated cultic ablutions or through the temple cult or animal sacrifice. In baptism, however, believers are "washed and sanctified" (1 Cor 6:11), "anointed and sealed" (2 Cor 1:21-22).

2. Righteousness is not attained through ritually correct religious actions but results from divine action (cf. 1 Cor 6:11; Rom 3:25; 4:25; Rom 6:3-4).

3. The Spirit as the power and presence of God/the gods is appropriated in baptism (cf. 1 Cor 6:11; 1 Cor 12:13; 2 Cor 1:21-22) and is now powerfully active in worship (cf. 1 Thess 5:19; 1 Cor 12; 14).

4. The interpretation of the cross as a once-and-for-all sacrificial cult that renders all other sacrifices superfluous must be understood as a fundamental break with both Jewish and Greco-Roman concepts (Rom 3:25).

5. The baptism tradition in Gal 3:26-28 develops a revolutionary and simultaneously utopian concept.[67] The change in status bestowed through baptism includes a transformation of actual social relationships! These new viewpoints may have originated in those Hellenistic cities that already constituted the mission field of Antioch and in which the invalidation of old traditions is most conceivable.

6. A new "holy day" is defined, Sunday.[68] The oldest literary reference appears in 1 Cor 16:2, where, in the context of the collection, Paul speaks of the "first" day of the week. According to Mark 16:2, the first day of the Jewish week that follows the Sabbath is Resurrection Day, when worship services were celebrated (cf. Acts 20:7) and which was considered "the Lord's Day" (cf. Rev 1:10).

Connection with Gnosticism?

Bultmann dated Gnosticism before the Hellenistic church and contemporary with Paul and saw in it a definitive religious and theological presupposition for Pauline and Johannine theology. "At first, Gnosticism probably penetrated into the Christian congregations mostly through the medium of a Hellenistic Judaism that was itself in the grip of syncretism" (1.171). Specifically, according to Bultmann, gnostic thought influenced early Christianity in its formation of an eschatological dualism, in its concept of sin (Rom 5:12ff.; 8:20ff.: the fall of Adam and of creation), in its terminology for depicting the saving event (the descent and ascent of the Redeemer), in the liberation from the demonic rulers of the world, and in its idea of unity. On the one hand, Paul and John adopted the terminology and even motifs of Gnosticism, but, on the other, their theological schemes broke gnostic thought open in many cases.

In relation to Bultmann's views, scholarship has changed the most with regard to the question of Gnosticism. While Bultmann still assumed the existence of a pre-Christian, syncretistic Gnosticism, there is broad consensus today that Gnosticism was primarily a second- and third-century C.E. phenomenon.[69] There are no pre-Christian sources for Gnosticism, and, in the New Testament, only 1 Tim 6:20 mentions it. Similarly, it is not possible to jump across centuries (in one's head!) and to postulate from predominantly third-/fourth-century C.E. texts (Nag Hammadi/Mandaean Scriptures) presuppositions for the New Testament that one cannot find there at all![70] In addition, it is clear now that, concerning the understanding of Gnosticism, its character and its proximity to the New Testament will determine the definition of what Gnosticism is supposed to be. The definition of Gnosticism as a specific ancient understanding of existence (a view elaborated by Bultmann's student Hans Jonas) has been very influential.[71] This broad definition of the term "Gnosticism" led to the subsummation of very different movements in late antiquity under this heading, which makes specific research in the history of religion difficult. In current research, four basic ideas seem to be considered the definitive characteristics of gnostic thought/a gnostic system:[72]

1. Both the supreme God and the Redeemer are perfectly transcendent beings. By definition, they cannot come into contact with anything earthly and are not subject to any change whatsoever.
2. The logically consistent result is a protological dualism according to which a division between a first/superior and a second/inferior god already occurs on the level of deity/deities before the origins of the world. Only the second/inferior deity (usually the "Jewish" god) appears as creator of material reality.
3. By necessity, the negative understanding of the material world and its origins results in cosmologies that further inform an understanding of the character of the supreme deity and the world (its becoming/being) and point the way to the higher worlds.
4. In the background of this worldview stands the experience of otherworldliness and the wish to overcome the world; it is supported by the consciousness that one actually belongs to "another," "better," and "higher" world to which one may return with the help of the Redeemer.

If one applies these four basic ideas to the New Testament, no book evidences convincing similarities to them. Therefore, one can dispense with the notion of Gnosticism as a presupposition for New Testament theology.

Summary

Rudolf Bultmann's concentration in his *Theology* on Paul and John involves both strengths and weaknesses at the same time: strengths because Paul and John are indubitably the most significant theologians of early Christianity, weaknesses because the theological and sociological developments before Paul, along with the driving persons, places, and ideas, do not come sufficiently into view. From the outset, early Christianity was a very mobile and creative movement. Already before Paul, decisive theological points were established and new concepts of identity developed. Anyone who joined the new movement of believers in Christ between 35 and 60 C.E. inevitably restricted his religio-cultural world. This restructuring did not occur as an absolute break with the past but, as a rule, as a process of linkage, demarcation, reinterpretation, rejection, and redefinition. These concepts do not represent strict opposites but could be in process sequentially and/or concurrently. The foundations for this must have been laid within the earliest form of Christianity. The life, death, and resurrection of Jesus Christ were subjected to adaptive interpretation; rituals such as baptism and the Lord's Supper, and Spirit-led worship, created a new identity; and the love ethic demanded by Jesus was actually lived out in the churches. Prior to and contemporary with the time of Paul, many men and women in many places engaged in this project. They created a new religious and ethical world, from which Paul definitely profited and which he developed further.

Chapter 4

HUMANITY
PRIOR TO THE REVELATION OF FAITH

Richard B. Hays

"Man Prior to the Revelation of Faith," the title of the first major section of Rudolf Bultmann's treatment of "The Theology of Paul," already hints at the contours of his interpretation of Paul's thought. Bultmann proposes a reading that focuses on "Man"—that is, on theological *anthropology*. And the "plot" of this reading is scripted by an *ordo salutis* in which everything hinges on the existential decision of the individual person to respond in faith to God's grace. As I shall explain, this approach to interpreting the theology of Paul—an approach meant to address the apologetic concerns of the mid-twentieth-century German academy—now seems deeply problematical.

The task of composing a critical evaluation of this section of Bultmann's hugely influential *Theology of the New Testament* has been, for me, a trip back in the time machine to a very different era in New Testament studies—an era that formed the ethos of my own early theological education, but that now seems remote and rather strange. It is a bit like the disconcerting experience of going back to one's high school reunion after more than forty years: there are familiar and welcome memories, but one also quickly becomes aware of how much has changed, how one's own view of the world has been altered across time, and how impossible it is to go home again.

I first read Bultmann in 1967, as an undergraduate. My now dog-eared and taped-together paperback copy of Kendrick Grobel's English translation subsequently accompanied me through the years of seminary, served as a frequent reference and sparring partner during my doctoral studies, and came off the shelf often when I later taught seminars on NT theology. Yet to read through the whole thing freshly now is to be confronted anew by the strangeness and instability of Bultmann's ambitious project. Is it really possible to "translate" Paul's Christ-centered Jewish apocalyptic discourse into the idiom of a demythologized twentieth-century existentialism? When the question is posed that way, a negative answer seems inevitable.

Yet anyone seeking to pursue the theological interpretation of Scripture is faced with a formidable task analogous to Bultmann's project: to give a faithful descriptive explication of the historically situated content of the biblical texts while at the same time seeking to be guided, as Bultmann put it, by "the presupposition that they have something to say to the present."[1] The critique that I shall offer in the following pages may therefore, precisely in and through its severity, serve as a chastening and cautionary word to all of us who try to meet the challenges of theological hermeneutics in our own day, and to grapple with what these texts have to say to us.

In the compass of this brief essay, I cannot possibly engage all the exegetical issues raised in Bultmann's extended treatment of "Man Prior to the Revelation of Faith."[2] I propose, therefore, to focus attention on four of Bultmann's major methodological decisions, key structural choice points that shape his presentation of Paul's thought. They are as follows: (1) Bultmann's decision to explicate Paul's theology chiefly as anthropology, (2) the decision to read Paul against the history-of-religions backdrop of a hypothetical Hellenistic Christianity influenced more by mystery religions and Gnosticism than by Israel's Scripture, (3) the decision to focus on individual words and concepts as the primary vehicle for interpreting Paul's theology, and (4) the explicit decision to employ a demythologizing hermeneutic to unfold the "real intention" underlying Paul's explicit statements. Our discussion of these interrelated methodological moves will identify several substantive theological issues that demand scrutiny. But at every point, it should be recognized, Bultmann's treatment of the issues in Pauline theology is heavily conditioned by the *methodological* commitments that frame his analysis.

Theology as Anthropology

In the opening pages of "Man Prior to the Revelation of Faith," Bultmann describes his reasons for focusing his discussion on Paul's *anthropology*. Observing that Pauline theology is "not a speculative system," he affirms that Paul is concerned not with some notion of God *in se*, but "only with God as he is significant for man, for man's responsibility and man's salvation." Thus, "[e]very assertion about God is simultaneously an assertion about man and vice versa. For this reason, and in this sense, Paul's theology is at the same time anthropology." Likewise, "every assertion about Christ is also an assertion about man and vice versa; and Paul's christology is simultaneously soteriology" (1.190–91). These statements—reminiscent of the famous methodological meditation at the beginning of Calvin's *Institutes*[3]—are certainly accurate observations about Paul's thought. Paul's discourse about God and Christ is always concerned to explicate God's action *pro nobis*, and therefore his theological and christological affirmations do necessarily entail anthropological and theological corollaries.

Having begun, however, with these unimpeachable observations, Bultmann suddenly leaps to an assertion that seems unwarranted and one-sided: "Therefore, Paul's theology can best be treated as his doctrine of man: first, of man prior to the revelation of faith, and second, of man under faith, for in this way the anthropological and soteriological orientation of Paul's theology is brought out" (1.191). Why is this approach "best"? Why not the other way around? Why are the anthropological and soteriological dimensions of Paul's theology not best explicated as entailments of his proclamation about God's action in and through Jesus Christ (as Bultmann's contemporary Karl Barth insisted they should be)? This is a fateful decision, because it determines the vantage point for all that follows. Everything in Paul's complex theological reflections is seen, as it were, from the side of the human experience, rather than from the side of the narrative proclamation of the gospel. Here Bultmann is following a well-established trajectory in German Protestant theology that dates back at least to Friedrich Schleiermacher. But I would venture the suggestion that this methodological decision causes him to place the accents of Paul's thought in the wrong places. Indeed, I would suggest that—contrary to Bultmann's own intention—he risks reducing Paul's message to an anthropocentric meditation on human religious psychology, its limits, and its possibilities. (I am mindful of the small irony that here I am applying a bit of Bultmannian *Sachkritik* to the master of the method.)

To take a particularly striking example, after citing 1 Cor 15:24-26, a dramatic passage that declares that Christ will hand all things over to God the Father after triumphing over all powers, including death as the final enemy, Bultmann remarkably comments, "In reality, he is thereby only [!] expressing a certain understanding of existence:[4] The spirit powers represent the reality into which man is placed as one full of conflicts and struggle, a reality which threatens and tempts" (1.259). Here Paul's proclamation of God's eschatological triumph over evil and death is converted through Bultmann's anthropocentric emphasis into a message about our human *Daseinsverständnis*; consequently, it becomes a rather banal affirmation that we live in a world where we are surrounded by conflicts and difficulties.

One can find similar examples strewn throughout the pages of "Man Prior to the Revelation of Faith," not always so dramatically reductive as this one, but consistently focusing on *human experience* as the chief subject matter of Paul's thought. We shall return to a further consideration of this *Tendenz* in Bultmann's interpretation when we consider his methodological commitment to demythologizing the texts. Here, however, I am calling attention to the way in which he systematically focuses on the *anthropological* content of Paul's writings as their real and primary sense. This primary focus on anthropology is, it seems to me, a significant reversal of the polarity of Paul's proclamation. Paul emphasizes again and again that his message is a word of revelation—*apokalypsis*—from and about God as disclosed in Jesus Christ. To cite just two examples, consider the following emphatic passages:

> For I want you to know, brothers and sisters, that the gospel that was proclaimed by me is not of human origin (*kata anthrōpon*); for I did not receive it from a human source (*para anthrōpou*), nor was I taught it, but I received it through a revelation of Jesus Christ (*di' apokalypseōs Iēsou Christou*). (Gal 1:11-12)

> And we also thank God continually because, when you received the word of God, which you heard from us, you accepted it not as a human word [literally, "a word of human beings," *logon anthrōpōn*]

but as it actually is, the word of God, which is indeed at work in you who believe. (1 Thess 2:13)

Bultmann would no doubt say, with justification, that each of these passages is concerned with "God as he is significant for man, for man's responsibility and man's salvation." But this statement runs the risk of misconstruing the *directionality* of Paul's soteriological grammar: the gospel for Paul is a proclamation of good news about *God* and *God's* action for the salvation of the world. This is of course the precise point of controversy in Ernst Käsemann's well-known critique of his teacher: Bultmann's anthropological focus fails to grasp the gospel as the *power* of God for salvation and domesticates it into a word about the possibility of a new self-understanding.[5] It may be a telling fact that neither of the above passages (Gal 1:11-2 and 1 Thess 2:13) appears in the index of scriptural passages cited in Bultmann's *Theology of the New Testament*—an omission all the more startling in a presentation that purports to take "the *Revelation* of Faith" as a hinge point for understanding Paul's thought.

The Hellenistic Thought World and the Erasure of Israel

At the very outset, Bultmann situates Paul "within the frame of Hellenistic Christianity," influenced by its thought forms but also at the same time calling attention to "the problems latent in the Hellenistic proclamation" (1.187). To be sure, Bultmann duly notes Paul's own roots in Hellenistic Judaism. But he questions the tradition that Paul was a pupil of Gamaliel in Jerusalem (Acts 22:3), and finds the most significant fact about Paul's upbringing to be the fact that he was a native of Tarsus in Cilicia, for "in his home city he came into contact with Hellenistic culture and became acquainted with popular philosophy and the phenomena of religious syncretism." Bultmann is not certain whether it was "in his pre-Christian period" that Paul absorbed "theological ideas of this syncretism (those of the mystery-religions and of Gnosticism)," but he opines that such ideas do surely "come out in his Christian theology" (1.187). As this preliminary summary would suggest, Bultmann's account of Paul's history-of-religions background exercises a major influence on his analysis of Paul's thought. Repeatedly in the pages of "Man Prior to the Revelation of Faith," Bultmann explicates various elements in Paul's conceptual world as arising from Hellenistic influences of one sort or another, even when he sees Paul critically qualifying these elements.

Particularly striking is the number of instances in which he identifies hypothetical "Gnostic" sources or backgrounds for Paul's ideas and images. In 2 Cor 5:1-8, Paul "comes very close to Hellenistic-Gnostic dualism" in his deprecation of present embodied existence, but avoids this problem by his wish to be "further clothed" in a heavenly body rather than "unclothed" (1.201–2). Again, in 1 Cor 15:44-45, Paul is "influenced . . . by Gnostic usage, with the result that he uses *psyche* in a deprecatory sense. . . . *Psyche* is now (as in Gnosticism) the merely natural, earthly vitality in contrast to the divinely given capacity for eternal life" (1.204).

Indeed, Bultmann (remarkably) finds Gnostic motifs throughout Paul's emphatic discussion of the resurrection of the body in 1 Cor 15. For example, "the drama described in 1 Cor 15:20-28 does not come from the tradition of the creation-story, but from Gnostic cosmology and eschatology" (1.228). On the contrary, most NT scholarship today would see this text as one of the passages in Paul that most robustly gives expression to *Jewish apocalyptic* tradition, but Bultmann affirms repeatedly that the notion of God's cosmic triumph derives from a Hellenistic Gnostic milieu. Not only in 1 Cor 15 but also in Rom 8:18-39, "Paul is able to appropriate the cosmological mythology of Gnosticism because it enables him to express the fact that the perishable 'creation' becomes a destructive power whenever man decides in favor of it instead of for God" (1.230). Or again, in Paul's account of Adam's transgression as the universal cause of human bondage to sin (Rom 5:12-19), "Paul is unquestionably under the influence of the Gnostic myth" (1.251). (Interestingly, neither here nor in any of the other passages cited in this paragraph does Bultmann specify *what* Gnostic myth he has in mind or cite any actual textual evidence for it.) To cite one last example, Bultmann explains the notoriously difficult Gal 3:19 as follows: "Paul can take up the Gnostic myth of the giving of the Law by angels in order to prove that the Law of Moses is not attributable to God himself" (1.268).

All of this is deeply problematical for at least two reasons. First, the older hypothesis of a well-developed pre-Christian Gnosticism, a hypothesis beloved by the *Religionsgeschichtliche Schule* of the early twentieth century, has foundered on the rocks of subsequent scholarly investigation, chiefly because of the absence of textual evidence for such a phenomenon. All the texts that attest a developed system of Gnostic mythology date from a historical period demonstrably later than Paul's letters.[6] Many of the narrative or dramatic elements that Bultmann ascribed to a hypothetical Gnosticism are much more easily explained as developments within Paul's own native Jewish tradition, particularly in its apocalyptic forms.

More deeply troubling than Bultmann's speculative hypotheses about Paul's Hellenistic intellectual horizons, however, are the *absences* and gaps in the picture he draws of Paul's thought world. One can read through page after page of "Man Prior to the Revelation of Faith" and find only the most cursory nods to the importance of Israel's Scripture for Paul's theology. Bultmann's Paul has turned his face primarily toward the worlds of Hellenistic philosophy, mystery religions, and Gnostic speculation; he seeks in various ways to counter or transform the mythological elements in those worlds, but their symbolic universe nonetheless provides the conceptual furniture for Paul's imagination. By contrast, the story of Israel's election, the fate of God's elect people, the reliability of God's covenant promises to Israel, the Jewish hope for resurrection of the dead, and the actual language of Israel's scriptural story appear only on the periphery of Bultmann's portrait of Paul.[7]

Indeed, while Bultmann does take note of Paul's wrestling with the significance of the Law, the role of that Law has become almost entirely a negative one for the person who has come to faith. Bultmann offers a lengthy and convoluted discussion of the role of Law for "Man Prior to the Revelation of Faith" (1.259–69), but the bottom line of that discussion is this: "*the ultimate purpose of the Law is to lead man to death* and thereby to let God appear as God" (1.267, emphasis original, both in German and in the English translation).

In order to arrive at this conclusion, Bultmann offers a whole series of highly debatable exegetical judgments about particular passages. He interprets Rom 10:4 to mean that Christ is the *termination* of the Law, rather than its goal (*telos*; 1.263). As I have argued elsewhere, this is almost surely a misreading of the text; within the argument of Rom 10, Paul is asserting that Christ is the true end to which Israel's Law points.[8] Again, referring to Gal 5:4 ("You are severed from Christ, you who would be justified by the Law; you have fallen away from grace"), Bultmann asserts that the very effort to keep the Law is already in itself sinful in principle, because it presumes that one can thereby achieve salvation through "self-powered striving" (1.264). But, as much recent commentary has shown, this reading superimposes the Reformation's concern about "self-powered striving" upon an argument that actually is chiefly concerned with whether Gentiles must adopt the practices and markers of Jewish ethnic identity.

To give one more example, Bultmann argues that Paul's image of the Law as a *paidagōgos eis Christon* (Gal 3:24) means that "the 'educating' done by the Law leads . . . into sin" and that this leading into sin is precisely "the purpose of the Law in the history of salvation" (1.266–67). All this is based on the doubtful assertion that Gal 3:19 ("Why then the Law? It was added because of transgressions [*tōn parabaseōn charin*]") means that the Law was given "to evoke transgressions"—a reading clearly at odds not only with the internal logic of the metaphor of the *paidagōgos* but also with Gal 3:24, which affirms that "before faith came . . . we were imprisoned *and guarded* until faith would be revealed."[9] Paul is arguing that the Law had a protective and propaedeutic function, not that it tempted the Jewish people into sinful self-powered striving that led to pride and alienation from God.[10]

What is almost entirely missing here is adequate attention to Paul's insistence that "the Law is holy, and the commandment is holy and righteous and good" (Rom 7:12). And more fundamentally, what is missing on Bultmann's radar is any recognition that Paul's argument in Romans is passionately concerned to show that "God has not rejected his people, whom he foreknew" (Rom 11:2a). The ongoing significance of Israel as a people is simply elided (or erased) throughout Bultmann's ingenious reading of Paul, and the notion that Paul is concerned to uphold the integrity of God's promises to Israel seemingly plays no role in his interpretation. At every point, instead, the discussion focuses on "Man" (*der Mensch* or *die Menschen*) as a naked generic subject, not significantly conditioned by a specific history (unless it is "the history of mankind," 1.266), and certainly not by God's election of a specific people. I would suggest that Bultmann's neglect of the story of Israel is but one aspect of his larger inattention to the significance of narrative in Paul's thought.[11] But that observation leads directly into our third set of methodological observations.

Theology as Word Study

In retrospect, one of the most curious and unfortunate features of Bultmann's presentation is his methodological decision to approach the exposition of Paul's theology of "Man Prior to the Revelation of Faith" through stringing together a series of word studies on individual terms and concepts: *sōma, psychē, sarx*, and so forth—in other words, his decision to approach the topic through a study of "anthropological concepts" (*die anthropologischen Begriffe*). Of course, this approach was influenced by the methodology then current in the field of biblical studies, as reflected in Kittel's *Theologisches Wörterbuch zum Neuen Testament*—a methodology that has subsequently come under severe criticism and fallen decidedly out of favor.[12] What I have to say on this matter, therefore, will hardly come as a surprise to most readers today.

The word-study approach has two closely related drawbacks. First, words do not carry semantic freight apart from contexts in which they are used. The Kittel approach tends to treat words as concepts whose sense is to be determined through a diachronic investigation of their history, rather than through careful synchronic observation of their usage in particular arguments or contexts. It would be unfair to say that Bultmann completely ignores the contexts in which Paul's anthropological terms occur, but it would be fair to say that he is more interested in developing an understanding of the terms themselves than in explicating the arguments in which they actually appear. So, for example, Bultmann can quite remarkably declare in the very beginning of his explanation of *sōma* ("body") that it would be a "methodological error" to allow our understanding of the term to be influenced by Paul's use of it in 1 Cor 15:35-50, because in this passage "Paul lets himself be misled into adopting his opponents' method of argumentation," and so in this text "he uses the *soma*-concept in a way not characteristic of him elsewhere." Paul's usage of the term here is in fact "un-Pauline" (1.192). The underlying assumption here is that Paul must have an ideal or normative *concept* of *sōma* that transcends his actual use of the term in any particular context—even, in this case, a context where he is making repeated and emphatic use of it in an effort to correct what he regards as the misunderstanding of his readers.

Bultmann's assertion that Paul has been "misled" by his opponents would suggest he recognizes that in 1 Cor 15 the apostle is addressing a particular pastoral situation, a situation that has created certain rhetorical exigencies. But Bultmann neither outlines his understanding of that situation nor attempts to show clearly how Paul's argument confronts it. Instead, he immediately starts surveying other passages more congenial with his own proposal that *sōma* in Paul most fundamentally indicates that *"Man is called soma in respect to his being able to make himself the object of his own action or to experience himself as the subject to whom something happens"* (1.195, emphasis original). If Paul's passionate discussion of the resurrection body in 1 Corinthians fails to fit this definition, it can simply be set aside as uncharacteristic of Paul's genuine theology. In sum, Bultmann's methodology undervalues both the historically contingent character of Paul's letters[13] and the rhetorical function of the anthropological terms as he actually uses them in his arguments.

The second major drawback of Bultmann's word-study approach may be illuminated by asking a simple question: why should an exposition of Paul's theology take its starting point from an exposition of the concept *sōma*? This choice of starting point seems both arbitrary and fragmenting in its effect. If we look to Paul's own discourse, we do not find him launching into disquisitions on the meaning of isolated anthropological terms. Instead, when he identifies the fundamental themes of his own message, he offers concise summaries of a kerygmatic narrative focused on God's saving action in Christ. Consider the following examples:

> [Y]ou turned to God from idols, to serve a living and true God, and to wait for his Son from heaven, whom he raised from the dead— Jesus, who rescues us from the wrath that is coming. (1 Thess 1:9-10)

> But when the fullness of time had come, God sent his Son, born of a woman, born under the law, in order to redeem those who were under the law, so that we might receive adoption as children. (Gal 4:4-6)

> For I tell you that Christ has become a servant of the circumcised on behalf of the truth of God in order that he might confirm the promises given to the patriarchs, and in order that the Gentiles might glorify God for his mercy. (Rom 15:8-9a)

For I handed on to you as of first importance what I in turn had received: that Christ died for our sins in accordance with the scriptures, and that he was buried, and that he was raised on the third day in accordance with the scriptures, and that he appeared to Cephas, then to the twelve. (1 Cor 15:3-5)

After citing these examples of Paul's encapsulations of his gospel, I decided to look them up in the index of Bultmann's *Theology*. Here is what I found: according to the index, none of them is discussed anywhere in Bultmann's exposition of "The Theology of Paul." In the preliminary opening pages ("Presuppositions and Motifs of New Testament Theology"), there are just a few glancing references to 1 Thess 1:9-10 and 1 Cor 15:3-5 as part of the kerygma of the earliest church and/or the Hellenistic church prior to Paul. But Bultmann does not treat them as part of his exposition of Paul's own theology. And, again according to the index, there are no references at all anywhere in Bultmann's book to Gal 4:4-6 or to Rom 15:8-9. These are astonishing omissions.[14]

My point is this: by focusing his exposition of "Man Prior to the Revelation of Faith" on isolated anthropological terms, Bultmann submerges the *story* that constitutes the heart of Paul's gospel. He offers a number of luminous insights into the meaning of this or that term that Paul uses. (See, to cite a single example, his lovely paraphrase of Rom 8:13: "He who derives life out of the transitory must, himself, perish with the perishing of the transitory" [1.247].) But the overall shape of Paul's proclamation is simply lost, replaced by Bultmann's own preoccupation with how human beings can find authentic existence. The stripping away of the kerygmatic narrative allows Paul's anthropological terms to be factored out of his narrative world, paraphrased in modern terminology, assigned a new prominence as proto-philosophical concepts, and eclectically reconstructed into a twentieth-century existentialist theological program whose contours would have been perplexing to the first-century apostle. This reconfiguration of Paul's theology is facilitated by the word-study method, which is particularly well suited to extract concepts (*Begriffe*) while discarding the narrative—or "mythic"—framework in which the concepts originally are found. But this observation leads to the final methodological decision that we must consider in assessing Bultmann's treatment of Paul: his demythologizing hermeneutic.

Demythologizing the Gospel

Bultmann's hermeneutical program of demythologizing the New Testament has been exhaustively debated by New Testament scholars and theologians—or at least it was a generation ago. Even if the intensity of the debate has waned in recent years, the importance of the issues raised by Bultmann is perennial. The fundamental problem, as Bultmann saw it, is that the New Testament writers lived and wrote within an ancient worldview characterized by a primitive cosmology that is no longer believable for modern persons living in a scientific age. Consequently, theological interpretation of the New Testament requires that its "mythological" stories and concepts be translated into different philosophical and linguistic categories that nonetheless preserve and reveal the "real intention" that is implicit in the mythological language employed by the New Testament authors.

Bultmann's *Theology of the New Testament* is neither an explanation nor a defense of the program of demythologizing; rather, it presupposes the necessity of such a program. The book therefore functions as a *performance*, an embodiment, of the sort of interpretation that Bultmann had advocated in his earlier essays on hermeneutics.[15] The task of such an interpretation is chiefly, as Bultmann pictures it, "the explication of believing self-understanding" (2.251). This conception of the task of New Testament theology explains, in part, Bultmann's pervasive anthropological focus and his palpable discomfort with the Jewish apocalyptic elements in Paul's proclamation. But it also leads to theological difficulties.

All of this is well-worked ground. My chief task in the last section of this chapter, therefore, is simply to illustrate the way in which Bultmann's demythologizing program manifests itself in his account of "Man Prior to the Revelation of Faith," and to assess the consequences of this approach.

Near the beginning of his discussion of Paul's anthropological concepts, in the discussion of the concept of *sōma*, Bultmann explicitly flies the flag for his hermeneutical agenda. He is grappling with Paul's discussion of the resurrection of the body—an idea that Bultmann finds distinctly problematical. He writes as follows:

> If man were no longer *soma*—if he no longer had a relationship
> to himself—he would no longer be man. Since Paul's capacity for

abstract thinking is not a developed one, and he therefore does not distinguish terminologically between *soma* in the basic sense of that which characterizes human existence and *soma* as the phenomenon of the material body, he connects the idea of somatic existence in the eschatological consummation with a mythological teaching on the resurrection (I Cor. 15). . . . In distinction from this mythology, the real intention of Paul must be made clear. It is that he asserts specific human existence, both before and beyond death, to be a somatic existence in the basic sense defined above [i.e., an existence in which man has a relationship to himself]. (1.198)

One must credit Bultmann with putting his hermeneutical cards on the table. Paul, says Bultmann, not having had the benefit of education in a German university, had not developed the "capacity for abstract thinking" necessary to conceive of an existence beyond death in which human beings, having no material body of any kind, will still be capable of having a relationship to themselves. (Whatever that might mean.) Therefore, the "unfortunate consequence" (1.198) is that Paul has recourse to a "mythological teaching on the resurrection" in which he imagines the existence of a "spiritual body." But Bultmann somehow knows that Paul's "real intention" lies not in what he actually wrote but in the abstract idea of a nonmaterial self "determined by the power of God which reconciles the cleft between self and self within a man and hence does presuppose a relationship of man to himself" (1.199).

I can only register the impression that Bultmann's interpretation of Paul at this point is both condescending and reductionistic. In addition, it is unclear whether Bultmann is still envisioning an existence "beyond death" in any temporally future sense, or whether Paul's apocalyptic eschatological vision of the resurrection hope has been subtly replaced by the concept of an integrated personal selfhood that might be attained, or anticipated, within life as we know it in the present age. I say intentionally that this is "unclear," because in the passage cited above we find, as often in Bultmann, a certain slippage between Paul's mythological/apocalyptic language and Bultmann's existentialist reappropriation of it. Whether the ambiguity is intentional or not, there remains a gray area in which Bultmann distances himself from the literal-referential sense of Paul's theological affirmations while still inhabiting them confessionally in some transferred metaphorical sense. At the same time, Bultmann asserts that this transferred sense is Paul's "real intention," even though the conceptualities he employs would have been unavailable to Paul or anyone else in the first century. Perhaps Bultmann's argument would be better served if he had avoided the language of "intention" and argued instead that Paul's formulations are groping dimly toward a reality that can now be more adequately named in a different (modern) linguistic register.

We find something similar in the later discussion of "flesh" and "sin" as "powers to which man falls slave." Bultmann writes,

> Paul can speak of both as personal beings as if they were demonic rulers—but in such a way that we do not have the right actually to ascribe to him a mythological concept of "flesh" or "sin." . . . Little as all this constitutes realistic mythology—it is not that but figurative, rhetorical language—it is, nevertheless, clear that this language stamps *flesh and sin as powers to which man has fallen victim* and against which he is powerless. The personification of these powers expresses the fact that man has lost to them the capacity to be the subject of his own actions [*sein Subjekt-sein*]. . . . [T]he subject-self, the true self of a man, is inwardly split. . . . Therefore, "I" and "I," self and self, are at war with each other. (1.244–45, emphasis original).

In this instance, Bultmann judges that Paul is already speaking figuratively, rather than in the language of "realistic mythology." Thus, strictly speaking, no demythologizing hermeneutic is necessary at this point. When Paul speaks of flesh and sin as "powers," he is in fact deliberately talking about an inward division in the human subject. But if that is the case, does it really make sense to say that the individual has "fallen victim" to these powers, and that he or she "has lost *to them [an sie]* the capacity" to be the subject of personal action? What, in this case, is the antecedent of the pronoun "them"? Does Paul really mean nothing more than that the rational will is overridden by other elements within the human psyche? Or should we instead consider the possibility that Paul really does believe in the existence of suprapersonal forces that oppress and enslave human beings?[16]

In light of this analysis, it is not hard to see why Bultmann can conceive of salvation chiefly as "a new understanding of one's self" that takes place through a process of individual decision. The individual sinner "is confronted by the gospel [the German here is actually *Botschaft*—not *Evangelium*] when it reaches him with the decision whether or not he is willing to understand himself anew and to receive his life from the hand of God" (1.269). It is important to get the balance right here: Bultmann is not saying that individuals can simply decide, as a project of self-improvement, to overcome their own dividedness or master their own baser impulses. Rather, the "decision" (*Entscheidung*) for a new self-understanding is always a "decision in regard to the grace which encounters man in the proclaimed word" (1.269). So the decision for a new self-understanding is always responsive in character, always answering God's offer of grace. But Bultmann is very clear that "[t]hrough Christ . . . there was brought about no more than the *possibility* of life," a possibility that must be embraced and actualized by the individual decision of faith (1.252).

It remains notoriously unclear exactly *how*, for Bultmann, the proclaimed word of Christ's death and resurrection enables or facilitates this new self-understanding, since this message is for Bultmann neither an account of Christ's death as a blood atonement that enables forgiveness of sins nor a true story about a cosmic event in which Christ has liberated humanity from the grip of hostile powers. But since the task of this essay is only to focus on Bultmann's treatment of "Man Prior to the Revelation of Faith," we need not attempt here to resolve this puzzle. The central point for now is that the human predicament is for Bultmann one of inward division and self-misunderstanding; accordingly, salvation is to be conceptualized in noetic terms as a transition into a new integrative interpretation of one's own self before God.

The besetting theological danger here is that of the reduction of theology to anthropology *simpliciter*. Both Barth and Käsemann leveled precisely this charge at Bultmann. On the basis of his account of Pauline theology, I would judge the charge to be justified. As we have already seen in the opening section of the present essay, Bultmann can astonishingly interpret Paul's account of Christ's eschatological triumph over the powers of sin and death (1 Cor 15:20-28) to express "only . . . a certain understanding of existence" that portrays our human reality "as one full of conflicts and struggle" (1.259). Or to take another example, he can write, "knowledge of God as Creator contains primarily [*vor allem*] knowledge of man—man, that is in his creatureliness and in his situation of being one to whom God has laid claim" (1.228–29). Does Bultmann really mean *vor allem*, or is this a case of rhetorical exaggeration to make the more modest point that the doctrine of creation should never be isolated from human recognition of our finitude and dependence upon God? Whatever judgment one makes about questions of this kind, it is at least clear that Bultmann repeatedly leaves himself open to being understood in reductionist terms.

Conclusion

In sum, we have seen that the opening section of Bultmann's treatment of Pauline theology makes a series of consequential methodological decisions that project an image of Paul filtered through the hermeneutical lenses of a philosophically sophisticated blend of twentieth-century existentialism and dialectical theology. Bultmann's Paul is a man of the Hellenistic world, immersed in critical dialogue with Gnosticism and mystery religions and only tangentially linked to his own Jewish heritage—except insofar as that heritage is the source of a lethal boasting that must be renounced in order to arrive at the new self-understanding made possible by the gospel. The narrative kerygmatic confessions of the early Hellenistic church belong to the presuppositional background of Paul's thought, but his real theological contribution lies in his nuanced development of a series of anthropological concepts that insightfully depict the human condition. For this reason, Paul's theology is first of all to be understood as anthropology—or, more precisely, as the exposition of "believing self-understanding." This line of interpretation is made possible through a demythologizing hermeneutic that reads beneath the surface of Paul's mythologically laden language to expose the "real intention" of his message. That real intention focuses on the possibility that individuals may attain a new self-understanding by making a decision in response to the proclaimed word, a new self-understanding that overcomes divided personal identity and receives life as a gift from the hand of God (1.269).

In this demythologized account of Paul's thought, certain crucial elements are dramatically downplayed or missing altogether: the election of Israel, the constitutive role of Israel's Scripture, the cosmic centrality of the *narrative* of the death and resurrection of Jesus (except as a stimulus to new self-understanding), the corporate character of redemption in Christ (and consequently the role of the church in God's eschatological purposes), the breaking down of the barrier between Jew and Gentile, and the radical hope for resurrection of the body and God's apocalyptic triumph over death and evil in the world. Some of these themes will resurface at least briefly in Bultmann's exposition of "Man under Faith" (1.270–352). But because the soteriological *solution* offered by the gospel must correlate with the diagnosis of the *problem* confronted by "Man Prior to the Revelation of Faith," the positive depiction of the condition of the believer in the latter part of Bultmann's account will remain individualistic and focused on a revised self-understanding.

It will be evident to the reader that in my judgment there would be "a more excellent way" to describe Paul's theology. That way would start by telling the story of God's action in Christ to fulfill the scriptural promises to Israel and redeem the creation that is in bondage to sin and death; the corollary analysis of the human condition would follow from that fundamental narrative. Christological narrative would assume primacy over anthropological concepts, and Paul's "real intention" would not be disjoined from the stories and images that are the primary content of his kerygmatic summaries. Whatever we might say about the human condition prior to the revelation of faith would be situated within the story of God's self-disclosure to Israel, as hermeneutically reconfigured by the cross and resurrection.

Of course, to work out such a presentation of Paul's theology would be a huge undertaking. In any case, such a presentation would be significantly sharpened and refined by respectful attention to Bultmann's wide-ranging and theologically sensitive depiction of Paul's thought. May the present volume of essays serve as a stimulus to new engagements with Paul that will emulate Bultmann's conviction that Paul still has much to say to the present—even if what we hear him saying is rather different from what Bultmann heard.

Chapter 5

HUMANITY UNDER FAITH

John M. G. Barclay

Bultmann's discussion of the theology of Paul (part 2 in the English translation) constitutes the climax of the first volume of his *Theology of the New Testament*, the goal and touchstone of all that has gone before. It forms two chapters, "Man Prior to the Revelation of Faith" and "Man under Faith," which require to be read together. As Bultmann indicates at the start of the second chapter, "Since Paul regards man's existence prior to faith in the transparency it has gained to the eye of faith, therefore man's existence under faith has already been indirectly pre-sketched in the presentation of pre-faith existence."[1] Thus I cannot avoid making some reference to the material discussed above by Richard Hays; each chapter illumines the other. Together they represent the culmination and distillation of Bultmann's work on Paul.[2] They also constitute, as a comprehensive, integrated, and compact whole, one of the most powerful readings of Pauline theology ever formulated, and one of the most profound.

Bultmann's analysis of Pauline soteriology ("Man under Faith") takes us to the heart of Paul and, simultaneously, to the core of Bultmann's theology: the close fit gives this chapter a particular intensity. In what follows I will analyze first the context and arrangement of the Pauline chapters (1), before exploring their entry point (2), and the contents and methods of "Man under Faith" (3). We can then consider some critiques of this construction (4), before offering a preliminary response to the challenge that Bultmann poses to contemporary readers of Paul (5).

The Context and Arrangement

As a theologian Bultmann was also a historical critic, and his Paul is accorded a precise historical location in the development of Christian theology. The authentic Paul of the seven letters (1.190) is kept wholly distinct from the later deuteropaulines (discussed in vol. 2, part 4), as from the image of Paul in Acts.[3] Equally significantly, Bultmann is careful to identify the traditions Paul inherited and incorporated into his letters. These include materials Paul cites as tradition (e.g., 1 Cor 11:23-26; 15:3-7), but also formulaic passages using terminology uncharacteristic of Paul, such as "the Christ hymn" (Phil 2:6-11), mini-creedal statements (e.g., Rom 1:3-4; 4:25), and standard lists of vices (e.g., Gal 5:19-21).[4] Identifying what Paul inherits but also develops or adapts enables the historian to place Paul within but also beyond the thought and preaching of the early "Hellenistic Church."

Part 1, titled "Presuppositions and Motifs of New Testament Theology," traces the development of early Christian thought from Jesus onward, climaxing in the long and wide-ranging chapter on "The Kerygma of the Hellenistic Church Aside from Paul." Here many Pauline texts appear in the discussion of traditions and concepts shared by other early Christians. The understanding of the church as the "new covenant" people of God, the notion of baptism as participation in Christ, the acclamation of Christ as "Lord," the experience of the Spirit as a wonder-working power—all these Bultmann discusses first in *this* context (before noting them again in the chapters on Paul); they were neither invented by nor unique to Paul. Throughout this part it is clear that Paul's handling of these motifs will be the central focus of interest. Key sections finish with questions asking how early Christian ideas might develop, and how their problematic features might be solved, and in almost every case Bultmann adumbrates the development or solution he will find in Paul.[5] Thus Paul is the theologian who clarifies or develops the common but inchoate (or dangerous) concepts taking shape in the first generation of Christian thought.[6]

Part 1 thus provides a *foil* for Paul,[7] since it clarifies not only the origin of many Pauline motifs but also the points at which he *went beyond* his inherited materials.[8] In identifying what Paul takes for granted, presupposes, and neither argues nor defends (as in his "do you not know?" questions on baptism in Rom 6), one can identify what is "specifically [*spezifisch*] Pauline" (1.84; *Theologie*, 84), what is "peculiar to Paul" (*für Paulus charakteristisch*; 1.85; *Theologie*, 85) or a "pecularity of Paul" (*eine Eigentümlichkeit des Paulus*; 1.154; *Theologie*, 153), like his "distinctive understanding of faith" (*das eigenartige Glaubensverständnis*; 1.90; *Theologie*, 89). Thus Bultmann recognizes mystical, apocalyptic, and "Gnostic" motifs in Pauline theology but is always alert to where Paul supersedes these motifs and develops his distinctive theological ideas. In a comparative weighting, such inherited notions need not be considered of definitive significance. It is the specifically Pauline clarifications and interpretations that count for most, because it is here that Bultmann identifies the chief contribution of Paul.

The analysis of Paul falls, as we have noted, into two chapters, whose relationship is dialectical.[9] The temporal scheme ("Man *Prior to* the Revelation of Faith") corresponds to a Pauline pattern of speech (Gal 3:23-25), but it is clear to Bultmann that Paul perceives the "ontic" human condition under sin and death only from the perspective of faith. The prominence of "faith" in the title of both chapters is a sign that Bultmann's arrangement of his material takes its shape not from a historical narrative (e.g., from the place of Christ in salvation history) but from the impact of the gospel on human existence. The Christ-event has not been displaced (to the contrary, it is the specific and singular source of faith), but the center of attention is its meaning for humanity.[10] Thus the first chapter begins with a famous analysis of Paul's anthropological terms/concepts (*Begriffe*), starting with the crucial, and problematic, discussion of "body" (σῶμα) as the individual's relationship to his or her self (sec. 17). In Bultmann's analysis human beings have forfeited their proper existence by looking to themselves, their assets, and their achievements as the ground of their security and life.[11] This quintessential, death-dealing sin is expressed in "boasting," found in a heightened form in Jewish boasting in law observance, a "striving after a righteousness of [one's] own" (1.267). Thus what is required in salvation is not some "magical or mysterious transformation of man in regard to his substance, the basis of his nature" (1.268-69), but a new self-understanding, a new relation to the possibilities of human existence: it is this decision in faith "in regard to the grace which encounters a man in the proclaimed word" (1.269) which our chapter, "Man under Faith," is designed to elucidate.

The Entry Point

Bultmann's point of entry is clear in the preliminary remarks that form the preface to both chapters on Paul (1.190–91; *Theologie*, 186–88). Here he insists that Paul's "basic theological position" (*theologische Grundposition*) is not a system of "theoretical" ideas that speak of the world, God, or Christ as they are in themselves: Paul's theology "deals with God not as He is in Himself but only with God as He is significant for man, for man's responsibility and man's salvation. . . . Every assertion about God is simultaneously [*zugleich*] an assertion about man and vice versa. For this reason and in this sense Paul's theology is, at the same time [*zugleich*], anthropology" (1.190–91; *Theologie*, 187). The same may be said about Christology: Paul's focus is not Christ's relationship to God, nor Christ's "natures," but his agency in the salvation of humanity. "Thus every assertion about Christ is also [*auch*] an assertion about man and vice versa; and Paul's Christology is simultaneously [*zugleich*] soteriology" (1.191; *Theologie*, 188).

The negative thrust of these statements is crucial. Bultmann denies that Paul is able to stand apart from his subject matter in some "objectifying" manner, as if it could be known or discussed without the self-involvement of the viewer.[12] At the same time, he distinguishes Pauline theology from "speculation," a pursuit of truth for its own sake, unrelated to its meaning for salvation or faith.[13] Paul is not interested in defining the nature of God (Trinitarian or otherwise), as if God's existence were an "objectively" perceptible thing: he announces what is true about God or Christ "for us" (1 Cor 8:6; 1.229). Nor is he concerned with apocalyptic "speculations" about the end times; where he draws on traditional motifs, he generally relates them to the present proclamation of the gospel (1 Cor 15:23-28; 1.307). The "new creation" is the person in Christ (2 Cor 5:17); any future drama can only confirm the eschatological moment that has already begun (2 Cor 6:2; 1.306–7; cf. 1.302). Paul has no investment in a "philosophy of history" or a cosmological plan: he does theology only out of and on behalf of faith, to challenge our understanding of ourselves and force us to the point of decision.

Bultmann here seeks to echo not only Paul's deep and subtle analysis of the human plight but also the fact that his theology is performed in the service of proclamation, a form of speech which does not primarily *describe* past or present facts but issues an *address* (*Anrede*), a challenge demanding not cognitive assent but personal decision (*Entscheidung*). Thus, in discussing the varied forms in which Paul presents "Christ's Death and Resurrection as Salvation-Occurrence" (sec. 33), Bultmann asks how the Christ-event can be "recognized and experienced by man as the deed of grace. . . . Only then can it take effect as a compelling and transforming power, when it can be understood as directed at man, reaching him, happening to him—i.e. when the challenge to accept it as salvation-occurrence thrusts him into genuine decision" (1.294–95). It is not enough to announce that God has sent the preexistent Son of God: that would be simply information and would reside "in a mythical sphere outside the realm of human experience" (1.295). Paul utilizes motifs of various religious background in describing the death of Christ, but his "real intention" (1.301) is not to delineate facts that one first "believes" as objectively true, before believing in the proper Pauline sense of surrendering oneself to the grace of God. Pressing beyond his inherited concepts, Paul interprets the death and resurrection of Christ in such a way as to show that the announcement itself raises "the decision-question whether a man is willing to give up his old understanding of himself and henceforth understand himself only from the grace of God" (1.300–301).

Bultmann here develops a characteristically Lutheran emphasis that the gospel is neither factual record nor academic speculation about God but good news *pro me* ("the Son of God loved me and gave himself *for me*"; Gal 2:20).[14] In radicalizing this tradition, Bultmann was strongly influenced by his teacher, Wilhelm Herrmann (1846–1922), for whom faith could be neither identified with nor dependent on objectively provable "facts" (that would constitute an epistemological form of "justification by works"). Exploring the difference between external "history" and the "historicality" of human existence (the immediacy of our daily encounters with each other, and with the gift and demand of God), Bultmann's dialogues with Martin Heidegger in Marburg during the 1920s provided a set of concepts for understanding human existence and a vocabulary of "self-understanding," "decision," and "authentic existence" (*eigentliches Sein*).[15] Some such conceptuality was a necessary tool for exploring the question of human existence, which Bultmann took as his entry point into Pauline theology. That Paul's theology amounts to his "new grasp of man's existence before God" (1.270) represents Bultmann's "pre-understanding" (*Vorverständnis*) of the text: it shapes the questions he brings to the text and identifies the subject matter (*Sache*) with which the text is primarily concerned.[16] Bultmann is self-consciously a theological interpreter of Paul, and his anthropological starting point reflects his view that theology's proper focus is not the propositional statements of the New Testament but the self-unfolding of faith that, under the impact of the gospel, has come to expression in those statements.[17] Whether this anthropological focus gives due weight to what Paul says about other matters and whether Bultmann's anxieties about "objectifying" language result in a one-sided or even reductionist representation of Pauline theology are questions that have been raised from the very beginning.[18]

The Contents and Methods

"Man under Faith" is divided into four sections: A. The Righteousness of God, B. Grace, C. Faith, and D. Freedom. Other motifs in Pauline soteriology are included within these sections, but such themes represent what Bultmann identifies as the characteristic marks of Pauline theology. There is some overlap (grace is discussed first in section A), but the sequence reflects Bultmann's reading of Rom 1–8, stretching from the righteousness of God (Rom 1:16-17) to freedom from death (Rom 8:12-39).[19] Material is drawn from all the authentic letters, with no interest in tracing developments or situational differences. Bultmann is explicit about inconsistencies in Paul's letters, but these led him not to fragment the Pauline corpus but to probe where amid the contrary statements Paul's real intentions are to be found.[20]

Section A, "The Righteousness of God," explores Paul's "new grasp of man's existence before God" (1.270). The genitive δικαιοσύνη θεοῦ is taken as a genitive of the author (1.285): Paul's concern is not with God in himself but with what God confers as a gift.[21] "Righteousness" refers not to ethical character but to relationship: as in Judaism, this is a forensic term, indicating a person's acknowledgment by God. Moreover, Paul here speaks of God's *eschatological* judgment, which he uniquely takes to be *already* pronounced in the present. Thus to be "righteous" before God is not to become sinless, by some magical transformation of substance, but to receive God's word of forgiveness. This word, Bultmann stresses, is a word of "sheer gift" (*reines Geschenck*; 1.281; *Theologie*, 277). In contrast to the human effort to accomplish righteousness ("the works of the Law") and to gain salvation, Paul announces the *grace* of God—an initiative that is wholly God's, both *without* and *before* our own (the latter emphasized in sec. 31 on reconciliation). This grace is paradoxical—given to the sinner, not to the righteous—and its effect is to judge the deepest refuge of human sin, the illusion that we can live from our own resources (1.282–85). Thus the grace of God encounters us as a crucial question: "Will you surrender, utterly surrender, to God's dealing—will you know yourself to be a sinner before God?" (1.285). Faith is the affirmative answer to this question.

Section B, "Grace," is focused on the death and resurrection of Christ, since grace is not, for Paul, a divine quality or emotion but an event. (Since it is not an emotion, grace is perfectly compatible with Paul's depiction of God's wrath and judgment—it is, in fact, the grace decision of the judge.) The core of this section is the long section 33 on "Christ's Death and Resurrection as Salvation-Occurrence," mentioned above. Here Bultmann surveys the range of thought complexes employed by Paul in expressing the meaning of the Christ-event. Notions of propitiation, cultic sacrifice, and redemption are clearly present, but such categories are "broken through" by the idea of redemption from the power of sin, law, and death. The concept of participation in the death of Christ (in baptism) is derived from the mystery religions, while the cosmic dimensions of salvation are influenced by Gnostic myth (1.298–300). But Paul "found none of these thought-complexes and none of their terminologies adequate to express his understanding of the salvation-occurrence" (1.300). He does not merely glue together these different ideas but in using them presses beyond them. In particular, he wraps the salvation-occurrence into the proclamation of the gospel: "the salvation-occurrence is eschatological occurrence just in this fact, that it does not become a fact of the past but constantly takes place anew in the present" (1.302). Thus "the salvation-occurrence is *nowhere* present except in the proclaiming, accosting, demanding, and promising word of preaching" (1.302).[22] Paul is not a history teacher but a preacher of the gospel, and what he wants to speak about is the challenge of the Christ-event, accosting hearers with the demand to be crucified with Christ, to surrender their previous understanding of themselves. Thus the purpose of the church and the sacraments (sec. 34) is not the preservation of a creedal tradition, nor the mediation of a magical transformation of the self (although Paul retains some such notions), but the communication of the challenge and promise of the gospel.

Part C, "Faith," develops what has already been implied. Faith is not assent to dogma nor acceptance of a narrative but a self-involving and thereby transformative act. In particular, it is an act of *obedience*, an abandonment of self-reliance in surrender to God's judgment and to the future opened by the Christ-event. Bultmann can speak of faith as an act (*Tat*) or attitude (*Haltung*) without it becoming a human accomplishment or a new form of self-dependence. The issue is not mere *agency* (does God act, or do we?) but reliance: as a human deed of surrender to God, faith is the opposite of work (*Werk*) or accomplishment (*Leistung*; 1.315–17; cf. 1.283–84).[23] In renouncing all works as the ground for security, faith looks not to itself but to "God's prevenient deed of grace which preceded faith" (1.319). Since faith is obedience, it is an active decision, not a fate imposed on believers by God, but the decision is to renounce one's own resources in reliance on Christ.[24] One may properly speak of faith as a "condition" (*Bedingung*) of salvation, since it appropriates and receives the gift of God,[25] but faith "lives out of the divine deed of salvation" such that one is "determined" by the grace of God in Christ (1.328). Thus faith shapes the whole of life (not special categories of behavior): every day demands a constantly renewed decision and a constant movement from the past of self-reliance to the future created by God, surrendering all to God's power and care.

Part D, "Freedom," gathers together the Pauline themes of redemption from sin, law, and death. The Pauline combination of indicative and imperative is interpreted dialectically: Paul's statements that believers have "died to sin" describe neither an aspirational ideal nor a magical alteration of nature but the grace-effected possibility of a new self-understanding, actualized by faith and appropriated in obedience, the imperative founded on the indicative (Gal 5:25). Although Paul can use "animistic" language of the Spirit, as if it were some material substance (*Stoff*), he characteristically presses beyond these "naïve" and "popular" ideas: the Spirit represents "the possibility of eschatological existence" (1.337), expressed in the "free, ethical obedience" of love. The Spirit may be a wonder-working "power," but there is no "magical compulsion" (*Zwang*; 1.336; *Theologie*, 332): to be "led by the Spirit" (Gal 5:18) "does not mean to be dragged along willy-nilly" (*ein entscheidungsloses Hingerissenwerden*; 1.336; *Theologie*, 333). "Mythological expressions," which accord to the Spirit a "mind" (Rom 8:6) and "desires" (Gal 5:17), should not be taken literally: they mean to say (*wollen sagen*) that "the Spirit founds a new will, whose origin is not within man but within the salvation-deed of God" (1.336; *Theologie*, 333).

Pauline freedom is by no means freedom from demand; even freedom from the law does not mean the end of the law tout court, since "so far as it contains God's demand . . . it retains its validity" (1.341). Liberated from the effort to establish his or her own righteousness, the believer is free for the radical obedience of faith, which surrenders the whole self to God and to his or her neighbor in love.[26] Pauline ethics are distinguished both from license (1 Cor 6:12) and from ascetic withdrawal: the believer is freed from the world not by withdrawing from it but by participating without investment in, or dependence on, its resources (1 Cor 7:29-35). With regard to death, Paul uses the language of the mystery religions and Gnosticism to speak of sharing the resurrection of Christ. But this does not mean that Christ, like some "natural power" (*naturhafte Kraft*), is infused (*eingeflößte*) into a person as a power of immortality (1.345; *Theologie*, 341). It means that in faith the believer lets himself or herself be determined by the word of the risen Christ, a word that speaks not just of the future resurrection (as in the apocalyptic expectations inherited by Paul) but of a present "life" already made possible in faith.

As this summary has indicated, Bultmann's interpretation of Pauline theology—which is always an *interpretation* and not merely a repetition or rearrangement of Pauline statements—involves a range of attempts to press beyond Paul's tradition-derived concepts to his "real intention," what he "wants to say," what is "characteristic" and "decisive" in the shape of his theology. By placing Paul within the stream of early Christian tradition, numerous motifs can be identified as inherited and not coined by Paul; it is reasonable to ask if he develops them in distinctive ways. No Pauline scholar would give as much weight to Paul's (inherited) phrase "the kingdom of God" as to his expression "the righteousness of God," although he uses them roughly the same number of times: the latter is much more clearly linked to themes and expressions characteristic of Paul. Some motifs are also more strategically located, more central to Paul's argumentation, than others. Bultmann's observation that Paul thinks of sin more as a power from which the believer needs deliverance than as transgression requiring repentance and atonement is now widely accepted. More controversially, where he finds contradictory ideas, he both explains such phenomena (e.g., as the clash of incompatible inherited traditions) and identifies which ideas are more characteristic of Paul (e.g., 1.250–51, 300, 329–30, 346). The result is a beautifully consistent reading of the whole of Paul. Bultmann docs not leave Pauline theology as a tangle of varied threads, nor does he merely select certain theological strands and disregard the rest. He includes *everything* but *weighs* it all, and although critics might carp at this procedure, no one has since produced a reading of Paul that is simultaneously *comprehensive* and theologically *coherent* to the same degree.

Of course such *weighing* is an act of judgment, of interpretation. No serious interpreter of Paul can escape this task: it is hard to imagine anyone judging Paul's statements in 1 Cor 11:2-16 on male and female heads to be the *center* of his theology. Bultmann demands a decision about the questions that drive Pauline theology and the issues of central importance; he is not content with a mass of Pauline ideas that cohere only loosely, if at all. His willingness to venture this hermeneutical judgment reflects his understanding of "New Testament Theology": its task is not to gather and describe the varied theological motifs but to identify the subject matter of the New Testament and its most appropriate means of expression. Bultmann's Lutheran heritage gave him the freedom (and responsibility) to exercise discrimination in this matter, what he called *Sachkritik*—a critical evaluation of theological expressions as judged by their subject matter (*Sache*).[27] All interpreters assess the centrality and helpfulness of Pauline expressions to some degree—witness the ways they variously maximize, minimize, or "explain" Pauline statements on predestination (Rom 9:14-23) or on the salvation of "all Israel" (Rom 11:25-32), according to their wider configuration of Pauline theology. Bultmann is simply more explicit about his interpretative judgments and more willing to voice his judgment that Pauline expressions are sometimes inadequate or misleading, when judged by the subject matter he is trying to express.

Thus exposed, his method is an easy target for those who disagree with his construction of Pauline theology.

Every hermeneutical decision carries a cost, and the price for Bultmann's discovery of deep coherence in Pauline theology is the demotion of those motifs that he positions away from the center. "Gnostic" notions of the primal human, popular notions of a material Spirit, mystical notions of participation in a dying and rising deity, apocalyptic speculations about the future—all these Bultmann recognizes as present in Paul. He simply judges them of lesser significance, since Paul appropriates and interprets them in his own distinctive way. Up to a point everyone could concur: no one is interested in Paul's eschatological trumpet (1 Thess 4:16; 1 Cor 15:52), and most Pauline scholars disregard Paul's assumption that Adam was an historical individual (Rom 5:12-21). It is when Bultmann's *Sachkritik* cuts much deeper than this that we are entitled to wonder whether he has judged the *Sache* aright. Paul's discussion of Israel in Rom 9–11 is noted in passing (1.282), but Bultmann's entry point (the question of human existence) and his disjunction between national/world history and the individual decision of faith mean that the history of God's promises to Israel cannot feature near the center of his Pauline theology.[28] He also minimizes the future orientation of Paul's theology, with its hope of bodily resurrection and the redemption of the cosmos: he recognizes that Paul speaks in such apocalyptic terms, but "the details in his picture of the cosmic drama have no theological importance," and the important point is that "life is already here" (1.346, 347).[29] In this respect, John's theology, with its radically "realized" eschatology, is more amenable to Bultmann than Paul's (see 1.36, 178; 2.6–10).

The place where the Bultmannian performance most conspicuously fails to fit the Pauline score is where Paul speaks of the resurrection of Jesus. Paul's catalogue of evidence in 1 Cor 15:1-11 makes Bultmann uneasy: Paul is "pushed" to provide this by Gnosticizing objections in the Corinthian church, but "is such a proof convincing?"[30] Bultmann's discomfort arises from his conviction that "faith, being personal decision, cannot be dependent upon a historian's labor" (1.26). More than that, "the resurrection, of course, simply cannot be a visible fact in the realm of human history" (1.295): it "cannot . . . be demonstrated or made plausible as an objectively ascertainable fact on the basis of which one could believe" (1.305). Paul's attempts to describe the resurrection body in 1 Cor 15:35-49 are similarly mistaken: he "lets himself be misled into adopting his opponents' method of argumentation" (1.192) and ends up speaking in mythological terms of the πνεῦμα as a bodily substance. This is not "characteristic" of Paul (1.192, 202), "genuinely Pauline" (1.192), or what "determines his fundamental discussions" (1.202). "Paul's capacity for abstract thinking is not a developed one" (1.198), but "in distinction from this mythology the real intention (*die eigentliche Intention*) of Paul must be made clear" (1.198; *Theologie*, 195). The point of speaking of the resurrection of Jesus is not to relate, still less prove, a past freakish occurrence, but to express the fact that "Christ himself, yes God himself, speaks in the proclaimed word" (1.305).

The identification of Paul's "real intention" is of course a hermeneutical construction—as Bultmann would have been the first to recognize. Bultmann took theological statements to be not timeless objectifying propositions but "thoughts of faith" (2.237). Thus the task of theological interpretation of the New Testament is not to repeat its time-bound and often mythological expressions but to unfold, in contemporary terms, the meaning of the early Christian faith response to the gospel (see 2.237–41). Bultmann's famous essay "New Testament and Mythology" struggles mightily with how to interpret New Testament statements on the resurrection in a context where "we moderns cannot understand Jesus' resurrection as an event whereby a power to life is released that we can now appropriate through the sacraments."[31] But what if we judge that some such conception of the resurrection is actually central and load bearing in Pauline theology, not just an inherited concept but core to, and characteristic of, Paul's thinking? If the resurrection of Jesus can be conceptualized *both* as a past event that is externally "true" *and* as a message that challenges the hearer, demanding submission to the risen Lord—as an event that is both *extra nos* and *pro nobis*—the antithesis Bultmann posits between "external" history and faith-evoking address may prove false.[32] He would still be entitled to ask whether this notion can be given coherent theological sense in a form communicable in contemporary terms—and to insist that without some such interpretation one cannot claim to have *understood* Paul.[33] But it is here in relation to the resurrection that Bultmann's exercise of *Sachkritik* was the least satisfying and has understandably raised the greatest alarm. If the cross is (primarily, for Bultmann) an act of judgment on human pride, and if the resurrection is emptied of its *content*, such that it is present only in the Word that summons us to a new self-understanding, has the grace of God become merely the gift of a new "possibility" without any substantial content to be *received*?

Contemporary Critiques

Bultmann's construal of the theology of Paul is widely recognized as a masterpiece and has deeply influenced followers and critics alike. Critical questions have arisen from a number of directions and may be summarized under four heads:

Developments in Historical Research

Since Bultmann's theological reading of Paul depended on historical research (to a far greater degree than Barth's), it has been vulnerable to advances in historical scholarship. The full publication of the Qumran texts has challenged some claims about Pauline uniqueness;[34] the Nag Hammadi library has undermined the hypothesis of pre-Christian "Gnosticism"; appeal to the "mystery religions" as a source of Pauline ideas has been questioned. Not all of this would be fatal to Bultmann's reading. He was more interested in what Paul did with inherited concepts than with the sources of those concepts, and Käsemann could maintain many of Bultmann's readings of Paul after replacing "Gnosticism" with "apocalyptic" as the origin of key Pauline ideas.[35] Nowadays Pauline scholars compare Paul with a range of religious and philosophical traditions, but the interest is more in profiling Paul (by similarity and difference) than in tracing the *sources* of Pauline ideas. A loss of confidence in source criticism makes it harder to identify pre-Pauline formulas, and on all fronts there is simply less interest in identifying how Paul pressed beyond the concepts he borrowed. While Bultmann's boundary between the authentic and deuteropauline letters has been largely maintained, the current tendency is to grant equal weighting to all the motifs in the undisputed letters. This policy is certainly less vulnerable to changes in historical judgment, but it also makes it harder to offer a coherent reading of Paul.

While Bultmann was fully aware of the diverse contexts of Paul's letters,[36] he assumed the possibility of constructing Pauline theology from a mixture of letters. The subsequent tendency to distinguish epistolary contexts and rhetorics has rendered such a synthesis questionable to some.[37] An allied critique charges Bultmann with abstracting Paul's theology from its original context in his mission to the Gentiles. Dahl charged Bultmann with a tendency to "dehistoricize" Pauline theology and thus adumbrated the effort to contextualize that theology, even (in fact, especially) the theology of justification, within Paul's Gentile mission.[38] The difference here is partly one of goal: where most scholars after Bultmann aim only to render Paul comprehensible in his first-century context, Bultmann pressed beyond this to theological interpretation. In his view, writing a "Theology of the New Testament" was inescapably a hermeneutical, and not simply a descriptive, task. The question is not whether this goal is legitimate but whether his theological interpretation of Paul is adequately supported by recent historical research.

Reevaluation of Judaism

For Bultmann, Paul's analysis of flesh, sin, and law comes to its most acute expression in his critique of Jewish "boasting," the ultimate example of the perverse human tendency to look to our own resources and accomplishments as the source of our security and "life." His interpretation of ancient Judaism, as tending to "legalism" and "rebellious pride," was indebted to a theologically loaded historiography of ancient Judaism common in late nineteenth- to early twentieth-century Germany.[39] That representation now seems historically illegitimate and ideologically unacceptable, following changes of perception in European scholarship and the publication of Sanders' *Paul and Palestinian Judaism*.[40] Paul's critique of Judaism is now taken to be directed at "ethnocentrism" rather than "works-righteousness"—or it is insisted that Paul has no critique of Jews or Judaism at all. Bultmann's statements about the law as a "path to salvation" (*Heilsweg*), dependent on human "effort" and "achievement," now appear to many embarrassingly outmoded.

This critique runs deep. Bultmann's reading of Paul is based on a contrast between perverted confidence in oneself and surrender to the judgment and gift of God in Christ: to unpick Bultmann's reading of Judaism might unravel everything else. Either Paul's anthropology and soteriology would have to be (implausibly) disconnected from his statements about the law and Judaism, or the whole would need to be reframed. Pauline scholars have sought different solutions. Some have jettisoned the Bultmannian frame, rereading Paul's statements on Judaism such that "the works of the law" represent social markers of Jewish identity, not achievements necessary for salvation. Others have defended some Bultmannian elements, claiming either that he was not so wrong about the tenor of ancient Judaism or that ancient Jewish self-understanding is one thing but Paul's *interpretation* of Judaism another.[41] In this debate the theme that Bultmann justifiably made central to his theology of Paul, the motif of *grace*, has received less attention than it deserves. When Paul is placed within ancient Jewish debates about divine goodness or grace (in which Jewish voices constitute neither a harmony nor a simple foil to Paul), one can appreciate Paul's remarkable emphasis on the *incongruity* of grace, in which his understanding of the Christ-event as gift to the unworthy matches his conduct and experience of the Gentile mission. A better understanding of ancient Judaism (and the ancient practice of gift) might reveal that the sharp edge of Paul's critique cuts against not individuals' self-achieved virtue but collective pride in socially defined criteria of worth.[42]

Questions Concerning the Starting Point

As we have noted, Bultmann is unapologetic about the fact that his project begins with a preunderstanding of Paul's subject matter and is guided by the question about human existence before God (1.270). Käsemann, Bultmann's most independent pupil, properly challenged the individualistic focus of Bultmann's anthropology: Paul's term σῶμα ("body") evokes one's relationship not to oneself but to the world, and Pauline anthropology concerns human existence on a social and not just on an individual level.[43] This shift in perception was hastened by social and intellectual changes in European culture during the 1960s, such that Bultmann's "existential" interpretation of Paul began to lose its appeal. In fact, mainstream Pauline scholarship has eschewed not only Bultmann's individualism but also his presumption that Paul's theology begins with the question of human existence. Many aspects of his reading now look one-sided. Why does Bultmann give so little attention to Rom 9–11 and to Paul's engagement with the Scriptures and the history of Israel? Why do church and the sacraments appear only as the context in which the word is preached? Why are Paul's ethics analyzed only in individualistic and not also in corporate terms? More broadly, in drawing out the *connection* between theology and anthropology in Paul ("Paul's theology is at the same time [*zugleich*] anthropology"), does Bultmann subtly shift from a relation of *coincidence* (Paul's theology and anthropology are conjoined) or *inclusion* (Paul's talk of God includes his talk of the human condition) to *identity* or even *interchangeability* (Paul's language about God is semantically identical to his language about humanity), such that theology is *reduced* to anthropology? Is not Paul *also* interested in God, Christ, the cosmos, Israel, and history, in dimensions wider than that of "human existence," even if he continually relates them to the content and the address of the gospel? Such questions, arising in new cultural and theological contexts, represent aspects of our current dissatisfaction with the anthropological question from which Bultmann started and to which he perpetually returned.

Alternative Readings of Paul

Since Bultmann, many good books have interpreted *parts* of the Pauline corpus and many have offered lengthy treatments of the whole, but none has matched the combination of economy, coherence, and depth achieved by Bultmann. We may identify four (partly overlapping) paradigms in reading Paul today, whose profile becomes clear in their distinction from Bultmann.

First, in contrast to Bultmann (who followed the order of Romans and the theological trajectory of Augustine and Luther), many Pauline scholars focus their reading of Paul with the notion of *participation in Christ* rather than justification by faith (e.g., Sanders, Hooker, Gorman, Campbell, following Schweitzer). For such interpreters, participation in (or union with) the death and resurrection of Christ, life in the Spirit, belonging to the church, baptism, the Lord's Supper, and a Christomorphic ethic stand at the heart of Pauline theology; justification is either interpreted in participatory terms or relegated to the margins. It is less clear in these readings what Paul's participatory language really means—a major weakness for a thinker as rigorous as Bultmann, for whom not to be able to articulate the meaning of a concept supposedly central to Pauline thought is to fail in one's responsibility to *interpret* Paul.[44] Bultmann was certainly aware that

Paul thought of baptism and the Lord's Supper as participation in Christ (1.140–44, 147–48), but he took these to be ideas that Paul's predecessors adapted from the mystery religions and that Paul surpassed. He may be charged with underestimating their significance and thus with missing the sense in which Paul regards believers as recentered by an event outside of themselves, but it is incumbent on Pauline interpreters to give some account of what it might mean to live such an "eccentric existence."[45]

Second, challenging Bultmann's focus on the self-understanding of the individual, a number of interpreters have taken the *apocalyptic* invasion of the cosmos in the Christ-event as the framework of Pauline theology (e.g., Beker, Martyn, de Boer, following Käsemann). For these interpreters, the cosmic scope of Paul's theology is not to be dismissed as mythological packaging: rather, it indicates Christ's universal claim on the physical, social (and political) domain. Emphasizing divine agency and power, a contrast is sometimes drawn with Bultmann's language of "possibility," while the proposal to translate πίστις Χριστοῦ as "the faith/faithfulness of Christ" (rather than "faith in Christ") has focused attention away from the believers' faith (e.g., Hays; Campbell). In fact, Bultmann was clear that faith is made possible only by the Christ-event,[46] and often speaks of the power (*Macht*) of grace, determining and freeing human existence (e.g., 1.291–92, 294). Nonetheless, "apocalyptic" readings that refuse to demythologize Paul's language of the powers (such as flesh and sin) have resonated with contemporary understandings of the "emergence" of evil and of forces that influence human behavior and thought, and their interest to contemporary theologians in the Barthian tradition indicates that the Bultmannian legacy has proven to be, comparatively, less enduring.

A third strand in Pauline scholarship, influenced by Reformed theology and/or by postliberal forms of "narrative theology," stresses the *narrative* framework on or beneath the surface of Pauline discourse (e.g., Hays, Dunn, Wright). Since Bultmann examined human existence in individual terms, he certainly undervalued the larger narrative dimensions of Pauline theology: Paul's use of Scripture, his interest in Abraham as the start of a narrative line, and his multiple readings of Israel's story are rightly now accorded far greater weight. For Bultmann these are the bass notes in the Pauline melody, hardly unique to Paul and not what made Paul a distinctive and creative theologian. His reading can fairly be charged with muting such notes altogether, but he forces one to examine Paul's understanding of history: does the Christ-event add another chapter to the narrative of Israel, or does it, as the eschatological event (which for Bultmann does *not* mean simply the *final* event), transcend and reconfigure all history? If Bultmann downplays Paul's engagement with Scripture, he is right to insist that the Christ-event has made history resound with a distinctive tune. If we are right to find "echoes of Scripture in the letters of Paul," Paul also found echoes of the gospel in the Scriptures of Israel, and that hermeneutical dialectic is certainly more complex than straightforward readings of "salvation-history" might suggest.

Finally, current *political* readings of Paul (emancipatory, anti-empire, and postcolonial) repudiate practically everything in Bultmann's reading of Paul, from his individualistic starting point to his apolitical conclusions. It is proper to object that Bultmann failed to register the importance of community in Paul's theology and ethics; what he noticed, he considered hardly distinctive of Paul and bound to disappoint the modern interpreter.[47] Bultmann demythologized Paul's language of powers to reveal embedded in such language faith's understanding of human existence; he did not discover a "hidden transcript" with coded references to Caesar. The first interpretative strategy may be flawed, but the second is hardly more plausible.[48] When Käsemann broke the Bultmannian mold, sensing the political potential of Pauline and of New Testament theology, he caught the intellectual turn from existentialist to sociopolitical categories of analysis. But there has yet to emerge a political reading of Paul that matches Bultmann in coherence and in the ability to encompass the whole range of Pauline motifs.

The Bultmann Challenge: A Preliminary Response

Bultmann was aware that his was neither a definitive nor a permanently satisfactory reading of Paul's theology: he was self-consciously engaged in a *theological* task, which "permits only ever-repeated solutions, or attempts at solution, each in its particular historical situation" (2.237).[49] Thus the most searching question he poses to a contemporary reader of Paul is not "was Bultmann's interpretation right?" but "can we offer in our day an interpretation as well conceived and executed as he offered in his?" Bultmann's reading excelled on at least five fronts: it was historically responsible, textually comprehensive, hermeneutically sophisticated, theologically relevant, and of immediate kerygmatic significance. Historically, he used the best available evidence and the sharpest critical tools to understand Paul's theology in its ancient context. Textually, he accounted for every feature of the Pauline letters, while identifying an inner coherence amid the mass of Pauline motifs. Hermeneutically, he was self-conscious about the preunderstanding he brought to Paul and about his goal to offer an interpretation appropriate to Paul's central subject matter. Theologically, he engaged contemporary cultural and philosophical questions, to help faith "master its constantly new historical situation" (2.237). And—of enormous importance to Bultmann—he sought to actualize the challenge of the gospel, which is not information about past or universal truths but "personal address in a concrete situation" (2.240). Whatever his weaknesses, it is hard to identify a current reading of Paul that matches Bultmann on more than one or two of these five fronts.

How might we rise to the Bultmann challenge? I conclude with the outlines of one possible answer, which would start with a central Pauline motif—grace—also dear to Bultmann, and with a question not unlike Bultmann's but posed in a different key: what would it mean to interpret ourselves—our world, our social relations, and our individual lives—as the product of a gift that does not match our worth but accords worth to us? Philosophical fascination with the theme of gift (Derrida, Marion, etc.), the search for a sociality based on reciprocity rather than legal right, the recognition that what gives human life worth and meaning is more than longevity and wealth—all these contemporary questions can be brought into relation with the Pauline kerygma, which declares God's act in Christ as a gift that challenges and refashions human existence, in both individual and social dimensions. The centrality of this theme in the Pauline letters can be amply demonstrated, crisscrossing Paul's metaphorical fields and linking theology to ethics (both social and individual). If the Christ gift were given without regard to worth, ethnic differentials between Jews and Gentiles are rendered irrelevant, and Torah observance (the "works of the law") is no longer the criterion of value ("righteousness") in the sight of God. Justification by faith, whose radical expression is the justification of the ungodly, expresses this incongruity between the divine gift and the worth of its recipients, liberating communities of mixed ethnicity from the cultural values which cause competition and division. Christian existence is thus participation—by faith—in the Christ-event, an "eccentric existence" suspended from the resurrection life of Christ, which is conceived by Paul as both objectively real and subjectively present in the life-transforming work of the Spirit. The present paradoxical existence of believers—at once doomed to death and alive in Christ—involves no physical transformation but takes place in (among other things) the formation of a new *habitus*—a deep structuring of dispositions and perceptions—which reshapes human life in the formation of countercultural communities.

This reading of Paul is historically grounded, contextualizing his theology in first-century thought and social practice and correlating his radical theology of grace with his practice as apostle to the Gentiles. There is a dialectical relationship between Paul's social practice, forming communities regardless of ethnic origin or social status, and his proclamation of a gift that disregards human criteria of worth. Paul's relativization of cultural traditions, his ethic of reciprocity, and his rejection of the quest for differential honor can all be connected to his theology of grace, which renders his communities "rich" in generosity. Where Paul's vision is impeded by hidden cultural assumptions (e.g., that it is "natural" and "decent" for men to have short hair; 1 Cor 11:14) a *theological* reading of Paul, dedicated to exposing the subject matter of his theology, is required to exercise some form of *Sachkritik*; how far this extends to his wider assumptions about gender and sexuality is a matter of theological judgment. Like Bultmann's, the goal of this reading is not to parrot Paul but to expose, with Paul, what it means for human life to be transformed by the gospel.

To position grace at the center of Pauline theology does not mean to revive Bultmann's outdated construction of Jewish "works-righteousness." Research on Second Temple Judaism reveals no simple contrast with Paul, nor a unified ideology of "covenantal nomism" (Sanders). Diverse Jewish convictions regarding divine goodness, mercy, and justice differ in their assessment of the operation and distribution of grace. Paul stands in the midst of these Jewish disputes, not in singular isolation, but his stress on (and experience of) the incongruity of the Christ gift combines with his practice of the

Gentile mission to challenge Jewish cultural norms. What he opposes is not the individual's self-confidence in achievement (Bultmann) but the social and cultural pride of a Jewish tradition that fails to submit to the newly creative gift of Christ—an event that for Paul is the definitive expression of God's relation to Israel. Echoing the sin that fails to acknowledge the giftedness of life, "boasting in the law" represents pride in the Torah's criteria of excellence, parallel to Greek pride in eloquence and appearance. There is no anti-Jewish edge to Paul's theology: he reworks his Jewish tradition to challenge the absolute authority of the Torah, in the light of a gift that constitutes the core identity of Israel.

This sketch is intended to indicate how Bultmann's remarkable reading of Paul may provoke us to interpret Paul quite differently today, in a contemporary post-Christian context. It is not clear if there is anyone alive today competent to match Bultmann's achievement. Although dated and one-sided, his work still remains a challenge, inviting others to render Paul's voice powerful and relevant, not only for the sake of New Testament scholarship, but also for the sake of the church and of an increasingly endangered world.

Chapter 6

JOHANNINE CHRISTOLOGY
AND ESCHATOLOGY

Jörg Frey

Exegesis and Systematics in Bultmann's Theology

Rudolf Bultmann is widely considered the most important New Testament scholar of the twentieth century. His *Theology of the New Testament*,[1] which appeared in three installments from 1948 to 1953, is still a classic even more than sixty years after its appearance. This work must be understood not simply as a summa of exegetical work but at least as much as a work of systematic theology, indeed a presentation of Bultmann's own theology via the interpreted biblical texts.[2]

In this regard, the structure of the work places central importance on the "theologies of Paul and John," which constitute the load-bearing columns at its center.[3] It is no accident that Bultmann speaks of "theology" in relation to Paul and John but does not use the term in any of the other chapter titles. The first section offers only "Presuppositions and Motifs of New Testament Theology." It does not consider the proclamation of Jesus (traditionally a focus of attention) as a component of New Testament theology but solely as a presupposition for it. It does not develop the kerygma of the early church (with which New Testament theology begins, according to Bultmann)[4] nor the kerygma of the Hellenistic church as theology, but discusses them only in terms of individual motifs. The third section of the work, after the treatment of the Pauline and Johannine theologies, also no longer speaks of "theology," but only of a "development" toward the early church. This development clearly appears to be a deterioration, a departure from the eschatological consciousness that alone deserves to be called theology and that, according to Bultmann, is present only in Paul and then—in even purer form—in John the Evangelist.

The fact that Bultmann's work represents a systematic and not a historical conception is also evident in the fact that the historic-chronological arrangement of the material evokes little interest. If one occasionally finds clearly post-Pauline concepts incorporated in the first section, one also finds references to texts that date before the Gospel of John in the third section. Bultmann does not independently consider the period between Paul and John, in which many New Testament writings originated.[5] Instead, as theologians, Paul and John stand alongside one another at the center and in largely parallel treatments. In both cases, Bultmann elaborates the human encounter with the message of faith before or without Christ, so that in the end he depicts "the human being [man] under faith" (for Paul)[6] or "faith as eschatological existence" (for John). Disregarding all the admitted terminological and structural differences between the thought of Paul and that of John, Bultmann systematically formulated the two portrayals with a view to a strict comparability. The question must arise as to whether the exegesis really receives primacy here or whether systematic theology has gained the upper hand over exegesis.[7] In my view, one should read Bultmann's *Theology of the New Testament* at least as much as a work of systematics as of exegesis.

In essence, this observation also applies to his commentary on John,[8] which summarizes in concentrated fashion the older discussion of the Fourth Gospel and, in its combination of exegetical and hermeneutico-systematic elements, offers a whole whose coherence has not since been attained and probably never will be attained again in a commentary. Bultmann's interpretation was and continues to be a grand theological schema—even if its historical, source-critical, and religio-historical presuppositions and the picture of the Gospel of John constructed from them has long since been recognized as untenable. Few Johannine exegetes complied with its entirety even in Bultmann's time.[9] Bultmann's view of Johannine theology certainly depends to a great degree on preliminary historical and exegetical decisions: for instance, on the presupposition of the existence of Gnosticism as a pre-Christian movement, including the Gnostic Redeemer Myth, and on the reconstruction of a text of the pre-redactional Gospel that contained no futuristic-eschatological and sacramental statements. John the Evangelist ultimately appears in Bultmann's reconstruction as a mirror image of the interpreter himself—that is, a modern Protestant theologian of the Word who can forgo wonders and sacraments, who long ago abandoned futuristic eschatology, and who practices a form of existential interpretation of the myth. In Bultmann's view, the reaction of John the Evangelist over against the Gnostic worldview dominant in his time prefigured the manner in which Bultmann's contemporary Christian proclamation should answer contemporaneous philosophy. Thus, John essentially offers a biblical legitimization for Bultmann's own theology. Unmistakably, such a hermeneutic *circulus virtuosus* runs the risk of itself becoming *circulus vitiosus*: Bultmann did not always escape this danger, at least not when he had reconstructed his object, the Johannine text, in a manner that he found "suitable."[10]

In the following, I discuss essential elements of Bultmann's interpretation and its presuppositions in the history of theology and exegesis and, against this background, present his depiction of Johannine eschatology, and Christology.

Systematic and Historical Presuppositions of Bultmann's Interpretation of John

Bultmann's Understanding of Eschatology with Recourse to Heidegger and the History of Modern Theology

The Primacy of Eschatology

The primary framework for Bultmann's interpretation of John is not Christology but *eschatology*.[11] Eschatology is the center of all of Bultmann's theology:[12] The coming of Jesus is "the eschatological event" (2.37; *Theologie*, 389), and faith is "transition into eschatological existence" (2.78; *Theologie*, 427). Yet, in contrast to older forms of theology, Bultmann understands eschatology in a radically new manner: It is no longer the concluding doctrine "of the last things" that is subsumed as a subset within other doctrines; rather, theology as a whole is now eschatology and "the eschatological" is the truly Christian.

Various lines merge in this viewpoint. From the perspective of the history of religions, Bultmann had already quite early on followed his teacher Johannes Weiss in comprehending the primitive Christian movement in the categories of eschatological expectation.[13] Still, in contrast to Weiss' and (especially) Albert Schweitzer's view of "consistent eschatology,"[14] eschatology also gained increased relevance for *systematic* theology with the rise of dialectical theology in the early 1920s. After the collapse of the Protestant cultural synthesis of God and the world in World War I, God was conceived as radically unworldly via the concept of eschatology.[15] This change of thought occurred for Bultmann initially under the influence of Wilhelm Herrmann, then (especially) Søren Kierkegaard,[16] and finally, after 1927, in explicit reference to the analysis of the temporality of human existence developed by his Marburg colleague Martin Heidegger in *Sein und Zeit*.[17] For Bultmann, then, it is of utmost importance that eschatology be placed at the center of Christian theology and that everything specifically Christian be seen as "eschatological."[18]

Recourse to Heidegger's Existential Ontology

The fact that Bultmann adopts Heidegger's ontology in this fashion has grounds in the conviction that the theological interpretation of texts must be performed with reflective, content-appropriate, and time-appropriate terminology and thus is directed to the analysis of the formation of concepts by contemporary philosophy. The phenomenological ontology of Heidegger was not, in Bultmann's judgment, a competing "worldview" but was purely formal, thus theologically neutral, and particularly well-suited to the character of the New Testament message.[19]

Heidegger posed the question of the meaning of being as a question about *existence* (*Dasein*), characterized by a *network of ontological structures*, by *existentiality*, and by the quality of *mineness*. That is, "being" always means one's own existence, is given to the possibility of choice, can be gained or lost, and can exist authentically or inauthentically.[20] In actuality, existence is only the precursor to one's own death, in "being until death." Here, it can "fully apprehend [one's own existence] in its thrownness."[21] Heidegger formulated special terms that confront a "vulgar" understanding: *historicity* versus history, *temporality* versus time, *futuricity* versus future. In the structure of "temporality," the temporal modes of past and future meet in the now. Future and past are not merely something yet-to-be or having-been; rather, the treatment of the future and the past opens possibilities for existence in the now.[22]

Bultmann's concept of eschatology and his understanding of history, time, and the future bear the strong imprint of Heidegger's analysis of existence. "History" would be "improperly" understood and inconsequential if we only wanted to portray how it was. Instead, history is properly understood only as historicality, as the "occurrence of being-in-the-world"[23] or as "the fact that one's being is not at one's disposal, is sometimes at risk in the concrete situations of life, goes through decisions in which one does not choose something for one's self, but chooses one's self as a possibility."[24] Thus, for Bultmann, *two ways of perceiving history* contrast with one another,[25] the "proper perception of history, which confronts one with decision, and the improper, which deals with the mere historical data."[26] Only the former merits consideration for the interpretation of God's revelation as an occurrence beyond one's control and with existence as its goal. When history is treated as an objective matter (and this also pertains to the investigation of the so-called truths of salvation from the New Testament), the consideration remains "improper"; it does not touch on existence, nor does it open the way for freedom in the now. Therefore, Bultmann formulated the goal of his historical work as "to interpret the phenomena of past history from the possibilities of the human understanding of existence and, thus, to bring these possibilities to consciousness as the possibilities of the current understanding of existence, too."[27] It definitely does not focus on the past, the "then," but on the present, the "now"—and, precisely on this point, Bultmann saw himself in agreement not only with Paul (2 Cor 6:2) but also and especially with John.

The situation with *eschatology* is analogous. For Bultmann, it does not involve a still outstanding future per se, nor the end of the world (such as the classical locus, *de novissimis*); instead, with strict reference to human existence, eschatology involves the end of the world *in* the world, that which occurs decisively in the revelation of God (and thus in the saving activity of God).[28] Indeed, revelation is not the communication of knowledge but a historical occurrence that is simultaneously, in "paradoxical identity,"[29] the eschatological event. In it, the worldly self-understanding enters into crisis. It calls one to decision and establishes one's authenticity. That is, in the revelatory event, in the coming of Christ, or in the proclamation of this coming, an eschatological event occurs in the now. In this understanding, too, Bultmann saw himself in agreement with John the Evangelist, in particular.

Fundamental Problems and Decisions with Regard to the History of Religions

In addition to recourse to Heidegger, Bultmann presupposes a series of additional central *insights and problems in the recent history of theology* that can be mentioned only briefly here and cannot be explored further.

1. In the first place, we need to keep in mind the modern *critique of primitive Christian eschatology* that traces back to the beginnings of modern exegesis.[30] The history of religions school and the so-called consistent eschatology clearly demonstrated this critique. If Jesus and Paul expected the imminent end, they were disappointed in this expectation, and all attempts to dispense with this disappointment must be abandoned as intellectually dishonest and incredible apologetics. The apocalyptic hopes in a future *parousia* of Christ as a cosmic drama, in a bodily resurrection, a Last Judgment, and an end of the world must, therefore, be considered mere speculation and a mythology unacceptable to the modern worldview. They remain external and irrelevant for faithful existence if one does not succeed in relating them to internal processes and contemporary self-understanding.

2. A second set of problems central for Bultmann was the *modern critique of metaphysics and epistemology*, which formed the background on which Heidegger's analysis of existence could be applied as a particularly suitable path toward the solution of the so-called subject-object-problem. Kant's critique of reason, in particular, posed the problem that God cannot be the object of human knowledge. In his dogmatic theology, Friedrich Schleiermacher felt that he could only legitimately speak about pious self-consciousness. The characterization of dialectical theology sharpened the problem. If God is conceived radically as "the all-determining reality,"[31] any objectifying discourse "about God" must be "not just error and delusion, but . . . sin."[32] God and his activity are not "objectifiable," but

neither is faith. Adapting a core statement of the Reformation, Bultmann's teacher Wilhelm Herrmann had already stated, "We can only say of God what he does to us."[33] Along these lines Bultmann phrased his maxim that discourse about God (i.e., theology) can be discourse only about a human being or about one's existence as determined by God. Only if a theological statement is simultaneously a statement concerning humanity does it truly pertain. Consequently, Bultmann consistently treats Christology as soteriology in which he does not make statements concerning the nature of Christ but discusses his functional significance for human beings.

3. An essential problem raised especially by historical scholarship on the New Testament is the question of the *relevance of historical data*. Lessing had already established the principle that "accidental historical truths" cannot substantiate "necessary rational truths."[34] Therefore, one cannot establish that something has religious validity through historical demonstration, and a belief substantiated by historical "data" would not be an actual belief. Conceived in Reformation categories, such a belief would not be God's gift but a human work. The path of historical apologetics often chosen in contrast to historical critique is, therefore, a retreat (and all too often also an intellectually dishonest retreat) into an internal, false security. Consequently, Bultmann can accept historical criticism and the skepticism in Synoptic Gospel research that accompanied *Formgeschichte*, in particular, because faith is ultimately independent of historical critique, just as it is independent of historical justification.

4. Bultmann's late liberal teachers had already made use of this separation of *faith and history*. Liberal theology was still in a position, however, to extract the "essence" of the Christian religion from the New Testament witnesses following a "core-and-shell" model, for example, by removing Jesus' simple gospel core from its time-bound shell (that is, the shell of Jewish apocalypticism or primitive Christian interpretation).[35] With Albert Schweitzer's *Geschichte der Leben-Jesu-Forschung*,[36] this synthesis collapsed and it became impossible to find the Christian essence in a specific epoch of early Christianity or even

in the "religion of Jesus." The discussion given impetus by Karl Barth's *Römerbrief* and the new movement of dialectical theology caused the chasm between history and faith to continue to grow. Bultmann now placed attention on the text as "address"; later he speaks of the "kerygma," the message: This kerygma can now "no [longer] . . . be comprehended from the perspective of the history of religion or of ideas; rather it concerns human beings in this existence. . . . The connection between history and faith is reduced to a single point, namely the kerygma."[37]

5. Bultmann adopted the concept of *existence* from the thought of Søren Kierkegaard, who was very important especially for early dialectic theology in general. Bultmann now specified the position already developed by Wilhelm Herrmann that theology is to be done in the context of the "realities of life," in reference to the concept of existence.[38] In existence, in the moment, one understands that it involves oneself (*tua res agitur*), revelation occurs here, and here faith has its place. Thus Bultmann understands revelation and belief in a strictly dialect manner. Revelation is not something that could occur before or behind current existence, in past history or in a mystical beyond, and then be noted, accepted, or rejected. Instead, it occurs only in paradox, in the here and now, in human existence, and only so is its unworldliness and intractability preserved. Against this background, it becomes clear why Heidegger's analysis of existence in *Sein und Zeit* could seem to Bultmann an appropriate foundation for explicating his own theology.

Bultmann's Understanding of Time and Immanent Eschatology

In the context of these problems and with recourse to Heidegger's ontology, Bultmann placed *two understandings of time* in a dialectical-polar relationship. As the understanding marked by objectivity, accessibility, and self-protection, as time without authentic decision, world time appears as the counterimage to eschatological time because the event conceived in the linear course of time as past or future means nothing for one's own existence. In contrast, by means of the eschatological now of the faith decision, the essence of the historical moment becomes perceptible. In the act of faith, "by recognizing revelation, the now becomes free from the past and from death, and the future opens up,"[39] while unbelief is linked to the past since sin persists via unbelief (cf. John 3:36).[40] In the now of decision, the absolute future and the absolute past meet as alternatives.

In Bultmann's understanding, time as temporality is characterized by its *punctiliar* and *alternative* nature. The theological yield of this time concept consists first in the fact that *eschatology can speak about the end of time and of history, although the sequence of events continues*; paradoxically, then, "existence" can be depicted as "subject to the end of time and history . . . even in the midst of the sequence of empirical time and history."[41] While the history of the world continues, it comes to its end in each moment.

Bultmann's concept of time shapes his theological statements. In contrast to an understanding of time as a linear process between before and after, Bultmann starts from a purely punctiliar understanding of time as *temporality*, as the now of decision. He considered this concept of time the only one appropriate for comprehending the reality of historical existence.[42] Bultmann's concept of *kerygma* links his concept of time as the punctiliar now with his understanding of the revelation of God in the coming of Jesus Christ. The saving event that occurred once, which would have no significance for human existence as merely a past event, becomes current and relevant as an eschatological event in its current proclamation. By becoming present in the kerygma, existence becomes authentic.

In principle, eschatology on this foundation can only be *present*. Contrariwise, the salvation-historical/futuristic eschatology of the New Testament writings (except for John) is inauthentic and mythological, thereby requiring demythologization or *existential interpretation*. Just as a merely past event cannot lead human existence to decision, so too a merely future event cannot lead human existence to decision and certainly not into the presence of God. Only existential interpretation can make these mythological statements comprehensible in relation to an event in existence. According to Bultmann's conviction, the saving event (and thus eschatology in the proper sense) comes into view only in the existential modification of the apocalyptic picture of the future. After all, Bultmann could point historically to the fact that such a modification already took place in the New Testament and led to an increasingly purer development of the eschatological consciousness.

The Development of the Eschatological Consciousness in Early Christianity

Bultmann's eschatological concept is the material criterion by which he measured the statements of the New Testament text and the means by which he sought to distinguish what was said from what was meant.[43] Thus, despite the disparities within the New Testament, he can conceive of the New Testament's eschatological (and thus truly Christian) self-understanding as ultimately uniform, which shines through the Christian kerygma but is then encountered most purely in the work of the Fourth Evangelist.[44]

From Jesus to Paul

In the ministry of *Jesus*, the coming of the kingdom of God was still a wondrous, future event that, according to Bultmann, already determines the present, in contrast to Jewish apocalypticism. The eschatological progression is separable from the progression of history and is understood as radically unworldly.

By contrast, in the kerygma of the *earliest church*, the essence of the eschatological event still appears largely concealed under the manifest expression of the expectation of a cosmic final drama. The dissolution of Jewish salvation-history thinking occurs only in the Hellenistic church, which Bultmann (following the history of religions school) placed at a wide distance from the Palestinian church. The expectation of the coming of the *parousia* becomes transformed at this point into the veneration of the present *kyrios*. In the place of Jewish salvation-historical thought, there appeared a conception according to which history in the present will be transcended by the *eschaton*. The cause of this transformation, according to Bultmann, was the encounter between the conceptualization of history evident in the Old Testament and the atemporal mythology of Gnosticism. The Old Testament salvation-historical tradition was able to correct Gnosticism's naturalist understanding of the saving event while preserving awareness of its historicity; in contrast, *the Redeemer Myth displaced the old expectation of the* parousia *and replaced the end of history envisaged mythologically in time with an event that transcends history in the present.* The clarified understanding of eschatology (as found in John) appears, then, as the result of the mutual interdependence of the Old Testament and early Christian understandings of salvation on the one hand and of Hellenistic and Gnostic conceptualizations on the other.[45]

This rethinking from apocalypticism to present eschatology occurred primarily in the theology of Paul, who recognized in the cross and resurrection of Christ the fulfillment of the eschatological expectation of salvation and the presence of the new aeon.[46] With Paul, the originally futuristic eschatology becomes soteriology, the doctrine of justification, and it unfolds as a present eschatology.[47] For Bultmann, the fact that Paul still holds to "saving truths" and expects the resurrection of the dead, for example, merely reflects a minor inconsistency in Paul (2.127; *Theologie*, 347).

The Eschatological Consciousness and Present Eschatology in John

This understanding finally becomes apparent most clearly and purely in the work of *John the Evangelist*. Here, the fact that "authentic eschatology" exists "only in the radical recognition of its presence" finds expression in the consistent theological penetration of the reality of Christ and the clever reinterpretation of traditional eschatology.[48] Fundamental for John is the notion that the sending of Jesus instigates the crisis that decides the fate of every person. This decision takes place in Jesus' revelatory work, "in the way one reacts to the revelation" or in "one's attitude toward the word of Jesus."[49] Thus a bold reinterpretation brought eschatology into the present and eliminated traditional eschatology. The world may take offence that "a contingent historical event should be the eschatological event,"[50] yet the revelation of its unworldly essence and its power for separation and decision lies precisely in this paradox. Revelation consists, ultimately, in nothing other than the "bare fact of it," in the statement "that the Revealer has come and gone, has descended and been re-exalted" (2.66; *Theologie*, 419).

With the incorporation of the eschatological event into the now of revelation, Bultmann saw in John the present and the future fusing together and the events separated in the linear understanding of time collapsing into a unity. As *the* eschatological event, the sending of Jesus must be a punctiliar entity "framed by his coming and his departing" (2.48; *Theologie*, 400);[51] that is, his coming and going "separated in earthly time, are simultaneous in eschatological 'time.'"[52] Thus, the saving events of Easter, Pentecost, and Parousia, which traditionally were conceived of as sequential events, collapse into one single event. The evangelist is supposed to have interpreted them as "one and the same." The one event "meant by all these," however, "is not an external occurrence, but an inner one: the victory which Jesus wins when faith arises in man by the overcoming of the offense that Jesus is to him. The victory . . . is the fact that now there exists a faith which recognizes in Jesus the Revelation of God" (2.57; *Theologie*, 410).

The story of Jesus, understood as an eschatological event, does not become a piece of the past but remains ever present because, in its very proclamation, it is an eschatological event. In proclamation, Jesus himself becomes present; in hearing, the crisis occurs; thus every moment has new eschatological character. Being in faith (understood as eschatological existence) also participates in the paradox of revelation. It is never complete existence but is existence newly apprehended in each moment—ever new is the "decision against the world," and in this very process it is "'in the world' . . . [but not] 'of the world'" (2.76–78; *Theologie*, 430). In faith, the possibility of human existence to understand itself in ζωή (life) is realized.[53] Thus definitive salvation is present in faith. In principle, nothing new or superior can still ensue. Yet the believer may "never look back. . . . Nothing is 'finished,'" and "in a certain sense," Easter lies "ever before the believer."[54]

For Bultmann the foundation for a critical treatment of the mythological eschatology of Jewish and Christian apocalypticism is the paradoxical concept of revelation and the recognition that the eyes of the world can neither see nor identify paradoxical eschatology. For moderns, apocalypticism's images of a future in time are untenable speculation and ideals that make the transcendent imminent, thereby rendering the otherworldly both secular and accessible. For Bultmann, John the Evangelist is at least a predecessor of this insight. In conscious opposition to an unrefined conceptualization that predominated among ecclesial circles, John carried out a consistent interpretation of the reality of Christ that "mainstream ecclesial" circles soon recognized as dangerous and consequently mitigated against.[55]

Thus Johannine eschatology appears as a paradigm for a "purified
. . . eschatology of faith"[56] that refrains from any depiction of eschatological salvation in terms of objective content and, for the most part,
consistently transposes the futuristic eschatology into the eschatological present. Bultmann denied the evangelist all statements that do not
evidence such a reinterpretation and attributed them to a redactor that
misunderstood his theology. The extent to which Bultmann's historical and exegetical judgments were determined by content and theological perspectives becomes particularly evident here.

Exegetical Predecisions in Bultmann's
Interpretation of John

Bultmann's interpretation of John rests on literary-critical and religio-
historical predecisions that trace back to his works from the 1920s.
Even though Bultmann banished historical detail in his commentary
to footnotes and opted not to provide an introduction,[57] these decisions are by no means theologically inconsequential (as Bultmann himself thought) but are indeed foundational for his interpretation. Only
the isolation of source documents and the separation of a secondary
redactional layer permitted him to interpret the work of the evangelist
in a form "cleansed" of supposed additions against the background of
the edited sources. Bultmann's interpretive interests pertained to this
work, which he presented in his commentary in the purported original arrangement, not to the transmitted Gospel.

According to Bultmann's reconstruction, the evangelist created
a work that was extremely uniform in style and theology, for which,
besides smaller source fragments, he primarily employed (1) a collection of miracle stories (*Semeiaquelle*), (2) a collection of Gnostic
revelatory discourses, and (3) a Passion narrative document. He incorporated these sources in his portrayal with a magisterial technique of
glossing interpretation, such that Bultmann thought he could largely
reconstruct even the scope of these sources. The evangelist's work is
supposed then to have become disarranged for unexplained reasons
and been discovered somewhere as a torso,[58] when an ecclesially oriented redactor brought it rather poorly into an order, supplemented
or corrected it by introducing the majority church's eschatology and
sacramental doctrine, and then disseminated it in this form.[59]

The conclusion in John 20:30-31 suggests that the Gospel was published by a redactor. Bultmann then infers the interests of the redactor from John 21.[60] They involved harmonization with the synoptic portrayal (Peter), futuristic eschatology (John 21:22-23), and the doctrine of the sacraments (John 21:1-14). Bultmann then excised other passages in John 1–20 that served these concerns on grounds of content. This included all traces of an apocalyptic-futuristic eschatology (John 5:28-29; 6:39c, 40c, 44c; 12:48), the sacramental conclusion of the bread saying in John 6:51c-58, and (with no text-critical justification whatsoever) the two words ὕδατος καί (water and) in John 3:5, which Bultmann saw as a sacramental correction.

These excisions are unsupportable from a style-critical perspective. The idea that the evangelist did not give the sacraments independent significance and the rejection of futuristic eschatology both result from Bultmann's concept of time. If all salvation is to be localized in the punctiliar now of the coming of Christ or its proclamation, the two notions Bultmann excises would be inappropriate "objectifications." The true believer needs no such "objective" signs. For a perfect theologian like Bultmann's John, they are essentially superfluous.[61] Whatever does not correspond to the refined concept of revelation presupposed for the evangelist is thus to be excised as an addition. The "ecclesial" redactor that is supposed to have supplemented the Gospel and incorporated futuristic eschatology and the church's sacraments as "corrections" also exemplifies, then, a rather poorly profiled "both-and theology." He, in Bultmann's view, grossly misunderstood the true eschatological self-understanding.

For the picture of how the evangelist worked, his treatment of his supposed sources is decisive. The revelatory Discourse Source, which Bultmann first encountered in the Prologue and in 1 John,[62] is most important. Basing his case on stylistic differences and substantive tensions, Bultmann isolated from the glosses of the author or the evangelist an earlier form (which was in parallel structure) and then extended this observation to all of Jesus' discourses in the Gospel.[63] Bultmann regarded the source to be a Semitic poem whose antithetical parallelism also points to the dualistic thought standing behind it, while he regarded all "prosaic" clauses that disturb the rhythm or explicate the source to be additions by the evangelist. Thus Bultmann recovered his source through a relatively mechanical process of subtraction.[64]

Conversely, this approach also gives a picture of the manner in which the evangelist worked. He largely adopted his (Gnostic) source and glossed it with clarifications and allusions.

This source-critical hypothesis is linked with the religio-historical hypothesis of the acceptance of the Gnostic Redeemer Myth. Bultmann also interpreted this acceptance biographically. The evangelist is supposed to have come from the milieu of Gnostic baptismal sects, as suggested by Mandaean parallels in particular.[65] He would have been, then, a "convert" to the Christian faith, formerly a Gnostic disciple of the Baptist, who introduced the Discourse Source from this milieu into the Christian community.[66] He then will have transferred the discourses, originally attributed to a beloved revealer figure, to the historical figure of Jesus. Thus, by connecting it with historical Jesus tradition, he historicized and "demythologized" the Gnostic myth. Consequently, Bultmann saw at work in the act of the composition of the Gospel, independently of Paul, that syncretistic process of critical encounter between the Gnostic myth and early Christian historical thought. In that process alone the radical understanding of the eschatological event as a historical event, introduced by the story of Jesus yet currently effective, could come into being.[67] This parallelism of the presupposed religio-historical processes and the accompanying hermeneutical situation then also supported Bultmann's portrayal in his theology, in which Paul and John stand at the center in remarkable parallelism.

The Gnostic Redeemer Myth, which Bultmann presupposed historically as a pre-Christian phenomenon,[68] appears in John in modified form, and the theological contribution of the evangelist lies in altering the original myth. The evangelist omits the preexistence of souls and the essential connection of Redeemer and redeemed, just as he does the cosmological teachings and the understanding of redemption as a cosmic event. In Bultmann's judgment, the Gospel of John is, therefore, *not* a Gnostic document. It employs Gnostic diction but only in a broken fashion. It does not understand the redemptive event naturalistically but as a historical event, and it transforms the cosmological dualism of Gnosticism into a dualism of decision. While the Gnostic myth recalls one's true nature, the Johannine call is to the decision of faith. Bultmann was convinced, however, that the myth offered "the right terms for understanding the Word of revelation," for it knows "that human beings are lost in the world" and "the unworldliness of the human self," and it already saw the saving event as desecularization.[69] Yet the myth only formulated the "question" that the Gospel answers; the myth described the *possibility* of redemption, while the Christian kerygma proclaims it in the historical Jesus of Nazareth as a paradoxical *reality*. Thus, the eschatological consciousness (in its "pure" and radical form) develops in continuity and opposition—that is, in critical comparison to the understanding of Gnosticism. This stance also prefigures the structure by which Bultmann himself drew upon the philosophy of his time—the existential philosophy of the early Heidegger in order to explicate the eschatological self-understanding of Christian faith.[70]

The Portrayal of Johannine Christology and Eschatology

As in his programmatic essay on Johannine eschatology from 1928,[71] so too in his *Theology of the New Testament* it is "dualism" that constitutes the starting point for Bultmann's portrayal of Johannine theology (secs. 42-44; after brief preliminary remarks on the historical situation of John, sec. 41). The opposites of world and God, and darkness and light, and the division of human beings into those "from above" and those "from below" offer the framework necessary for the discussion of revelation. In the background stands Bultmann's conviction that Gnosticism was the originating milieu of Johannine thought (especially of the "Revelation Discourses"). In it one finds not only an awareness of the necessity of redemption and revelation but also the terminological material that assists the Christian proclamation of the revelation issued in Christ—the proclamation of the "fact of Jesus 'having come.'" The myth does not, indeed, answer the question of revelation itself (no more so than did Heidegger's analysis of existence); it tells about nonhistorical redeemer figures. Only the kerygma that this Redeemer has appeared in the specific and historical person of Jesus of Nazareth "historicizes" (and to this degree "demythologizes") the myth. Only it juxtaposes the possibility of revelation with the message of revelation issued and the "question" of salvation with the answer of faith.

Christology as Soteriology and Realized Eschatology

"*Within this world of death life appeared*" (sec. 45; 2.33; *Theologie*, 385). Bultmann begins his portrayal of Johannine Christology with this statement, adapted from 1 John 1:2 and formulated entirely as an assertion. Here, a characteristic element of Bultmann's portrayal becomes evident. Bultmann does not present Johannine theology as if it is an object distanced from himself but as something with which he is in substantial agreement. In the style of assertion, the evangelist and his interpreter close ranks, and description mutates somewhat into proclamation.

It is further remarkable that Bultmann rarely speaks explicitly of "Christology." This circumstance reflects the fact that, substantively, Bultmann is not concerned with the doctrinal statements about the "nature of Christ" but, strictly functionally, with the significance that the revelation or the coming of Christ has for the world or for believers. Consequently, the subsections under the major heading "The κρίσις of the World" deal with "The Sending of the Son" (sec. 45), the "Stumbling Block of the ὁ λόγος σὰρξ ἐγένετο" (sec. 46), "The Revelation of the δόξα" (sec. 47), and, as a point in time, "Revelation as the Word" (sec. 48). Thus the arrangement already makes it clear that, for Bultmann, one can only appropriately discuss soteriology precisely because speech about Christ (even in the Reformation) expresses what Christ is "for us."

Bultmann begins the discussion of the sending (or the coming or appearing) of the Son with the assumption that the sending statements (derived from a Gnostic milieu) also constitute the historical basis of Johannine Christology. He represents this sending as "the κρίσις of the world,"[72] as the eschatological event that, not just in the future but already in the past, brought the human world into this crisis and to decision. As such, wherever it is preached, this sending leads to decision and signifies ever anew the end of the world within the world. Johannine theology as interpreted here agrees entirely with Bultmann's own thought.

The discussion of the *sending* of God's Son and, even more, of his preexistence is a mythological statement, of course, and the question of whether it should really be understood mythologically is for Bultmann little more than rhetorical. It does not involve the graphic description of a path or even a transformation in the "status" of Jesus; it has nothing to do with an objective christological statement. In substance, it deals only with the fact that, in Jesus, "the transcendent divine reality became audible, visible, and tangible in the realm of the earthly world" (2.33; *Theologie*, 386). The decisive content of all statements concerning his sending or coming is that the Sent One is not to be understood as a this-worldly figure. Furthermore, a departure corresponds to the coming. The Sent One is only a guest in the world between coming and going; he "does not become . . . a figure within world-history" (2.34; *Theologie*, 387) or a part of the "world" but remains ultimately remote. The Johannine statements about Jesus' farewell, return, exaltation, and glorification ultimately make clear the otherworldliness of the Revealer.

A second section deals with the connection between God's sending of his Son and his love (1 John 4:9; John 3:16) and takes up the Johannine interpretation of the sending of Jesus as *an act of God's love*. For Bultmann, of course, this is not a statement about God "per se" or his "essence," which, after all, is not "objectifiable." Instead, this statement defines only the purpose of the coming of Jesus with a view to the world and humanity. Jesus comes to deliver the cosmos. Here, Bultmann also briefly discusses the classical christological titles Savior, Lord, Messiah, and Son of Man. All of these derive their meaning solely from the Judeo- and early Christian or Hellenistic conviction "that Jesus is the eschatological salvation-bringer, that *his coming is the eschatological event*" (2.37; *Theologie*, 389).

Then Bultmann returns to the motif of κρίσις. By means of the ambiguous relationship of "judgment" and "decision" (John 3:19; 9:39), John is supposed to have "radically executed the historicization of eschatology initiated by Paul," since now the judgment occurs "in the encounter with Jesus and the decision between belief and unbelief that it necessitates."[73] What the tradition envisioned as a dramatic cosmic event at the end now occurs in the present, in the encounter with Jesus or his word, perhaps even without the world noting it.

The Offense of the σάρξ and Revelation

With the coming of the Son of God having been functionally interpreted, the "how" is now to be defined more precisely. Here, Bultmann summarizes concisely what he had written in his commentary on John 1:14 (as a brief presentation of his understanding of revelation).[74] The Revealer comes "as a human being," indeed, "as a specific historical human being, as Jesus of Nazareth." The pointedness of this statement must not be misperceived. "His humanity is authentic,"[75] not restricted by special "supernatural" qualities. "He is the Revealer in pure humanity."[76] Bultmann presents this offense as clearly as possible—the offense of the paradoxical identity of human being and Revealer, of σάρξ ("flesh") and δόξα ("glory"). Revelation is thus radically veiled. Nothing could identify the historical human being Jesus as "Messiah" or Revealer—not an impressive religious personality, not superhuman powers, and not an aura. Moreover, any intention (no matter how pious) to see the δόξα along with or through the σάρξ would be a mistaken act of unbelief, an attempt to ground faith through external or internal evidence. Yet true belief is manifest precisely when a human being takes no offense at the pure humanity of Jesus—and yet believes.

In the background of these statements stands more than Bultmann's judgment concerning the earthly Jesus, who is supposed to have appeared in an "un-Messianic" fashion.[77] Bultmann saw the Johannine emphasis on the radical paradox as antithetical to Christian Gnostics who regarded the union of Son of God and human being as only temporary (from the baptism until before the crucifixion) or who even saw the incarnation as a natural process of the union of human and divine. If this were the case, the humanity of the incarnate one would not remain intact.[78]

A second aspect also differentiated John from the Christian Gnostics. The Revealer also differs from a teacher or mystagogue who communicates doctrines and formulas and, through his teaching, ultimately renders himself dispensable. To the contrary, Jesus as a person is not dispensable. "He does not *communicate anything*, but *calls men to himself*" (2.41; *Theologie*, 394). He is himself the gift that he promises; life is not a body of lore that one could learn from Jesus, but ultimately it is only he himself.

The core question, then, is how the vision of the δόξα (John 1:14b) should be understood. One could think that the Johannine portrait depicts Jesus as a Hellenistic "god man" (θεῖος ἀνήρ). He had access to wondrous knowledge about Peter, Nathanael, and the Samaritan woman, did astonishing wonders, and escaped the traps of his opponents in wondrous manner. Yet for Bultmann, all of these narrative elements only appear to call his humanity into question. Jesus' wondrous knowledge is an expression of the fact "that the believer feels himself searched and known by God and that his own existence is exposed by the encounter with the Revealer" (2.42; *Theologie*, 394). The fact that the Revealer could not be seized demonstrates that the fate of the Revealer lies beyond human will. According to Bultmann, Jesus' wonders, interpreted as signs (σημεῖα), are ambivalent even for the evangelist—being open to misunderstanding and ultimately being only images and symbols of what takes place in the totality of Jesus' work.[79] They do not offer any external legitimization of Jesus, for when the signs are not understood as such, they become only an offense and create animosity and persecution.

Yet not only Jesus' deeds but also ultimately his words are open to misunderstanding. The offense they also occasion finds clearest expression in categorizations of Jesus' claim as demonic or blasphemous (John 5:17-18; 8:48). Finally, the presentation of the one crowned with thorns as king (John 19:5, 14) and the inscription on the cross (John 19:19) give particularly drastic expression to the radical paradox of his claim despite his pure humanity.

Thus Bultmann understood the Johannine portrayal of Jesus as a peculiar extension of the Markan theory of the Messianic Secret. In this regard, the offense lies not in Jesus' silence but precisely in the fact that, as a human being, he announced this claim publicly. Indeed, the concentration of the discussion of the glory or glorification of Jesus in the hour of his farewell, or in the "now" (νῦν; John 13:31-32), points to the fact that the relationship of faith in Jesus is ultimately "a relationship to the Exalted One"—but this relationship is such that the Exalted One is also always the Earthly One. "Jesus' life on earth does not become an item of the historical past, but constantly remains present reality. The historical figure of Jesus, i.e. his human story, retains its significance of being the revelation of his 'glory' and thereby of God's. It is the eschatological occurrence" (2.49; *Theologie*, 401).

John's Gospel describes the unity of Jesus with God through a number of expressions: in the mythological statement about the sending and in mystical formulas concerning mutual being in one another. Yet, according to Bultmann, these statements represent neither mythology nor mysticism and certainly not metaphysics in the sense of the later Doctrine of Two Natures.[80] Instead, even these statements ultimately illustrate only the idea that "God Himself encounters men in Jesus, a Jesus moreover who is a man in whom nothing unusual is perceptible" and thus, once again, "the *paradoxical nature* of the *concept of Revelation*" (2.50; *Theologie*, 403).

Attention falls now on the "works" or "the work" that Jesus performed. These expressions can refer (as in the kerygma of the Hellenistic church) to the death and resurrection of Jesus as "saving truths." Paul already counted the incarnation among the saving events and for John it is now "the decisive salvation-event" (2.52; *Theologie*, 405). Yet, while Paul subordinates the incarnation to Jesus' death, for John the incarnation as the "coming" of the revealer forms a unity with his death as "going." In this regard, however, the focal point is no longer his death, which has no particular saving significance for John but is only the completion of the work begun with the incarnation, "the last demonstration of . . . obedience" (2.52; *Theologie*, 405). This distinction is also evident in John's interpretation of the crucifixion, which he treats from the outset by way of the terms ὑψωθῆναι ("to be raised up") and δοξασθῆναι ("to be glorified"). John does not thereby regard Jesus' death as an event from which the subsequent resurrection removes the character of catastrophe. Rather, it is "already his exaltation" (2.53; *Theologie*, 406).

In contrast, in Bultmann's judgment the common Christian interpretation of Jesus' death as atoning sacrifice for sins is not definitive for John. He admits an exception regarding 1 John 1:7, yet he suspects a redactional gloss here, as he does in the substantively parallel statements in 1 John 2:2, 4, 10. In the end, he asserts, "Whatever may be the origin of these passages, the thought of Jesus' death as an atonement for sin has no place in John, and if it should turn out that he took it over from the tradition of the Church, it would still be a foreign element in his work" (2.54; *Theologie*, 407). Apparently Bultmann sensed that, textually speaking, he stood on shaky ground here, and he ultimately made his decision not by way of exegesis but on ideological grounds.

If Jesus' death does not stand out as a distinct event, the resurrection also "cannot be an event of special significance" (2.56; *Theologie*, 408). The cross is indeed victory over the world, and according to John Jesus did not receive the power to give life only upon his resurrection, because he carried life in himself from the outset (John 5:26). When the evangelist speaks of Jesus' resurrection (2:22), he does so "only" in a brief narrative aside.[81] In the Easter stories, the appearances of the Risen One only had the sense of signs (σημεῖα; John 20:30) that demonstrate Jesus' victory over the world, but these appearances are just as ambivalent as the wonders, being (as Bultmann freely admits) "not indispensable" and only "a concession to man's weakness" (2.56; *Theologie*, 409). That is, true faith can even forgo the Easter appearances; they have no theological value. The interpretation of John 20:29 as a criticism of Thomas, who in his unbelief wants to see and thereby does not embrace the paradox of the revelation concept (as Bultmann represents it), justifies this understanding. Here, too, systematic interests that lead to the marginalization of extremely important statements within John's Gospel seem largely to determine the interpretation.

According to Bultmann, the Farewell Discourses, where the promise of the *parousia* merges into the promise of Easter so that resurrection and *parousia* become identical (John 14:18-19 and 16:16-24), demonstrate that Easter is not a distinct "event." From the fact that the promise of the Spirit also parallels Easter in 14:15, it follows that Easter, Pentecost, and *parousia* are ultimately all "one and the same." "An external occurrence" is not involved "but an inner one: the victory which Jesus wins when faith arises in man by the overcoming of the offense that Jesus is to him" (2.57; *Theologie*, 410). According to Bultmann, then, " 'the facts of salvation' in the traditional sense play no important role in John" and "[t]he entire salvation-drama—incarnation, death, resurrection, Pentecost, the parousia—is concentrated into a single event: the Revelation of God's reality (ἀλήθεια) in the earthly activity of the man Jesus . . . in faith" (2.58; *Theologie*, 411). Correspondingly, the sacraments, too, no longer play a role. Already in his commentary on John, Bultmann had interpreted the words ὕδατος καί in John 3:5 as an insertion by the ecclesial redactor and conjectured that John 3 originally treated only birth from the Spirit and not by baptism with water. Similarly, he also attributes John 6:51b-58 and John 19:34b-35 to the redactor. In the simple attitude of the church, the redactor reintroduced the sacraments into the "radical" theology of the evangelist, who had treated them in a manner that, although not polemical, was nonetheless lackadaisical.

Under the heading "Revelation as the Word" (sec. 48), Bultmann now decisively defines the content of the revelation as *self*-revelation. The works that bear witness to Jesus are his words; the content of his words is what Jesus saw and heard with the Father. The concrete content of this revelation is never communicated, however. It evidently does not involve heavenly knowledge or religious mysteries but only the person of Jesus. He himself is his word; he is the Logos. Jesus ultimately reveals nothing "other than that he is the Revealer," who brings in his person what human beings crave (salvation or, metaphorically, the light, the true bread, etc.).

Bultmann traces this situation, too, to the Gnostic myth for which the "simple fact" is decisive. Yet, while John eliminates the cosmological presuppositions from the myth and does not speak of the relationship between the Redeemer and the redeemed, there remains for him only the "bare fact of Revelation" (2.67; *Theologie*, 419)—which contains the negation of all human self-assertion and therein the fulfillment of human longing for life.[82] This understanding of revelation also rules out any authentication of Jesus' sayings. The question as to why precisely this specific historical person should be the Revealer "must [!] not, may not, be answered" if one does not want to remove the offense (2.69; *Theologie*, 421). Here, the intensely radical nature of Bultmann's *Theology of the New Testament* becomes evident, which certainly extends far beyond the New Testament texts, even beyond the Gospel of John. Bultmann even reckons with the notion that John wanted to interpret a (synoptic) picture of Jesus (which was probably already present in his communities) in the light of his concept of revelation. John was certainly not concerned with the transmission of historical tradition or the reproduction of the past but with the actualization of the eschatological event (in remembrance through the Spirit). Thereby, according to Bultmann, John stood in diametrical opposition to "salvation-historical" thought (found, for instance, in Luke's works).

Belief as Overcoming the Offense and as Eschatological Existence

In terms of content, nothing more precise can be said here in relation to the revelation. "Its meaning can only be further clarified by

124 — Jörg Frey

demonstrating the movement that issues in belief" (2.69; *Theologie*, 422)—that is, in the description of faith as "eschatological existence" (2.75; *Theologie*, 427) defined by the revelation.

In this regard, Bultmann defined (Johannine and simultaneously Reformation) faith as "the hearing of the Word" (2.70; *Theologie*, 422). According to John 20:31, belief is the goal of the Gospel; the call to belief and the promise of belief permeate the Gospel. The objects of faith are Jesus' words (or works) and, ultimately, Jesus himself. "To have faith *in him*" (πιστεύειν + dat.) and "to believe *in him*" (πιστεύειν εἰς . . .) are identical, because in the preached word one encounters the Preacher himself. Thus, belief results from hearing—indeed, it *is* hearing itself. Of course, a distinction must be made here between real (i.e., believing) hearing and mere acoustic perception.

The relationship between seeing and believing is more complex since belief does not come from seeing. Verbs of seeing can denote a general sensory perception, but in specifically Johannine usage, they involve "the inner perception of matters having no sensory perceptibility . . . the 'sight' which recognizes the Son of God in the Incarnate One," that can paradoxically coincide with sensory perception (John 1:14) but can also be detached from it (2.72; *Theologie*, 424). This seeing is not a mystical vision, nor does it "mean that 'we' were 'eye-witnesses' in the sense that is meant in historical inquiry; for in that sense the unbelieving Jews were also eye-witnesses and yet saw nothing of the 'glory'" (2.72; *Theologie*, 424). Faith is not rooted in sight, then; a "faith" that comes superficially by Jesus' deeds would only be false faith. Conversely, seeing is an implication of faith; it is *"the knowing* that is peculiar to faith" (2.73; *Theologie*, 425), with regard to which Bultmann decidedly rejects the idea that recognition can lead beyond the "mere" belief and simultaneously constitute a higher level of faith. There are no levels of *pistikoi* and *gnostikoi* in the Christian church, no insight into higher knowledge that extends beyond simple faith. "Faith is everything," and "knowing is a structural aspect of believing" (2.74; *Theologie*, 426).

Bultmann discusses this faith as "eschatological existence" in the concluding section (sec. 50), where he emphasizes the difference between John and Paul. While Paul discussed the question of the *path* to salvation (faith vs. works), this was no longer a topic of discussion for John. He dealt with salvation itself. "He addresses himself to man's longing for life and attacks a false understanding of life" (2.75; *Theologie*, 427). Here the categories that Bultmann had acquired in dialogue with Heidegger found renewed application. Faith is "turning away from the world, the act of desecularization, the surrender of all seeming security and every pretense, the willingness to live by the strength of the invisible and uncontrollable" (2.75; *Theologie*, 428). The "overcoming of the offense" takes place as "human beings encounter life only in the Word that a mere human being, Jesus of Nazareth, speaks to them" (2.75; *Theologie*, 428)—a Word that cannot be further demonstrated in a worldly manner. It is the overcoming of the offense of the ὁ λόγος σὰρξ ἐγένετο, and therein lies the "decision against the world" and for God (2.77; *Theologie*, 429).

Here, Bultmann's systematic understanding of faith came to bear upon his exegesis. According to his conviction, faith is not holding some content or historical "facts" to be true, nor is it a dualistic worldview—in the sense, for example, of believing in an "afterworld" to which a person can turn in flight from the world. Indeed, it is not a "work" that a person freely does and certainly not an "accomplishment." When Bultmann speaks of "decision," it is an act understood in a paradoxical identity as simultaneously affected and granted by God. Thus Bultmann can also adopt the "predestinarian" statements in the Gospel of John. The disciples are chosen (John 15:16), they are in the hands of the Good Shepherd, who keeps them (John 10:28). The assurance of faith does not lie in them, nor in worldly circumstances or reasons, but in what they believe—and that is that Jesus, "who knows his own," establishes an assurance that differs from and far surpasses any worldly assurance.[83]

As the overcoming of the offense, then, faith is "desecularization" and the transition into eschatological existence. Although faith is in the world, it is nonetheless removed from the world and from worldly existence (John 17:11). This dialectic manifests itself then in the description of what for Paul is the relationship between indicative and imperative. Believers are "in the light" and still confess their sins (1 John 1:5-10). As sinners, they require constant forgiveness, but they know at the same time that their relationship to God is determined and continued through Christ. No false security or perfectionism can arise; the purity of believers is determined and granted *extra nos*. Thus keeping the commandments is the same as keeping the word, and love is nothing other than faith—just as John does not develop an independent ethics and does not further specify the content of the love commandment.

Bultmann then cites additional terms traditionally employed for the salvation of the end time, such as peace (John 14:27) and joy (John 15:11; 17:13), as characteristics of eschatological existence, although neither term refers to a possibility within the world or a condition of the soul. Instead, they refer to something that can be perceived only as reality in faith, in the overcoming of the world and of the anxiety experienced in it. Something similar applies to the formulas that describe communion with God and Christ as reciprocal recognition and communal existence. Here, too, no direct mystical relationship is involved, because of the distance between Jesus and the believer established by Jesus' departure. In fact, the notion of remaining "in him" or "in his words" finds expression in prayer that is certainly aware of the exaltation and is characterized by confidence in it (παρρησία; 1 John 5:14).

Finally, the criterion of eschatological existence is the possession of the Spirit. Yet John speaks about this differently than elsewhere in the New Testament. For John, the Spirit is not "the power that causes miracles and striking mental phenomena," nor "the power and norm of Christian conduct," but "the power within the Church which brings forth both knowledge and the proclamation of the Word" (2.88; *Theologie*, 440). In this regard, the Spirit teaches no new, supplementary, or superior knowledge, but recalls what Jesus taught. He works such that the revelation is a constantly new experience in the proclamation of the church.

In conclusion, Bultmann treats, with remarkable brevity, the Johannine understanding of the church. Once again, Bultmann presupposes that the fundamental Johannine perspective originated in Gnosticism, according to which the pneumatics, in whom the preexistent rays of light live, constitute a potential unity (2.91; *Theologie*, 443). For Bultmann, this presupposition explains why John does not speak about the church in terms of salvation history (that is, in terms of the eschatological people of God) but conceives of the church as the "invisible church," as the community of those who heed the voice of the Good Shepherd but whose unity in a flock is, once more, only an eschatological entity.

The church is identifiable on earth neither through external characteristics nor in a specific lifestyle; instead, it experiences its distance from the world only negatively, in hatred and persecution. Therein, by overcoming the offense and in faith, the church must once again comprehend its God-determined existence and, in the power of the Spirit, preach to a world, confronting its unbelief.

Exegetical Reflections

With a view to Bultmann's portrayal of Johannine theology, one must first grasp the great earnestness with which Bultmann took and read the Gospel of John as a theological work. In this regard, Bultmann continues to be exemplary. As historical criticism reawakened increasingly within New Testament studies, the theological density and intensity of interpretation often disappeared, with a more descriptive and distanced style predominating. In those instances, the interpreter's position is advanced cautiously as the author devotes himself to the description of historical and literary processes and ancient circumstances. In Bultmann's eyes, this approach is a deficient and "improper" understanding of history, the results of which may be historically interesting but remain ultimately irrelevant for one's existence and conduct of life.

In my opinion, Bultmann is entirely correct on this point. The text of John in particular (but not exclusively) requires a reading that takes seriously its theological claim and "extends" its "remembering" interpretation of the Christ event into the present. One must ask, however, whether it is possible to identify the intention of John the Evangelist so directly with the proclamation relevant for the present.[84] At least the "difficult" aspects of Johannine thought, most clearly the anti-Jewish statements in John 8, stand in the way of such an identification. They recall the fact that, despite every legitimate interest in the theological significance of a text, this text is still from a distant author in a world that has become foreign to us.

Already among his students, and all the more so in the discussion that has become increasingly international and interconfessional, the history of the interpretation of John since Bultmann has shifted many accents considerably.[85] Here, one should mention the following features:

1. The *historical interest*, with a view to both the historical validity of Johannine traditions and the historical context of the Johannine communities, that reawakened shortly after Bultmann;
2. The increased *interest in Jewish tradition* as the background of the Gospel of John (stimulated not least by the Qumran discoveries);
3. The growing *caution regarding overly detailed literary-critical reconstructions*;
4. The *rise of new methods of interpretation* under the influence of the nontheological disciplines of linguistics, social sciences, and cultural studies.

Admittedly, all of these tendencies have also led to the fact that the Gospel of John is rarely interpreted in the theological density that Bultmann exercised, especially in the text of his commentary.

Some Problems of Interpretation

With a view to the interpretive tendencies and details, I can name only a few problems:

1. Soon after Bultmann, the focal point of interest among his students already shifted back to *Christology*, and current scholarship is largely agreed that eschatology or a presupposed dualism did not form the framework of Johannine thought, but Christology did, as is evident not only in John's christological titles and the "I am" sayings but also in narrative elements and traditional figures of speech.[86] In my opinion, it is very doubtful whether the Gospel of John really avoids "ontological" statements as consistently as Bultmann thought. I think that both the language concerning the preexistence of Jesus or the Logos (e.g., John 8:58) and Jesus' "I am" sayings (ἐγώ εἰμι), which trace back to the Old Testament revelation formula אֲנִי-הוּא, show that Jesus' existence overarches time and that he, as a consequence, is distinguished from all other human beings.[87] With his purely functional interpretation, Bultmann markedly underestimated the weight of Johannine Christology.

2. Bultmann's interpretation depends on the dogmatic pre-supposition that revelation must occur in paradox, that the Revealer is a pure, concrete human being—and nothing more. In accordance with this presupposition, he also interpreted the traditions concerning the earthly Jesus minimalistically, concluding that he appeared "unmessianically," which ultimately renders essential aspects of the passion tradition and the pre-Pauline confession tradition historically incomprehensible. Admittedly, the interest in the unmitigated humanity—indeed more—in the strict nondisclosability of the revealer hardly corresponds to the thought of the author of John. This lack of correspondence manifests itself, for example, in the treatment of the "signs," which are certainly ambiguous and open to misunderstanding for John but still have a positive revelatory function and should actually lead to faith (cf. John 12:38-41). Bultmann's confusion becomes even clearer in view of the Easter appearances, which he ultimately evaluates as only a concession to human weakness. The dogmatic formulation associated with the notion of revelation finally comes to almost grotesque exaggeration when, according to Bultmann, the question of why Jesus in particular should be the revealer *must* not be answered. All the Gospels pursue this question, and in the context of ancient religions, this question inevitably must have been asked in the early Christian mission and been answered—with various arguments. Bultmann's position at this point clearly evidences the dependence of interpretation on the epistemological parameters of his own theology.

3. Derived from the model of the Redeemer Myth, the consolidation of all the acts of the Christ event (from the sending and incarnation to the exaltation and sending of the Spirit) into a single "eschatological" event is also problematical. From the perspective of the history of religions, this model functions only on the assumption that John adopted a Redeemer Myth. Even the narrative, however, presents the contradictory interpretation that John does indeed want to speak about different acts—after all, he reports the burial between the cross and the resurrection. John emphatically transposes the imparting of

the Spirit to Easter (John 20:22), but the Exalted One is not simply identical with the Paraclete, and even the *parousia* idea is at least still evidenced in John 16:16-19 and 14:3, and even more clearly in the supplementary chapter (John 21:22-23), and in 1 John (2:28; 3:2).

4. Finally, Bultmann's ecclesiology is also clearly underdefined. Even if it is the case that John hardly mentions ecclesial structures and "offices," one can still perceive traces of church life in individual images and in the transparent portrayal of the disciples. These traces appear significantly more prominently in the direct treatment of congregational problems in the Letters of John, and the explicit love ethic there may take up the very concrete questions of mutual solidarity. Bultmann's assertion that only the invisible church appears here results from his disinterest in any concrete historical classification. Ultimately, he presupposes a markedly Gnostic ecclesiology for John.

The consequence, however, is that questions of religious and literary origins, which Bultmann regarded as irrelevant, nonetheless significantly determine his portrayal of Johannine theology. The choice of the language of dualism as the starting point, the reduction of the acts of the Christ event to a single punctiliar event, and the understanding of the church (and of ethics) all rest on the assumption that an essentially Gnostic source lies behind the Gospel, a source whose language and manner of presentation the evangelist is supposed to have adopted in modified form.

The Historical Problem

To be sure, neither the so-called Revelation Discourse Source nor even the phenomenon of pre-Christian Gnosticism in the background of the Gospel of John can be verified historically. Most of his students have already rejected the source,[88] and the widespread acceptance in the twentieth century of a pre-Christian mythological Gnosticism based on Mandaean texts is no longer tenable for chronological reasons.[89] Bultmann assembled the Redeemer Myth in a "concordance mosaic"[90] out of various texts from Jewish wisdom to late Mandaean texts; in its full form, this myth cannot be located before third-century Manichaeism. Hermeneutically, mythological Gnosticism has central importance as the presupposition of Bultmann's interpretation; historically, however, one must assume that the Gnostic myth formed only later and did not even exist at the time of the creation of the Gospel of John.

Not only is the religio-historical "screen" (against which Bultmann explained the development of authentically Christian eschatological consciousness, for example) historically dubious, but even more so is the figure and method of operation of the evangelist, whom Bultmann characterized as the great "model theologian." He towers above all the other New Testament authors and stands as a singular figure, even in contrast to the tradition of the Johannine community and the "church" redaction. He is indeed supposed to have made wide usage of preexistent sources but also to have compiled them in overarching manner and utilized them in the service of his own concerns. His "purified" understanding of revelation distanced him from all other early Christian authors, and no interpreter before Bultmann had understood him in his radicality. This evangelist is a Protestant theologian of the Word, who needed no sacrament and understood the wonders that he himself recounted as merely symbolic. He is the precursor and biblical model of an existentialist interpretation; indeed, he is—in a word—the mirror image of his interpreter.

Historically, all of this is extremely unlikely. *This* evangelist never existed, no more than the greater portion of the presupposed sources; even the process of redactional "arrangement" and publication (with the textual rearrangements) can hardly be imagined. The text that Bultmann interpreted, like the screen against which it was interpreted, is an implausible construct, even a fiction.

What Remains?

What remains, therefore, of Bultmann's "Theology of John"? Bultmann's theology remains an impressive structure of persuasive power and with many thought-provoking accents. Bultmann depicted it from specific hermeneutical presuppositions (for instance, his understanding of time) with the aid of the New Testament texts. Yet one can hardly characterize this as exegesis. All too often the text is not permitted to say what it says, and the assumption that it means something other than what it says has extratextual grounds. Thus Bultmann does inappropriate violence to the texts. The question of whether an interpretation based on such an untenable construct can still be relevant at all must be left open here. Finally, there remains the phenomenon that Bultmann's theology continues to fascinate in its coherence, and that no interpretation of John can now attain such coherence if it takes seriously the texts as they are and in their historical context.

Chapter 7

DUALISM AND SOTERIOLOGY IN JOHANNINE THEOLOGY

Richard Bauckham

Reading Bultmann's interpretation of the Gospel of John,[1] even in the light of the kinds of critique that must be applied to it at the present day, is still an exhilarating experience. As an attempt at a truly theological interpretation of the Gospel, it has few rivals in more recent writing. This is because of Bultmann's thoroughgoing attempt to penetrate to *what is really going on theologically* in the evangelist's work. Though primarily a historical exegete, trained in the history of religions school with its commitment to history unencumbered by dogma, Bultmann had the express aim of uniting exegesis and theology. He did this most successfully in the case of the Gospel of John, both in his *Theology of the New Testament* and in his remarkable commentary on the Gospel,[2] because he believed that, among the New Testament writers, the Johannine evangelist himself grasped most clearly the essential core and character of the Christian message, the *kerygma* of the early Christian movement, and presented it in a way that most readily enabled the modern interpreter to distinguish this essential core from the "mythological" forms of expression that the evangelist deployed. In other words, this early Christian writer had already carried out, to a large extent, the program of "demythologizing" the kerygma that Bultmann held to be essential if Western people in the second half of the twentieth century were to be able to hear it aright. Bultmann's attempt to get inside the dynamic of the Johannine evangelist's thinking was at the same time his attempt to locate and to express the Gospel message for his own contemporaries. This means that it is certainly not a "purely historical" report of the thought of the Gospel (unlike many more recent accounts of Johannine theology), but it is an interpretation that is importantly rooted in Bultmann's historical reconstruction of the background and development of the Gospel.

Three key factors give Bultmann's interpretation of Johannine theology its distinctive character. One is the source analysis by which he isolated the sources the evangelist incorporated in his Gospel and the later redaction of the evangelist's work by an editor who, by adding material, brought the Gospel more into line with conventional Christian teaching. Second, behind the Gospel, according to Bultmann, lies the Gnostic myth of the Revealer, which the evangelist found in one of his main sources, the "revelation-discourses," and which Bultmann reconstructed from Mandaean literature. According to Bultmann, it is the Johannine evangelist's use of this pre-Christian Gnostic myth that explains the distinctiveness of the Johannine literature as compared with the other main theological trends in early Christianity. It is important for Bultmann's interpretation of Johannine theology both that the evangelist took over this already existing mythological framework for his Christology and soteriology but also that he adapted it considerably to suit his own purposes. Third, the philosophical resource that Bultmann brought to his work of identifying and expressing the core message of the Gospel was the existential analysis of Martin Heidegger. This enabled him to understand the Christian kerygma not as a propositional statement belonging to myth or dogma but as an understanding of human existence. Just as the Johannine evangelist himself formulated the kerygma as essentially a radical challenge to decide for a new possibility of human existence, using the Gnostic mythology merely as a framework for expressing this, so Bultmann was able to demythologize the Gospel's message by reexpressing it in the conceptual framework of a Heideggerian distinction between authentic and inauthentic existence. It may need to be stressed that Bultmann did not suppose that he drew the message itself from Heidegger, any more than the evangelist derived the kerygma itself from Gnosticism. Rather, Heidegger provided the conceptual tools for expressing the message.

From Gnosticism, then, the Johannine evangelist took over the idea of the Redeemer who came from heaven into the world and returned to heaven, a Redeemer who came in order to reveal and only to reveal. The evangelist was also indebted to the cosmological dualism that provides the framework for this Gnostic soteriology of revelation, a dualism expressed by the opposing pairs of light and darkness, truth and falsehood, life and death, freedom and bondage. This myth of the Revealer and this dualistic picture of reality are what give this Gospel its peculiarity. But the Johannine evangelist did not in fact share the Gnostic view of reality. Crucially, what the Johannine Jesus reveals is not some secret about the true nature and destiny of a predetermined category of people, whom he thus frees from their bondage to demonic powers in this world. The "mythological statements have lost their mythological meaning" (2.62).[3] The Johannine Jesus in fact "reveals nothing but that he is the Revealer" (2.66)—that he has come from beyond the human world of thought as the authoritative word of the Creator confronting his hearers with the necessity for the decision of faith.

That the Gospel's use of the Gnostic myth is in service of a non-Gnostic theology is nowhere clearer than in its claim that the Word became flesh (1:14), which is coherent with its view of the world as God's creation. Accordingly, the dualistic terminology that the evangelist has taken over from Gnosticism no longer expresses a cosmological dualism that would explain the origin of evil by a myth of cosmic origins. Rather, these terms "take on their specifically Johannine meaning only in relation to the idea of creation" (2.17)—by which Bultmann means that they represent the two possibilities of human self-understanding: either understanding oneself as a creature, dependent on and open to the transcendent reality of God, or understanding oneself as autonomous and shutting oneself against the reality of the Creator. The world is in darkness in that the second form of self-understanding is prevalent in human society until the Light comes to open up the possibility of an authentic form of existence in relation to God. Jesus as the Light confronts humanity with the life-or-death decision for or against this possibility of existence—the decision to believe or to reject. Thus the dualism of the Gospel is not a cosmological one but "the dualism of decision."[4] It does not describe some extrahuman cosmic reality, nor a predetermined division of humanity into two categories, but expresses the significance of the existential decision with which God's word, incarnate as Jesus, confronts all people.

Bultmann's understanding of the Johannine dualism requires a little more explanation. "The world" (κόσμος) or "this world," which means primarily the human world, has appropriated darkness and falsehood (the terms are equivalent) and made them its own essence, that is, its way of being (which Bultmann distinguishes from nature).[5] Darkness and falsehood thus comprise a power to which the world is in bondage. That is to say, it is in the grip of an illusory self-understanding. It is this "illusion about itself, not some immoral conduct, that is the lie" (2.18). A self-understanding of oneself as sovereign, in revolt against God, cannot but issue in evil conduct. In turning away from the reality of God ("the truth") the world "turns itself into a specious reality, which, being a lie, is simultaneously death" (2.19).

The two possibilities of existence open to humans are to live out of an origin in the world (to be "of the world," "of the earth," "of the devil," or "from below"), repudiating their true origin in God, or to live out of their origin in God (to be "of God," "of the truth," or "born of God" or "born from above"). The latter is to know the truth (that God is the Creator and thus the only true reality), while the correlative Johannine term "life" means "simply openness to God and to him who makes God manifest [Jesus]" (2.19). Only in acknowledging their creatureliness can humans acquire a true self-understanding and thus an authentic existence. In the face of the liberating revelation of truth in Jesus Christ, humans have only the two possibilities: to receive it in faith or to opt for self-delusion.

Bultmann acknowledges that there is much in the Gospel that makes it seem that the two categories of humanity are determined from the outset but explains this by supposing that in the Gnostic myth from which the Gospel's dualistic language came, it did indeed refer to a predetermined division of humanity. In the Gospel, however, the language has been refunctioned to express the "dualism of decision": "John's predestinatory formulations mean that the decision of faith is not a choice between possibilities in this world that arise from inner-worldly impulses, and also that the believer in the presence of God cannot rely on his own faith" (2.23). Since faith is precisely a renunciation of self-assertion, it has to be understood as God's gift.

The Johannine Jesus says that it is only in rejecting the light he brings, by opting to remain in darkness, that people become sinners under judgment, because in "his decision between faith and un-faith a man's being definitively constitutes itself, and from then on his Whence becomes clear" (2.25). Thenceforth the two groups become recognizable by whether they follow the new commandment of love for one another. Because they effect this decisive division, the coming and going of Jesus are the eschatological event in which the judgment of the world takes place.

Salvation is the encounter with God that can be had only by faith. Bultmann is at pains to deny that the Gospel envisages a "mystical relationship" (2.84), by which he seems to mean a kind of unmediated union with the divine—the Hellenistic religious mysticism that others in the history of religions school had identified in this Gospel. The believer's "eschatological existence" is a reality "only in faith . . . *not in any direct relationship to Jesus or to God*" (2.85, emphasis original). Here the traditional Lutheran insistence on "faith alone" meets a Heideggerian philosophy of existence. Nor is the new form of existence a new nature. The believer's freedom from sin should not be understood as "a new nature . . . to which sinlessness belongs as a natural quality [as in Gnosticism]. Sinlessness, rather, is inherent to faith," that is, "the overcoming of the world that must be done over and over again" (2.79). Here the emphasis on faith serves also to complete Bultmann's account of how Johannine theology, despite its use of Gnostic mythological categories, actually distinguishes itself sharply from everything that is distinctively Gnostic.

There is a final point of special interest in Bultmann's exposition of Johannine soteriology. The language of truth and life with which the Gospel speaks of salvation corresponds to the world's quest for reality and life. Since the world, despite its rebellion against God, cannot cease to be God's creation, it longs for what it must have in order truly to exist, even though it does not know what this is until it encounters the light (2.26, 65). When Jesus presents himself as the bread and water of life, the light of the world or the good shepherd, he "is presenting himself as that for which the world is seeking" (2.26). He "assumes such a preliminary understanding as is expressed in mythology" (2.27). In this way Bultmann is able to acknowledge the broad resonance of the Gospel's images of salvation without deriving the Gospel's kerygma itself from the world of Hellenistic religion.

Assessment

There is much to appreciate in this interpretation of Johannine theology. In particular, in my view, Bultmann's account of "the dualism of decision" is an indispensible insight into the way Johannine dualism functions. But the three key factors that comprise Bultmann's approach to the interpretation of the Johannine Gospel have not fared well in subsequent study. The second factor—Bultmann's reconstruction of the Gnostic myth of the Revealer and the claim that this Gospel owes its distinctive character to its dependence on this myth—carries conviction with very few scholars today.[6] Reconstructing such a myth from Mandaean sources seems a dubious enterprise, while it is extremely debatable that there was what might be called "Gnosticism" or "Gnosis" prior to the writings we now know from the Nag Hammadi library. Above all, perhaps, later scholars have not found the need for such a speculative hypothesis in order to explain the Gospel we have. This is partly because, for many scholars, the Qumran writings provide a more plausible parallel to at least one of the features of the Gospel that Bultmann thought needed a particular sort of history of religions background to account for it, that is, its dualism (see the below section "Dualism in Qumran Texts and in John"). More generally, Judaism in forms not influenced by "Gnosis" is now very widely regarded as the only kind of "background" to the Gospel that we need to postulate. Another major trend has been to introduce sociological factors—the history and situation of the "Johannine community"—into the explanation of this Gospel's distinctiveness.

Many would also say that Bultmann exaggerated the difference between Johannine theology and other currents of early Christian thought. He did so because of the first of the three factors that made up his approach: his particular theory of sources and redaction. Bultmann excised, as due to the ecclesiastical redactor, those parts of the Gospel that especially make it less eccentric as compared with the other writings of the New Testament. For example, he was able to characterize the evangelist's eschatology as wholly realized or actually atemporal—that is, demythologized—by attributing expressions of future eschatology to the redactor. This looks like resorting to a source-critical explanation too quickly, where a more patient attempt to understand and appreciate the patterns of thought and expression that the Gospel as we have it exhibits might conclude that the evangelist put a strong emphasis on the present experience of eternal life without excluding a still future dimension. It seems to be a feature of the way this Gospel is written that it sets such seemingly contrasting themes as eternal life in the present and resurrection in the future side-by-side so that readers can see them as complementary dimensions of the matter.

Finally, Bultmann's use of a philosophical analysis of human existence to express the kind of self-understanding he found in the kerygma of the Gospel has found few followers in recent writing on John, though this is not to say that some of the exegetical insights that were facilitated or sharpened by Bultmann's use of Heideggerian analysis have not been appreciated and influential. Many scholars are simply not interested in a contemporary theological appropriation of Johannine theology, preferring to explore the thought world of the Gospel in other ways, especially social-scientific ones. Those who do have a serious theological concern tend to work with conceptual tools from the Christian theological tradition without seeing the need for anything so radical as Bultmann's demythologization. Indeed, it must be said that Bultmann's theological approach is reductionist in the sense that it deliberately leaves aside any information content, focusing exclusively on the divine word that challenges humans to faith, that is, to a self-understanding of the human being as creature dependent on and open to the transcendent Creator. Penetrating as this focus for reading the Gospel can be, is it really all there is to say about Johannine soteriology?

That said, one may also wonder whether, after Bultmann, something important has not been lost. If Bultmann could be accused of reducing theology to existential self-understanding, a theological assessment of recent Johannine scholarship might highlight a danger of reducing theology to sociology.[7] There are certainly many who resist that danger, but is there anything comparable to Bultmann's attempt to enter the dynamic of Johannine thought with such a thoroughgoing, though necessarily risky, determination to let it speak to contemporary people?[8] I merely pose the question. Of course, there are some who would say that, whereas Bultmann found John the most theologically congenial of the New Testament writings, it now poses almost insuperable problems for contemporary appreciation and appropriation.[9] The Gospel's dualism is certainly a key factor in such reactions.

Dualism in Qumran Texts and in John

For many Johannine scholars the place vacated by the Gnostic background to the Gospel postulated by Bultmann has been occupied instead by the Dead Sea Scrolls. It was the early publication of some of these (especially the *Community Rule* [1QS] and the *War Rule* [1QM]) that convinced many scholars that one did not need to seek the background to the Johannine Gospel and letters outside first-century Judaism. Although a range of similarities have been observed between the Gospel and the Qumran literature,[10] Raymond Brown speaks for many when he claims that "there is only one area of relatively precise similarity," that is, "dualism and its corollaries."[11] With a focus especially on the "Treatise of the Two Spirits" (1QS 3:13–4:26), a series of scholars have claimed that there is such a close correspondence in both concepts and terminology that there must be a close historical connection (or even direct literary dependence) between the two bodies of literature, especially since the dualism of the Qumran texts has been characterized as unique within ancient Judaism.[12] Other scholars, however, have found the contrasts more considerable than the resemblances.[13] I myself have argued that the resemblances can be explained as independent developments from scriptural texts and traditional Jewish imagery. With reference to the use of light and darkness imagery, the terminological correspondences are negligible compared with the key terminology present in each text and missing in the other. The theological significance of the imagery also differs decisively in ways that can be better explained from other sources in Scripture and late Second Temple literature than as some kind of adaptation of the Qumran usage. Moreover, the Johannine dualism is expressed not only in the light and darkness imagery, which it shares with the Qumran texts, but also in the spatial contrast between above and below and in the related contrast between God and the world. These are not shared with Qumran, and yet they are certainly as formative of the Gospel's dualistic worldview as the light/darkness imagery is.[14] My case has been supported, in greater detail, by Jörg Frey.[15] It should be noticed also that, whereas the case for a close connection between the Qumran texts and the Johannine literature worked with a simple account of "Qumran dualism," based mainly on 1QS 3:13–4:26 and supposed to have belonged to the central ideology of the Qumran sect, recent studies of dualism in the Qumran texts have considerably problematized this topic, arguing for a range of forms of dualism even in the texts usually attributed to the community itself and highlighting the exceptional character of 1QS 3:13–4:26.[16] Any fresh attempt to compare dualism in the Qumran texts with dualism in the Johannine literature will need to take full account of that discussion.

In the present context it is especially important to note that those who have strongly supported a close historical connection between Qumran dualism and that of the Gospel of John also insisted that John has made highly distinctive use of the concepts and images he shares with Qumran, focusing them on Christology and soteriology in a way quite unparalleled at Qumran and thereby shifting their meaning considerably. Charlesworth speaks of John's "amazing creativity,"[17] while, more prosaically, Fitzmyer asks, "[W]hy should one expect the light/darkness imagery to function in the same way in both bodies of literature?"[18] While intending a response to my critique, both scholars have failed to take account of my argument that the distinctively Johannine use of the light/darkness imagery has much better precedent in Jewish literature other than the Qumran texts.[19] There is indeed no reason why we should expect the light/darkness imagery to function in the same way in various different bodies of literature, but if we find plausible sources for the distinctive ways in which John uses the imagery, the hypothesis of John's dependence on the texts or traditions of Qumran becomes redundant. However, the most important point, in the present context, is that the more the distinctiveness of John's use of the light/darkness imagery is stressed, the less relevant the hypothesis of a relationship with the Qumran texts becomes for understanding the theology of the Gospel. Of course, Bultmann argued, rather similarly, that John radically refunctioned the Gnostic myth of the Redeemer, but the dualism of this (hypothesized) myth was already closely connected with a redeemer figure who came from the divine world in order to save people from this world. It had the christological and soteriological focus that the dualism of the Gospel has, and this gave it real explanatory power in Bultmann's interpretation of the Gospel.

The Qumran dualism, on the other hand, entirely lacks any such christological and soteriological focus. Thus it must be concluded that the Dead Sea Scrolls have failed to fill the place vacated by the Gnostic background to the Gospel that Bultmann postulated.

Types of Dualism and Duality in John

In discussions of dualism in the ancient world the term is used in narrower and broader senses. It can be usefully defined as "a mode of thought that separates reality into two opposing forces."[20] But when John Gammie lists a variety of kinds of dualism that scholars have identified in apocalyptic literature, it is clear that the term "dualism" embraces a wider range of contrasting pairs of concepts. He lists the following:

1. Cosmic dualism, in which the cosmos is divided into two opposing forces of good and evil (though in Jewish thought this always takes the form of a "modified dualism" in which God is ultimately sovereign and the opposition is not absolute);
2. Temporal or eschatological dualism, in which the contrast is between the present age and the age to come;
3. Ethical dualism, in which two categories of humans, the righteous and the wicked, are contrasted;
4. Psychological dualism, in which the contest between good and evil takes place within individual humans;
5. Spatial dualism, in which a contrast is drawn between heaven and earth;
6. Theological dualism, which entails a radical distinction between God and humanity, Creator and creation

In other discussions of dualism he identifies four more types:

7. Physical dualism, which draws an absolute distinction between spirit and matter;
8. Metaphysical dualism, which refers to the opposition between God and Satan;
9. Soteriological dualism, in which humanity is divided into two categories by people's acceptance or rejection of a savior;

10. Cosmological or ontological dualism, in which (in contrast to type 1) the dualism of opposing cosmic principles is original and absolute.[21]

It is clear that only some of these kinds of "dualism" qualify as "a mode of thought that separates reality into two opposing forces." Types 1, 3, 4, 8, 9, and 10 are all forms of the fundamental polarity of good and evil, while 2 can be classified with them because it distinguishes the two ages as that in which evil is dominant and the coming age in which good will no longer be opposed by evil. But 5, 6, and 7 do not necessarily posit *opposing* categories, merely *contrasting* ones. In 6 God is radically distinguished from but not opposed to his creation, as he is to evil. In Platonism, a version of 7, spirit and matter are radically different, superior and inferior, but not opposed to each other as good and evil are. Gnosticism, on the other hand, tended to assimilate its distinction of spirit and matter dualism to a dualism of good and evil. Finally, the spatial contrast between heaven and earth (5) may signify a relationship of radical difference or a hierarchical difference of superior and inferior, though it too can be assimilated to a dualism of good and evil if the earth is regarded as the sphere of creation in which evil is dominant. In most Jewish cases, this is allied to eschatological dualism (2), such that in this age the earth is subject to the powers of evil, but in the age to come, as God's good creation, it will be liberated from evil.

It may be useful to reserve the term "dualism" for the various forms that the polarity of good and evil takes in Jewish and Christian literature and to use the term "duality" for forms of thinking that divide reality into two contrasting, but not opposed, categories, such as Creator and creation. In fact, if we use this distinction, all versions of Jewish and Christian monotheism entail both some form of dualism (the good God is opposed to all evil) and some form of duality (the Creator is ontologically distinguished from creation). Since all versions of Jewish and Christian monotheism also hold that God's good creation has been in some way and to some degree corrupted by evil, there is also a correlation between the dualism (God against evil) and the duality (God and creation). However, this correlation is not identity. Indeed, any form of belief that God is rescuing or will rescue his creation from evil requires that the dualism and the duality are distinguished, as well as correlated. Were creation and evil identified, there could be no salvation.

These remarks may serve to suggest that generalizing about "dualism" in the Gospel of John is potentially misleading. We need to make careful distinctions between kinds of dualism and duality. In table 7.1 I have divided the terms and expressions that the Gospel of John uses in contrasting pairs into several categories.[22] (In most cases both components of the pair occur in the same context, but I have included some cases, such as "ruler of this world" and "kingdom not from this world," where the two components are in obvious contrast, even though they occur in widely separated contexts.) In addition to the major categories I–III, I have also listed a large number of "Miscellaneous Dualities" (IV; the list could doubtless be extended). In these cases the contrasting terms or phrases cannot easily be aligned with the major categories. Some compare good and bad alternatives, others superior and inferior, others temporal differences. In some cases of the pairing of a negative and a positive (e.g., "You did not choose me but I chose you"), the negative is purely hypothetical and serves merely to underline the positive. In some cases, the contrast belongs to the style of an epigram (e.g., 4:37; 8:35; 12:25). Indeed, this author has a strong tendency to express himself in a quasi-epigrammatic style, which may in part account for the prevalence of contrastive ways of speaking throughout the Gospel. More generally, what the examples listed in IV show is that the use of contrasting pairs of terms or phrases is a dominant habit of thought and expression in this Gospel. It is a way of formulating thought that is to some extent universal and seems to come naturally to the human mind. That the author of this Gospel is particularly fond of it may be part of the reason for the fact that the dualism that can be found to some degree throughout early Christian literature comes to unusual prominence in this Gospel. Perhaps this is less of a theological choice than a habit of mind.

Most of what is usually called Johannine dualism I have included in category II, but it is too often confused with some or all of the material I have put into category I. In category II occur the various forms of the fundamental polarity of good and evil. Here light is opposed to darkness, God to the devil, truth to lies, Jesus to religious imposters, his disciples to the world, faith and obedience to unbelief and disobedience, freedom to slavery. The category combines

Table 7.1
Dualisms and Dualities in the Gospel of John

I. Creation and Creator		
This world	The Father	13:1; 16:28; 17:11
Earth	Heaven	3:31
Earthly things	Heavenly things	3:12
From the earth	From above/heaven	3:31
Flesh	Spirit	6:63
Born of flesh	Born from above/of Spirit	3:3-8
Born of blood, will of flesh, and will of man	Born of God	1:13
Life (ψυχή) in this world	Life (ψυχή) for eternal life	12:25
Perish	Have eternal life	3:16; 10:28
Die	Live forever	6:50-51, 58
Die	Never taste death	8:51-53
Food that perishes	Food that endures to eternal life	6:27
This water (and thirst again)	Living water (and never thirst again)	4:10-15
II. Evil and good		
Darkness	Light	1:3-9; 3:19-21; 8:12; 9:5; 11:9-10; 12:35-36, 46
Walk in darkness	Walk while you have light	12:35
Night	Day	9:4; 11:9-10
Walk in the night	Walk in the day	11:9-10
Blind	Seeing	9:26, 39
Lies	Truth	8:44
To do evil	To do truth	3:21
To do evil	To do good	5:29
From this world	Not from this world	8:23
From what is below	From what is above	8:23
From the devil	From God	8:44-47; 7:29
Glory from humans	Glory from God	5:41, 44; 7:18; 12:43
Ruler of this world	Kingdom not from this world	12:31; 14:30; 18:36

Table 7.1 *(cont.)*
Dualisms and Dualities in the Gospel of John

II. Evil and good *(cont.)*		
Father of lies	Spirit of truth	8:44; 14:17; 16:13
Children of the devil	Children of God	1:12; 8:44
Thief and bandit	Shepherd	10:1-2
In his own name	In my Father's name	5:43
Do not know God	Know God	7:28-29, 8:55
Do not believe	Believe	3:18, 36
Disobey the Son	Believe in the Son	3:36
Slavery to sin	Freedom	8:33-36
The world	Jesus	17:25
The world	Those chosen from the world	15:19; 17:6-9
From the world	Not from the world	15:18-19
The world	Those whom you gave me	17:9
The world	You (the disciples)	14:17-19, 22; 16:20
Do not love Jesus	Love Jesus	14:23-24
Do not keep his words	Keep his words	14:23-24
In the world	In me (Jesus)	16:33
III. Provisional good and eschatological good		
Grace	Grace	1:16
Law	Grace and truth	1:17
Moses	Jesus Christ	1:17; 5:45; 9:28-29
What Moses wrote	What I say	5:47
Worship in Jerusalem	Worship in Spirit and truth	4:21-24
My Father's house (temple)	My Father's house	2:16; 14:2
Inferior wine	Best wine	2:10
Manna	True bread from heaven	6:31-32
Vine	True vine	15:1
IV. Miscellaneous dualities		
Baptize with water	Baptize with the Holy Spirit	1:26, 33

IV. Miscellaneous dualities *(cont.)*		
Destroy	Raise up	2:19
Needed no one to testify	He himself knew	2:25
Ascended into heaven	Descended from heaven	3:13
Judge the world	Save the world	3:17; 12:47
Resurrection of judgment	Resurrection of life	5:29
Increase	Decrease	3:31
On this mountain	In Jerusalem	4:20
Worship what you do not know	Worship what we know	4:22
Hour is coming	Is now	4:23; 5:25
Sow, labor	Reap	4:37-38
What you said	For ourselves	4:42
On his own	What he sees the Father do	5:19
On my own	As the Father taught me	8:28; 12:49
My own will	The will of him who sent me	5:30; 6:38
On his own	Prophesied	11:51
Lose	Raise up	6:39-40
Openly	In secret	7:4, 10
From God	On my own	7:17
Come on my own	Sent	7:28; 8:42
Slave does not remain	Son remains	8:35
Have the poor	Have me	12:8
At first	When Jesus was glorified	12:16
Love life—lose it	Hate life—keep it	12:25
For your sake	For my sake	12:30
Not understand now	Understand later	13:7
Servants do not know	Friends know	15:15
You did not choose me	I chose you	15:16
Speak on his own	Speak what he hears	16:13
Rejoice	Weep and mourn	16:20
Joy	Pain	16:20-21
Plainly	In figures	16:25, 29
Come from the Father	Go to the Father	16:28

Table 7.1 *(cont.)*
Dualisms and Dualities in the Gospel of John

IV. Miscellaneous dualities *(cont.)*		
Come into the world	Leave the world	16:28
In the world	No longer in the world	17:11
See—believe	Not see—believe	20:29
Were younger	Grow old	21:18

Dualisms and Dualities in 1 John

I. Evil and good		
Darkness	Light	1:5-7; 2:8-9
Walk in darkness	Walk in light	1:6-7
Is in/walks in darkness	Remains in the light	2:9-11
Hate	Love	2:9-11; 3:14-15; 4:20
The world	Those who do the will of God	2:17
Passes away	Remains forever	2:17
Lie	Truth	2:4, 21-22, 27
Lie	Do the truth	1:6
Not from us	From us	2:19
Denies the Son	Confesses the Son	2:23
The world	We	3:2
Children of the devil	Children of God	3:1-2, 10
From the devil/the evil one	From God/born of God	2:29; 3:8-10, 12
From the world	From the Father/God	2:16; 4:2-6
Do sin	Do righteousness	3:4-10
Evil deeds	Righteous deeds	3:12
Remains in death	Passed from death to life	3:14
The one who is in the world	The One who is in you	4:4
Spirit of error	Spirit of truth	4:6
Does not believe	Believes	5:10
Does not have the Son	Has the Son	5:12
Does not have life	Has life	5:12
The evil one	The One who was born of God	5:18

II. Miscellaneous dualities		
Old commandment	New commandment	1:7-8
Word or speech	Deed and truth	3:18
We loved God	He loved us	4:10

what Gammie lists as (1) cosmic dualism, (2) ethical dualism, (8) metaphysical dualism (not a very helpful term), and (9) soteriological dualism. In category I, on the other hand, I have placed expressions of kinds of "dualism" from Gammie's list that are not forms of the opposition of good and evil and that I have suggested we might therefore call "dualities." These are (5) spatial dualism and (6) theological dualism.

The spatial contrast between heaven and earth, "above" and "below," functions in the Gospel largely to make the contrast between God and creation. There is no interest in a heavenly world of angelic beings. Heaven is where God is, where the Father and the Son are united in glory, and where Jesus' own will go to be with him in the place he has prepared for them. Heaven is the space that represents transcendence. The distinction between Creator and creation is also the basis for the contrast between flesh and Spirit, mortal life and eternal life, which is integral to the Gospel's soteriology. "Flesh" is created human existence,[23] naturally mortal, while life from the Spirit or from above or eternal life is the gift of participation in the divine life that transcends death. While flesh left to itself dies, its true destiny in God's purpose is to be united with the divine life. The Son, who has eternal life in himself, becomes flesh in order to give flesh eternal life. Thus flesh is not evil, even in its weakness and mortality, but its natural mortality means that, if humans reject the Savior who can give them eternal life, they must die. At this point, it could be said, the contrast between creaturely, mortal life and eternal life converges with the ethical dualism of good and evil and the soteriological dualism that is created by human acceptance or rejection of the Savior. Those who choose to remain in their sins die in their sins. Death, the natural fate of creaturely life left to itself, becomes the actual fate only of sinners, because it is they who reject the Savior who brings eternal life from God.

There is one key Johannine term that bridges categories I and II: "this world" or "the world" (the two are used synonymously). On the one hand, the world is the "all things" that God, through the Word, created, and the created sphere into which the Word came in incarnation. On the other hand, the world is the sphere of darkness, the human world under the dominion of "the ruler of this world," ignorant of God and practicing evil. Since the latter is the actual condition of the world into which Jesus comes, the transition from one sense to the other is easily made, as in 1:10, which introduces the negative usage of "world": "He was in the world, and the world came into being through him, yet the world did not know him." Thus "the world" or "this world" becomes a key term in expressions of ethical dualism and also of soteriological dualism in that those who reject Jesus are "from the world," while his disciples are those he has "chosen from the world." The world that Jesus comes to save (3:16, 17; 4:42; 6:33, 51) is at the same time God's good creation, which he loves (3:16), and also that creation subject to evil and in need of salvation. Once again it is soteriology that requires the evangelist to work with both the duality of category I and the dualism of category II. For the Gospel's soteriology to make sense, the two must converge but remain different.

In category III I have brought together contrasts that relate the provisional good of the Mosaic covenant to the eschatological good that arrives with Jesus. It is important to distinguish these as a distinct category of duality because some interpreters tend to assimilate them to the true dualism of good and evil. When the Jewish leaders of Jesus' day reject Jesus, they do not represent the old covenant but betray it.

Dynamic Dualism

What holds together the various dualisms and dualities I have grouped and distinguished in categories I, II, and III is soteriology. Without soteriology the complexity I have highlighted might seem merely confusion. Johannine soteriology, however, requires just this complexity. The Gospel does not oppose one world of reality to another in order merely to separate eternally what have always been distinct. As C. K. Barrett observed, "The distinguishing feature of John's dualism is its mobility; it is dualism in motion, in becoming."[24] The dualism is essentially a framework for portraying how the divine Son became mortal flesh in this world in order both to overcome the world and to save the world.

We can illustrate this briefly in terms of each of the two most prominent ways in which the dualism is expressed: the opposition of light and darkness, and the opposition of Jesus and the world. The generative sources of the light and darkness imagery in the Gospel are not Qumranic but scriptural: the opening verses of Genesis (Gen 1:3-5) and the Isaianic prophecies of messianic light shining in the darkness of the world (Isa 9:2; 42:6-7; 60:1-3).[25] Conspicuously opening his Gospel at the same "beginning" that opens the Torah, the evangelist joins a Jewish tradition of speculation about the primordial light that inaugurated creation, identifying both the divine Word in the beginning and the primordial light that preexisted the universe with the eternal Son. The point is to claim that the same light that illuminated creation in its pristine state and persisted in spite of the darkness that opposed it (whose origin is not explained) is the light that has come into the world with the incarnation of the Word. The exposition of Genesis therefore prepares for the central and dominant focus of the Gospel's use of light and darkness imagery: a great light coming into the world, shining in the darkness of the world, giving light to all people, so that they may come out of the darkness into the light, and be able to walk in the light instead of stumbling in the darkness (1:5, 9; 3:19; 8:12; 11:9-10; 12:35-36, 46). It is notable that the imagery of light and darkness is confined to chapters 1–12, and, just as it is prominent in the Prologue, so it is prominent at the very end of his period of public ministry (12:3-5, cf. 40) and in his summation of his mission: "I have come as light into the world, so that everyone who believes in me should not remain in the darkness" (12:46).

Except for the hint in 1:5, the imagery of light and darkness in the Gospel is not used to describe a perennial conflict between light and darkness. Rather it is inspired by the prophetic picture of a messianic light with its overtones of eschatological novelty. The picture is of a world in darkness,[26] whose situation is changed when the light comes into it, floods it with light, and requires people either to live in it and walk by it or to stay in the darkness. This is what Bultmann's existential insight valuably called a "dualism of decision." It is all about the challenge of the new situation created by the incarnation and mission of Jesus. After chapter 12, Jesus no longer calls the world into the light (12:36). (Later his disciples, inspired by the Paraclete, will witness to the world, but the Gospel does not portray this in the language of light and darkness.)

Expressions of dualism that use the terms "the world" or "this world" function rather differently from those that use the imagery of light and darkness. As we have noticed, these terms are frequently used to refer to the world that the divine Son created, entered, and came to save. It is sinful and in need of salvation, but in a large majority of the occurrences of these terms the world is not explicitly portrayed as an entity opposed to God or to Jesus. The antagonism, when it occurs, is a consequence of the Son's coming into the world. It is how the world and its ruler respond to the salvific mission of the Son. So once again we are concerned with a dualism "in motion," a dualism that comes about and develops along with the eschatological divine invasion of the world. The opposition of the world to Jesus (and his disciples) emerges only gradually in the story, after its initial adumbration in the Prologue (1:10). As opposition to Jesus, it is found in chapters 1–12 only at 7:7, 8:23, and 9:31. It really comes into its own, when the light and darkness imagery has disappeared from the Gospel, in the Last Supper discourse (14–16), and in the prayer of Jesus in chapter 17. In these chapters, we find that Jesus' disciples, who are "not from the world" and "chosen from the world," become, along with Jesus, one of the two components of a dualistic contrast between them and the world. The coming of the Son into the world has divided the world into those who are born from above and so are no longer "from the world" and those who reject the one who comes from above and so become the world in this pejorative and dualistic sense.

Thus we discover that these two fields of dualistic discourse—the light/darkness imagery and the world/Jesus antinomy—function differently. The former is a "dualism of decision," calling people to live in and by the light that has come into the world. The latter is a "dualism of opposition," portraying the antipathy of those who reject Jesus toward him and toward those who accept him. Appropriately, the former predominates in chapters 1–12, the latter in chapters 14–18. With characteristic Johannine irony, the apparent victory of the powers of this world over the king whose royal authority is not from this world is in fact his "conquest" of the world (16:33) and the proclamation of his rule (19:19-22). Thus the "dualism of opposition" proves to be not only the consequence of the Son's salvific mission but the very means by which he brings eternal life into the world. The Gospel therefore uses its "dualism of opposition" in a much more theologically profound way than simply to bolster the identity of a sectarian group at odds with its social context.

Conclusion

This discussion has focused on dualism and on soteriology insofar as it relates to dualism. We have concluded that soteriology is the central concern in the Gospel's prominent use of both dualisms and dualities. In the Gospel's narrative of salvation, the coming of the divine Son into flesh sets its dualistic categories in motion. Light dispels darkness, requiring decision, while the world that rejects Jesus is conquered and saved by him through its very rejection of him.

A fuller discussion of Johannine soteriology would have to undertake two major tasks. One would be an exploration of the concrete imagery of salvation in the Gospel (water, bread, wine, shepherding, etc.), for where analysis of the Gospel tends to be abstract the Gospel itself is full of metaphors that "flesh out" its talk of eternal life in a way that relates to its most distinctive christological image: the "enfleshment" of the Word.[27] The second task would be to explore the Gospel's talk of intimate communion between believers and the divine Trinity—the "mystical" element in Johannine soteriology that Bultmann was anxious to downplay.[28]

Chapter 8

THE RISE OF CHURCH ORDER

Luke Timothy Johnson

I first read Bultmann's amazing book in my late twenties. I was then a Benedictine monk and a student of theology. At that time, *Theology of the New Testament* stood as a colossus, demanding to be taken into account. It would have been inconceivable to me—as it would to other young scholars in the 1960s—that Bultmann would ever come to resemble Ozymandias, needing excavation to be fully appreciated.

The same copy I read then lies before me now as I write. Every page is scarred and scratched with notes, queries, and objections.[1] Many of my questions arose because Bultmann was saying things much different from the views of scholars who were more familiar to me (Brown, Dupont, Cerfaux, Wikenhauser, Cullmann). Like another book I read and fought with in that same period of my life, Peter Berger's *Sacred Canopy*, I found Bultmann's *Theology* to be challenging, even threatening, to my (supposedly) stable monastic existence.[2] As so often happens when books stimulate such a fearful and angry response, Bultmann and Berger ended up shaping my perceptions far more profoundly than the Browns and Fitzmyers and Cullmanns who up to then had been my heroes.

My notes, queries, and objections to the *Theology*, however, came not only from an emotional reaction to the intellectual—shall I say existential—challenge Bultmann posed to my monastic certitudes, but above all through his stunning exposition of Paul. They arose as well from genuine difficulties I had even then with the construction of the book itself. And whenever I reread the *Theology*, as I often do in my doctoral seminars on the New Testament and theology at Emory, I find two convictions confirmed: the first is that Bultmann's is the only version of the odd enterprise in intellectual history called "New Testament theology" that is truly grown-up; other entries in the field pale in comparison, lacking either the sharp appreciation of the hermeneutical problem presented by the New Testament, or the energy to enucleate a genuinely "pure" biblical theology.[3]

The second conviction is that I remain deeply unconvinced by a number of aspects of his presentation. It is, I think, precisely the lack of *argument* within Bultmann's work that makes his book most frustrating. By "lack of argument," I do not mean that the *Theology* lacks a strong thesis or the coherent development of that thesis, much less that it is deficient in learning; the book bristles with the citation of specific texts from Scripture and other ancient writings and consistently locates itself within scholarly discourse. Any reader wanting to challenge Bultmann must be willing to be master of the same wide range of learning, and that remains a daunting task. I mean rather that the book proceeds by way of assertion more than by way of genuine analysis—seldom is a New Testament text presented as problematic and effort given to deciphering it. Much in the manner of his teacher Adolf Schlatter, rather, Bultmann tends to array textual evidence in support of meanings he has already determined; the reader is less often offered options to consider than conclusions presented as self-evident,[4] while the premises underlying the overall demonstration are seldom if ever exposed for critical assessment. His amassing of data is so apparently exhaustive, and his overall vision so apparently comprehensive, that a reader finds it difficult to find a vantage point from which to ask how things might have been read differently or what might have been left out.

In fact, his work is so constructed that the examination of any of its individual parts must be considered within the whole, and the treatment of any specific topic can adequately be assessed only by taking into account what Bultmann has said on the topic in other parts of his work. The chapter I have been invited to consider, "The Rise of Church Order and Its Earliest Development" (vol. 2, chap. 5), for example, must be placed in the context of Bultmann's treatment of the church in *The History of the Synoptic Tradition* and elsewhere in *Theology*.[5]

The Church as Historical Phenomenon

As the subject of historical inquiry, the church remains a consistent focus for Bultmann, especially since he is far more confident in a scholar's ability to reconstruct the history of the earliest church than he is in the ability to reconstruct the historical Jesus. In *The History of the Synoptic Tradition*, for example, he acknowledges that his formal analysis of Jesus traditions is as much in service of constructing a history of the church, as was Dibelius' study of the community and its needs. He declares that all historical work must move in a circle: "The forms of the literary tradition must be used to establish the influences operating in the life of the community and the life of the community must be used to render the forms themselves intelligible."[6] Thus, by distinguishing between those elements in the Jesus tradition that are apocalyptic or eschatological in character and those that are sapiential, he considers that a theory concerning ecclesial development is demonstrated: "An essential part of my inquiry concerns the one chief problem of primitive Christianity, the relationship of the primitive Palestinian and Hellenistic Christianity."[7] Bultmann pays minimal attention to the Synoptic Gospels as compositions: he sees them primarily in terms of how they organize and edit tradition; only Luke does he recognize as having a "literary" quality.[8] Much as the church itself, the Gospels appear primarily as the medium for the transmission of tradition.

The same presuppositions and procedures concerning the historical study of the church are found in *Theology*. Here is the same disinterest in the overall literary or rhetorical shape of the New Testament compositions in favor of a concentration on them as sources for historical reconstruction. Here also is the conviction that (in circular fashion) levels of tradition within compositions can be assigned to various stages of historical development of the church, so that the placement of the tradition and the securing of the development are mutually reinforcing. Here, finally, is the history of religions scheme (borrowed from Heitmueller and Bousset)[9] of geographical/cultural development in the church from Palestinian to Hellenistic to Paul, a development that continues after Paul—the subject of the chapter I am engaging—in the direction of institutionalization.

Before taking up the specific subject of institutional development, however, it may be helpful to add a few further comments on Bultmann's practice as a historian, specifically with respect to his historical knowledge, method, and perspective. I have already noted his impressive command of earliest Christian literature, even though he gives scant actual attention to some canonical compositions (James, Revelation) and makes much heavier use of some second-century evidence (Clement, Hermas, Ignatius) than others (the apocryphal acts and gospels). In contrast, the real but limited knowledge of the *Umwelt* displayed in the *Theology* shows how much information concerning that world has been discovered since Bultmann wrote. He alludes to "associations," for example, but does not have the benefit of the analyses that have shown how the structure of such associations parallels that of the Diaspora synagogue and the early church.[10] As is well known, Bultmann vastly overestimates the coherence and pervasiveness of Gnosticism as a pre-Christian phenomenon. He could not have used "Gnostic" so casually or so often had he known the cautions issued by later scholarship.[11] Similarly, his use of "the mysteries" would have benefited from the vast new knowledge concerning them made available since Bultmann's time.[12]

As for Second Temple Judaism, Bultmann does not appear aware of the complexities of "eschatological/apocalyptic" exhibited in the extant literature; instead, like his predecessors (Schweitzer, Weiss), he uses "eschatological" as an abstract category that can be put to many uses. Similarly, he does not know how mysticism and mystery occupied a place even at the heart of the rabbinic tradition.[13] In this and in other respects, such as the pervasiveness of what Sanders calls "covenantal nomism,"[14] the fact that the discoveries at the Dead Sea were not yet available to him at the time of his writing meant a major lacuna in his knowledge of Palestinian Judaism. He was not aware, for example, that a community could be at once eschatological, law observant, and mystical and have a highly elaborate hierarchical structure.[15] Finally, research in Judaism since the time of Bultmann has simply obliterated the easy linguistic and cultural distinctions between Palestine and the Diaspora that fueled the history of religion school's tripartite theory of development.[16] In short, the historical evidence for many of his assertions concerning the *Umwelt* is inadequate or wrong.

Bultmann can scarcely be blamed for such lack of knowledge. He worked with what was available to him, as do we all. It is simply unfortunate that his masterful synthesis appeared just as research into the world of the New Testament was about to change the perception of that world dramatically. More questionable—again in hindsight—is his historical method. He is utterly confident in form criticism as the key to historical reconstruction. Not only does this method demand treating compositions as repositories of tradition rather than as rhetorical arguments (more on this later), its actual handling of those traditions is sometimes maddeningly inconsistent: why, for example, is the Letter of James, with its strong eschatological expectation and vision of a community of solidarity, not considered as evidence for the early Palestinian church, or why is the collection for Jerusalem discussed as an aspect of the Hellenistic church rather than as an effort in which Paul was intimately involved? The method is almost always circular as well: the determination of what tradition is "early" or "late" depends on a prior conception of development, and that conception of development is also supported by traditions being assigned as "early" and "late." Finally on this point, Bultmann's fondness for notions of "self-understanding" is at best only loosely connected to the texts and structures he is describing: it is difficult to avoid concluding, for example, that his construction of the self-understanding of the primitive church as the "eschatological congregation" is anything more than a form of reification.

Most problematic in Bultmann's practice as a historian, however, is the way in which theological judgments intrude into his historical analysis. This may seem a strange complaint for a book that seeks to be a theology of the New Testament, but it is a complaint that cuts to the heart of his endeavor. Like his predecessors and peers, and in fact like many of his successors, Bultmann simply did not make an adequate distinction between the discrete epistemologies demanded for doing history and theology. The result is something of a muddle, in which theological presuppositions affect historical description, and historical developments are the subject of theological judgments. And as Nils Dahl observed in his classic review of Bultmann's masterwork, those theological presuppositions and judgments are entirely those of the Reformation.[17]

Eschatology and Church Structure

The topic of church structure is not entirely lacking in Bultmann's early historical analysis. His discussion of "The Earliest Church as the Eschatological Congregation" (vol. 1, chap. 2, sec. 6) is heavily dependent on the Gospels and the first chapters of Acts: the Twelve are "eschatological regents" whose leader possesses the keys of the Kingdom of Heaven (1.37).[18] But Bultmann says nothing more about any specific leadership activities, a surprising omission in light of Acts' portrayal of the apostles as administering the community of goods (4:32–5:11) and overseeing the mission (8:1-9).[19]

The subject recurs in "Beginnings toward Development of Ecclesiastical Forms" (vol. 1, chap. 2, sec. 8): since the eschatological congregation does not conceive of itself as a new religion—"a new historical phenomenon" (1.53)[20]—its main preoccupation is negotiating its boundary with Judaism, specifically with respect to observance of the Law and the inclusion of the Gentiles (1.53–56). With regard to the decision to include Gentiles by the apostolic council, Bultmann relies solely on Gal 2:1-10, dismissing the account in Acts 15 because "the source on which it rests told about another meeting and decision" (1.56). He discusses the first congregation's ties to synagogue and temple with respect to its place of meeting, its practice of baptism and the meal (1.57–58), and then turns to the subject of the "direction of the church." Although Jerusalem plays a symbolic role as the center for the entire church, the portrayal in Acts of "the legal right of supervision" over the church by Jerusalem "is certainly legendary" (1.61). The Twelve do not really hold an office: their task is the proclamation of the word (1.58–59). The elders, in contrast, serve as a real center of authority in the congregation, as they did in the synagogue (1.59). Bultmann stresses the necessity of tradition from the beginning but insists that this "need not be mediated by institution or sacraments" and declares that the idea of an "apostolic succession" based on the imposition of the hands appears only later with the Pastoral Letters (1.60). Nevertheless, even in the eschatological congregation there was need for a "certain regulation" with regard to the common life (1.61–62).

In the Palestinian church, then, Bultmann sees "tendencies and beginnings in the direction of institutional forms" that pose "questions which arise for the future" (1.62). I think it important to observe at once the decidedly nonhistorical considerations that Bultmann introduces from the start, since these considerations influence his later discussions. When speaking of the office of elders, for example, Bultmann asserts that the congregation is not constituted—as if it were a club or association—by its members "but is conscious of having been founded by God's deed," so that the question that really matters is "*what office can appropriately be instituted* for the direction of the eschatological Congregation? Undoubtedly, it can only be one *founded upon the proclamation of the word*" (1.59, emphasis original).[21] Even in these early descriptions, then, we see the ecclesial values that Bultmann espouses: institution must be measured by the community's eschatological calling—how it remains somehow "other" from the world—and specifically by the primacy of the proclaimed word over any form of human-based authority.[22]

Bultmann's discussion of "The Kerygma of the Hellenistic Church Aside from Paul," in turn, pays almost no attention to questions of ecclesial institution or authority. In "Church Consciousness and the Christian's Relation to the World" (vol. 1, chap. 3, sec. 10), his focus is entirely on the concept of church and the way in which the eschatological consciousness of the primitive community was translated into the Hellenistic context. The Hellenistic church grew out of the synagogue and carried forward the awareness of being the people of God (1.95–98); indeed, the concept of "church" applied first to the movement as a whole more than to particular assemblies (1.93–95).[23] In its emphasis on the community rather than the individual, the Hellenistic church showed itself superior to the mysteries (1.93). As the people of God, the church separated itself from "non-Christian cults of every sort" (1.99) and cultivated a dualistic view of outsiders (borrowing elements of Stoicism and Gnosticism) that expressed itself in forms of asceticism, eschatological expectation, and moral transformation (1.100–107). Everything in Bultmann's treatment of this "church concept" suggests that the Hellenistic church successfully maintained, mutatis mutandis, its identity as an eschatological community.

His subsequent discussion of "The Church's Relation to Judaism and the Problem of the Old Testament" (vol. 1, chap. 3, sec. 11) likewise pays exclusive attention to the spectrum of early Christian responses to the Old Testament (1.108–15) and raises a question concerning ecclesial structure only with reference to the nullifying of ritual commands while retaining the symbolic language of sacrifice. He asks whether cult and cult leadership would also be abolished and whether the office of priest would appear (1.116).

Bultmann's treatment of "The Word, the Church, the Sacraments" in the section of *Theology* devoted to Paul (vol. 1, chap. 5, sec. 34), as might be expected, focuses entirely on the church as eschatological community and is therefore also entirely positive. Paul's eschatology combines elements of Gnosticism and apocalypticism (1.306–7), but central to it is the proclamation of the word: "[I]n the 'word,' then, the salvation-occurrence is present. . . . the 'day of salvation' . . . is present reality in the Now in which the word encounters the hearer. . . . [T]he apostle," therefore, "belongs intrinsically to the eschatological occurrence" (1.307). It is the word that calls the church into being as an eschatological congregation, and as a result the church belongs to the salvation occurrence. Bultmann here speaks of the "peculiar double character of the eschatological Congregation. On the one hand, it is no phenomenon of the world but belongs to the new aeon; on the other hand, this eschatological Congregation, which as such is invisible, takes visible form in the individual congregations within the world" (1.308).

What kind of actual historical shape might such a "visible yet not visible" church take? It takes its "purest form" in the cultic gathering, "from time to time" (1.308). Bultmann emphasizes again that the church is "not a club in which like-minded individuals have banded together . . . [nor] a conglomeration of the Spirit-endowed, each of whom has and enjoys his private relationship to Christ." From the side of Judaism, the notion of the people of God stresses this communal character; from the side of Gnosticism, the image of the Body of Christ does the same (1.310). The structure of the church is determined by its eschatological holiness, defined by its rejection of worldly distinctions (Gal 3:28), but, Bultmann asserts, such rejection "does not mean a sociological program within this world; rather, it is an eschatological occurrence which takes place only within the eschatological Congregation" (1.309). From the center of this cultic gathering, to be sure, "there develops a secular faith-determined community of living" in which there are various reciprocal ministries and services, but Bultmann emphasizes that "official representatives" of the community (*episkopoi* and *diakonoi*) appear "for the first time" only in Phil 1:1 (1.309–10).

After this remarkably brief characterization of structure in the Pauline church, Bultmann turns to an extensive examination of Paul's language about baptism and the Lord's Supper, paying particular attention to the way in which Paul modifies the tradition regarding each so as to distance it from the practice of the mysteries—they are to be understood not mystically but eschatologically, and nothing of *ex opere operato* should be associated with them. He asserts, indeed, that "the sacrament of the Lord's Supper like that of baptism is also coordinate with the word-proclamation and ultimately only a special mode of it" (1.313; cf. 1.311–14). From Bultmann's historical analysis of the church to this point, it is clear that the church as eschatological congregation—the ideal—is corrupted when it is overly determined by outside influences (such as the Law or the mysteries) rather than the proclaimed word, or when its structures (of worship or leadership) are not subordinate to the proclaimed word. It might almost be said, paradoxically, that the church begins to lose its identity as soon as it becomes "historical," for to that extent it can no longer be fully eschatological. From this perspective, "development" must almost necessarily mean "decline." Such would be the logical conclusion to draw from Bultmann's analysis to this point, and such is the paradox within which he begins my target chapter.

The Rise and Development of Church Order

Bultmann begins his discussion with the commonsense observation that no human society can survive without regulations; it was therefore natural for Christianity to develop in structure, a process that eventually became the Catholic Church. But he then raises the question whether "the Ecclèsia in the New Testament sense" is a historical entity, a "thing of history at all." "Is it not, rather, the eschatological Congregation of those who are divorced from the world . . . ?" If that is true (and everything in Bultmann's presentation has sought to convince the reader that it is true), then if the Ecclesia should constitute itself as an entity within the world, having a history within which it works out its regulations, it would mean "a falling away from its own nature." It would fall even further if its regulations were a matter of coercion and were attached to specific offices. Such a development would "directly contradict the nature of the Ecclesia" (2.95). This set of statements perfectly summarizes the prior analysis and anticipates the rest of the chapter: one can have the authentic eschatological Ecclesia, or one can have a historical institution, but one cannot have both.

Bultmann locates his discussion within the debate between two influential predecessors, the great church historian Adolf von Harnack and the legal scholar Rudolf Sohm.[24] Sohm regards the development of ecclesiastical regulation as "the sinful fall of the church," a denial of its nature; Harnack, in contrast, argues that structure was there from the beginning and its development does not contradict the nature of the Ecclesia (2.95–96). Bultmann declares that in terms of history, Harnack is correct, but that in terms of what he calls "the decisive factor," namely the church's "self-understanding" as an eschatological congregation defined by separation from the world, Sohm must be considered correct (2.96). What this opening discussion reveals above all, I think, is Bultmann's deep ambivalence about the church as something other than a pure ideal. The more it moves from the invisible to the visible, the more problematic it is.

As his presentation proceeds, Bultmann considers from a slightly different angle some of the aspects of the starting point—the incipient regulations of the local church as they were "determined by the congregation's understanding of itself as an eschatological community ruled by the Spirit." The starting point must be the Pauline church, where the Spirit-endowed are the chief persons of authority and the Spirit-endowed are primarily the proclaimers of the word (2.97). Bultmann disagrees with Sohm that any and all regulation is a betrayal of the Spirit; Paul's churches show the proper alignment: the Spirit guides the proclamation of the word, and that proclamation guides everything else (2.98). What Bultmann sees as an ideal state of affairs, however, depends on a misreading of the evidence. He states that compared to the Spirit-endowed authorities, "those who act for the external order and welfare of the congregation's life play at first a subordinate role" (2.97).

But this is simply not what our earliest datable evidence (Paul's letters) supports. Four things should be noted. First, as Paul's own experience indicates, the claim to possess the Holy Spirit (1 Cor 7:40) or to be an apostle called by God (1 Cor 9:1) by no means assured acceptance of the authority thus claimed. Second, those exercising leadership in the local assembly (1 Thess 5:12-13)—to whom the congregation should submit—are not identified as the Spirit-endowed.

The congregation in Corinth is told to be "subordinate" to the heads of household enumerated in 1 Cor 16:15-18, without any reference to their possession of the Holy Spirit. Third, in Rom 12:8 and 1 Cor 12:28 the gifts of the Spirit include the homely exercise of local leadership. Fourth, some of the Spirit-endowed, in turn, even those speaking a "word" in the assembly (such as glossolalists and prophets), require regulation and the discernment of the community (1 Thess 5:21; 1 Cor 14:29-32). By the selective and slightly tendentious use of the evidence, Bultmann has created an ideal starting point that does not actually appear in Paul's letters.

· Bultmann sees the starting point as an ideal as well because the Spirit was at work in congregations as well as in Spirit-endowed leaders. This is a critical point: the real question, he says, is "in what form will the rule of the Spirit, or of Christ, realize itself in history?" (2.99). For the earliest church, he speaks of a "congregational democracy" or "pneumatocracy" to describe the participatory role of congregants and explicitly contrasts this to the development of a monarchical episcopate and a distinction between priests and laymen. Bultmann dedicates a lengthy paragraph to the data supporting such democratic activity in the earliest church. What bewilders the reader is that, apart from the Pauline passages dealing with discernment (see above), the bulk of the evidence for such activity comes from Acts, Clement, Ignatius, and the Pastorals, writings that Bultmann otherwise assigns to the later stage of development (2.99)!

As Bultmann traces the development (or decline) toward ecclesiastical offices, then, the reader must keep in mind this primordial, Spirit-filled ideal and the criterion for the authentic authority to make regulations in the church it establishes: when leadership and regulations are Spirit-led, they are appropriate to the nature of the church as eschatological congregation, but to the degree that "authority behind the regulations is represented by individuals, then the ecclesiastical office arises." And for Bultmann, that is what becomes what Sohm called the "sinful fall of the church" (2.100).

Bultmann finds no fault with the organization of the elders in the Palestinian church or the equivalent structure in the Hellenistic churches, where the use of ἐπίσκοπος (taken from associations) probably is roughly equivalent to πρεσβύτερος; a real distinction comes only with the monarchical episcopate in Ignatius (2.101–2). But his nonchalance here is at first puzzling: are not such boards of elders precisely offices based on persons rather than Spirit? The reason Bultmann does not object to them is that they are simply local authority structures; the "church" as a whole—remember his insistence that this was the initial "conception" of church from the start—continues to be directed by the Spirit-endowed leadership of the apostles, and such charismatic leadership, he insists, is *not* an office. It is, rather, their proclamation of the word that constitutes the church (2.103). The charismatic leader is not one appointed by a local church but "is the inspired man endowed with miraculous power" (2.104).

Things begin to go awry when the double stream of authority (charismatic/general and institutional/local) become merged and appointment to office comes to be seen as the transmission of charism. Now, the proclamation of the word becomes "an affair of congregational officers," and local bishops come to be seen as successors of the apostles: "The decisive step has then been taken: henceforth the office is regarded as *constitutive of the Church*. The whole Church rests upon the office-bearers, whose office is held to go back in uninterrupted succession to the apostles (= the twelve)" (2.107, emphasis original). The final stage is when bishops become leaders of the sacramental cultus (2.108–9), and an absolute distinction is drawn between clergy and laity. The church has now become an institution of salvation: "*the regulations of the Church all together become ordinances of divine law* and make the Church into an institution of salvation" (2.110, emphasis original). The only remaining step in the church's decline is the development of a system of discipline (see 2.221–26).

There is much that can be challenged in this section of Bultmann's historical/theological reconstruction. One is his focus on the presence/absence of office or institution as the most important criterion for the church's authentic identity. Even if one allows that "eschatology" is the enemy of history—a concession not all find easy to make—and that "eschatological consciousness" is the mark of authentic Christianity, an intense eschatological consciousness is perfectly compatible with hierarchical and even legalistic structures, as Qumran and many subsequent communities have shown. It is by no means obvious, furthermore, that the elaboration of ecclesial structure in Christianity completely routinized the work of the Spirit: second-century literature above all is replete with examples of Spirit-filled leadership—evidence is provided by the apocryphal Acts, by the Acts of the Martyrs, by Montanists, and by Gnostics. The struggle between charism and order was real in these instances, but it is a historical falsification to reduce Christian existence in the second and third century to a caricature of institutional cult and hierarchical order.

Bultmann's use of sources also requires attention. He recognizes that the last stages of development take place after the New Testament, and the earliest explicit evidence for them is Clement and Ignatius. But he sees a key role also played by the New Testament compositions called the Pastoral Letters. Here, he says, we find the laying on of hands as charism; here we have the offices of bishop, elder, and deacon; here we have the command to appoint others to office (2.106–8). Because Bultmann—like the great majority of scholars of his generation—regarded the inauthenticity of the Pastorals as self-evident, he was confident that they served as witnesses to the critical stage of development he called "decisive": the collapse of charismatic authority into institution. Indeed, from F. C. Baur to Walter Bauer, the so-called church order in the three letters to Paul's delegates was regarded as the clinching evidence for their inauthenticity.[25] Some present-day scholars, however, continuing a long tradition of resistance to the "assured result" of critical consensus in the nineteenth century, consider it possible that the Pastorals were written within the frame of Paul's ministry.[26]

But even those who think they are inauthentic must agree on several points with respect to their so-called church order. First, the elements dealing with ecclesial structure amount to two chapters in 1 Timothy, and at best one line each in 2 Timothy and Titus; there is much more to these letters than church order. Second, the depiction of community organization in 1 Tim 3 and 5 is utterly simple and finds parallels in contemporary associations and Diaspora synagogues. Third, what is said about leadership and its functions, moreover, agrees substantially with the fragmentary evidence in Paul's undisputed letters (see 1 Thess 5:12; Gal 6:6; 1 Cor 6:1-8; 12:28; 16:15-18; Phil 1:1; Rom 12:7-8; 16:1-3). Fourth, in sharp contrast *both* to Qumran and Ignatius, these letters totally lack any theological legitimation for the exercise of leadership; it is entirely straightforward and functional. Finally, more than that, because the letters portray the delegates as under the direction of the apostle, they agree completely—in terms of literary presentation—with Bultmann's portrayal of the ideal relationship between apostolic/charismatic authority and local leadership.

Just as Bultmann began with the self-understanding of the church as an eschatological congregation, so does he bring the tale of development to a conclusion with a discussion of what he considers the transformation in the church's understanding of itself (2.111). The portrait he draws is essentially that which has become familiar in scholarship under the rubric "early Catholicism" (*frühkatholizismus*).[27] Rather than an eschatological community shaped by the transcendent proclamation of the word, the church as institution claims possession of salvation. Eschatology is transmuted from a stance of opposition to the world in response to the proclaimed word, to an expectation of a future return in the far distance, so that the church stands now as the ready and available instrument of grace through its sacraments and is ever more comfortable facing a prolonged existence within secular history: "the Christian faith, losing its eschatological tension, is becoming a Christian-bourgeois piety" (2.114; cf. 2.12–16).

And just as Bultmann began his treatment of the primitive church by insisting that it did not conceive of itself as a "new religion—i.e. a new historical phenomenon" (1.53) he concludes his discussion of the development of church order by asserting that the church now conceived of itself precisely as a new historical phenomenon, and indeed "*as a new religion* existing side by side with the Jewish and the heathen religion (the latter regarded as a unity)" (2.116, emphasis original). The fullest literary expression of this new consciousness is the Acts of the Apostles. The author of Luke and Acts, Bultmann asserts, "is guided in his presentation by *a conception of Christianity as an entity of world history*" (2.116, emphasis original). The very composition of a historical account, which in Bultmann's view would have been incomprehensible to those seeing the church as the eschatological congregation, reveals Luke's own understanding: "the history of salvation continues" in "the history of Christianity" (2.117). The story of the early church's development, according to Bultmann, is a tragic one: the Spirit is imprisoned by institution, and eschatology is stifled by history. By becoming more humanly visible and real within the ancient world, Christianity inevitably lost its true identity, becoming not a challenge to the world through the word but a part of the world through the machinery of salvation.

Beyond Bultmann

Moving "beyond Bultmann" demands more, I think, than correcting what one regards in his account as incidentally inadequate or in error. It demands asking in a more fundamental way how to provide a responsible account of two separate things that Bultmann treated as one. One task is to attempt a historical description of the Christian movement from its diverse first-century beginnings to the time of its first real consolidation in the middle to late second century. Another task altogether is to engage theologically the understanding of church as it is found in the discrete compositions of the first and second centuries. Although these two tasks intersect in many ways, they nevertheless require distinct modes of knowing and different methods of engagement.

History

The task of historical description has its own importance, but it is not fundamentally a theological enterprise. In this regard, Harnack's position—with which Bultmann partially agreed—is better than Sohm's—with which Bultmann more fundamentally agreed. To carry out the task more adequately, I think, the following principles need to be operative.

First, the accurate dating and the appropriate use of sources is imperative. Although the practice of tradition criticism need not be abandoned altogether, greater skepticism concerning it is required; by no means is the "prehistory" of Rom 3:21-26 or Phil 2:5-11 certain. Paul's letters give us our earliest evidence, together, perhaps, with James and Hebrews. Colossians, Ephesians, 2 Thessalonians, and the Pastoral Letters may also need to be considered within the Pauline framework. The Synoptic Gospels and Acts must be treated with the greatest caution as providing information concerning Christianity before Paul. In any case, dates and location of traditions need to be argued for, rather than assumed. Even for the Pauline letters, furthermore, it cannot be assumed that the same structures, practices, and images were at work in every one of his churches.

Second, the historical account must be inclusive. This means that more than the presence or absence of structure should be analyzed. Rather, the entire range of practices and images concerning the assembly found in the respective compositions needs to be considered, without reference to how they do or do not meet or fall away from a supposed ideal. Inclusivity means as well the willingness to acknowledge the multiple ways in which believers interacted with the symbolic worlds within which they lived and from which they entered the assembly. In this regard, Bultmann is relentlessly either/or in his perspective: the eschatological congregation must be distinguished from the mysteries or from Judaism. But history is usually much more a matter of both/and: just as there were a variety of ways of being Jewish, so there were a variety of ways of being religiously gentile, and Christians from the beginning brought aspects of those worlds into the believing assembly.[28]

Third, the diverse geographical location of early communities is also important, for development happens in different places in different ways and at different speeds. Bultmann's Palestinian/Hellenistic distinction is too simple and serves more as a way to organize data than as description of datable and locatable communities. Rather than start with a single place (Palestine) with a universal conception of church that precedes local assemblies, which then undergoes a transformation, proper historical method would begin with all the diverse communities (and their conceptions) and recognize that through a variety of exchanges (leaders, goods, letters, convictions) a broader fellowship and a more inclusive sense of Ecclesia developed.[29]

Finally, from a historical perspective, institutional development is simply natural to communities as they grow in size and complexity. From a historical perspective, there can be no asking of what structures are "appropriate" to the proclamation of the word or "endowed" by the Spirit or consistent with an eschatological self-understanding. From a historical perspective, institutional development may be measured by effectiveness or by sustainability, but it cannot be measured by theological criteria. The development of the early church in the direction of Catholicism cannot in historical terms be regarded as a "fall from grace," or a "corruption," or a "decline." It is, in historical terms, simply what happened.

Theology

The large problem of how best to read the New Testament theologically can clearly not be addressed fully in this essay.[30] But I think the way forward is in a different direction than that taken by Bultmann (and all other "New Testament Theologies"), namely, seeking to locate historically some principle of unity that can give usable coherence to the diverse New Testament compositions within a single book. I think the right direction rather lies in affirming two complex realities and working to put them in an ongoing dialectical conversation. The first complexity is the world of readers, who approach these texts for a variety of reasons and from a variety of perspectives. The second complexity is the irreducible diversity of the New Testament compositions themselves, which resist reduction to a single historical or thematic unification. The best possibility for an authentic theological engagement with the New Testament is not to be found in a book, however learned, but in a living conversation among believers who take the otherness of the canonical texts with full seriousness.

It is as a collection of diverse literary compositions with distinct literary and rhetorical shaping, moreover, that the New Testament must be engaged by contemporary readers. The "otherness" of the texts is secured not simply by their historical distance from readers but also by the resistance posed by their specific rhetoric. Consequently, whatever any of the New Testament compositions has to say on any specific topic—such as the church—must be assessed within its rhetorical shaping and purposes. The true inadequacy of Bultmann's historical method is that it does not enable him to get at much of what the New Testament writings have to say theologically about the church.

Because Bultmann does not read Romans rhetorically, he does not see how Paul's discussion of Jew and Gentile in God's plan (Rom 9–11) has everything to do with Paul's vision of how his readers are to live within community with mutual acceptance of differences (Rom 14). Because he does not read Hebrews rhetorically, he fails adequately to appreciate its powerful vision of the church as a people on pilgrimage to God. Because he does not read James rhetorically, he does not grasp that it challenges readers to the most radically countercultural stance in the New Testament. Because he considers Ephesians only from the point of view of its (presumably) late date and does not read it rhetorically, he misses the New Testament's most powerful evocation of the church as the place of reconciliation in the world and the sign of the world's possibility. Finally, because Bultmann does not read Luke-Acts as a literary whole, but considers Acts separately as a

172 — Luke Timothy Johnson

historical source alone, he considers it the supreme expression of the church's transformation of consciousness from eschatological congregation to historical church. He fails to see that Luke continues in his second volume the same prophetic challenge that he began with the portrayal of Jesus in his Gospel: the church in Acts embodies and enacts the same radical challenge to the world as a Spirit-guided institution that Jesus did as God's Spirit-anointed prophet.[31]

I conclude by suggesting that quite different perspectives on the church past and present are offered in turn by Bultmann's historical reading, and the literary engagement I have proposed. From Bultmann's tale of development as decline, the church appears as most authentic when least visible, and the Christian reality as the sad loss of an eschatological dream. From the ongoing engagement with the New Testament's diverse compositions in all their literary and rhetorical complexity, in contrast, emerges a set of visions that are various indeed and, precisely in their variety, offer diverse possibilities for authentic expressions of the church and a diverse set of challenges to corruptions of the church.

Chapter 9

THE DEVELOPMENT OF DOCTRINE

James D. G. Dunn

In the first volume of his *Theology of the New Testament* Rudolf Bult-mann had dealt briefly with the message of Jesus, not as part of the theology of the New Testament but only as a "presupposition" for it (1.3; 30 pages).[1] Then with equal brevity he dealt with "the kerygma of the earliest church" (another 30 pages), again not really as part of the theology of the New Testament, since it was also presupposition and had to be reconstructed from traditions drawn upon by Acts, Paul, and the Synoptic Gospels. Chapter 3 dealt with "The Kerygma of the Hellenistic Church Aside from Paul," a more substantial 120 pages. But this was basically in preparation for the major part of the first volume, "The Theology of Paul" (165 pages). And in it he reveals one of his controlling presuppositions, that already before Paul early Christian theology (the Hellenistic church) was heavily influenced by Gnostic motifs, including an already developed Gnostic redeemer myth. Then follows, in part 2, the principal focus of volume 1, in which it becomes clear that when we talk about the theology of the New Testament we are talking primarily about the theology of Paul. For all his critical scholarship, Bultmann remained to the core a Lutheran, or perhaps more precisely a Lutheran Paulinist.

In volume 2 it becomes equally clear that John has an almost equivalently central role for Bultmann's *Theology*. Part 3 is devoted to "The Theology of the Gospel of John and the Johannine Epistles" (ninety pages). No other New Testament author or writing is given the same attention. The Epistle to the Hebrews, for example, is given close attention only twice in the two volumes: briefly in chapter 3 of volume 1 in one page on the subject of "The Church's Relation to Judaism and the Problem of the Old Testament," inserted among equally brief comments on the *Epistle of Barnabas, 1 Clement,* the Valentinian *Ptolemy to Flora,* and Justin Martyr; and in just over two pages in chapter 7 of volume 2 on "Christology and Soteriology" as "the core of the development toward the Ancient Church," where the primary concern seems to have been to compare Hebrews rather negatively with Paul.

I mention this as a way into discussion of Bultmann's understanding of the development (of theology?) toward the ancient church, since it helps make clear that for Bultmann the center and substance of the theology of the New Testament are to be found in Paul and John, with all else within the New Testament and extending into the Apostolic Fathers to be viewed in the shadow particularly of Paul, in comparison with and reaction to Paul. Much as Bultmann is to be congratulated for refusing to draw a sharp dividing line between canonical and noncanonical/postbiblical literature, as William Wrede had strongly urged,[2] it is difficult to regard the title, *The Theology of the New Testament,* as a sufficiently accurate description of the task to which Bultmann had set himself. In part 4 it is not only Hebrews that is evaluated by measuring it against Paul, but all the other writings of the New Testament and the Apostolic Fathers, where Bultmann is happy to advance the discussion, for example, of soteriology by reference to the Shepherd of Hermas, the epistle of James, *Didache, Barnabas,* Hebrews, 2 Peter, *2 Clement,* the *Letter of Polycarp,* the Revelation of John, Colossians and Ephesians, 1 Peter, the Pastoral Epistles, and Ignatius in that rather higgledy-piggledy manner.

So what is lacking is a genuine engagement with the individual non-Pauline, non-Johannine writings of the New Testament, with Ignatius as something of an exception. In contrast with Bultmann's typically existentialist engagement with Paul (the undisputed Pauline letters) and John, the review of such other writings is more descriptive, at arm's length, and, frankly, rather boring in a way that introductions to the New Testament are often boring when they are content to summarize the writing's teaching on particular doctrines.

One of the chief indicators of where Bultmann's heart lies is his treatment of eschatology. Clearly the eschatological character of Jesus' preaching and of earliest Christian (Paul's) theology was a principal feature. The expectations regarding the age to come were already being fulfilled: the blind were seeing, the deaf were hearing, and good news was being preached to the poor; the kingdom of God was at hand and already upon them; the resurrection of Jesus was the beginning of the resurrection of the dead; the (Pentecostal) outpouring of the Spirit was in fulfillment of one of the principal hopes for the age to come; Christ would soon return. Bultmann was not unwilling to embrace fully this dimension of earliest New Testament theology, despite the obvious theological problem of making sense of such an eschatological emphasis at over nineteen hundred years' distance. The reason he could so embrace the New Testament's eschatology was simply because he had found a way to handle it theologically. Earliest eschatology, and possible questions of failed expectation (the delay of the *parousia*), did not trouble him, because he believed that this eschatological dimension could be readily mapped into an existentialist concern for the ultimate. This was why John was so central to his conception of New Testament theology—because John demonstrated precisely that such mapping was already being done before the end of the first century and within the New Testament ("Faith as Eschatological Existence"). The *krisis* had already entered the world; the light which determined that judgment (by individuals' reaction to it) was already shining in and through Jesus, the Word become flesh. The future eschatology had been absorbed into the present significance of Jesus.[3] The eschatological challenge of Jesus and the first Christians still came over in the existentialist challenge of the preached word. This too was why the influence of Gnostic motifs on Paul was of little concern for Bultmann. For as Hans Jonas was to show, Gnosticism mapped still more readily into existentialist philosophy—Jonas' characterization of Gnosticism in *The Gnostic Religion* as stemming from a sense of alienation translated without much difficulty into an existentialist sense of the "thrownness" (*Geworfenheit*) of one's place in life.[4]

As a faithful Lutheran, Bultmann in effect regarded "justification by faith" as the "canon within the canon" of the New Testament. But as a twentieth-century Heideggerean, Bultmann concluded that existentialist philosophy was the "canon within the canon," or the hermeneutical key for appreciating and interpreting the theology of the New Testament in contemporary language. And in consequence he judged the post-Pauline, post-Johannine Christian writings, whether in the New Testament or written later, by the criterion he had in effect drawn from Paul and John, and for the most part found them wanting in one degree or other. Bultmann would have denied that he was a biblicist who regarded all post–New Testament writings as subapostolic, as a falling away from the apostolic authority of the New Testament. But in effect he regarded (the undisputed) Paul and John as the authors who expressed the theological heart of Christianity and the other New Testament writings and Apostolic Fathers as a downhill development.

Paradosis and Historical Tradition

This becomes apparent quite quickly in part 4 of Bultmann's *Theology of the New Testament*, and not least in chapter 6, "The Development of Doctrine." In section 54, "Paradosis and Historical Tradition," the issue posed is the degree to which the tradition is concerned with history. For Bultmann, however, this is not a primary concern of the two Pauline passages, which deal expressly with the tradition that Paul inherited. The fact that 1 Cor 11:23-25 claims to include historical information ("on the night he was betrayed") is ignored—presumably because the focus of the eucharistic liturgy, as also of the baptismal liturgy, is not on the historical past, but on the sacramental moment in the present. In the case of 1 Cor 15:3-4, Bultmann of course accepts that the tradition is making historical statements: "the occurrence of salvation, of which the Christian formulas speak, is peculiarly bound up with history, with world history. It took place not in some mythical time, neither is it a timeless occurrence in some transcendent sphere, but it took place here on earth, and not long ago, either" (2.121). So Luke's setting the story of Jesus and the beginnings of Christianity into the context of world history "is understandable," but "in the process the eschatological character of this history gets lost" (2.121). So, Luke's theological error was to dissolve the eschatological into the historical, whereas, for Bultmann, the better way was to transpose the eschatological into the existential, as John had demonstrated.

Bultmann poses the issue as "the problem of the relationship between history of salvation and world history, or [Bultmann's preferred way of posing it] between revelation and history." Somewhat surprisingly, "history-of-salvation" for Bultmann is not history like "world history" but is equivalent to "revelation" or eschatology. For Bultmann it was important to be able to say that "the 'new covenant,' unlike the old, is not the founding event of a people's history, but . . . an eschatological event, and the 'People of God' with which this covenant is made is an entity not of world history but of eschatology. . . . For Christ is the end of history" (2.122). What Bultmann means is that eschatology is the end of history, that revelation is not, strictly speaking, historical. Focusing the event of Jesus on its eschatological significance allows Bultmann to avoid historical questions regarding Jesus—the historical Jesus—to escape what he saw as the danger of making the existential impact of the preaching of Jesus (the kerygma) depend on being able to demonstrate the historical facticity of this or that feature of his mission. So the Gospels, where they focus on fulfillment of OT predications (as with Matthew), forsake "the history-of-salvation point of view," and in an historical account of the life of Jesus and the history of the Church, "their eschatological meaning" has been sacrificed (as with Luke-Acts).

The more positive way forward, for Bultmann, is signaled by passages like 2 Cor 5:18-19 and 8:9 and Phil 2:6-11, which indicate that "it was possible *to formulate statements of the paradosis without mentioning historical facts*" (2.123, emphasis original). Here he falls back on the misleading interpretation of 2 Cor 5:16, that Paul no longer wanted to know "Christ according to the flesh," whereas "according to the flesh" should most probably be read adverbially, qualifying the verb ("know") rather than adjectivally, qualifying the noun ("Christ").[5] Paul was not decrying historical interest in the prepassion Jesus but a perception of Jesus uninformed by the Spirit, by the revelatory significance of his death and resurrection. But once again, for Bultmann, it is John who shows the way forward, in his handling of the Jesus tradition with a freedom that was untrammeled by a concern for historical detail.

Of course they were speaking about a historical person, "the Word became flesh" (John 1:14). But did it follow that information about the manner of his historical life was also necessary (to faith)? Certainly Luke thought so, but again Paul provides the key. For when Paul refers to the obedience of Christ (Phil 2:8; Rom 5:19) or to his exemplary love (2 Cor 8:9; Rom 15:3), he is thinking of "the self-abasement and sacrifice of the pre-existent Christ and not of the concrete conduct of the historical Jesus" (2.123). And when appeal is made to the sayings of Jesus, as in the Apostolic Fathers, it is not motivated by historical-biographical interest but by concern to regulate the life of believers and to keep their hope alive. "The one whom they heard speaking in the words was not the historical Jesus, but the Church's heavenly Lord" (2.124).

"That neither Matthew nor Mark wrote his Gospel out of histori-cal interest, as Luke did, is clear" (2.124). "[T]he Jesus whom he [Mat-thew] depicts is to be understood not as a figure of world history but as its conclusion. . . . [H]is historical account expresses that fact (that eschatological salvation became history) by making the reader con-scious that the present is eschatological in character" (2.125). As for Mark, he "expresses the kerygmatic character of the historical account . . . : Jesus' life is not an episode of world history but the miraculous manifestation of divine dealing in the cloak of earthly occurrence" (2.125) (note the almost gnostic language of Bultmann here).

Bultmann continues to struggle with the issue of how important was the historical fact of Jesus to the kerygma. Matthew and Mark suc-ceeded in making the historical account serviceable to the kerygmatic character of the "gospel." By rooting both baptism and the Lord's Supper in his account of Jesus, Mark gave "the history of Jesus the character of occurring revelation" (2.125). That is, what was impor-tant was not the historical fact or account of Jesus' baptism or Last Supper but the encounter here and now which the kerygma and the celebration of baptism and Lord's Supper made possible. The histori-cal "thatness" rather than the "whatness" of such events in Jesus' life, as also of his death and resurrection, was all the history that need be retained or emphasized. Bultmann's criticism of Gnosticism was that it sacrificed from the kerygma this reference to the historical occur-rence, divorcing it from history, surrendering "the historical reality of the Redeemer" (2.126). Yet, even so, the clue that Gnosticism gave to Bultmann's existentialist appropriation of the kerygma means that he could not leave his criticism of Gnosticism there. For "the intent of

Gnostic teaching" was, after all, appropriate: "in opposition to a historizing [*sic*] of the eschatological occurrence, it expresses a legitimate interest in faith" (2.127).

Here again it is John who shows the way forward: in dealing so freely with the Jesus tradition, "he most sharply made clear the meaning it has for the kerygma by reducing the revelation of God in the man Jesus to the mere fact that He so revealed Himself" (2.127)— echoing his earlier pronouncement that in his Gospel "John presents only the fact of the Revelation without describing its content" (2.66). "He presents this person not as a reliably testified person of the past but as he is constantly present in the word which proclaims him." For John "the tradition is not historical transmission . . . but is the Church's preaching." Even Paul falls short at this point, since, inconsistently with his basic insight, he "still tries to guarantee the resurrection of Jesus by the enumeration of witnesses, as if it were an historical visible fact" (2.127).

In reading this (sec. 54) it is almost impossible to escape the impression that Bultmann is reading these New Testament texts with existentialist spectacles with a gnosticizing warp in them.

1. The New Testament Gospels are part of the New Testament. They are evidence of how the earliest churches theologized about Jesus. A New Testament theology should take seriously their concerns and should consider their theology with a greater degree of dispassion than Bultmann shows. Instead he in effect critiques them (particularly Luke) by what he regards as the inadequacy of the way they represent Jesus. That is, he takes his own existentialist response to a Jesus who is only the presupposition of New Testament theology and in effect uses that as the criterion by which to critique the Gospels. He does not ask whether that fairly represents the Evangelists' concerns (apart from John) or whether he in writing a theology of the New Testament should first describe as sympathetically as possible what they understood to be their task before he grappled theologically with them.

2. It is now agreed that the Gospels, at least the Synoptic Gospels, are most fairly categorized as biographies, not modern biographies with typical modern concerns regarding personal

identity, but ancient biographies concerned to demonstrate a person's character by what he did and said.[6] Bultmann's attempt to dismiss historical-biographical interest from the earliest churches was always unrealistic—and all too Gnostic in character! Gentile believers in particular, being called to believe in a Jewish Jesus, as the Messiah/Christ of Jewish expectation, after whom they would be called once baptized in his name ("Christians"), would of course have wanted to know about this Jesus. And the Gospels were a way of responding to that need for basic information. Bultmann makes no attempt to engage with that concern, except to dismiss it as a misunderstanding of what faith is and how it works.

3. By using the word "gospel" at the opening of his Gospel (Mark 1:1—"the beginning of the gospel"), Mark integrated the mission and teaching of Jesus into the "gospel," which for Paul had indeed focused primarily or even exclusively on the death and resurrection of Jesus. And in so doing, Mark ensured the character of what was and became a new genre— the Gospel—an account of Jesus' mission and teaching, leading up to the account of his death and resurrection. To deny any historical interest in so portraying the gospel is at best tendentious, and at worst mischievous. Nor should it be forgotten that the Gospel form that Mark gave to the recounting of the gospel was copied by the other Evangelists, including John. It was the *Gospel of Thomas* that most matched the retention of Jesus' teaching for which Bultmann was reaching.

4. It is entirely questionable as to whether Paul had no interest in "the historical Jesus."[7] I have already critiqued Bultmann's use of 2 Cor 5:16. And Paul's reference to the historical character of Jesus' mission can certainly not be limited to his death (and resurrection). For example, the echoes of Jesus' readiness to have table fellowship with sinners are sufficiently clear in Gal 2:14-15. Paul's claim to imitate Christ almost certainly looks beyond Christ's passion (1 Cor 11:1). The exhortation to "please one's neighbor" (the only time Paul refers to the "neighbor" apart from his quotations from Lev 19:18, in echo

of Jesus' own unique exaltation of that part-verse) naturally appeals to Christ's example (Rom 15:2-3).

5. It is unjustified to take the Apostolic Fathers' use of the Jesus tradition (*Didache, 1 Clement,* etc.) as the only model for the way the Jesus tradition functioned and was used in the oral, prewritten Gospel phase. That was primarily material collected for catechetical purposes. But the evidence of Paul, James, and 1 Peter suggests that the Jesus tradition had been absorbed into the lifeblood of the earliest assemblies and informed their values and life models, without the assemblies having to remind themselves explicitly every time that it was Jesus who had said this or that. Likewise how stories are told about Jesus in the Gospels, Jesus and the Sabbath, Jesus and table fellowship, and so on, can assuredly be taken as exemplifying the way such episodes in Jesus' life were recalled in order to give guidance to the first Christians in similar situations.

6. And John, for all the freedom he displays in handling the Jesus tradition, also preserves various geographical notes and has information about the overlap between the missions of the Baptist and of Jesus that we would otherwise lack. The extended discourses that he attributes to Jesus can again and again be seen to be expanded meditations on particular Jesus sayings and images used by Jesus (as indicated in the Synoptic tradition). And the "signs" that he shows Jesus perform are likely to be modeled on typical miracles of Jesus as recorded also in the Synoptic tradition.[8]

In short, rather than an engagement with the development of doctrine, with the way the paradosis was used and with the question of the extent to which the historical facticity of Jesus' mission and message was a factor of any importance for second (and third) generation Christians, Bultmann has seen his task as defending his own view of what authentic faith is, and his own view, therefore, of which second generation faith may be regarded as "authentic." This is not *The Theology of the New Testament,* so much as Bultmann's Theology of the New Testament.

The Problem of Right Teaching and the
Rise of the New Testament Canon

Bultmann begins section 55, "The Problem of Right Teaching and the Rise of the New Testament Canon," in characteristically Bultmannian fashion. "Christianity did not become a mystery-religion, because in it salvation rests primarily . . . upon the proclamation of the word. . . . The proclamation, telling of God's deed in Christ, is at the same time personal address to the hearer" (2.127–28). Here again the two key elements in Bultmann's theology come through clearly: salvation happens through the proclamation of the word (not in a historical event) and comes to the hearer of the word as existential challenge. "Faith must prove itself to be living faith by reaching in each case a right judgment as to what is required of the man of faith" (2.128)—a classic expression of Christian existentialism. And lest the gnostic dimension of Bultmann's "faith" be lost to sight, he immediately emphasizes that " 'knowledge' (whether ἐπίγνωσις or γνῶσις) scarcely differs in substance from 'faith,' except that it emphasizes *the element of knowing which is contained in the very structure of 'faith'* " (2.128, emphasis original).

For Bultmann "the origin of Christian theology" was the earliest Christian wrestling with the implications and consequences of the "special knowledge" or "wisdom" whose content is the divine plan of salvation, the mystery revealed to Paul, and even more so for Colossians and Ephesians (2.129). This seems a little late to date the *origin* of Christian theology, which surely began with the first questions raised by Jesus' mission, his death, and its aftermath: What has God done or been doing in and through Jesus? Was soteriology first, or was Christology first? Or were they too much bound up with each other from the start, so that to pose such an alternative is inevitably misleading? But Bultmann is probably on the right track when he asserts that "[t]he critical question for the development of theology is how far it sticks to being an unfolding of the knowledge contained in faith" (2.129). Also, that "[m]otivation for the development of a Christian theology was furnished not only by the necessity of interpreting the kerygma but also by the Old Testament, which . . . also required interpretation" (2.130). In support, one might add, it is all too easy to underplay the importance and role of the OT in the dynamic of the earliest Christian theology—the Old Testament as the "the substructure of New Testament theology," in the words of C. H. Dodd.[9] And it is certainly true that the development of theology included the exposition of earlier authoritative Christian writings, as indicated by the fact that Paul's literary heritage quickly became text to be interacted with and interpreted—consider the Pastorals, *1 Clement*, Ignatius, and Polycarp, though I would not go along with Bultmann in arguing that "II Thessalonians is a commentary on I Thessalonians" (2.131).

However, the topics of "knowledge" and "wisdom" inevitably bring up once again the question of Gnosticism and Bultmann's assumption that Paul himself was "already under the influence of *Gnostic thinking*" (2.132, emphasis original). Here again Bultmann confuses the kind of speculation evident in early Jewish apocalyptic thought and wisdom tradition with the redeemer myths found in later Gnostic systems. But the knowledge of subsequent Gnostic thought is of the "I" of the individual as a spark of divinity trapped within a material body and physical world—quite different from the knowledge of God, and being known by God, in OT and early Jewish thought. And Wisdom is not an emanation at several removes from the unknown God, as in the Gnostic systems, but is a way of speaking of God's immanence without calling in question his transcendence, a way of asserting the knowability of the unknown God, through the Torah (for Sirach and Baruch)[10] and through Jesus (for Paul and the first Christians).[11]

Bultmann's view that Paul was engaging with gnosticizing Christians in Corinth is now passé, though he has more grounds for his claim that the later New Testament writings (the Pastorals, Jude, and 2 Peter in particular) simply dismiss "false teaching" without engaging with it (2.133). Since this contrasts with Paul's struggle with the "gnosticizing wing" of Christianity, the implication is that these later writings do not actually engage in theologizing—an interesting corollary for a *Theology of the New Testament*. Notably, Bultmann also claims that 1 John, unlike Paul, does not engage in theological discussion with the false teachers, but at least it "makes clear the existential meaning of faith"—so that's all right then.

The treatment of Colossians and Ephesians is also passé, since it assumes that the "philosophy" against which warning is given (Col

2:8) is "Gnostic speculation" (2.133), and that Ephesians, like Colossians, uses "the cosmological terminology of Gnosticism ([Eph] 1:10, 20-22; 2:14-16)" (2.134). But in Colossians it should be apparent that what is in mind is the reaction to the distinctively Jewish claims being made by the Colossian church (Col 1:12), a reaction that is even more distinctively Jewish, where the Colossian Christians were being "disqualified" because they did not observe the food laws, festivals, Sabbaths, and ritual purity (2:16, 20-21). And interpretation of the puzzling 2:18, "worship of angels" or "worship with angels," has now the benefit of Qumran's "Songs of the Sabbath Sacrifice," expressing the worshipers' sense of participating in the "angelic liturgy"—a benefit that Bultmann lacked. The most obvious solution is that the church in Colossae was suffering some heavy criticism, disqualifying criticism (2:18), from the local synagogue communities, indignant that this bunch of nonproselytes, even non–God fearers, were claiming a share in Israel's distinctive heritage.[12] And Ephesians so well represents Paul's commission to take the gospel of Israel's Messiah to non-Jews (Eph 3:1-12)—to those called "the uncircumcision" by those who are called "the circumcision," and hitherto regarded as "strangers to the covenants of promise, having no hope and without God in the world" (2:11-21)—that it is hard indeed to strip away the characteristically Jewish context of the letter, let alone replace it with a Gnostic context.

The next section (sec. 55.4), on the great "diversity of theological interests and ideas" (2.135), is a good deal more credible. Bultmann had been able to take on board the central thesis of Walter Bauer,[13] that a concept of " 'right' or 'orthodox' doctrine stands at the end of a development" or is the result of a conflict between various shades of doctrine, where "orthodoxy" is the version which triumphed and "heresy" is the divergent teaching which was rejected—or as Bultmann puts it provocatively, "the 'great Church' is only the most successful heresy" (2.137–38). So Bultmann is able to argue that there was no "norm or an authoritative court of appeal for doctrine" (2.135). Well, yes, it is true that a concept of "the rule of faith" did not really emerge till Irenaeus, but Bultmann was also well aware that Paul had a concept of "right walking" (ὀρθοποδεῖν) (2.136), where the norm was the gospel itself (Gal 2:14).

Still, Bultmann is correct that "in the beginning, *faith* is the term which distinguishes the Christian Congregation from Jews and the heathen, not *orthodoxy* (right doctrine)" (2.135) and that "*pistis* takes on the meaning of right belief" only with the Pastorals, perhaps also with Eph 4:5, and pretty clearly with Jude 3 (2.135–36). The "good confession" of 1 Tim 6:12 can be taken to imply a "right confession in contrast to heresy." But is Bultmann really justified in his insistence that, in contrast, the "confession" of Rom 10:9 can be so clearly distinguished from a "*right* confession in contrast to a heretical one" (2.136)? Paul presumably thought of the confession, "Jesus is Lord," as a necessary(?) expression of saving faith, with the implicit corollary that other expressions could/should be deemed insufficient or inadequate (not yet "heretical," but not "right").

Even so, it is salutary to be reminded that the term αἵρεσις meant simply a "sect, party, school, or faction," not to mention the fact that the earliest believers in Jesus were described as a sect (αἵρεσις), like the sects of Pharisees, Sadducees, and Essenes (2.137).[14] And though the sense of "heretical" may be recognizable in Titus 3:10 (2.137), the more important point to draw out is that there was no single truth statement that defined earliest Christian theology; diversity of faith expression and "right walking" was characteristic of a Christianity of believing Jews and believing Gentiles from the mission of Paul onward. It is also important to appreciate that in the second century, as both emerging Christianity and emerging (rabbinic) Judaism were trying to define themselves, not least over against each other, it was almost inevitable that a concept of "right belief" (orthodoxy) and "wrong belief" (heresy) should emerge, on both sides(!), as each tried to establish their own identity by distinguishing themselves from the other.[15] I wish Bultmann had found himself able to address such issues. It would have been an entirely appropriate concern to expound writings like Ignatius and *Barnabas* in their own terms (and entirely justifiable as part of the theological reception of the New Testament), rather than simply treating them as variously inadequate successors to Paul. But, I accept, that would begin to stretch "The Theology of the New Testament" too far beyond the New Testament.

Bultmann quite justifiably turns to the issue of "*the authority which might determine 'right' doctrine*," reasoning, also quite justifiably, that the role of "reliable tradition" was naturally central, and that the apostles were naturally regarded as the bearers of that tradition (2.138, emphasis original), so that we are hardly surprised that the Church's first manual of ethics and congregational order was given the title the "Teaching (*Didache*) of the Twelve Apostles" (2.139–40). He goes on to remind us that the Gnostics also appealed to authoritative tradition but draws the false corollary that "[i]t was Gnosticism particularly which made oral tradition suspect" (2.139, 140). That is an unjustified corollary; we know that the oral Jesus tradition continued to be in lively use in the postapostolic churches as late as the middle of the second century. It was not the oral character of Gnostic tradition that made it suspect. It was the claim that the tradition concerned had been given in secret to some apostles (Thomas as the most obvious example), after Jesus' resurrection, which made "the great church" (to use Celsus' phrase) so suspicious of that tradition. Additionally, the narrative of the human condition and its resolution which this secret revelation presupposed and expressed was so different from the Jesus tradition which the Synoptic Gospels had transcribed and made basic to Christian discipleship and assembly. Bultmann was probably too enticed by the existentialist character of Gnosticism to see this point clearly. Nor did he take sufficient note of the fact that a concern for "reliable tradition" inevitably included a concern for reliable information about Jesus' mission and message; but for Bultmann this would have meant recognizing that the "reliable tradition" was also "historical tradition" and would have tied faith too tightly to reliable history.

Otherwise Bultmann is himself quite reliable in his discussion of the transition from oral to written tradition. In dealing briefly with the process of canonization of the New Testament writings, he recognizes that Paul's letters were read at worship services and passed to or shared with other churches (1 Thess 5:27; Col 4:16) and that "relatively early there must have been collections of Pauline letters" (2.140). Thereafter he rehearses the familiar reasoning that the criterion for canonical authority was apostolic authorship, including close disciples of apostles (Mark, Luke), that is, the tradition that in effect had been established as deriving from the apostles by the New Testament Gospels and Paul in particular. Apostolicity was sufficient to exclude documents like *1 Clement* and *Barnabas* from the canon, and the established tradition represented by the Synoptic Gospels in particular was sufficient to exclude a document like the *Gospel of Peter*. But, again justifiably, Bultmann ends his discussion of New Testament canon by citing Ernst Käsemann's reminder that " '[t]he New Testament canon, as such, is not the foundation of the Church's unity. On the contrary the canon, as such . . . is the foundation of the multiplicity of confessions' " (2.142). It would be fairer, however, to put it not as a kind of "either-or" but as a "both-and," the unity and the diversity of the canon constituting the New Testament and its theology.

Motifs and Types

Section 56, "Motifs and Types," incites no special controversy—with one exception. Bultmann rightly points to the "special influence [that] emanates from the Pauline letters" (2.142). That includes, of course, the letters that Bultmann attributes to the Pauline school—2 Thessalonians, Colossians, Ephesians, more remotely the Pastorals, but also 1 Peter. And to the same influence could be attributed the writing of other epistles, 1 John, the letter form appended to Hebrews, perhaps the letters of Rev 2–3, and the later apocryphal letter to Laodicea, the novelistic correspondence with Seneca, and so on. But also the form used by Clement, Ignatius, and Polycarp attests the influence of Paul, who was obviously venerated by them.

"The tradition of the Hellenistic synagogue" gave much paraenetic material, notably the doctrine of the Two Ways, notable particularly in the *Didache* and *Barnabas*. Nor should it be forgotten that the Apocalypse of John (Revelation) attests the influence of the apocalyptic literature of Judaism—bearing in mind also that the Apocalypse of John is, like the two greatest apocalypses of Judaism (*4 Ezra* and *2 Baruch*), a response in at least some measure to the catastrophe of 70 C.E. and evidence of how much the first apocalypse (Daniel) was drawn on for inspiration.

"The influence of *Hellenistic popular philosophy*" (2.144, emphasis original) is passed over in three sentences. But when one considers the attention Bultmann pays to Gnostic influence, this is not a little surprising. A fuller discussion of the influence of Stoic thought on Paul would have been highly appropriate, and the possible influence of Platonic thought (through Philo?) would have merited at least some reference to or preferably some discussion in regard to Hebrews and John's Gospel. Unfortunately Bultmann had failed to appreciate the extent to which Greek/Hellenistic philosophy (not yet Gnosticism) had already influenced Jewish thought (notably Philo), his attention too much distracted by the quest for the myth of the Gnostic redeemer.

But it would not be Bultmann if he did not conclude this brief section (sec. 56) by claiming that "the tradition of Gnostic mythology which had already affected even Paul and John continued to have effect"—referring particularly to "the fact that the central motifs of christology, ecclesiology, and eschatology were worked out in Gnostic terminology—as we find them in Col., Eph., and the letters of Ignatius" (2.144). It is true that Bultmann thinks that it was only subsequently, in the apocryphal gospels and acts, that the "Gnostic fantasy was let loose" (2.144). But, sadly, his own preoccupation with the "Gnostic fantasy" distorted his own perspective.

Theology and Cosmology

In section 57, "Theology and Cosmology," Bultmann gives a summary of "the theological thoughts of the New Testament organized according to traditional *loci* in the form of a dogmatic" (2.145). He delays his study of "Christology and Soteriology," or at least of the latter, till chapter 7 (sec. 58) and starts with the more presuppositional or background ideas of God ("theology in its narrower sense") and of God in relation to the world.

He starts with the Jewish creedal understanding "that only one is God," rightly noting that the New Testament writers never saw it as necessary to argue that God exists. He notes also that "thoughts taken from the natural theology of Stoicism are put to service" (Bultmann did not share Barth's unwillingness to recognize Paul's indebtedness to the Stoa's "natural theology" in Rom 1:19-20), though he maintains that "natural theology is never treated by and for itself, as if in the interests of a theodicy." Here again, in his judgment, post-Pauline epistles never reach the depth of Paul's handling of the problem of suffering in 2 Corinthians (he could have added the not unrelated issue of God's apparent unfaithfulness to Israel in Rom 9–11); "in the main, the idea gets no further than the notion of the suffering Christ as an example to be followed (I Pet. 2:21, 3:18, 4:1; Heb. 12:1f.; Ign. *Eph.* 10:2f.; Pol. *Phil.* 8:1f.)" (2.146). All this is not unfair.

Once again, however, Bultmann's entrancement with (what he regarded as) the probability of Gnostic influence leads him to dismiss the influence of early Jewish apocalyptic and Wisdom/Logos specula-tion on New Testament Christology. So he misses the significance of glorious angel imagery evident in the portrayal of the exalted Christ in Revelation (particularly the vision of Rev 1:13-16). More important, in consequence, he misses also the significance of the fact that whereas the angel interpreter in Revelation forbids John to worship him (19:10; 22:8-9), as in other Jewish apocalypses, in contrast the glorious figure of the Son of Man, the Lamb, is also worshipped together with the one seated on the throne (5.11-14). Likewise the background to talk of the (divine) Word, which Philo in particular provides, is put to one side so far as the Johannine prologue is concerned, because John's usage is drawn "not from the philosophical but from the mythological tradition." Like the reflection on angelic beings, the "origin lies not in the genuine Old Testament-Jewish tradition but in that of Gnosti-cism" (2.146, 147).

None of this bodes well for Bultmann's discussion of late New Tes-tament Christology, since the assumption of dependence on Gnostic mythology seems to blind him to the tension between early Christian claims for Christ and their inherited conviction that God is one. This tension is integral to the developing Christology in the second half of the first century and well into the second century—we need instance only Paul's reference of YHWH texts to Jesus (as in Rom 10:9-13) or Ignatius' uninhibited reference to Christ as "our God" (as in *Eph.* inscr.) or the Apologists' Logos-Christology. Consequently, one of the most important and defining developments of earliest Christian theology (in what sense is Christ "God"?) is neglected.

Bultmann's handling of the figure of the devil is also somewhat puzzling. He assumes the figure to have originated "in the mytho-logical dualism of Iranian religion" but to have become "an inferior opponent of God" (2.147-48). In so arguing, he presumably deemed the portrayal of Job 1–2 as inadequate to explain most New Testa-ment talk of the devil. But this is an unnecessary assumption, since there was plenty of precedent in Jewish angelology and apocalyptic for earliest Christian references to Satan and for Revelation's visions of the beast.

Typical of Bultmann is the fact that the talk in Colossians and Ephesians of Christ's work in "reconciling all things" and "uniting all things" (Col 1:20; Eph 1:10) is distanced from any allusion to a concept of the "fall" of creation (cf. Rom 8:19-22), and the assertion is made without qualification that "[h]ere Biblical tradition has been forsaken and Gnostic mythology is at work" (2.149). For Bultmann, all talk of "elemental spirits" (Col 2:8, as in Gal 4:3, 9) and "principalities and powers" (Col 2:10, 5; Eph 1:21; 3:10; 6:12) immediately evokes the Gnostic systems of aeons emanating from the unknown God and indicates that "a mythological cosmology has been taken over" and that the author has taken over Gnostic concepts (2.150, 151). According to the same perspective, the idea of Christ's victory over the cosmic powers (as already in 1 Cor 2:6-8; 15:24-26) owes nothing to reflection on Ps 110:1 (as in 1 Cor 15:25!) but is "in keeping with Gnostic thinking" (2.153). Likewise, in Eph 4:8-10, the description of Christ's ascent and descent, drawing explicitly on Ps 68:18, far from being inspired by such poetic reflection on Moses' ascent of Sinai (somewhat like the second-century B.C.E. *Exagôgê* of Ezekiel the Tragedian), can only be explained as use of Gnostic terminology, "especially the myth of the Redeemer's descent to earth and his reascension" (2.151).

The giveaway comes when Bultmann makes so bold as to claim that Jewish apocalyptic thought betrays "a feeling about the world . . . which is no longer determined purely by the tradition of the Old Testament faith in God and creation" but by the Gnostic diagnosis of the human condition. "It is the feeling of people who feel themselves prisoners in a world pervaded with sinister powers—or if not prisoners, at least strangers in an enemy's land. Upon the soil of such a feeling it is quite understandable that the dualism and mythology of Gnosticism could take root and become influential" (2.152). Such a feeling, most probably, was precisely the root of the Gnostic worldview, the sense of alienation and longing for release from the trammels and incapacities of human existence. To be sure, apocalyptic dualism has some similarities to Gnostic dualism, but the former is primarily a soteriological dualism while the latter is inescapably a cosmological dualism. But it was not the dualism that appealed to Bultmann so much—indeed he believed that "the intellectual power of Paul" prevented such a full-blown Gnostic mythology from taking over Christian theology. Rather, it was the Gnostic "understanding of human existence" that appealed to Bultmann's existentialism and which he, regrettably, was all too ready to read into Jewish apocalyptic thought and to earliest Christian use of such imagery.

Summary and Conclusion

One moves on from Bultmann's treatment of Paul and John to his treatment of the "development of doctrine" with a rather heavy heart. For what made his treatment of Paul and John so stimulating, despite his assumption that they were both influenced by Gnostic motifs, was precisely that both rose above the Gnostic mythology and presented a gospel and a theology that still challenged twentieth-century thought. But in the subsequent "development of doctrine," the genius of Paul and John and the eschatological/existential challenge are largely lost to view, mired by the influence of Gnosticism. The comparison of the post-Pauline and second-century documents with Paul and John leaves these documents almost entirely with a negative sign against them—unsatisfactory. And yet in that period two great and identity-forming developments were taking place: the growing attempt to assert the deity of Christ and to do so without questioning the understanding of God as one, where that was a factor; and the relation of emerging Christianity to emerging (rabbinic) Judaism, including in effect competing claims to the same Scripture and to Israel's heritage. A discussion more sharply focused on these developments would/ should have brought out how crucial was the determining factor of a direct continuity with the tradition that had been given its enduring shape particularly in the Synoptic Gospels and the theological acumen of Paul (yes, Bultmann, you were right there). In other words, such a discussion would have been highly appropriate to a *Theology of the New Testament* in that it confirmed and demonstrated what a critical factor the chief writings of the New Testament were already in the second century, effectively exercising canonical authority well before their canonical status was formally recognized.

Chapter 10

CHRISTOLOGY AND SOTERIOLOGY

Larry W. Hurtado

In the section of Bultmann's *magnum opus* titled "The Development toward the Ancient Church" comes the chapter on "The Core of the Development," subtitled "Christology and Soteriology."[1] It is clear that Bultmann saw the development in question (placed in the late first and early/mid-second centuries C.E.) as largely a deviation or decline from what was for him the theological high point and standard represented in Paul and John. For Bultmann, of liberal Protestant background, "the Ancient Church" meant the early stages of what became the Catholic Church, with its emphasis on sacraments, institutional offices, creedal formulations tied to particular ancient philosophical categories, and a loss of spiritual fervency, and so development in that direction would never have his favor. Moreover, Bultmann approached this period and the texts that he addressed in this chapter with a tightly focused view of the theological criterion by which all should be judged, essentially his particular recasting of what he claimed was the heart of Pauline (and Johannine) theology. So his discussion in this chapter largely consists in a critique of some seventeen early Christian authors/texts as to how well they measure up to this criterion. But it is by no means clear that Bultmann's characterization of Pauline theology is adequate or even sufficiently faithful to Paul. In any case, his single-minded use of it as a criterion by which to judge all else seems arbitrary, reflects little effort to take account of the situations addressed in the various texts reviewed, and at least in some cases seriously fails to do justice to the theological content of the texts.

On the one hand, as is true of the larger work in which it appears, the chapter reflects the breadth of Bultmann's scholarly scope and the cohesiveness of his own theological outlook, with a survey of an impressive number of what became canonical or extracanonical Christian writings of the late first and/or early second century C.E. On the other hand, it also indicates the particularity of his preferred theological stance and his readiness to wield it as a criterion by which to judge sharply texts that he took as insufficiently in accord with it. So, before I do anything else, the first task here is to identify briefly that theological stance.[2]

The Theological Emphasis

We may begin by noting that, although the title of Bultmann's chapter 7 posits "Christology and Soteriology" as the theological focus, it is immediately clear that (as more fully reflected in earlier chapters and in his other writings) for Bultmann Christology was mainly subsumed in soteriology. Indeed, one wonders if Christology in itself mattered much to him at all. He devotes only the first three pages of the chapter to christological matters as such (2.155–57), rightly noting there the ubiquity and important place of the worship of Jesus in early Christian circles, briefly citing key christological titles, and offering a few paragraphs on how "Christ's person" was understood. Thereafter, the chapter is given over entirely to discussing how "salvation" is treated in the various texts surveyed. That is, although the New Testament rather consistently foregrounds Jesus as the definitive revelation of God's purposes, the essential content of the gospel message, and the key basis and pattern for salvation, Bultmann equally consistently focused on how early Christian texts present the proper *human response* to the proclamation of Jesus' significance, and for Bultmann the core of that proper human response was a particular conception of one's situation before God.

In the Epilogue (2.237–51), Bultmann considers "The Task and the Problems of New Testament Theology," emphasizing and justifying there his focus on the "new self-understanding" that he saw depicted in the New Testament, "an existential understanding of myself which is at one with and inseparable from my understanding of God and the world" (2.239). Although he then asks whether one can "concentrate upon faith without seeing at the same time that toward which it is directed, its object and content," it is clear that for Bultmann New Testament theology is essentially a "self-understanding" formed in response to "the proclamation of Jesus Christ" in the kerygma (2.239). To be sure, Bultmann recognized that for the earliest Christians Jesus was "a decisive event," his death, resurrection/exaltation, and future appearance as eschatological judge and savior central in their proclamation.[3] But Bultmann was concerned more with how the New Testament refers to the life of faith, how believers see themselves in light of the gospel message of divine grace.

One reason for Bultmann's preferred focus was that the New Testament references to Jesus' redemptive death, his resurrection and exaltation to heavenly glory, and the hope of Jesus' future return all involved expressions in what Bultmann regarded as mythological language that could not readily be meaningful for modern people.[4] In Bultmann's view, the eschatological claims in these expressions were particularly a problem. For example, how could moderns continue to expect Jesus' return in glory after so many centuries?[5] So, concerned to promote an engagement with the Christian gospel in a form that could be made meaningful to moderns, Bultmann directed attention away from these christological statements and onto how the New Testament presented their consequences for believers. That is, he concentrated on how the New Testament writings depicted the life situation of those who choose to live in response to the proclaimed significance of God's acts in Jesus.

In the New Testament, Jesus' death and resurrection/exaltation are typically presented as themselves eschatological events and as inaugurating a new stage in God's redemptive program. That redemptive program is to find consummation in Jesus' future return and its consequences for believers (resurrection and eternal life). Crucially, in Bultmann's view, the present time of believers is, thus, one of living between the decisive inception of eschatological salvation (in Jesus' death/resurrection) and that future completion. So, for Bultmann (especially in the chapter we consider here), in assessing early Christian texts the decisive question was "how the *relation between salvation's present reality and its futurity is conceived*" (2.161, emphasis original). In the New Testament texts that he approved, Bultmann found an emphasis that the present is already affected by the redemptive power that is to be consummated in the future hope of resurrection and eternal life. In these texts, though believers remain in a world of mortality and sin, they are offered not only forgiveness from past sins, but also "emancipation from the power of sin" (2.161). That is, believers are depicted as in a new situation and as having a new sense of themselves as forgiven and enabled to respond with a new freedom (including freedom from striving for righteousness) and a new empowerment. Yet the eschatological hope has not been fully realized, and they continue to inhabit a world of frailty, the real danger of sin, and the continuing need for divine grace.

In short, Bultmann emphasized that in those New Testament writings that he thought most adequately express matters (essentially, those by Paul and John), the believer lives "between the times" in an interim period of "paradoxical character . . . in which the powers of the new aeon are already at work," and yet mortality and sin remain realities as well.[6] So the believer must heed the "imperative" of God's behavioral demands but does so in response to God's prior "indicative," that is, the redemptive revelation and the new spiritual power conveyed through Jesus' death and resurrection and made available in the proclamation of the gospel.[7]

As noted already, for Bultmann, however, the New Testament eschatological framework and basis for the view of Christian existence as "between the times" was "mythological," no longer credible, and so his entire theological program could be seen as a kind of rescue operation aimed at distilling out of the deeply mythological outlook of the New Testament a faith stance that could be seriously considered and embraced by moderns. Essentially, Bultmann urged that what he saw as the proper faith stance of existence under God's grace, regarding oneself as forgiven, somehow freed from guilt and one's past proclivities and somehow opened to and enabled for new life possibilities, could be embraced by moderns. Simply in response to the clear proclamation of this faith stance, so it seems, Bultmann believed that people could still choose to see themselves with both humility and with new possibilities, as fallible but not confined by their shortcomings. In short, it appears that Bultmann thought that this life stance could be made sufficiently cogent and attractive on its own to secure this response, even if the original bases (especially the resurrection of Jesus) were mythological, and so no longer meaningful as stated in the New Testament.

In the chapter we consider here, Bultmann used this faith stance as a criterion by which to assess the developments reflected in the texts that he considers. In this survey of early Christian texts, Bultmann insisted that this paradoxical situation of the believer is inadequately represented in those texts that emphasize the "imperative," the divine demand for obedience, without grounding it adequately in the proclamation of the divine "indicative," the declaration of God's redemptive initiative and empowering grace. This, he urged, reduces Christian existence to ethical striving, with the attendant dangers of self-condemnation for failure and/or a self-congratulatory works righteousness that boasts in merely observing a set of commandments in the strength of one's own will. As indicated earlier, I find Bultmann's discussion problematic. I have some reservations about his theological program, and I think that his discussion of early Christian texts is tendentious and seriously flawed.

Bultmann's Theological Program: Some Critical Observations

There have been numerous critical comments in response to Bultmann's theological and hermeneutical program, and I claim no great originality or completeness in those that I pose here. Instead, I simply underscore in what follows a few objections that I believe are particularly relevant.

My first criticism is directed at Bultmann's effort to distill the essence of a Christian faith stance from Paul's letters. Bultmann's treatment of Paul is the subject of another contribution to the present volume, and so I shall be brief.[8] My main comment is that Bultmann's reading of Paul seems too much shaped by his German Lutheran theological heritage (at least, too much for anyone not a fellow German Lutheran) and inadequately grounded in Paul's historical setting.[9] Bultmann devotes a mere three pages to "The Historical Situation of Paul" (1.187–89) and in that brief discussion seems to me to make more than one crucial error. A prime example is Bultmann's claim that Paul was "won to the Christian faith by the kerygma of the Hellenistic Church" (1.187; to which Bultmann devoted 120 pages, 1.63–183), which Bultmann distinguished sharply from the "Earliest [Jerusalem] Church."[10] In fact, however, Paul says that his zealous efforts against "the church of God" (Gal 1:13-14) were aroused by and initially directed against "the churches of Judaea" (Gal 1:22-23) and elsewhere insists that he and Jerusalem Christian leaders preached the same gospel (1 Cor 15:1-11).

Likewise dubious is Bultmann's characterization of the cognitive focus of Paul's religious reorientation as a recognition that "the Torah was called into question by the Hellenistic mission" (toward Gentiles?) and that his "Jewish striving after righteousness by fulfilling the works of the Law" stood under God's condemnation (1.187), which was directed also against "all human accomplishment and boasting" (1.188). In fact, Paul's own references to his reorientation emphasize the christological content of the experience, a divine revelation of God's Son (Gal 1:15-16). Similarly, in Phil 3:4-11, Paul's contrast is not between his "previous understanding of himself" and some new sense of freedom from "human accomplishment and boasting" but, instead, between his former Pharisaic reliance on Torah as the definitive revelation of divine purposes and the subsequent recognition that Christ is. Paul's passion in this passage is not over some new "self-understanding" as stated in Bultmann's somewhat abstract and quaintly Lutheran terms but instead is directed toward a deep relational knowledge of Christ, for whom Paul was willing to forgo all else.

It is another failing in Bultmann's discussion of Paul that he gives inadequate attention to the Gentile mission, which was the crucial context in which Paul's theological emphases were developed. To cite one important matter, Paul's critique of Torah seems to me heavily prompted by the need to defend the legitimacy of his Gentile converts and his opposition to those Jewish Christians who thought that Gentiles had to complete their conversion by taking on full Torah observance in addition to faith in Christ. So, for example, in addressing the Galatian churches where this issue had surfaced, he hammers away on the surpassing significance of Christ and the relativized role of Torah. But in letters to churches where agitators for Torah observance apparently had not (or not yet) been active, for example, 1 Thessalonians and 1 Corinthians, we do not find Christ and Torah counterposed in such a sharp manner or an emphasis on "justification" and faith.

To be sure, Paul's reasoning in Galatians and Romans about Christ and Torah and about faith in Christ is important and certainly is to be engaged theologically. But Bultmann's efforts to do so rest heavily on

Protestant (especially Lutheran) theological tradition, in which Paul's situational critique of Torah was taken out of context and refashioned into a timeless and generalized critique of human "self-righteousness." Bultmann developed this further in an existentialist direction without adequately considering the theological bases on which he worked. It is ironic that Bultmann, so heavily shaped by the historical emphases of Bousset and others in the *religionsgeschichtliche Schule*, seems to have been so ready to abstract Paul's statements from their historical setting, refashioning them (somewhat simplistically, in my view) into a modernizing theological program shaped heavily by insufficiently examined theological traditions and his own philosophical prefer-ences. The result was a dubious distillation of the putative essence of Pauline theology, in which Paul's consistent and robust emphasis on the significance of Jesus Christ as the supreme expression of God's purposes and the core of believers' devotional life was replaced with a rather more bland focus on believers' "self-understanding."

One could also complain about the highly individualistic emphasis in Bultmann's theology. One finds many references to the faith stance of individuals, as they individually ponder themselves and their life orientation. But there is scant treatment of the corporate nature of Christian life, the mutual edification, forgiveness, and encouragement so much urged in the New Testament, and the emphasis that God's purpose for individuals is to make of them a new humanity to be exhibited provisionally in the *agape* relationships that are to character-ize the *ekklēsia*. Indeed, I wonder if Bultmann's apparent lack of inter-est in the corporate dimension of Christian life dulled in some ways his appreciation of some of the early Christian texts that he found theologically deficient.

I register one further general criticism that has to do with Bult-mann's way of engaging in what he called "*content-criticism* (Sachkri-tik) such as Luther, for example, exercised toward the Epistle of James and the Revelation of John" (2.238). Bultmann conducted this "content-criticism" probably most sharply in the chapter that I focus on here, where he examined critically various early Christian texts as to how faithfully he thought they maintain the faith stance that he ascribed to Paul (and John).

Surely all serious students of the New Testament are well aware that it is a collection of texts among which there are notable differences in emphasis. Indeed, in some cases, these differences among texts may well reflect differences among the early Christian circles from which they derive. It is, therefore, entirely appropriate (indeed, even necessary) that a serious study of New Testament theology should note differences and avoid a simplistic homogenizing or harmonizing of them. In some cases, these differences may be such as to raise questions about how the respective texts came together to form part of the New Testament canon. One might well consider, for example, how the Epistle of James came to be included in the New Testament along with the Pauline epistles.

But Bultmann went much farther. He did not simply note differences among early Christian texts and consider what might have prompted them; he used his claimed core of Pauline theology about Christian existence "between the times" as the criterion by which to judge the texts. The sole question in Bultmann's analysis of these texts was how well they reflected this theological emphasis. If one judges it sufficient simply to cite Luther as one's authorizing precedent (as it may have been in Bultmann's German setting), then perhaps one can simply select Paul as the "canon within the canon," against which the rest of the New Testament can be assessed. And, then, if one is sufficiently confident in positing the specific core of Paul's theology, one could follow Bultmann's procedure. But, apart from Luther's precedent, what theological basis is there for making Paul or any particular New Testament author/text play such a role? However much Paul's letters have been influential in Christian theology down the centuries (and they have been) and however much they may strike us as particularly profound and/or moving in their articulation of Christian faith, one needs to offer a cogent *theological* basis for assessing every other text by how clearly or completely it affirms Christian faith in the same manner as Paul.

From its earliest observable stages, the formation of what became the New Testament canon seems to have involved the progressive incorporation of a certain variety of texts and emphases. The preference for a fourfold Gospel (over against Marcion's exclusive acceptance of Luke and Tatian's harmonizing *Diatessaron*) illustrates this readiness to affirm and draw upon a certain diversity, in the case of the Gospels, various "renditions" of the Jesus story. Our earliest reference to Christian texts being treated as Scripture is likely in 2 Pet 3:15-16, the Petrine voice here portrayed as affirming Paul's letters, which in itself represents an interesting effort to treat differences positively. Then, across the second and then third centuries C.E., we see further a growing variety of texts coming to be treated as Christian Scriptures (e.g., 1 John, 1 Peter, and others).[11]

I contend that this deliberate incorporation of diversity in the New Testament canon reflects an early Christian view that there is something to be gained from them all and that *for theological purposes* they are best read in conversation with one another, their various emphases preserved and their diversity seen as enriching the scriptural resources for theology and Christian life. One certainly should allow each text to have its own voice, and I repeat that it is fully appropriate to note where texts/authors exhibit differences of emphases or even seem to go in different directions. In this sense, "content-criticism" is both legitimate and even necessary. But Bultmann's heavy privileging of Paul (or, more accurately, Bultmann's privileging of his own characterization of Paul's view of Christian existence) seems to me questionable, or at least requires more justification than Bultmann provided. In any case, one can practice "content-criticism" in which the differences among texts are noted and taken seriously without making one author/text the criterion by which to judge the rest.

Moreover, any assessment of the theology reflected in a given text should surely also involve an attempt to take account of the historical circumstances and the particular issues or setting addressed in the text. As I have noted already, even among Paul's undisputed letters there are some that do not project the same emphases on "justification" and the contrast between "faith" and Torah observance that we find in Galatians and Romans. Clearly, Paul's emphases varied and were likely shaped in each letter by the particular issues and situations that he intended to address. Just as it is important to take account of the occasion and concerns prompting Paul's individual letters, so it is surely as important to do so in the analysis of the sort of variety of texts and authors surveyed by Bultmann. But it seems to me that he did not do this and instead either praised or condemned texts simply on the basis of whether they seemed to him to affirm a recognizably Pauline emphasis that is in fact not even consistently expressed in the same terms across Paul's own several letters.

Neglected Riches

Bultmann's approach to the many early Christian texts surveyed in his chapter on "Christology and Soteriology" not only represents a somewhat arbitrary way of proceeding, however; it also results in a serious neglect of, or a failure to appreciate, the significant contributions that at least some of these texts can make to New Testament theology. In light of the limited scope for this discussion here, I focus on two selected texts that particularly reflect the riches neglected in Bultmann's treatment. It is difficult to know whether his method prevented him from recognizing adequately the contributions that these texts (and others) can make to our appreciation of early christological emphases or if his own prior theological decision to focus on the human existential situation simply made less relevant for him the christological material in these texts. In any case, among the writings that Bultmann surveyed and found wanting there are some significant expressions of the rich and powerful Jesus devotion that characterized earliest Christianity.[12]

Hebrews

As an example, consider the Epistle to the Hebrews, Bultmann's discussion of which (2.166–68) is illustrative of the problems in his approach.[13] Though Hebrews bears an epistolary ending (13:22-25), the author describes this writing as a "word of exhortation," and it is often seen today as a sermon or homily, a treatise reflecting rhetorical skill.[14] Various passages convey the author's concern that intended readers, who have suffered abuse for their Christian profession (10:32-35), may now be tempted to defect and/or may be in danger of waning in their commitment. So, the author urges them to maintain their profession in the hope of divine reward for their faithfulness (e.g., 10:36-39; 12:7-13). This concern rather clearly prompts the author's combination of warnings (e.g., 2:1-4; 3:12–4:11; 10:26-31) and exhortations to persevere (e.g., 4:14-16; 6:9-12; 10:19-25; 12:1-13; 13:13-16).

Bultmann complained that in Hebrews the "faith" by which "my righteous one" should live (10:38) is simply "endurance" and "can hardly be defined in any other way than simply belief in God" (2.167). But, for one thing, this fails to take account of the situation that the author of Hebrews engages, in which endurance in the face of opposition and other forces is what is required of the believers addressed. In such a situation, surely what is called for is exhortation to a believing and obedient response and an acceptance by believers of their responsibility before God. But the author does not really portray this simply as sheer unaided effort. Believers are made partakers of "the heavenly gift," are given the Holy Spirit and a foretaste of "the powers of the world to come" (6:4-5), and their perseverance is further energized by the specific "hope" that is "a sure and steadfast anchor of the soul" and based in Jesus' transcendent and eternal efficacy (6:19-20).

Moreover, it should be abundantly clear that in Hebrews the faith called for is quite specifically based on the singular significance of Jesus, who is variously presented as the unique Son who outranks angels and Moses (1:1–3:6), the uniquely valid high priest (esp. 7:1–9:28) whose sacrificial ministry and intercession surpasses and renders obsolete all that went before him (e.g., 9:23–10:10), and the "pioneer and perfecter of our faith" who serves as both exemplar and enabler of the perseverance that the author urges (e.g., 12:1-3, 18-24; 13:8-16). In Hebrews, as Attridge observed, "Jesus makes possible for the addressees their life of faith. It is the function of the christological exposition of the text to indicate how this is so and thereby to ground the exhortation to faith and with it the whole paraenetic program of the text."[15] As I wrote in a previous discussion of Hebrews, "Repeatedly the discussion moves from setting forth christological claims to underscoring their behavioural consequences."[16] The faith urged in Hebrews is most certainly not "simply belief in God"!

Indeed, Hebrews is widely (and justifiably) regarded as one of the most impressive and distinctive presentations of christological claims in the New Testament, which comprise "[t]he creative heart of the doctrinal reflection of Hebrews."[17] From the initial, elegantly constructed first sentence (which comprises the whole of 1:1-4) onward, Hebrews reflects and affirms a remarkable double emphasis on Jesus' uniquely exalted and divine status and his genuine sharing in human nature. In Jesus, God has now superseded all previous revelations attested in the Old Testament Scriptures (1:1-2). As both the agent of God's creation of the world and the unique bearer of God's glory and being (*hypostasis*), and having made final purification for sins, Jesus is now uniquely exalted (1:3-4). In a seven-link catena of biblical citations, the author lyrically declares Jesus' superiority to angels (1:5-14), brandishing several christological titles, among them some of the boldest that we find in the New Testament: "Son" (vv. 5, 8), "O God" (v. 8), and "Lord" (v. 10).

Thereafter, just as robustly the author turns to emphasize Jesus' genuine participation in human existence (2:5-18), which makes him a fitting redeemer of those who share "flesh and blood" (2:14). Following on from the presentation of Jesus' exalted nature and status in Heb 1, we have in Heb 2 forthright references to Jesus' sufferings and death (2:9) and how these things serve further to make him all the more appropriate and efficacious as the priest on behalf of believers (2:10, 18). This makes somewhat puzzling Bultmann's claim that in Hebrews and the other texts he surveyed in his chapter 7 "reflections about the relation between the divine and human nature in Christ" are "remote" (2.157). To be sure, we do not have the intricacies of christological debate of the fourth and fifth centuries, but it is curiously myopic to miss the rather clear dual emphasis of Hebrews on Jesus' divine status and full partaking in human existence. This surely constitutes "an important early expression of a duality about Jesus" that was developed later in the "two-natures" debates.[18]

But Hebrews is likely best known for its elaboration of Jesus as the uniquely qualified priest who has offered "once for all" the efficacious sacrifice that secures redemption for believers and now is also their heavenly intercessor. In Rom 8:34, Paul briefly reflects what was already then a belief shared among Christian circles that the risen/exalted Jesus "at the right hand of God" there intercedes for believers. So the author of Hebrews drew upon what was an element of Christian tradition, but he developed it more programmatically than in any other early Christian text. In what may have been a new wrinkle, however, Hebrews links Jesus' priesthood with the Old Testament figure Melchizedek as part of an argument for Jesus' priestly superiority to the Aaronic priesthood. The prompt for this link is almost certainly Ps 110, the single most frequently cited and alluded to Old Testament passage in the New Testament.[19] There was interest in Melchizedek in some ancient Jewish circles as well, but in Hebrews the unique association of Jesus with Melchizedek is driven and shaped by the author's convictions about Jesus.[20] The author, however, did not come to think of Jesus as superior after linking him with Melchizedek. Instead, based on convictions that erupted amazingly early after Jesus' execution about the redemptive efficacy of Jesus' death and about Jesus' resurrection as involving his exaltation to heavenly glory and his intercession there for all who call upon him, the author either hit upon (or developed) the midrashic connection with Melchizedek in Ps 100:4.

Simply put, in this, as in the larger fabric of exposition and exhortation in Hebrews, christological convictions are foundational and determinative. Although perhaps drawing upon traditional acclamations, it is no glib line in 13:8 that "Jesus Christ is the same yesterday and today and forever."[21] Just as the author opens his treatise in 1:1-14 with one of the most sustained declarations of Jesus' exalted status in the New Testament, so in the concluding portion he makes Jesus the one with whom and by whom believers are to identify themselves, their perseverance inspired and modeled by Jesus, and Jesus the one through whom their worship of God is to be distinctively shaped (13:8-15).

In light of the remarkable christological thought in Hebrews and its role in the author's view of Christian life, I find Bultmann's cursory treatment of the writing curiously deficient, as if tone-deaf to the powerful notes of its exposition.

Revelation

I turn now to another writing that Bultmann seems to have underestimated (2.173–75) and one that likewise in fact expresses a noteworthy christological stance, Revelation. Characterizing Revelation as "a weakly Christianized Judaism," Bultmann alleged that in this text Christ's significance is little more than "that he gives the passionate eschatological hope a certainty which the Jewish apocalyptists lack."[22] Bultmann complained that "the peculiar 'between-ness' of Christian existence has not been grasped" in Revelation, because "the author does not reflect about the past which in Christ has been brought to its end and out of which believers have been transplanted into a new beginning" (2.175). But, once again, it seems to me that Bultmann's monocular approach, his judging everything by his own formulation of Christian existence derived from his somewhat selective and ahistorical reading of Paul, and not really engaging the historical concerns reflected in Revelation, led to a serious failure to appreciate this remarkable early Christian writing.

In the case of Revelation, we are able to identify the real author (a certain early Christian prophet named "John") and the actual initial readers/recipients (the seven churches addressed in Rev 2–3), which makes the text particularly valuable for historical study of early Christianity and invites us also to take adequate account of the present and future situations of believers projected by the author.[23] As I noted in an earlier publication, the primary purpose of the author was not to engage in doctrinal development or to offer reflections on the nature of Christian existence but above all "to urge perseverance in faith among the intended readers," as explicitly reflected in the exhortations to the seven churches and captured directly in the appeals for "the endurance of the saints" in 13:10 and 14:12. Nevertheless, Revelation is also "a noteworthy statement of beliefs about Jesus," comprising one of the most exalted christological views in the New Testament.[24] And if, as I hold, what makes an author/text identifiably Christian is first and foremost an affirmation of the unique significance of Jesus, then Revelation is by no means "weakly Christianized."

From the opening words, which probably functioned as the original title of the work, "The Revelation of Jesus Christ," onward, it is clear that Revelation is centered on Jesus. Another early and remarkable indication of the high status of Jesus for the author is the doxology directed to him in 1:5-6, all the more significant as it is a special form of praise more customarily reserved for God elsewhere in the New Testament (e.g., Gal 1:5; Rom 11:36; Eph 3:21; Phil 4:20; 1 Tim 1:17). The initial vision of the glorified/glorious Jesus in 1:12-19, followed by prophetic oracles issued by Jesus to seven churches in 2:1–3:22, combine further to indicate the commanding place of Jesus for the author. But perhaps a still more astonishing passage comes in 5:1-14, where the author depicts a heavenly scene of divine sovereignty and worship, God represented as seated on the heavenly throne, and then with God "the Lamb," who is obviously Jesus.[25] The climax of the scene is the inclusion of the Lamb with God as recipient of praise and worship in 5:9-14, initially offered by the heavenly "elders," then joined by angels and then "every creature in heaven and on earth and under the earth." As Richard Bauckham noted several decades ago, this inclusion of Jesus as rightful corecipient of heavenly worship is all the more remarkable in Revelation, because the author emphatically rejects the worship of other beings as idolatry, this concern about

God's uniqueness reflected also in the scenes where the author is warned against worshiping God's angel sent to him (19:10; 22:8-9).[26]

The elect are consistently described as having been redeemed through Jesus' redemptive death. In 1:5-6, Jesus is praised as the one who "loved us and freed us from our sins by his blood, and made us to be a kingdom, priests to his God and Father." Their names stand in Jesus' "book of life" (e.g., 3:5; 21:27). In the vision scene in 7:9-17, they are portrayed in robes washed and made "white in the blood of the Lamb" (v. 14). The name of the Lamb and "his Father" is written on their foreheads (14:1), and they "follow the Lamb wherever he goes" (14:4).[27] Clearly, for this author Jesus is crucial, which makes it dubious for Bultmann to treat the text as essentially sub-Christian.

Granted, as is the case in Hebrews, Revelation does not explicitly articulate Christian existence in the terms that Bultmann required. But, once again, this seems to be a red herring. Revelation is not a discourse on the nature of Christian existence but instead an urgent summons to live and die for Jesus. Most of Revelation by far is given over to the author's depictions of what the future holds for the earth and its inhabitants, with warnings about "the beast" and his demands and about the divine judgments that will be poured out upon those who give their allegiance to "the beast" and his evil and oppressive regime. In light of the looming threats to believers foreseen by the author, he warns his intended readers to prepare themselves to suffer for their faith and urges them to remain steadfast and endure it all in the sure hope of God's vindication. In short, the author's sense of urgency moves him to emphasize strong admonitions to believers to give their all.

So if we treat the text with a reasonable sympathy for the situation addressed (contra Bultmann, 2.174–75), it would be unfair to impute to the author a deficient sense of standing under divine mercy, as if everything depended simply on believers' own efforts. The author directs urgent exhortations to his readers because, having been redeemed and made acceptable to God by Christ, they are now facing a situation in which they must follow Christ and endure whatever may come in the confidence that God will remember them. Simply put, the situation envisioned by the author required this emphasis. He was not theologically deficient but directly focused on what would be necessary in his intended readers.

Moreover, in Revelation we have an early Christian writing that projects a particularly robust Christology. Indeed, along with the Epistle to the Hebrews, Revelation reflects one of the boldest, "highest" christological stances that we have in the New Testament. Furthermore, for this author Jesus is also central in his understanding of soteriology. The salvation of believers rests on Jesus' redemptive suffering, and through him they acquire a new relationship with, and status before, God as royal priests. They comprise "the bride, the wife of the Lamb," and "the holy city Jerusalem" from God that will enjoy the direct presence of God and the Lamb (21:9-27). That the author does not deploy the particular articulation of Christian existence sought by Bultmann is no basis for treating the text as somehow inferior. That Bultmann did so tells us more about him than about the Christian authenticity and worth of Revelation.

Conclusion

It would require more space than available here to reconsider similarly all the other early Christian writings so peremptorily surveyed by Bultmann, but I hope to have illustrated through this brief consideration of two of them why I think Bultmann's discussion in chapter 7 of his *Theology of the New Testament* is inadequate and misleading. To be sure, the writings in question do not all project the same outlook or emphases, and some of them may well be subject to theological critique as reflecting a deficiency in this or that matter. But in engaging early Christian writings, it is not appropriate to wield one particular emphasis as an iron rule by which to assess them. That would be a curiously sectarian approach. Instead, we can judge early Christian writings adequately only if (with some sympathy) we take account of the situation addressed and the likely reasons that the various authors chose to underscore what they did. We should not read too much into what was not said, unless the situation addressed seems to have called for something lacking.

Moreover, if any criterion is used to judge early Christian writings, it is far more appropriate to focus on how they project the significance of Jesus. Devotion to Jesus (however diversified it was) is surely the key distinguishing feature of earliest Christian circles and was far more significant and crucial than any particular way of framing Christian existence. In any "New Testament theology," therefore, Christology is more appropriately the crucial matter. Indeed, for many early Christians, Jesus was not only the basis of redemption but also the pattern for the life of believers and the embodiment and guarantee for all their own hopes for the consummation of that redemption.

Chapter 11

THE PROBLEM OF CHRISTIAN LIVING

Wayne A. Meeks

Anyone who has read the whole of Bultmann's *Theology of the New Testament* is likely to feel, upon arriving at the concluding part, a letdown.[1] After the excitement and passion expressed in Bultmann's account of Pauline and Johannine theology, the "Development toward the Ancient Church" is anticlimactic. One senses from the author an air of disappointment: he has been let down by history itself, particularly the history of the church. That is especially true in the final chapter, "The Problem of Christian Living." Here we learn that, for the church of the second century, those transformative paradoxes that united the indicative of God's grace with the imperative of responsive life, the "already" of the new age with the "not yet" of promised fulfillment, have faded. The eschatological community loses its nerve and lapses into institutional self-preservation and legalism.

For anyone who hopes that Christians might find in the New Testament impetus and guidance for the living of a moral life—*eine christliche Lebensführung*—in our world, Bultmann's unflinching assessment is not encouraging, to say the least. This is especially true for those who hope that the church might speak and act prophetically to affect the social, political, and economic forms and forces that shape our common life. From the very first chapter of the *Theology of the New Testament* Bultmann is at pains to disabuse us of the hope (so central to the nineteenth-century Protestant liberalism against which he was reacting) that either from the example and message of Jesus or from the kerygma of the earliest community of his followers one might find directives either for "the molding of human society" or for "the formation of character" (1.19). Though the image of Jesus as prophet is central to the description of his mission here—in many ways Bultmann's conception of the prophet resembles that of the nearly contemporary work by Martin Buber[2]—Bultmann's Jesus "does not, as the prophets did, raise the demand for justice and right," because Israel under Roman occupation no longer has any significant national life (1.12–13). Here in the final chapter, we find that we can also expect no help from the church as it has evolved by the end of the second century. The scope of its moral concern is mostly domestic, because the Christian appeal is limited by and large to "people in humble circumstances or at least to the lower middle class" (2.227). Matters of politics are beyond their ken. "They also lack any regard for the problems and tasks of social life" (2.227). "How far the Christian Church was from thinking of remolding the world, of adopting an economic or political program, is indicated by its attitude toward property, slavery and the state" (2.229), namely, effectively hands-off and conservative. That is true even of the Apocalypse, for while it may urge hatred for the Roman state, it contains no notion that the Christians ought to be responsible for improving the state or managing it more justly. For people of their status "such responsibility was out of the question" (2.231).

Our disappointment is the greater because our expectations are so high. Throughout the *Theology*, Bultmann wrestles with the question of how an "authentic" ethic can be formulated in accord with his existentialist hermeneutic. Throughout, even at the distance of half a century and the transformation of our discipline, one is awed by Bultmann's command of details, in the primary texts and in the scholarly literature, and by the brilliance of his synthesis—even in those cases where we must now say that he was surely wrong. And the heart of his effort, in this capstone of his life's work, is aptly signaled in the Epilogue, a magisterial, concise analysis of the development of "the science of New Testament theology." He assesses the accomplishments of each of his predecessors by one touchstone: Adolf Schlatter's famous insistence that "the act of thinking" (*Denkakt*) must not be separated from "the act of living" (*Lebensakt*). To prevent that separation, he urges, it is essential to find the right relationship between *historical reconstruction* and *interpretation*. For Bultmann, "reconstruction stands in the service of the interpretation of the New Testament writings under the presupposition that they have something to say to the present" (2.251). We are thus presented with two sets of questions: (1) Does the existentialist interpretation, centering on the lonely, decision-making, individual self, really succeed in keeping *Denkakt* and *Lebensakt* together—or, to put it another way, is "authenticity" (*Eigentlichkeit*) the best model for ethics? (2) Has Bultmann—or have we—discovered an adequate model for using the New Testament as authority in moral formation and practice?

Authenticity or Responsibility?

Our first question is outlined succinctly and poignantly in an essay that Bultmann published in 1955, just two years after the appearance of the final fascicle of the *Theology of the New Testament*, on "The Forms of Human Community."[3] Here he reacts directly to the perversion of human community that he had witnessed close at hand in the Nazi program and, more distantly, in Stalinism. He distinguishes "four forms of human community": that "transmitted by nature," that "which has developed in history," that "which has been founded by the intellectual world of art and science," and that "founded by religion."[4] It is the first of these, which includes marriage, family, race, and people, in which National Socialism, with its ad nauseam talk of *Blut und Boden*, most conspicuously destroys "the specifically human element." As his highest example of the natural community, Bultmann chooses erotic love, of which there is "perhaps no more magnificent example" than Shakespeare's *Romeo and Juliet*. In this most intimate of communities we see, according to Bultmann, that "the will to selfhood is the presupposition for genuine communion; for only those who are persons, that is, each a self can join in true communion."[5]

Here we find stated in its shortest compass that passion for authenticity that is at the heart of Bultmann's existential definition of faith—and his insistence on the priority of the individual decision to any consideration of community. The implied paradox is stated explicitly when Bultmann comes to discuss the fourth form of community, that created by religion: "Community with God, which is intended to be the basis of true human community, first of all tears man out of every human community and places him in a radical *loneliness* before God."[6] This radical loneliness seems all the more poignant when we read the penultimate paragraph of this essay, in which he avows "that faith brings to light the hidden community of all men." Indeed, he envisions a community that would embrace all those represented by the diverse company of poets and philosophers he has cited throughout the essay, "all of them—nihilists, atheists, mystics and philosophers— . . . linked together in a pilgrimage, in the search for God."[7]

Historical Context

While we must obviously avoid oversimplifying the intellectual influences at work in Bultmann's resolute focus on the individual's quest for authentic existence, I think we cannot fail to see behind the statement just quoted, of the impossible possibility of real community, the reflected pathos of his personal engagement in the world crisis of the early twentieth century. There are two factors at work. Narrowly, within the subculture of Protestant theology, Bultmann's position was formed by the movement we usually call Dialectical Theology. That movement reacted against nineteenth-century progressivism, with its "subtle secularism," its idealist notion of social and cultural progress that denies "the *skandalon* of the Word of God which is the absolute judgment on any human activity."[8] Dialectical Theology can be seen as a reflection of and a response to a larger disillusionment that pervaded European thought in the aftermath of World War I. In theological circles, that disillusionment neatly coincided with a new historical understanding of eschatology, a topic central to Bultmann's reconstrual of the theological task and a topic to which we must return further below.

More broadly, the 1955 essay reminds us of Bultmann's horror at the manipulation of mass movements by National Socialism, the submersion of the individual into *das Volk*. Bultmann was an early member of the Confessing Church, the countermovement organized in 1934 in opposition to the German Christians controlled by an Imperial Ministry of the Nazi government, and he spoke out strongly against the "Aryan Paragraph," legislation designed to remove persons tainted with any Jewish lineage from all government positions, including ordained clergy.[9] His own brother died in a concentration camp. In a society intent on mobilizing every segment of German society toward the realization of its racially based imperial destiny, how could one preserve, not merely one's life, but any sense of personal integrity?

How could one continue to be fully a person, a *self*, if not by some Kierkegaardian leap of faith that lifted one out of that society gone mad? In this respect we may place Bultmann among that uncounted number of European intellectuals of his time who, if unable physically to escape, performed what some of them called, using Kafka's phrase, an "interior emigration."

We are thus able to imagine, however distantly, the tragic context in which Bultmann finds it necessary to speak of faith as a lonely and, at least initially, *isolating* act. Nevertheless, I think we must agree with Heinz-Horst Schrey that by focusing exclusively on "the I-Thou relationship and decision" as definitive for "man as a historic being," Bultmann empties both human "historicity" and ethics of concrete realization. The exclusive focus on "the new self-understanding as the core of the ethical" fails to do justice "to the ethical problem of how the Christian is to live in historical time," that is, in community and in institutions. "Authenticity" is not an adequate model for life in community.[10] If we are to work toward a more adequate model, we must begin by addressing the twin paradoxes that frame Bultmann's whole discussion of ethics: the paradoxical relation between "the indicative" and "the imperative" (the subject of the whole of sec. 59), which, in turn, centers on "the Christian self-understanding" caught in "the paradoxical situation of the Church: as the eschatological entity . . . [which] yet must lead its life within the old world between 'no longer' and 'not yet' " (2.203).

Demythologizing Eschatology

Bultmann's statement of the second and more basic of these paradoxes brings us back to his involvement with the Dialectical Theology discussion, and it depends upon a very specific understanding of eschatology. As a student at Marburg, he became close to Johannes Weiss. Weiss was the teacher who encouraged Bultmann to go on to doctoral studies and who later suggested the topic for his dissertation.[11] Weiss came to Marburg from Göttingen, where he had been a prominent member of a group of young students and untenured instructors in the 1890s who identified themselves as the "History of Religions School." And it had been Weiss who used his emerging understanding of apocalyptic eschatology to undermine one of the central pillars of the liberal theology that had drawn him and his fellow students to Göttingen.

The best-known proponent of that liberal theology was Albrecht Ritschl. Weiss and his friends had come to Göttingen especially to study with him. At the heart of Ritschl's theology was the concept of "the kingdom of God," which he took to be the center of Jesus' own message. As Ritschl understood it, the kingdom of God was that ideal social order in which human flourishing could reach the potential intended by the Creator and which would be progressively realized as faith responded to God's grace in daily, loving action. Johannes Weiss was deeply moved by the power of this concept to transform the religious life of his contemporaries. Orthodox Lutheran preaching, with its near-exclusive emphasis on the doctrine of justification, left the majority of Weiss' contemporaries cold. Grace was identified in the popular mind with a punctiliar act, with no corresponding experience in the lives of those brought up in the church. As a result, Weiss thought, education was neglected, and the whole doctrine of grace seemed either a matter of indifference or the cause of "pietistic self torment." In contrast, Ritschl's interpretation of the kingdom of God seemed the best possible way "to awaken and to cultivate a sound and sturdy religious life."[12]

No wonder, then, that the young Weiss' first major scholarly investigation (after his *Habilitationsschrift* on *Barnabas*) focused on the concept "kingdom of God," seeking to understand how the phrase would have been heard by Jesus' contemporaries. Weiss' findings plunged him into "a distressing personal conflict," for he discovered "that Ritschl's concept of the kingdom of God and the like-named idea in Jesus' proclamation were two different things."[13] Far from being a call to progressive personal and social morality, Jesus' announcement of God's kingly reign pointed to a miraculous invasion of the human sphere by God's transcendent power. It was an *eschatological* image, and Weiss' book placed Jesus' proclamation and, indeed, Jesus' entire mission within the context of Jewish eschatological expectations. Specifically, they were to be interpreted from the special eschatological scenarios that had developed within the *apocalyptic* movement, a movement reconstructed by Weiss and others of the school from a variety of sources.

The "personal conflict" was peculiarly acute for Weiss, because he had married Ritschl's daughter. Even so, it was nothing compared to the shock waves that his book's publication would send through the theological world. Years later Bultmann recalled one of his other teachers saying, "If the kingdom of God is an eschatological entity, then it is a concept unusable for dogmatic theology."[14] In the event, Weiss' viewpoint was taken up with enthusiasm by his colleagues in the history of religions school and by their students and successors— Bultmann not the least among them.

Silence about Society

If Jesus' message and mission were to be understood within the context of apocalyptic eschatology, as reconstructed by the history of religions school, that would have revolutionary consequences not only for the historian's understanding of Jesus himself but also for picturing the earliest forms of the movement that arose after his crucifixion. Bultmann was profoundly aware of these challenges. It is not the case that his adoption of existentialism as "the right philosophy" blinded him to the centrality of community formation in early Christian self-understanding. Not only have we seen his own expressed concern for forms of human community that would enable human flourishing, but as a historian he was also aware that "church consciousness" was a defining aspect of the earliest movement. Already in the second chapter he describes "the Earliest Church as the Eschatological Congregation" (sec. 6). In his chapter on "the Kerygma of the Hellenistic Church," he declares that it was "a decisive question" for "Hellenistic congregations" to find continuity with the notion of the "true Israel."

> Does the salvation proclaimed by the Christian message mean only the salvation of the individual, the release of the individual soul from the contamination of sin and from suffering and death? Or does it mean salvation for the fellowship of God's people into which the individual is incorporated? The fact that the earliest Church in its mission simply took the latter for granted essentially differentiates it from the propaganda of other oriental religions of redemption; and, viewed historically, therein lies a basic reason for Christianity's triumph over them. (1.93)[15]

But what is an "eschatological congregation"? Today, with the Qumran documents and archaeology at our disposal, we might say that we know what a community looked like that organized itself around the imminent expectation of "the End of Days." The *yahad* of the Qumran covenanters was trying to shape every aspect of its daily practice—its

worship, its calendar, its interpretive activities, its structure of authority and discipline—into forms suited for the anticipated end. That,
to be sure, is not the kind of eschatological congregation Bultmann
envisioned. At the ideational level, the Qumran group experienced
nothing like the "already" of the early Christian kerygma: the Prophet
of the End Time and the Anointed Ones of Aaron and Israel were still
to come. Still, the palpable eschatological tension that we sense in the
Qumran texts propels us to explore the relationship between their
ideology and their social practice, and a half-century's scholarship,
despite many unresolved and disputed questions, has given us some
general picture of what that "eschatological community" looked like.

We do not have from Bultmann any clear description what the
early Christian communities looked like *as social entities*. The nearest
we come is in "the still unconcluded discussion once held between
Rudolf Sohm and Adolf Harnack" that Bultmann summarizes in
order to frame the final part of the *Theology of the New Testament*.
As he sees it, "Harnack focuses upon the Ecclesia as historical phenomenon; Sohm understands it from the point of view of its own
understanding of itself" (2.96). Thus the contrast between Sohm and
Harnack corresponds to what a modern ethnographer might identify
as the "emic" over against the "etic" description of a culture—though
Bultmann would certainly never have adopted such terms, had they
been available to him—and, not surprisingly, Bultmann sides unequiv-
ocally with Sohm. "Self-understanding" must be the starting point of
all interpretation. To be sure, he criticizes some aspects of Sohm's
position, for he knows that the self-understanding of the early community, as we saw above, also included the sense of being part of the
People of God, a translocal fellowship, and Harnack had made that
point clearly. Nevertheless, Sohm's picture of a *charismatic* community, led by Spirit-imbued individuals, seemed to fit better Bultmann's
notion of a group that was eschatological and therefore *unworldly*,
essentially *invisible*.

It would be interesting to compare Bultmann's discussion here,
of the transition from charismatic, locally centered leadership to institutionalized, geographically inclusive leadership, with Max Weber's
discussion of "routinization of charisma" in *Wirtschaft und Gesell-
schaft*—which also took the Sohm-Harnack debate as its starting
point.[16] But to ask sociological questions about the development

would be to take Harnack's side, to regard the *ekklēsia* as a "historical phenomenon," "an object for historical, sociological, psychological consideration" (2.96). Bultmann's lack of interest in the social sciences is not surprising, for it was common in the German university culture of his time. The political scientist Franz Neumann, in exile in America, wrote that the study of "social and political reality found virtually no place in German university life" of his youth. Weber was the one notable exception, but he had little influence at home; it was only "in the United States that Weber really came to life."[17] However, it is not merely disdain for the social sciences that prevents Bultmann's following Harnack in some "historical, sociological, psychological" description of authentic Christian community. It is a dilemma posed by his fundamental conception of human identity, which threatens to make the paradox of "eschatological community" into a simple oxymoron. If eschatology means the end of the world, then the community does not belong to the world and therefore is no part of history. Here, as Nils Dahl pointed out in his review of the *Theology of the New Testament*, to demythologize means to *dehistoricize*.[18]

When Bultmann does talk about community, significantly he speaks only of the "Church *concept*," "Church *consciousness*." The experience of *being* a social movement or group of a certain kind, the facts of its organization and the practices and habits that constitute or facilitate that experience, are outside the picture until they appear in that inevitable fall into the dreaded "early Catholicism." It seems, after all, that the *eschatologische Gemeinde* exists only as a *Denkakt*, not a *Lebensakt*. And where does Bultmann find this rare entity? Where was the already/not yet paradox actually realized, in Bultmann's view? I think we must say candidly that he finds it only in his synthesis of Paul's theology and in the hypothetical first edition of the Fourth Gospel, thoroughly Paulinized in his interpretation. Not only did the whole second-century church fall short of understanding the crucial paradox, even the "ecclesiastical" editor(s) of the Fourth Gospel missed the point and so did members of Paul's own school writing later in his name. One begins to suspect that this act of thinking was very difficult to connect with any lasting act of living.

If the already/not-yet paradox tends to disappear as we seek to discover any social realization of it, so too the other paradox at the center of Bultmann's ethics, the indicative/imperative nexus, is equally problematic, for the two are inextricably linked. The linkage is emphatically stated in the introductory section to the final chapter of the *Theology of the New Testament* (sec. 59), titled "The Understanding of the Imperative." "The problem of Christian living" is not primarily a practical one but a matter of *self-understanding*, set by "the paradoxical situation of the Church: as the eschatological entity . . . [which] yet must lead its life within the old world between 'no longer' and 'not yet.' As a new life no longer belonging to the old aeon it can be described in the indicative; but as long as it must be led in the old world, it stands under the imperative. Paul had solved the problem . . . and John likewise" (2.203). And Bultmann clearly declares the issue here to be whether the Pauline and Johannine solution (!) to this problem

> would be retained—whether Christian freedom would be understood as the freedom to obey, obedience itself then being understood as the gift of grace or of the Spirit, or whether obedience would be conceived as an accomplishment and hence as the condition to be fulfilled in order to obtain salvation . . . , and then whether the imperative would receive again the character of law in the sense that had been demolished in Paul's doctrine of justification: the character of a way to salvation. (2.203)

Thus the developments in organization and moral sensibility that Bultmann discusses here will all be tested (and found wanting) by the same criterion by which, in the preceding section, theological developments were measured. That had to be the case, for, as he says, "on account of the peculiar nature of the Christian understanding of salvation the themes of soteriology and ethics cannot be separated" (2.203–4). That, in a nutshell, defines the perspective from which Bultmann's whole understanding of ethics must be seen.[19]

What is at issue here is Bultmann's understanding of grace. His soteriology is effectively reduced to atonement.[20] Grace appears in the unconditional declaration of God to the believer, "Your sins are forgiven." That declaration is the simplest form of what Bultmann means by "the indicative." It was perhaps not quite fair of Karl Barth to say that in Bultmann's description of the "Christ event" soteriology threatens to swallow up Christology, for Bultmann is at great pains to say, repeatedly, that it is the prior act of God *in Christ* that works salvation.[21] Nevertheless, Barth puts his finger on an essential weakness when he suggests that Bultmann's attempt to purge the New Testament kerygma of all "objectifying" talk about God leads finally to a new docetism.[22]

That docetism emerges when we ask how the act of God's grace is mediated to the believer. For Bultmann the answer is, emphatically and exclusively, "through the kerygma." But what *is* the kerygma? Unlike several English-speaking theologians, notably C. H. Dodd, Bultmann resists defining the kerygma in any quasi-credal form, as a set of statements. One of the reasons for avoiding that kind of definition is closely related to the project of "demythologization." Those creed-like statements that form critics discovered in the New Testament and other early Christian literature take the form of myths. The mythic pictures of the world, which early Christians shared with their contemporaries, are a stumbling block to "modern" believers—but not in the sense that the kerygma was a *skandalon*. On the contrary, the offense of myth obscures and displaces the offense of the cross, which calls each person out of every self-contrived security. The other major reason Bultmann avoided identifying the kerygma with "objectifying" statements is that such an understanding always threatens to identify the act of faith with the act of accepting those assertions. And that would make the act of believing into a *work*, undoing the radicality of Paul's central doctrine, as Luther and Bultmann understood him, justification by grace alone.

To preserve the radicality of the proclamation of grace, it was essential to *demythologize* the kerygma, and that meant to find a way, not to *remove* the myths, as nineteenth-century liberalism attempted, using philosophical idealism, but to *translate* them, using the philosophy of existentialism. The trouble is that Bultmann is so chary of any and all "objectifying" language that in his own translation the kerygma becomes little more than a formal operator, a ghostly signal, an *Anrede* that has scarcely more to say than "be authentic." Consequently the dialectic of indicative and imperative is self-emptying. The imperative swallows up the indicative by denying every social construct or ritual act that could make the indicative real to ordinary people and thus consumes the ground of its own possibility.

The fundamental issue turns on the question of how we construe personal identity. In the existentialism of Bultmann's time, to speak of identity meant to speak of an individual, self-consciously extracted from every institutional and communal context. The existentialists shared this focus on the isolated self with the long idealist tradition against which they were, in part, reacting—epitomized for moderns by Descartes' bold retreat into his own doubting mind to establish a new foundation for rational confidence. The most interesting turn in moral philosophy of the past several decades is the growing persuasion, from a variety of quarters, that the modern individualist self is an illusion. Succinctly described by some ethicists as a recovery of the Aristotelian description of the human person as a "political animal" against the Socratic-Platonic notion of the self-abstracting *nous*, this revised conception of the moral agent is reinforced by long-term trends in the social sciences, which yield a model of personal identity as a social and transactional process. Each of us comes to know "who I am," not just by sitting and thinking about myself but, beginning in earliest childhood, by responding to other persons who respond to me. My personal identity is not a hidden essence to be discovered but an emerging story to be lived and told, in a language not private to me but shared with all who live in the culture into which I am born. It follows that we do not become moral agents except in the relationships, the transactions, the habits and reinforcements, the special uses of language and gesture that together constitute life in community. Our moral intuitions are those unreflective convictions about what is right or wrong, fair or unfair, noble or despicable, with which all the more complicated moral decisions must begin and which they must take into account. These intuitions are not given by nature, nor are they imprinted upon a tabula rasa by the austere thinking of an autonomous mind, but are shaped in the same communities and by the same kinds of interpersonal processes by which we become conscious and competent selves.[23]

If all identity is social and all morals are communal, then the grammatical paradox of "indicative and imperative" may not be the best way to describe the making of a Christian moral agent. Certainly the hyper-Reformation focus on preaching as the fundamental way of thinking about the communication of the indicative has to yield to some larger conception. David Horrell has said it well, urging that the indicative/imperative conundrum is "best understood as related to the construction of an always vulnerable social identity: the indicative describes the new identity of group members, an identity constructed via the rituals in which the central myth is embodied; the imperative urges them to continue to make this designation of central and defining importance for identity and practice."[24]

Toward an Ethics of Response

In one of his last publications, the late Abraham Malherbe leads us back to the first Christian writing known to us, Paul's First Letter to the Thessalonians, to show us that in Paul's missionary practice there was never any separation between the indicative of proclamation and the imperatives of forming a moral community.[25] This is a key insight. If we look again at that letter with our questions in mind, we discover that there the goal of moral formation of a newborn Christian community is succinctly defined: "to the end that you walk in a way worthy of the God who called you into his own kingdom and glory" (1 Thess 2:12). This is a form of admonition that we hear in many variations in early Christian literature. As in the quoted sentence, the name of God is often followed by a relative clause that specifies what action or attribute of God believers are to have in view as they devise a "worthy" or fitting way of acting. Or in a different grammatical form, the point is made that the prior action of God provides the possibility as well as the direction and shape of the action required of those who recognize and respond to that action. Thus, "Be kind to one another, tenderhearted, forgiving one another, as God in Christ forgave you" (Eph 4:32).

The specific action of God that is most often privileged in the early texts, particularly in the Pauline and Johannine circles, is the crucifixion and resurrection of Christ. Thus the "new commandment" that echoes through generations of the Johannine circle is "that you love one another, as I [Jesus] have loved you" (John 13:34), for the love of Jesus is specified as his laying down his life. It is a short step to construe the believer's response as a response not only to the action of God but to the being of God that is manifested in the action. So the little poem constructed by the author of 1 John 4:7-10 backs the admonition to love one another with the assertion, "God is love."

While many have noticed the responsive structure of much early Christian moral discourse, no one has seen its systematic potential so clearly as H. Richard Niebuhr. In his Robertson lectures, which with some additions from other manuscripts were published a year after

Niebuhr's death as *The Responsible Self,* he sketched out the beginnings of a phenomenology of responsibility. Fragmentary though it is, it seems to me still unsurpassed in its suggestiveness and clarity. He proposed setting alongside the familiar teleological and deontological forms of ethical theory one he called sometimes the *katechontic,* deriving the label from the Stoic tag for what is "fitting." But while Stoic ethics tended toward both a social conservatism and a radical individualism, Niebuhr's notion of the responsive self entailed both a dynamic conception of the reality to which action should be fitted and a "fundamentally social character" of the self that acts. He sums up part of his proposal like this: "Monotheistic idealism says: 'Remember God's plan for your life.' Monistic deontology commands: 'Obey God's law in all your obediences to finite rules.' Responsibility affirms: 'God is acting in all actions upon you. So respond to all actions upon you as to respond to his action.' "[26] The conception of Christian ethics as an ethics of response provides us with a perspective that can enable us to reclaim many of the results of exegetical and historical research both on the biblical texts and on their subsequent deployment and influence, their *Wirkungsgeschichte,* and to put these results to work again in the shaping of a Christian moral life. If the moral life is defined as the sum of fitting responses to a reality defined by God's being and God's acting, then everything, in a sense, hangs on the way we understand that prior action and being. And that means that ethics is fundamentally an interpretive enterprise. Furthermore, the interpretive process is conducted not by transcendent minds but by persons embedded in societies and communities that have their own distinctive histories and languages. The formation of the interpretive—and moral—community is prior to the agent's decisions about the moral thing to do. And within that community as well as between that community and other moral communities that it may encounter directly or indirectly, in the present world or in history, many voices legitimately contend for a part in defining the reality of which a moral act or habit is "worthy."

The Quest for Biblical Authority

We must turn now to the second of the central questions with which we began, namely, whether we can find for our time, as Bultmann struggled to formulate for his, a way of interpreting "the New Testament writings under the presupposition that they have something to say to the present" (2.251).

The Golden Age Fallacy

The starting point for Bultmann's inquiry into the way in which Scripture may appropriately be employed to authorize a Christian way of living is a historicized version of Luther's quest to find, within the multiplicity of scripture, *was Christum treibt*. That is, his program implicitly assumes that, by rigorous application of all the tools of modern historical inquiry, the interpreter can specify the canon-within-the-canon by which each individual passage of scripture is to be judged. Bultmann shares this starting point with virtually all twentieth-century Protestant biblical interpretation and, after mid-century, most Roman Catholic interpretation as well. An enormous part of this scholarship has fixated on the attempt to describe "the historical Jesus," but Bultmann had no illusions about the ultimate usefulness of that quest: witness his criticism of Schlatter in the Epilogue (2.250). Nor does he imagine that some putatively objective description of the earliest groups of Jesus' followers, *die Urgemeinde*, can provide the ultimate criterion for theology and ethics. As we have seen, the touchstone by which all Christian theology and ethics is to be measured is that "believing self-understanding" which responds to "the kerygma." And clarification of that self-understanding "takes place directly in the analysis of the theology of Paul and John" (2.251).

We have here an extraordinarily sophisticated version of what I have called "the golden age fallacy."[27] This fallacy, which has infected much of modern biblical interpretation, leads us to imagine that there was once a moment when the Christians had it exactly right but that moment then was lost: the religion of Jesus became the religion about Jesus; the apocalyptic community of the end time was institutionalized into a bourgeois religion; revolutionary solidarity with the marginalized classes was supplanted by the otherworldliness of apocalyptic fanaticism; a Jewish ethical monotheism was corrupted by "Hellenistic" metaphysics and sacramentalism; a universal ethic of love was straitjacketed by "rabbinic" concepts of merit and retribution and legalism—the list of ways we may conceive the "fall" is endless.

The notion of a fall from pure beginnings is not modern at all but very ancient. According to Eusebius, Hegesippus taught already in the second century that the church had been a pure virgin (cf. 2 Cor 11:2) until the martyrdom of James the Just, after which a disappointed candidate for succession to his leadership "began its corruption by the seven heresies to which he belonged" (*Hist. eccl.* 4.22.5). Even earlier the Pastoral Epistles envisioned a "deposit" of "healthy doctrine" laid down by Paul, which his successors ought to guard against contamination by "heretical persons." It was only in the eighteenth century, however, that the notion of *das Urchristentum* began to dominate historical imagination, and into this originally polemical strategy was injected the hubris of "scientific" historiography: we now imagine that we have a system of *methods* that enable us to uncover the primeval moment of truth.[28]

Compared with many of his contemporaries, Bultmann was not so naïve as to think that method alone could ensure the recovery of the ultimate criterion for judging theological affirmations. He knew that even good history cannot substitute for responsible interpretation and that interpretation is a complex, self-involving task. Nevertheless, the entire shape of the *Theology of the New Testament* is determined by the conceit that there was *once* a moment—fleeting and fragile— when the kerygma was rightly understood and effectively received. That moment is enshrined in Paul's letters and in the (hypothetical first edition of) John's Gospel. Everything since has been to a greater or lesser extent a corruption.

The notion of virgin doctrine subsequently corrupted has been a useful polemical ploy, but it is difficult to square with what we know about the historical development of the early Christian communities. Textual and archaeological discoveries since Bultmann's day have reinforced the trend that had begun already in the history of religions approach he knew so well, to see the early centuries of the Christian movement as the age of experimentation. Many voices contended, many rival schools jostled for influence in the ongoing process of invention, offering different conceptions of "salvation" and of the life that embodies it. Bultmann was fully aware of this diversity. That is shown by the importance in his work of the categories constructed by the History of Religions School, by which they thought to describe the real world of religious movements in and around early Christianity: Gnosticism, Apocalypticism, the Hellenistic Mysteries, and so on. Yet, looking back on the whole historical armature of Bultmann's

oeuvre, we see the brittleness of these hypostasized theoretical entities, and we observe again that they are forced into the old purity-
and-fall pattern. That is not good history, and it does not make for the
kind of interpretation needed to inspire a responsible ethics.

Responsible Reading

If, as I suggested above, the way to get beyond the self-consuming
paradox of the indicative and imperative is to adopt a version of Richard Niebuhr's ethics of response, then it follows that all ethics entails
interpretation and that interpretation is the fundamental, constitutive activity of the community of faith. The interpretation of scripture is the paradigmatic instance of that activity, but interpretation
is always multidimensional and dialectical. By reading ourselves into
the scriptural narratives, we interpret ourselves. We bring our own
social worlds with us in the very way we read, yet that world may be
reconfigured as we discover new ways of interpreting it. New events,
new experiences, new contexts all give us new questions to bring to
the texts, and the texts may provoke counter-questions of which we
had not dreamed.

We see abundant examples of this self-involving interpretive process in the early Christian communities—and in other groups contemporary with them, especially among the Jews struggling to live
faithfully in the Greco-Roman world. For example, the first Christians
read scripture in order to discover language that can render intelligible events they have experienced or about which they have been told.
Thus their own story gets told, in large part, in the language of Jewish
scripture. The most vivid details of the crucifixion narrative are echoes
of certain psalms of lament. Not only is the group's story shaped by
the texts but the community's perception of what the texts are about
is shaped by the requirements of their story. Moreover, the reading of
the texts not only shapes the story; text and story together shape the
community's understanding of itself and its world. So, to continue
with the same example, the community that hears incessantly repeated
the scripture-shaped passion and resurrection narratives sees itself in
the sort of world that has crucified God's anointed one. When the
converts experience some hostility from their neighbors, it is easy for
them to understand their own suffering by analogy with the story of
Jesus. That homology of experience, in turn, reinforces the validity of

the story and sends them often back to the scripture in search of additional understanding and hope. One thing that happens then is that members of the new movement, whether they are Jews or Gentiles, find themselves within the biblical story of Israel. The new community becomes, as it were, a character within the narrative—Israel itself, or Abraham, or the "you" addressed by Torah and prophets, or the "I" and "we" that pray the Psalms. When that happens, naturally the scripture itself is transformed—even before new writings are added to it and a "New Testament" emerges. For "scripture" exists not merely as words on papyrus or leather but as a communicative process within interpretive traditions and the communities that bear and are borne by those traditions.

The new communities of Christians are not shaped only by scripture. They live in a certain environment that sets limits and defines opportunities for their existence, and they each have their own history. When a householder in Ephesus or in Corinth offers hospitality to one of the wandering apostles who bring the gospel and then permits the converts to that gospel to form within his or her household a meeting, an *ekklēsia*, a familiar social pattern is invoked with common expectations about the group and about relationships and obligations. It is then precisely that kind of group with those expectations that then interprets and is interpreted by scripture. And they are not the first to have had this experience nor to have attempted such interpretation. Many immigrants to these cities, in the mobile world of the late Hellenistic and early Roman period, have found a bit of home in similar fashion, and among them particularly the Jews have engaged in the same kind of dialectical interpretation of their old scriptures and traditions in the new Greco-Roman world. And from that Greco-Roman world they have brought to their interpretation not only the practical dimensions of the Greek and Roman city, not only the pervasive assumptions that underlie popular magic and the ubiquitous and manifold presence of public religion but also some dimensions of the high culture, of philosophical reflection on the moral life as popularized and broadcast by the orators and by their own preachers, like Philo of Alexandria and the author of the Wisdom of Solomon.

The moral community is a community that responds to the action of God. The action of God, however, can be recognized only by interpretation, and that interpretation is extraordinarily complex.

Experience of the community shapes the questions addressed to scripture, which in turn interprets the experience. This reciprocity occurs within other dialectics: between social forms and normative images; between group-specific and broad cultural forms of language, relationships, and norms; between texts and traditions of interpretation; between traditions of interpretation and new social and cultural contexts.[29]

By this summary description of activities constitutive of the earliest Christian communities, I hope to reaffirm and to exemplify my conviction that indeed the New Testament texts "have something to say to the present," and, furthermore, that critical historical scholarship has a role in helping them to say it. At the same time, I have tried to frame the example in such a way as to disarm the perilous metaphor which we cannot completely avoid: that the text "says" something. It does not. Without a responsible, interpretive community, the text is silent. The fallacy of "textual agency," as Dale Martin pointedly insists, misleads by masking the real locus of authority, the true warrants for moral and theological assertions.[30]

The final question is whether the enterprise of constructing "New Testament theology" is still viable or even desirable. As we celebrate in these pages the twentieth century's most impressive monument of that two-centuries-old movement, it may seem almost impious even to raise the question. My rereading of that monument reminds me yet again how much my generation owes to Rudolf Bultmann's vast learning, his bold syntheses, his passionate commitment to the integrity of scholarship, and his unshakable confidence in the grace that calls and enables each of us to respond. Nevertheless, that rereading also reconfirms my growing conviction, already expressed on other occasions, that "New Testament theology" is a category mistake.[31] The New Testament does not have a theology. The second-order procedures by which the practices that constitute the Christian community must be ordered and corrected in every generation—the procedures we name "theology" and "ethics"—are ours to carry out, and we must take responsibility for them and for the ways in which we may use the New Testament (and the Old) in the process.

PART II

BULTMANN IN HISTORY AND THEOLOGY

Chapter 12

BULTMANN'S
THEOLOGY OF THE NEW TESTAMENT
IN CONTEXT

Angela Standhartinger

The Americans moved in on the 28th of March, welcomed in calm
hearts as liberators. . . . On the morning of the 28th, I sat at my desk,
hearing the shooting first in the distance and then ever closer—it
did not continue for long, however—and finally I saw the tanks and
other vehicles entering Marburg. . . . The university (converted into
American barracks) closed down and I benefited from it personally.
To the extent that I was not occupied with daily tasks, I worked on
my *Theology of the New Testament*. I am already well into the final
corrections and I hope to be able to complete it in a few weeks.[1]

This statement comes from Rudolf Bultmann's letter to Friedrich
Gogarten written on June 10, 1945, a month after Germany's surrender. In the midst of collapse, after night bombings, uncertain as
to whether the order to defend the city of Marburg to the last drop
of blood might yet still be carried out, suffering from hunger, cold,
and privation, uncertain as to whether the liberators would prove
to be such and whether the expected liberation from the tyranny of
National Socialism would succeed, Bultmann sat at his desk "uncon-
cerned with reality,"[2] as though there were nothing more important
to do than finally to complete the *Theology of the New Testament*, due
by contract back in December 1929.[3] Despite or, indeed, because of
this self-portrayal, I would like to ask in what follows whether and to
what extent the historical, theological, and social context influenced
the production of Bultmann's *Theology of the New Testament*.

234 — Angela Standhartinger

One can deduce from Bultmann's letters that he had begun substantive work on his *Theology of the New Testament* immediately after concluding his commentary on the Gospel of John in September 1940—that is, one year after the war began with Germany's invasion of Poland.[4] According to Bultmann's own testimony, he made rapid progress with his work at first. He was already able in December 1940 to discuss the section on Johannine theology with his student and friend, Gerhard Krüger, professor of philosophy at Münster.[5] In December 1945, he expressed the opinion that he would be able to complete the work in a few weeks. The publication two and five years later (respectively) of the first two fascicles in German ("Jesus and Paul" in 1948; "John" in 1951) not only can be attributed to Germany's collapse, censorship, and restrictions on publication and the paper shortage, but also had something to do with Bultmann's involvement in education policy for the University of Marburg (reopened as early as September 1945) and its de-Nazification. The third and final section ("The Development toward the Ancient Church") was concluded only two and a half years after the formation of the Federal Republic in December 1952, thus in a time when Bultmann had aroused theological, ecclesial, and, especially, personal hostility because of his so-called program of demythologization.[6]

A number of Bultmann scholars hold the view that *Theology of the New Testament* contains nothing truly new, that Bultmann's thought was already "as good as finalized" with the dictionary article "Paulus" published in the *RGG²* in 1930.[7] In fact, Bultmann had already given the lecture course "New Testament Theology" ten times.[8] Bultmann first formulated the program of existential interpretation in the introduction to his 1926 book on Jesus, the basis of sections 1–3 of the *Theologie*. Even the famed first sentence of the theology has a precursor in the 1930 article on Paul.[9] Naturally, the commentary on Johannine literature published in the years 1937–1941 constituted the most important groundwork for the chapter on "The Theology of the Gospel of John and the Johannine Epistles." Is one to assume that there is no trace in the *Theology of the New Testament* of the dominance of National Socialism in Germany, World War II, the collapse of hopes, and the disappointments of the early postwar years? Such a circumstance would be astonishing for an author who wrote programmatically in 1955:

Only those are able to understand history who are themselves moved by sharing in history, that is, who are open to the language of history by their own responsibilities for the future. In this sense it is precisely the "most subjective" interpretation of history that is the "most objective." Those alone who are moved by the question of their own historical existence are able to attend to history's claim.[10]

In this essay, then, I would like to ask how the context in which Bultmann's *Theology of the New Testament* originated left an imprint on its execution. Why did Bultmann write his *Theology of the New Testament* at precisely this moment? Can one find in it reflections of political, social, and ecclesial debates, or does the very absence of concrete contextualization suggest the program by which Bultmann hoped to overcome the collapse and crisis of those years? In order to clarify these questions, I will first reconstruct Bultmann's life, work, and thought in the years of National Socialism and World War II and in the early postwar years. Following this reconstruction, I will examine select passages from the *Theology of the New Testament* with respect to their "contextuality." In conclusion, I would like to refer briefly to Bultmann's reaction to the attempt to interpret his theology as contextual in approach.

Bultmann's Context from 1933 to 1952

As one of the theologians with the closest ties to liberal theology and the history of religions school, Bultmann was called from Breslau and Giessen to the University of Marburg as professor of New Testament. In dialogue with the second edition of Karl Barth's *Letter to the Romans*, he became an adherent of Dialectical Theology between 1921 and 1924.[11] From his student days (1905–1916), Bultmann was already familiar with Marburg, a small city in the northern region of Hessen with a population of 28,439 in 1933. The city had a rural ambience and almost no industry, and thus the university was its most important economic sector. In 1932, about four thousand students (including about eight hundred women) studied with about one hundred fifty professors and lecturers, including one female professor, the Germanist Luise Berthold. Socially and culturally, Marburg had little to offer, so Bultmann cultivated active interaction with his colleagues on the philosophy faculty. These colleagues included Martin

Heidegger in his Marburg years (1923–1928); Heidegger's successor Erich Frank; the new generation of philosophers including Hans Jonas, Karl Löwith, Hans-Georg Gadamer, and Gerhard Krüger; the classic philologist and Plato scholar Paul Friedländer; the archaeologist Paul Jacobsthal; the Indo-Germanist Hermann Jacobsohn; the Romance linguist Erich Auerbach; and others. Bultmann was very popular as a teacher, such that as many as seventy students participated in his seminar, of whom one-quarter were women—which was by no means common at that time.[12]

Marburg was already a stronghold of National Socialism in 1924.[13] As early as the 1932 election for the Reichstag, the NSDAP won 49.2 percent of the votes there and thus exceeded the national average (33.1 percent) by 16.1 percent.[14] The mood also seized theology students.[15] The positions of the professors, in contrast, ranged from liberal to national conservative.[16] After the National Socialists seized power on January 30, 1933, they also restructured the university according to the Führer principle and replaced the rector and deans. On grounds of their anti-intellectual attitude and policy, the National Socialists reduced the size of the student population and, furthermore, established quotas for Jews and women at 10 percent. This policy led to a steady decline in enrollments at Marburg to approximately twelve hundred in the last prewar semester of 1939. Fifteen professors and additional instructors were dismissed because of their Jewish origins or political stances—including Bultmann's friends Erich Auerbach, Erich Frank, Hermann Jacobsohn, Paul Jacobsthal, and Karl Löwith and his colleagues Heinrich Hermelink and Hans von Soden—although, after successful protest, von Soden was reappointed two months later. The professor of religious studies, Friedrich Heiler, was transferred to the philosophy faculty as a penalty, and the Jewish lecturer, Samuel Bialoblocki, was removed from his lectureship.

Already in December 1932, Bultmann wrote Martin Heidegger, "Because, indeed, of the impressions I had gained from superb National Socialist students, I had placed great hope in the movement." Now, however, since "the movement" had become a party, his impressions were depressing.[17] In reaction to Heidegger's rectoral address "The Self-Assertion of the German University" on May 27, 1933, Bultmann wrote of his lack of confidence in the "achievements of the new Reich," continuing, "And my lack of confidence is not grounded in the fact, for example, that I think that these achievements will be predominated by errors or failures, but in the fact that an atmosphere of ὕβρις [*hybris*] and of concealed anxiety is spreading in a disturbing manner."[18] The conflict over Heidegger's rectorate in Freiburg and the failed attempt (even after 1945) to persuade Heidegger to distance himself publicly from his address delivered in the spirit of National Socialism cooled the cordial relationship between the two men. After Heidegger rejected the anthropological interpretation of *Sein und Zeit* in the letter "Concerning Humanism" (1947), Bultmann no longer wished to acknowledge connections between his philosophy and Heidegger's.[19]

Bultmann also reacted publicly to the National Socialists' seizure of power at the end of January 1933, although in an entirely different tone. One day after May 1, 1933, which the National Socialists celebrated as a "Holiday of National Work," Bultmann read a political statement at the beginning of his lecture on the Gospel of John in the summer semester. According to his own report, it was the first (and probably the only) time that he expressed himself in this manner regarding political affairs of the day. "The significance of political happenings for our entire existence has been brought home to us in such a way that we cannot evade the duty of reflecting on the meaning of our theological work in this situation."[20]

Bultmann did not distance himself entirely from the "grand possibilities" of the new situation. With the Pauline ὡς μή ("as though not") from 1 Cor 7:29-31, he emphasized, however, the distinction between God and the world order and the distance that faith must maintain from the world. "This does not mean that faith has a negative relation to the world, but rather that the positive relation that it has to it and to its ordinances is a *critical* one."[21] He saw the critical view of faith, first, as directed specifically against making persons into heroes as expressed, for example, in the renaming of a plaza in Marburg, Adolf-Hitler Platz. This view was directed, second, against the climate of denunciation, and, third, against the defamation of those with differing views. Then follows the famous passage:

> As a Christian, I must deplore the injustice that is also being done precisely to German Jews by means of such defamation. I am well aware of the complicated character of the Jewish problem in Germany. But, "We want to eradicate lies!"[22]—and so I must say in all

238 — Angela Standhartinger

> honesty that the defamation of the Jews that took place in the very
> demonstration that gave rise to this beautiful sentiment was not sus-
> tained by the spirit of love. Keep the struggle for the German nation
> pure and take care that noble intentions to serve truth and country
> are not marred by demonic distortions![23]

Finally, he criticized the religious claim of the National Socialists.
"And we should as scrupulously guard ourselves against falsifications
of the faith by national religiosity as against a falsification of national
piety by Christian trimmings. The issue is either/or!"[24]

The lecture manifests three fundamental themes that would shape
Bultmann's theological engagement with National Socialism in subsequent years. First, he adopted an attitude of critical distance over
against the world order and the state. Admittedly, he acknowledged
the political order in the sense of the Lutheran doctrine of Two Kingdoms; nonetheless, faith and the church are fundamentally different
to the political order. The believer lives at a distance from the world
according to the Pauline "as though not." First Corinthians 7:29-
31 became the motto for the years that follow.[25] Second, he advocated personally on behalf of his Jewish friends and fellow citizens.
Bultmann still spoke suggestively of a "complicated Jewish problem
in Germany," without making clear thereby his position "regarding
this problem" or stating whether this "problem" was actually real.
Only a few months later, however, he formulated an unequivocal antiracist position against the adoption of the Aryan paragraphs by the
church.[26] Third, Bultmann warned against "false security" and the
cult of personality that marked the National Socialists' veneration of
the Führer and that had been on vibrant display a year earlier during "the Führer's" visit to Marburg.[27] In the same year, in the maga-
zine *Neuwerk*, Bultmann published a sermon that dealt with National
Socialism's claim that "Individualism Is Finished!" He criticized that
claim on the basis of the historicity of existence—specifically with the
reminder that "our fathers were not significantly worse than we are,"
and, second, by observing that simply asserting the claim does not
make it true.[28] His critique applied equally to every form of socialism
to the degree that it extinguishes individualism.

Bultmann joined the Pastor's Emergency League, founded in
September 1933, and the Confessing Church that grew out of it and

became one of its leading thinkers. This also led to renewed association with Karl Barth. Bultmann frequently took a stance against the introduction of the Aryan paragraphs in the church.[29] This engagement in ecclesial politics brought students from the Confessing Church to Marburg, where they found support from Bultmann and von Soden.[30] It is no wonder, then, that after 1938 the Gestapo considered the faculty in Marburg "a collecting basin for the unsatisfied elements and the querulous among theology students."[31] Nonetheless, because of the National Socialists' university policy, student numbers decreased significantly. In 1939, there were only 79 still studying theology; in 1933, it had been 478.

At the beginning of the church struggle, Marburg's theology professors were still able to intervene with one accord on behalf of the confessing faction in the struggle. After the punitive transfer of Friedrich Heiler and the appointment of two German Christians (the church historian Ernst Benz and the practical theologian Alfred Uckeley), this unity shattered. In addition, the theologian Georg Wünsch, who feared for his chair because of his earlier membership in the Social Democratic Party of Germany, changed sides and conformed to the National Socialist ideology of race, as his *Evangelischen Ethik des Politischen* (1936) evidences.[32] Bultmann and his friend Hans von Soden protested against the prohibition issued in February 1933 that disallowed public participation in the church struggle, and they did not join the National Socialist Teachers League, as required.[33] In contrast to Karl Barth, however, Bultmann took the oath of allegiance to the Führer, required of all professors after August 20, 1934, because he saw himself as required fundamentally to acknowledge secular order in the sense of the Lutheran doctrine of Two Kingdoms—at least as long as the state were to respect the intrinsic rights of the church.[34]

Bultmann's theological writings from the time contain some political statements, albeit surreptitiously and implicitly. The essay "The Meaning of the Christian Faith in Creation," published in 1936, argues against equating the National Socialist state with God's good creation:

> No nation [*Volkstum*] is so unambiguous an entity that one can explain every stirring of the national will as a demand of a divine ordinance. Nor is nationality [*Volkstum*] a purely natural thing that

is given in one's blood; rather it is something that, though it has a natural basis, arises in history, and through history every nation is given the possibility of evil as well as of good.[35]

In the lecture "Jesus and Paul," also published in 1936, Bultmann criticized the claim made by the influential National Socialist ideologue Alfred Rosenberg, who advocated "[a]way from the Jewish Paul and to the Aryan Jesus."[36] Over against this position, also propounded in liberal theology, Bultmann emphasized, "All that one can do is to go to Jesus through Paul; i.e., one is asked by Paul whether he is willing to understand God's act in Christ as the event that has decided and now decides with respect both to the world and to us."[37] For the Karl Barth Festschrift in the same year, he interpreted Sophocles' *Antigone* as a political allegory concerning resistance against a ruler in which "the power from which true law is derived and by which all human law and its statutes is given a relative status."[38] On the one hand stands the tyrant, who lives in the illusion that he has the support of the people while simultaneously squelching all free speech in the people. On the other hand stands Antigone, for whom "the power of *Hades* is not acknowledged in mute resignation. On the contrary, submission to it means acting rightly in the concrete situation of the moment."[39] Yet, even for her, "who acknowledges *Hades* to be the power limiting human life," the power of death remains "the power of darkness and of horror."[40]

Two years later, after synagogues were burned down in Marburg during the night of November 9–10, 1938, and a few months after visiting the Jewish classicist Paul Friedländer in Berlin after his release from the Sachsenhausen concentration camp,[41] Bultmann's essay "Christ the End of the Law" appeared.[42] Bultmann attempted to challenge the theses that "Jewish religion is [for Paul] a stage in the development of the human mind which has now been surpassed" and that Paul's "rejection of the law" is an assessment of "the worthlessness of Old Testament ethics."[43] Whether Bultmann actually succeeded here in effectively criticizing the common stereotype of Judaism as a works religion remains open to question, for in his writing, universal human behavior and "typically Jewish" behavior seem to overlap imprecisely. Nonetheless, one must credit Bultmann at least with portraying Judaism also as a religion of grace.[44] In the lecture "Prophecy and

Fulfillment," delivered in 1940 at the plenary meeting of the Society for Evangelical Theology in Alpiersbach, which was published only in 1949, Bultmann posed the question of whether "Old Testament history [may] be legitimately understood as prophecy."[45] It is simultaneously a question concerning biblical hermeneutics and concerning the interpretation of contemporary history. By means of the concepts of covenant, kingdom of God, and people of God, he attempted to demonstrate how the New Testament adopts Old Testament concepts and interprets them eschatologically. He found it a "peculiar paradox" that Judaism seeks to equate the notion of the people of God and the notion of the people constituted as a state. "But the contradiction is that God and his actions are not understood in the radically transcendent and eschatological sense, but are brought into line with the empirical history of the people."[46]

Again, one recognizes simultaneously the reception of anti-Jewish stereotypes from the nineteenth and twentieth centuries and, in the same breath, allusions to the National Socialist theory of the mission of the German people. Yet Bultmann also concerned himself with the existential component of Jewish history.

> The encounter with the grace of God teaches man to conceive of God's activity as eschatological in the true sense, that is, as an activity withdrawing him from the world; and it endows him with the possibility of faith as that of eschatological existence in the world and in time. In the light of this we get the right to conceive of this Old Testament history of miscarriage as a promise, that is, the way in which God has led the people of the Old Testament; and we get the right to interpret that conflict not as that of two human ideas, but as one which belongs to human existence as such—the conflict of being created for God and called to God, and yet of being imprisoned in secular history. . . . [F]aith requires the backward glance into Old Testament history as a history of failure, and so of promise, in order to know that the situation of the justified man arises only on the basis of this miscarriage.[47]

At the same meeting, Bultmann also delivered the lecture "The Question of Natural Revelation," which he published together with the lecture "New Testament and Mythology," delivered in 1941, in the book *Offenbarung und Heilsgeschehen*, which appeared in the same year. "Natural Revelation" contains the most contemporary references. Alluding to National Socialist claims (some of which were also adopted by German Christians), Bultmann guarded here against making nature and history the criterion for the Christian revelation of God: "Even those whose faith is in Germany would not say directly 'Germany is God' but at most would express it in this way; that God confronts them in Germany—reveals himself in Germany."[48] With a view to human weakness and tentativeness, human beings know about God, but they attempt to evade the question. They do so, for example, by maintaining that the "blood, which binds together the individuals of a people and pulsates through all generations of the people conceived as an 'eternal' entity" or "that the power of blood is determinative of his destiny."[49] These formulations allude directly to National Socialist propaganda. The theory that God reveals God's self in history merits equal criticism from a Christian perspective because every historical phenomenon proves to be ambiguous. The theory that God reveals God's self in historical persons proves to be an "illusion in view of the knowledge that in a man nothing can be revealed to a greater extent than in heroism of that state of being a fighter."[50] Bultmann clearly rejected not only the Führer cult but also contemporary nationalism and national pride when he continued,

> In short, every phenomenon of history is ambiguous, and none reveals God's will in itself. . . . The essential nature of the German people is not present as a clear criterion by virtue of which we may clearly judge the rightness of our action. It is indeed itself an historical dimension, and it is repeatedly left to each generation, and each individual in it, to decide what is to be accounted typically German. What is to be taken as typically and inescapably German in the things we see in our history? As there are national virtues, so there are national vices: what must be reckoned as such? The real nature of what is essentially German lies before us as something which must first of all be laid hold of, in the same way as the individual's real self lies before him.[51]

In the year when Germany seemed blessed with military good fortune and, with the attack on the Soviet Union in 1941, attained its most extensive borders, this statement should be considered a courageous public criticism of National Socialist ideology and its friends among the German Christians. Admittedly, this essay has remained largely overlooked because of interest in the demythologization debate. After World War II, "New Testament and Mythology" was read as a critique of the National Socialist mythologies of the Führer cult and the "master race," but it contained no explicit allusions.[52] Rather, it addressed a "biblicist orthodoxy" widespread in the Confessing Church.[53] Although the ideas were by no means new, a controversial debate erupted immediately. Because the publication of theological works became practically impossible in 1943, Bultmann answered hundreds of letters and was subjected to several ecclesial heresy trials that culminated in 1953 in the circulation of a Pastoral Letter, disseminated in all Lutheran churches, against demythologization.[54]

With the invasion of Poland on September 1, 1939, World War II commenced. The theology faculty in Marburg was immediately closed as "unnecessary for the war." As had been the case in World War I, Bultmann was not conscripted because of his disability. Yet, he wrote his friend Gerhard Krüger stating, "One lives numb in time." After a successful protest, the theology faculty was reopened in January 1940. There were, however, only eight to twenty-five students (primarily women, Germans from abroad, and soldiers on leave to whom emergency examinations were administered). The faculty sought to maintain contact with other students through the military post. In 1941 and 1944, Bultmann worked on two essays that seem at first glance to be at cross-purposes. With recourse to a dogmatically correct but existentially disappointing Christmas sermon, he attempted in January 1941 to comfort his students "in the field" with the advice that, precisely there, they could become intimately familiar with the most important thing for preaching, and thus for theology—namely, unmasked exposure to human anxiety and distress. The gospel is, indeed, the same in all times, but it must "be preached specifically for each and every age!"[55] In November 1944, in contrast, to those who had fought on the front lines, some for five years, and who, concerned with their future, were counting the cost of their theological education, he touted the necessity of fundamental exegetical training, including the study of ancient languages since proficiency in them is the indispensable foundation of critical theological thinking.[56]

Beginning in the winter of 1943, the supply situation in Marburg was serious so that, in the final months of the war and, indeed, in the first years after liberation, people went hungry and cold. Marburg was bombed on February 22, 1944, and February 22, 1945, with a total of 142 fatalities. The train station and the surrounding clinics (only) were destroyed. The rest of the city, including Bultmann's neighborhood, was spared. Nevertheless, after 1943 many air battles took place over the city, occasioning air raid sirens and fear. In the final years of the war and in the initial postwar years, many persons came to the city (including some who had been bombed out, refugees, and displaced persons), and the Bultmanns, along with others, took in refugees. On March 28, 1945, Marburg surrendered without a fight to the entering Americans. Despite orders to defend the city, no defense was attempted, primarily because the munitions supplied for that purpose lacked detonators.

Bultmann stood on the "pre-occupation White List" as "a theologian, a liberal, an active supporter of our policies and program."[57] He formed a friendship with Edward Y. Hartshorne, the American officer responsible for the university, and Samson B. Knoll, the officer responsible for de-Nazification and intelligence, and collaborated in the reopening of the university in September 1945. The demand for university theological studies was great. As early as the winter semester 1945–1946, 100 students enrolled to study Protestant Theology, and their number grew to 273 in Bultmann's last semester in the summer of 1951.

From 1945 to mid-1946, Bultmann was a member of the "Planning Committee of the Philipps-University of Marburg for the Reform of German Schools of Higher Learning" and in this function was also concerned with the de-Nazification of the academy—that is, with the investigation of the National Socialist involvement of his colleagues. One-third of the professors were dismissed at first. Bultmann engaged with particular vigor against the reinstatement of the theologian Georg Wünsch and, in protest against the planned reinstatement, even published a report that demonstrated the National Socialist spirit in *Protestant Political Ethics*.[58]

His contribution in the report of the Planning Committee called for all students to study classical antiquity and, especially, Plato's philosophy, for they contain the origins of the idea of scholarship. From Plato, one learns how to make arguments, the λόγον διδόναι and διαλέγεσθαι. There is an inherent unity between university and antiquity that must be returned to consciousness in order to counter the National Socialists' misuse of knowledge. Thus the study of antiquity has pedagogical significance, and the study of ancient languages and literature is "a means for the development of the capacity to think that can hardly be replaced."[59] The study of antiquity would preserve the unity of the disciplines since antiquity exposed all the fundamental problems of human life. It would not involve the acceptance of the proposed solutions. "Rather, all tradition only becomes fertile through vibrant critical engagement with it."[60] Finally, familiarity with antiquity facilitates reflection on the fact that one has been shaped by one's historical heritage. The heritage of the university, however, also ultimately includes Christian theology, which has shaped another, new understanding of human existence. Familiarity with the Christian understanding of humanity is also a precondition of study and should be offered to auditors in all the disciplines of university study. Bultmann repeated this theory frequently, at the Marburg Conferences on Higher Education (Marburger Hochschulgesprächen), for example, where he found that humanism and Christianity share "a common front against modern relativism," which "dissolves the ideas of truth, goodness, and justice" and ends in the National Socialist doctrine of race and in the perversion of justice in the motto "justice is that which is useful to the nation."[61]

Moreover, Bultmann was also active in the revival of cultural and intellectual life. Bultmann contributed the essay "Adam, wo bist du?" to the first issue of the journal *Die Wandlung* founded in November 1945 by Karl Jaspers and others.[62] From the biblical concept of humanity, he developed the claim,

> However absurd it might be to turn this idea of equality into a programme of equalization for the sake of equalization in the visible world of change and differentiations, it seems just as childish, in contrast to that, to make protestations which—it may be in the name of the race—champion the inequality of men and races as something essential.[63]

While in this essay Bultmann continued to speak of "the tragedy in the history of Israel and Judaism" because Israel attempted "to identify the people of God with the specific, historical nation," he also wrote, "Israel is the holy people, alone of all peoples favoured with the knowledge of the one true God."[64] Bultmann contributed to the first German Congress of the International Council of Christians and Jews in May 1949.[65] Citing *Mimesis* (a book by his Jewish former colleague Erich Auerbach), he emphasized that Western culture is indebted to Judaism for the decisive impulse in the development of individualism.

> The Jewish Old Testament inheritance operates in the development of the West, to the effect that now, on the basis of this unique discovery of the radical otherness of human being over against the being of the world, a constant tension exists in man's relation to the world. . . . There is a tension in relation to the world which must basically be settled by the individual in isolation. Paul gives characteristic expression to it in the famous "as if not."[66]

Bultmann also participated in the reconciliation with France and England, and in the construction of a peaceful central Europe at the "Council of Europe" meeting in 1949, where he presented "Forms of Human Community."[67] Here, he envisioned the imminent danger that "community transmitted by nature" and "the community which has developed in history" may culminate in a National Socialist "Blood and Soil" ideology and a totalitarian concept of the state. He contrasted it with "community founded by religion," which through desecularization "reaches out far beyond the sphere of the church— the community of love, which embraces all men, in an effort to capture their hearts."[68] Last, Bultmann intervened in the conflict over the new church constitution and defended the general right to vote for all church members over against a delegation principle.[69] During his first journey to the United States in 1951, he spoke about freedom in a fundamental manner.[70]

Context in the *Theology of the New Testament*

Why did Bultmann write his *Theology* in the final years of the war and the early postwar period? How did his experience of National Socialism affect its specific conception and execution? Can the allusions to present circumstances evident in the contemporary essays also be found in the *Theology of the New Testament*?

First, one may conjecture that, with this work for the textbook series *Neue theologische Grundrisse*, Bultmann wanted to meet "the need" of theology students harmed by National Socialism and the war. He placed in their hands a textbook in which they could find both an overview and an overall outline of New Testament theology. He expected much from students. In contrast to his other publications, the German version contains a noteworthy overabundance of untranslated Greek quotations, which demand much of readers, not only of the poorly educated war generation but also of current students. In this regard, Bultmann gave consideration to the reconfiguration of the postwar university. Students should be forced to train their thinking by engaging with the Greek text of the New Testament, thereby attaining the capability to substantiate their theological judgments themselves.

In the epilogue, Bultmann gave an account of the method and program of his *Theology*. He placed himself in the tradition of the history of religions school.[71] With Johannes Weiss, he accentuated the centrality of eschatology in early Christian thought.[72] He followed Wilhelm Bousset not only in section 12, titled "Lord and Son of God," but also in the adoption of the model of the development of the "early Palestinian church" into the "Hellenistic church."[73] Regarding the sacraments, he adopted the views of Wilhelm Heitmüller.[74] Primarily, however, he followed Wilhelm Wrede's programmatic *Über die Aufgabe und Methode der sogenannten neutestamentlichen Theologie*. With Wrede, he found the preaching of Jesus and the theologies of Paul, of the Johannine School, and of the *Letters of Ignatius* to be central theological schemes.[75] Admittedly, Bultmann wanted to expand Wrede's definition of the task of a theology of the New Testament ("to present as New Testament theology the living religion of earliest Christianity"; 2.246; *Theologie*, 594)[76] so that the task included the "development of the self-understanding of the believers" (2.246; *Theologie*, 594).[77] In the end, however, he permitted his teacher Adolf Schlatter, who had called for "the connection between the act of living and the act of thinking," to predominate over Wrede (2.246; *Theologie*, 594):[78]

> [I]t is not possible to accomplish the theological task [of the science called New Testament theology] once for all—the task which consists of unfolding that understanding of God, and hence of the world and man, which arises from faith, for this task permits only ever-repeated solutions, or attempts at solution, each in its particular historical situation. Theology's continuity through the centuries

consists not in holding fast to once formulated propositions but in the constant vitality with which faith, fed by its origin, understandingly masters its constantly new historical situation. . . . Theological propositions—even those of the New Testament—can never be the object of faith; they can only be the explication of the understanding which is inherent in faith itself. Being such explication, they are determined by the believer's situation and hence are necessarily incomplete. (2.237–38; *Theologie*, 585–86)

The incomplete nature of New Testament theological propositions is grounded both in the "inexhaustibility of believing comprehensions, which must ever actualize itself anew" and in the fact that New Testament thought does not yet know modern developments in the areas of state, society, and technology (2.238; *Theologie*, 536). New Testament theological propositions are also only approximate when they speak of God's relationship to the world. Consequently, it is necessary to employ content criticism (*Sachkritik*, as Bultmann did, much like Luther) on portions of the canon. For him, there are only two theologians in the New Testament—Paul and John. The unity of the canon is for Bultmann "only a relative one"; following his student Ernst Käsemann, Bultmann states that "[t]he New Testament canon, as such, is not the foundation of the Church's unity. On the contrary the canon, as such . . . is the foundation of the multiplicity of confessions" (1.141–42; *Theologie*, 493–94). Bultmann's *Theology of the New Testament* not only profiles individual sections of the canon but also reaches beyond the New Testament canon. Already part 1, titled "Presuppositions and Motifs of New Testament Theology," and then part 4, titled "The Development toward the Ancient Church," incorporate the early Christian literature available to Bultmann up to Justin and Ptolemeus' *Letter to Flora* (1.112–14; *Theologie*, 115–16).[79] One must also note, however, that he concerned himself only cursorily with detailing the discussions and controversies within early Christianity, and does so more in sections 9–15 than in sections 51–61. In this regard, he fell short of the approach of Walter Bauer, whom Bultmann esteemed.[80]

Bultmann asked whether individual theological propositions prove to be explications of understanding that are given expression in the life of faith. This explication occurs when "the theological thoughts of the New Testament are the unfolding of faith itself growing out of that new understanding of God, the world, and man which is conferred in and by faith," which then lead the human being addressed by the kerygma to a new self-understanding (2.239; *Theologie*, 587). The model is not contextual and time-bound, but universal and transtemporal. The kerygma is "address to concrete existence" and "in a concrete situation," to be sure, but always and everywhere it has only one effect—namely, that "the self-understanding awakened by it is recognized to be a possibility of human self-understanding and thereby becomes the call to decision" (2.240–41; *Theologie*, 589). Thus, the kerygma always confronts the individual without regard to gender, to social and historical location, or to societal references and relationships.[81] In other words, the kerygma reveals itself in the respective concrete situation of existence, indeed always when one's previous existence becomes questionable, and it reveals itself as the possibility of a new self-understanding. This new self-understanding remains abstract and formalized, however, to the extent that the kerygma contains the (unchanging) call to decision whose respective enactments cannot be explicated because they must remain acts or deeds of concrete life.

Consequently, it is no wonder that only a very few subtle contemporary allusions appear in the *Theology of the New Testament*. Political disputes shine through only rarely. For example, Bultmann rejected the theory of a "communism" described in Acts 2:45 and 4:34-35. because those passages lack "both a social program and organized production." In this way Bultmann takes an indirect stance on the issue of the economic system to be established in the two Germanys that were in the process of formation.[82] In contrast to this, in Bultmann's 1926 book on Jesus, he commented critically on the "proletarian" movements of both the right and the left: "It is true that the poor and hungry are blessed, because the Kingdom of God will end their need (Luke 6:20, 21), but the Kingdom is no ideal social order. Subversive ideas and revolutionary utterance are lacking in Jesus' preaching."[83]

Concealed allusions to his experiences in the period of National Socialism, with its subordination of individuals and their fates to the supposedly greater good of the fate of the German people elevated to transcendence, may be revealed when Bultmann says,

> Undoubtedly, the Gnostic myth and its terminology offered the possibility . . . of comprehending the Church [ἐκκλησία; German: *Versammlung*—i.e., assembly] and the individual as placed in the

grand context of a process of disaster and salvation. But the question now is whether this cosmic occurrence is to be understood as only a sublime process of nature which takes place by-passing, so to say, my conduct, my responsibility, my decisions—a process which has me at its mercy for better or for worse. (1.181–82; *Theologie*, 185)[84]

In contrast, "existence responsible in its historicity" is a characteristic of freedom. Bultmann's consistent antiracist stance is also evident in his statement that

Christian freedom is freedom from all human conventions and norms of value. The social distinctions of freedom and slavery as well as those of sex and race [German: *Volkstum*] have lost their significance "in Christ" (Gal 3:28; I Cor. 12:13), and "do not become slaves of men" (I Cor. 7:23) applies to all desires for emancipation, for they stem from human evaluations. (1.343; *Theologie*, 344)

Finally, part 4 of the theology ("The Development toward the Ancient Church") is portrayed as a history of decline from a "congregational democracy" to the monarchical episcopate (2.98–99; *Theologie*, 451), from a "fellowship of salvation" to "an institution of salvation" (2.114; *Theologie*, 466) which no longer understands faithful existence as eschatological in the sense of Paul and John.[85] Thus, Bultmann also objects to and resists the "historization of the eschatological event" found especially in the Lucan two-volume work.[86] In opposition to this historicization stands Gnosticism, whose students, in Bultmann's view, included the letters of John and Ignatius. The extent to which this model of decline is due to Bultmann's high esteem for the eschatological *kairos* or to the experience of clericalization in postwar Protestantism and the trauma of the demythologization debate can hardly be determined.

Finally, in "the indignation" of the Apocalypse "over the demands of the emperor cult" Bultmann discovered the demarcation of the "natural boundaries" of Christian obedience to the state, which must have been understood in 1953 as an unequivocal Christian "No!" to the National Socialist Führer cult and its inhuman consequences.[87] He concluded the theology with a paragraph concerning the church's practice of penitence, and one can assume links to the virulent de-Nazification trials, which Bultmann also considered unsatisfactory.

Some have actually read Bultmann's *Theology* as a theological objection to political injustice.[88] One should not overlook the fact, however, that these allusions remain marginal on the whole. Consequently, one should also take a brief look at the modifications that Bultmann made in relation to his earlier preparatory studies.

The content of the epilogue of the *Theology*, although developed significantly further, draws on the introduction to the book on Jesus. Methodological considerations pertaining to research on the historical Jesus are drawn from the introduction of *Jesus* and assembled in section 4 of his *Theology* ("The Question of Jesus' Messianic Self-Consciousness"). Sections 1–3 follow the outline and contents of *Jesus* but have been significantly abbreviated, which hinders rather than enhances the nuanced consideration of Judaism in some passages. Thus in *Theology of the New Testament* Bultmann speaks of Jesus' "struggle against Jewish legalism," in which "the idea of obedience is not radical enough" (1.10, 12; *Theologie*, 10, 12).[89] In contrast, in the book *Jesus* Bultmann asserts the following:

> At the same time we should utterly misunderstand the Jewish ethic if we supposed that it was entirely dominated by thought of reward. However popular this idea may have been among the lower classes, it does not give Jewish religion its peculiar character. Rather the fundamental trait of this religion is *obedience*. Obedience which is not the fulfillment of a contract, but which arises from reverence before the majesty of the holy God. . . . "[I]n the name of" God, is again and again emphasized as a protest against the morality motivated by desire of reward.[90]

New in comparison to *Jesus* is the keyword *Entweltlichung* (renunciation toward the world, desecularization), which first appeared in 1940 and now is used to summarize Jesus' message.[91]

> For Jesus . . . man is de-secularized by God's direct pronouncement to him, which tears him out of all security of any kind and places him at the brink of the End. And God is "de-secularized" by understanding His dealing eschatologically: He lifts man out of his worldly ties and places him directly before His own eyes. Hence, the "de-historization" or "desecularization" both of God and of man is to be understood as a paradox (*dialektisch*): precisely that God, who stands aloof from the history of nations, meets each man in his own

little history, his everyday life with its daily gift and demand; de-historized man (i.e. naked of his supposed security within his historical group) is guided into his concrete encounter with his neighbor, in which he finds his true history. (1.25–26; *Theologie*, 26)

With the keyword *Entweltlichung*, Bultmann takes up the text of 1 Cor 7:29-31, which had become central for him after 1933. *Entweltlichung* (desecularization) accentuates the conclusions to the sections on "The Kerygma of the Hellenistic Church" and "The Theology of Paul" (1.182–83, 352; *Theologie*, 186, 353).[92] Both sections were already drafted in the 1930 article on Paul. The material summarized in 1930 as the "Conditions of [Paul's] Reality" has now been expanded into the self-contained sections 9–15.[93] In this way, the plurality of Hellenistic Judaism and Christianity is brought to light.

The treatment of Judaism (especially in sections 8.1-2, 11, and 27) remains ambivalent but takes up the syntheses attained during the war and early postwar years.[94] The early Palestinian church stood within Judaism and understood itself as an eschatological entity. One can indeed discern a critique of the law under the influence of the sayings of Jesus. Nevertheless, the early church "clung to the Law as a characteristic of the Chosen People which it was conscious of embodying" (1.55; *Theologie*, 57). Only in the Hellenistic church did "the principle of Christian faith" come to be "in antithesis to the principle of the Jewish Torah-religion" (1.109; *Theologie*, 110–11). In any case, Bultmann overviews seven positions surfacing in a spectrum of data (Gnosticism, *Barnabas*, Hebrews, *1 Clement*, Ptolemeus, and Justin) and demonstrates in various ways how the cultic law does not remain in force; instead, only the promises and commandments of the Old Testament remain in force, so that the possession of the Old Testament signifies a counterweight to natural theology (1.119; *Theologie*, 121). Finally, Paul propounded the theory "that even the demand of God embodied in the Law is grace only" (1.268; *Theologie*, 269).

As early as 1930, Bultmann had outlined Pauline theology as anthropology and explicated it with the assistance of anthropological terminology.[95] Statements concerning the person of Paul and his particular contribution are not repeated.[96] This disappearance of the person of Paul in favor of his theology can be interpreted as criticism of the heroization of historical individuals that led to catastrophe in the Germany of 1933–1945. It leads simultaneously to the opposite, however—namely, the isolating and decontextualizing of Paul the theological thinker, as well as his predecessor Jesus and his successor John.[97] It is thus no wonder that the objective of Jesus' message and of Pauline and Johannine theology is virtually identical: "Freedom from the World" (sec. 40.3) and "Faith as De-Secularization" (sec. 50.1).

The kerygma reveals itself, then, in the midst of a religiously plural environment and is formulated by theologians standing in various locations in the history of religions, but it remains ever the same and calls believers out of the world into the critical distance of the "as though not." Bultmann did not understand desecularization as escapism nor as asceticism, but as the "smashing of all human standards and evaluations" (2.76; *Theologie*, 428). In this regard, desecularization remains a formal concept. At the same time, however, it also remains free to resist any time-bound entanglement in the world.

Bultmann and Contextual Theology

For Bultmann, the three great theologians of the New Testament (Jesus, Paul, and John) agree that faith involves a critical distance from the world and "desecularization," and thereby they set the core and criterion for every early Christian theology. This ultimately leaves little cause for wonder that Bultmann's *Theology* seems nearly without context in its execution, despite the context in which it originated. It reflects its contextuality, however, precisely in the increasingly cited ὡς μή ("as though not") from 1 Cor 7:29-31, summarized in the keyword *Entweltlichung*—namely, the attempt to establish faith as an attitude of resistance to experiences and entanglements in unjust world affairs. In this regard, it reflects the experience of "internal immigration" by which Bultmann succeeded in surviving the years 1933–1945 and the disappointments of the early postwar years. It can hardly be accidental that Bultmann's *Theology* links to early twentieth-century concepts and formulates, thereby, the hope that achievements in science and culture have outlasted and resisted the barbarism of the "Thousand Year" Reich as undamaged as possible. Simultaneously, however, Bultmann's anthropological approach also makes available a critical capability against all universal social and ecclesial claims. Even if Bultmann's treatment of Judaism (despite great personal commitment) falls short, it nonetheless does not allow a foothold for such phenomena as racism, nationalism, the cult of personality, and totalitarianism that limit the freedom of individuals. With its combination of historical-critical, religio-historical, and theological thought, Bultmann's *Theology* constitutes a counterweight to the growing biblicism in postwar Germany.

Bultmann did not want the kerygma to be understood only formally as address in human crisis but also as a call to concrete response and to action in the concrete situation of human coexistence. This may be most evident in his engagement with his students. In 1971, Dorothee Sölle delivered a controversial lecture (the origins of her book *Politische Theologie: Auseinandersetzung mit Rudolf Bultmann*)[98] at the meeting of Bultmann's students, the so-called Alten Marburger. Sölle became familiar with Bultmann's *Theology* through her religion teacher Marie Veit, who received her doctorate under Bultmann in 1946. She began her critical discussion of Bultmann with the surprising assertion,

> The study in the sociology of religion by D. Goldschmidt and Y. Spiegel *Der Pfarrer in der Großstadt* (1969) comes to the conclusion that adherents to Rudolf Bultmann's theology among the pastorate push for the formation of the political opinions of the congregation more than other ecclesial functionaries do who lack such an education or who have a conservative education.[99]

Thus, there were students of Bultmann who understood his theology as a call and a manual for critical reflection on their historical, social, and political existence and their present. Sölle sent Bultmann, by then eighty-seven years old, her book, and he responded with an extensive letter, which unfortunately can be cited here only in excerpts. He wrote,

> I certainly do recognize a relationship between your "political theology" and my theological work, but also a distinct difference, indeed a contradiction. The contradiction obviously consists primarily in the fact that I speak of the dialectical relationship between an otherworldly, transcendental reality, while you deal only with this-worldly reality. Your understanding of faith as desecularization is oriented around the "pre-understanding of the fated nature of circumstances and orders" (p. 79). To the contrary, it is independent of them without meaning that it "abandons the

social and political rationality that regards the world as alterable" (p. 79). The opposite is the case: faith gives the freedom to alter the world. The saying applies: δός μοι ποῦ στῶ, καὶ κινήσω τὴν γῆν (Give me [a point] where I can stand and I will move the world). I am, therefore, entirely in agreement with you when you demand that theology connect theory and practice (p. 105). A "political" theology is not necessary for this purpose, however; rather, it is actually the task of any theology to the extent that it must consider the *responsibility* of faith for the structures of the present world.[100]

In the subsequent pages of his letter, Bultmann discusses Sölle's approach quite fundamentally and certainly does not simply reject it. His answer is "yes and no." Even if he does not always agree with her political concretization, he shares the concern that faith at a critical distance from the world must defend itself in the contexts of the world.

This seems to me the most important legacy to New Testament studies that Bultmann left in his *Theology*. For him, the theological schemes of early Christianity are not encyclopedias of Christian truths; rather, they can be understood only as address in one's respective concrete existence. As address, they contain a distance from the world that grants them the potential to be the ever-self-actualizing Word of God. They cannot, however, be contained in human language for all times; instead, in order to understand them as address, as kerygma, they must be considered and translated concretely in the historical, social, and societal realities of every historical present. Despite or perhaps even because of their apparent noncontextual character, Bultmann thereby elevates the call for a theology that is ever to be rethought, reformulated, and responsible in context.

Chapter 13

BULTMANN AND THE THEOLOGICAL
INTERPRETATION OF SCRIPTURE

Francis Watson

Bultmann in Perspective

In the course of a lengthy and troubled attempt to clarify his relationship with his former theological ally, Karl Barth states that in Rudolf Bultmann's work "the usual dividing-lines between exegesis, dogmatics, and preaching are in principle abolished."[1] The claim may seem exaggerated. No reader of Bultmann's major works—his *History of the Synoptic Tradition*, his book on Jesus, his commentary on John, his *Theology of the New Testament*—could overlook the dominating presence of standard exegetical and historical methods, pursued with great skill to often provocative and always lucid conclusions.[2] Theological concerns are directly or indirectly perceptible in these works, but it is left to Bultmann's essays to develop them more fully.[3] Barth, however, does not have Bultmann's exegetical works primarily in view. Like most of Bultmann's readers at the time of writing (1952), he is preoccupied with the "demythologizing" program first announced in a wartime essay dating from 1941 and entitled "New Testament and Mythology: The Problem of Demythologizing the New Testament Message."[4] Here the claim that Bultmann's exegesis is one with his theology becomes more credible. For Bultmann the *Entmythologisierung* of the New Testament's supranaturalist worldview requires an "existential interpretation," which is outlined systematically under headings such as "The Christian Understanding of Being" and "The Event of Salvation."[5] Much of the discussion is shaped by paraphrase or quotation of mainly Pauline texts. Here at least, Barth's assessment is correct: theology and exegesis are one.

From Barth's perspective this is so far all well and good—or rather, it *would be* all well and good *if* the theological commitments actually did arise out of the texts. In reality, they do not. The texts are read through the filter of the early philosophy of Martin Heidegger, with its concern to analyze the ontological structures of human existence and the possibilities of realizing or failing to realize one's true being. It is, says Barth, this philosophical straitjacket that prevents Bultmann from proceeding beyond *self*-understanding in relation to God and the world to the liberating knowledge of the divine Other opened up to us in Christ.[6] Bultmann himself makes his relationship to Heidegger explicit. He writes,

> Above all Martin Heidegger's existential analysis of being [*Dasein*] appears to be simply a secular philosophical presentation of the New Testament account of human being: the human exists historically in concern for self [*in der Sorge um sich selbst*] on the basis of anxiety [*Angst*], in the moment of decision between past and future— whether one will lose oneself in the sphere of the present-at-hand, the "they," or whether one will attain one's true self [*Eigentlichkeit*] in abandoning all securities and in unconditional openness to the future. Is this not also the New Testament view of humanity?[7]

For Bultmann the difference is simply that the philosophers believe that deciding for one's true self is an inherent human possibility, whereas the New Testament ascribes that possibility to God's liberating act in Christ. The difference is profound, but it is a difference within a common framework: both the New Testament and modern philosophy have independently discovered the natural human self-understanding that corresponds to the ontological realities of human being.

Bultmann, then, is a theologian and an exegete, a practitioner of theological interpretation of Scripture. Yet theological interpretations are not of a piece. They differ fundamentally, and some may be judged to be more appropriate to their object than others. In "New Testament and Mythology," Bultmann's naïve enthusiasm for his philosophical mentors makes it all too easy for his critics to view his theological minimalism as reductive, undermining the substance of the New Testament message. And it is the demythologizing essay that is widely regarded—especially in the English-speaking world—as the definitive statement and summary of Bultmann's entire project.[8] If Bultmann is to be rehabilitated as a theological interpreter of Scripture, this flawed wartime production must be dislodged from its central position in his oeuvre and replaced there with his real masterpiece, the *Theology of the New Testament*. This work became available in English at much the same time as the demythologizing essay and has been largely eclipsed by it.

"New Testament and Mythology" should be viewed in historical perspective as a piece of Christian apologetics composed under the conditions of the Third Reich. Its immediate occasion was the publication in 1940 of a deservedly forgotten book by the philosopher Wilhelm Kamlah, ominously entitled *Christentum und Selbstbehauptung* (Christianity and Self-Assertion).[9] The "and" in the title might be replaced by "or," for Christianity is presented here as the main obstacle to the "self-assertion" required of a national community bound by ties of blood as it strives to defend and extend its boundaries at the expense of a threatening other, thereby realizing its authentic historical destiny.[10] The (male) individual is called to realize his own natural self-assertion within that of the political community; he attains his own true self in turning from narrow self-interest to total commitment (*Hingabe*) to the cause of the Fatherland.[11] The problem with Christianity—exemplified in Augustine—is that it fails to differentiate between a purely individual self-assertion (*Eigenmächtigkeit*), which it rightly criticizes, and the legitimate and necessary self-assertion of the *Volk*.[12] Also legitimate and necessary is the drive for recognition (*Geltungsdrang*) that accompanies this communal self-assertion. *Hingabe* includes the aspiration to perform deeds that further the community's well-being and freedom, meriting praise and securing fame (*Ruhm*).[13] The turn from inauthentic to authentic existence is a movement from *Eigenmächtigkeit* to *Hingabe*, from self-centeredness to commitment to the cause.

Bultmann devotes over five pages of his 1941 demythologizing article to a review of Kamlah's book, emphasizing the structural similarity between Kamlah's ontology and that of Christian faith in the shared concern to differentiate true and false ways of being human.[14] Thus "commitment" corresponds to "faith," over against the individual self-assertion to which both are opposed. In commitment or faith one attains to what is original, natural, and authentic to human being, leaving behind the inauthentic sphere in which the original and natural is covered up. Kamlah's concept of commitment is defined here in purely abstract terms, and the political emphasis is ignored. The difference between philosophy and faith is simply that philosophy believes that true being may be attained by an unaided human decision, whereas faith insists that the human decision is grounded in the divine saving action in Christ. It is clear that Bultmann proposes an utterly different account of the truly human to Kamlah's version of the National Socialist "new man." But it is also clear that he does so from within the constraints of the National Socialist political order, and that, up to a certain point, he is able and willing to make common cause with one of its ideologues—before finally breaking with him.[15] Indeed, there are also echoes of Kamlah's book in the repeated references to the New Testament's "mythical worldview" in the opening pages of Bultmann's essay. In the very first sentence it is said that "[t]he worldview of the New Testament is essentially mythical," and references to "the mythical worldview" in its opposition to "the worldview of the natural sciences" recur like a refrain in the pages that follow.[16] In his own opening pages Kamlah had similarly contrasted the Christian "mythical worldview" with "the new worldview of mathematical natural science."[17] It is as if the Christian theologian strives to outdo the post-Christian philosopher in insisting on the great gulf that divides the world of the New Testament from our own.

It is tempting to speculate about Bultmann's motives for writing as he does. Perhaps he has in view the parlous future of the Evangelical Church within the Third Reich, which, after its spectacular victories in Western Europe, seems set to continue indefinitely. Perhaps his essay expresses a desire to be treated as an equal by philosophers such as Kamlah, Heidegger, and Jaspers, an aspiration to join an intellectual elite that looks with disdain on Christians who persist in believing the unbelievable.[18] For our purposes, what matters is that this essay is neither the whole of Bultmann nor the essential Bultmann. After the war, the demythologizing issue played a far less significant role in his own work than in its critical reception by others.[19] He himself gave priority to writing his *Theology of the New Testament*, which was to sum up his career as a New Testament scholar and theologian.[20]

The question is whether, in this work too, the usual lines of demarcation between exegesis and theology are eradicated. How far is Bultmann's construal of New Testament theology shaped by his own theology? In what sense is this New Testament theology itself a theological reading of the New Testament? If it is such, does that call into question its integrity as a work of exegetical and historical scholarship, or are history and exegesis actually enhanced by the theological framework in which they are housed? Bultmann does not claim that this theological framework is timelessly valid, acknowledging that it is provisional and subject to criticism and revision. Fundamental questions about the subject matter of the New Testament must be asked and answered again and again from within ever-new historical contexts (585–86; ET, 2.237). In this provisional character, theology is no different from any other scholarly endeavor. The most resolutely untheological, "purely historical" account of Christian origins will similarly be shaped by questions and concerns characteristic of its own time and place of origin. The situatedness of the interpreter—whether historian or theologian, or both—is a limitation that becomes increasingly visible as time passes and situations change. Yet situational limits also open up the possibility of dialogue between differently situated interpreters. A specific time and place represents a unique *vantage point* from which an object is viewed, and what is seen from there must be taken into account by those who view it from elsewhere.

Bultmann's construal of the New Testament is descriptive. It holds itself accountable to the texts, as is immediately evident from the hundreds of scriptural citations and references that throng the pages of *Theology*. Yet description is always also interpretation. Decisions have been made about which themes to elaborate and which to play down. Some developments within early Christianity receive tacit approval; others do not. The subject matter for a New Testament theology has had to be differentiated from that of a New Testament introduction or a history of the early church. There is no pretence of indifference, as though it could no longer matter to anyone how Jesus thought about God (sec. 4) or what John meant by "the word became flesh" (sec. 46). At every point one might—if so inclined—raise critical questions about Bultmann's interpretative decisions, finding fault with him for absences, prejudices, misreadings, and above all for a failure to realize that theology is one thing and historical reconstruction another.[21] A more fruitful approach is to try to *understand* the relationship between theology and history in *Theology*, observing how this relationship works in practice rather than rushing to evaluate. A good place to start is Bultmann's table of contents. Here, two terms—"kerygma" and "theology"—are especially prominent, and in the following sections of this chapter I shall offer an extended paraphrase of what Bultmann means by them.

Kerygma

Part 1 of Bultmann's three-part work deals with the *Voraussetzungen und Motive* of New Testament theology, its "Preconditions and Themes."[22] New Testament theology is not an autonomous enterprise but is dependent on historical realities that predate it and provide the subject matter for its reflections. The three sections of part 1 ("chapters" in the English version) are all concerned with *speech*: the "message" (*Verkündigung*) of Jesus, the "kerygma" of the earliest Christian community and of the Hellenistic church apart from Paul. Underlying the distinction between the apparent synonyms is the fact that the kerygma represents the transformation of the message. In the kerygma the messenger becomes the message,[23] Jesus the preacher and prophet is subsumed into Jesus the Messiah and as such becomes the content of the preaching.[24] There is no absolute disjunction between the kerygma and Jesus' call to live in the light of the coming kingdom of God. In proclaiming Jesus as the exalted Messiah and the coming Son of man, it is not forgotten that he is also prophet and teacher (36; ET, 1.34). Yet his post-Easter acknowledgment as the crucified and risen Messiah sets everything that preceded Easter in a new light.[25] What was proclaimed as future by Jesus is now proclaimed as present in Jesus. The boundary between this age and the age to come can no longer be clearly discerned, for Jesus is the one who was and is and is to come.[26]

For Bultmann, then, Jesus' *reception* by the post-Easter community is more fundamental to New Testament theology than the "historical Jesus"—if that expression is used to refer to a Jesus abstracted from his own reception and reduced to an individual consciousness of mission or relatedness to God, expressed in his preaching and teaching. In spite of his notoriety as an archskeptic, Bultmann does not deny the possibility or legitimacy of historical knowledge about Jesus.

Rather, he insists that *all* historical knowledge about Jesus is mediated by a community that viewed him as the crucified and risen Messiah and that aspects of his person or career that the community chose not to preserve must remain inaccessible to us.[27] Underlying the historical Jesus scholarship that Bultmann rejects is the illusion that historical research might enable a direct and transformative encounter with Jesus as he actually was, in the fullness of his own experience of the divine.[28] In subordinating the historical Jesus to the kerygma that reflects his messianic post-Easter reception, Bultmann claims to reassert the priorities of the New Testament texts themselves.

At its core, the kerygma is the announcement that an *event* has occurred, originating in divine rather than human initiative, in which the situation of humanity vis-à-vis God has been transformed. The event has its antecedents in the history of Israel and is foreshadowed in Israel's sacred scriptures; its cosmic significance will be revealed only when the existing world order is brought to an end; and this eschatological future and scriptural past serve to *establish* the definitive status of the event rather than relativizing it. The event is an *advent*, the coming of a recognizably human figure, belonging to a specific time and place, who lived out his own unique life between the universal human coordinates of birth and death. In itself the event of this human life can have only a limited and relative significance, but for faith it attains universal and definitive significance as it is affirmed by God "on the third day." That at least is what the earliest witnesses claimed, and their testimony continues to resound through the pages of the New Testament. The witnesses have themselves been caught up into the event, for the divine affirmation that occurs in the raising of Jesus is an *address* that requires the presence and the understanding participation of an addressee if it is to fulfill its intended function as a speech-act. The New Testament texts trace their own possibility back to this participation of the witnesses, that is, to the *faith* of those addressed by the divine speech-act of Jesus' resurrection. This original faith is communicated in the form of tradition, and for Bultmann the crucial question is how this communication of tradition is understood. Does the tradition simply hand down claims about events experienced by others in an ever-receding past, events that must be taken on trust as items of belief? Or is the original divine speech-act somehow *reenacted* as tradition is communicated in the preaching of the gospel? Insofar as the second is the case, the saving event will be a reality of the present no less than the past and will make good its claim to final, unsurpassable, "eschatological" significance. The faith evoked by the kerygma will be no less original than the faith of the first witnesses. In the kerygma the saving event will be announced, but it will also be realized.

According to Bultmann, the kerygma announces that the Jesus whose life belongs to the past remains decisive for the present—not just because his disciples chose to keep his memory alive but because (as they came to believe) *God* has decreed and announced his decisive significance. The apostolic preaching is the repetition and reenactment of the divine announcement. That is the theological point secured by Bultmann's historical reconstruction of the kerygma of the earliest community, presented as a basic *Motiv*—a "theme" or "component"—of New Testament theology. It is also a *Voraussetzung*—a "*pre*-condition"—of New Testament theology, since the rationale for the divine decision has not yet become clear. Christological or messianic claims are made, the earliest community constitutes itself on the basis of these claims, but the kerygma will become theology only when set in the context of a developed *soteriology*. According to Bultmann, that is the contribution of just two of the New Testament writers; part 2 of *Theology* is therefore devoted no longer to the kerygma but to the *theology* of Paul and John. Yet fundamental theological points are already made throughout part 1, in the historical reconstructions of the proclamation of Jesus and the kerygma of the Jerusalem and Hellenistic communities.

While major theological and especially christological issues come to light in these initial analyses, the kerygma for Bultmann remains a *pre*-theological entity. The moment of transition from the early kerygma to New Testament theology occurs as the figure of Paul is introduced at the beginning of part 2. According to Bultmann, Paul was brought to Christian faith by the kerygma of the Hellenistic community (188; ET, 1.187). As with any other hearer of early Christian preaching, he was confronted with the question of whether he was willing to recognize in the crucified Jesus the Messiah whom God raised from the dead. Paul, however, was "a zealot for the ancestral traditions" (Gal 1:14) who persecuted the church because its message seemed to undermine the Law as he understood it and thus to threaten the fundamentals of Jewish identity. The question posed by the kerygma concerned Paul's willingness to accept not only its positive content (that Jesus is the Messiah) but also its negative judgment on his previous identity and conduct. Characteristically, Bultmann stresses the negative: "This then is the meaning of his conversion: the abandonment of his former self-understanding, i.e. the abandonment of what had been until then the norm and meaning of his life, his pride and joy" (189; ET, 1.188).

Paraphrasing Phil 3, Bultmann here highlights the kerygma's impact on an individual biography. In opening up the possibility of a new life lived in the light of Jesus' messiahship and resurrection, the kerygma also passes judgment on the old life—even where that life has been one of devoted service to God. There is gain, but there is also loss, and the gain is inseparable from the loss (Phil 3:7). The kerygma brings Paul a "knowledge of Christ Jesus my Lord" (3:8), and theological reflection leads him to articulate its implications and rationale in terms of his own transformed self-image. Paul is exemplary in this respect, in spite of the biographical particularities he lists "circumcised on the eighth day, of the people of Israel," and so on (3:5-6). His readers are to think of themselves as subject to essentially the same revaluation of gain and loss; if they fall short of the transformed self-image intended by the kerygma, God will reveal it to them (3:15). Here, then, the kerygma begins to develop into theology as Bultmann understands it: an account of the transformed situation of the kerygma's addressee.

Theology

Only in an account of its addressee does the kerygma's underlying logic come to light. Within the New Testament Bultmann finds such an account especially in the Pauline and Johannine texts, to which the second and longest of the three main divisions of *Theology* is devoted. The relatively brief presentations of the message of Jesus and of the earliest community, together with the much fuller analysis of the kerygma of the Hellenistic community, are intended to prepare the way for the *theology* of the New Testament, virtually identified with the theology of Paul and of John (part 2). In part 3, later developments in belief and practice are assessed on the basis of criteria derived from Paul and John. Thus Bultmann interrogates texts such as the Pastoral

Letters and the *Shepherd of Hermas* to see "how far the Pauline and Johannine understanding [of salvation] was maintained" (510–11; ET, 2.158). New Testament theology seems to have no place for the theologies of Matthew, Mark, Luke-Acts, or Hebrews.[29] This apparently arbitrary exclusion is rooted in what Bultmann thinks theology is. If one identifies the theology of a text merely by summarizing its ideas about God, Jesus, the eschaton, the church, and so on, as appropriate, then every New Testament writing would have its own theology. But if, as Bultmann argues, theology is the attempt to give conceptual clarity to the kerygma by analyzing the situation of its addressee, then it is plausible to claim that only Paul and John offer any such account. The crucial point is that, in both writers, the kerygma is explicitly said to be addressed not to a particular community or individuals but to humanity as such. In John the universal scope of the kerygma's address is conveyed by the term κόσμος, "world," while for Paul the most significant of his anthropological terms is σάρξ, "flesh."[30] Such terminology enables both writers to construct an account of the total human context presupposed in the kerygma and so to bring to light the logic and rationale of its word of judgment and grace.

Bultmann presents New Testament theology as "anthropology," an account of the human condition. The two main subdivisions of his Pauline theology section both take *der Mensch*, the human being, as their theme. That is not to say that Christology is here subordinated to anthropology, losing its authentically Pauline and Johannine primacy. Fundamental to Bultmann's account of human being is that it is addressed by the kerygma derived from the event of Christ's incarnation, death, and resurrection. The existence of *der Mensch* is the existence of the being addressed in the kerygma, the one in whom the kerygma enables the decision of faith for which it calls. Since the kerygma is always an event in time rather than a timeless wisdom, it is possible and necessary to speak of human existence prior to as well as subsequent to the Christ-event. Yet this before/after structure is inseparably linked to the Christ-event that both differentiates and unites the "before" and the "after." Christology is not subordinated to anthropology any more than anthropology is subordinated to Christology; rather, they are *co*-ordinated with each other, and it is the task of theology to elaborate that co-ordination. In that sense Paul and John are already theologians. They provide an explanation of why the

Christ-event is needed and how it transforms human existence; their theology is *soteriology*. A three-stage soteriological sequence—fallenness, salvation-event, faith—underlies Bultmann's accounts of both his New Testament theologians.

Fallenness

For Paul, human existence apart from Christ is characterized by a perversion of an original human relation to the creator God (226–32; ET, 1.227–32; cf. Rom 1:18-23). To be truly human is to know one's own creatureliness and subjection to the Creator's claim, but humanity "has always missed its true being [*sein eigentliches Sein*]" (227; ET, 1.227). The term σάρξ sheds light on the ambiguous human situation. In Paul's usage, "flesh" stands not only for human materiality and weakness in relation to God but also for "the sphere within which one moves, which defines one's horizon, one's possibilities of acting or suffering" (236; ET, 1.235). The fleshly is the visible, the this-worldly, the natural, the given. While σάρξ is neutral in itself, "the conduct oriented to the σάρξ and normed by the σάρξ is sinful" (238; ET, 1.238) in that it is oblivious to God's claim. This conduct may be attributed to both Jews and Greeks. Jews may succumb to the sphere of the flesh even as they zealously observe the law; Paul himself "put his confidence in the flesh," that is, in his inherited privileges and the corresponding practice (Phil 3:4). Closed off against God, the flesh is the sphere of human self-sufficiency, confidence in one's ability to attain whatever one conceives as the good life, for example, "righteousness" (Phil 3:9) or "wisdom" (1 Cor 1:20). In either case, this confident self-sufficiency can be expressed in the form of "boasting" (Rom 3:27; 1 Cor 1:29). Of course, there are also less high-minded ways of living according to the flesh. The "works of the flesh" include the misuse of the body in sexual immorality or drunkenness, but the term "flesh" is still broad enough to include practices or attitudes such as idolatry, hostility, envy, anger, and quarreling (Gal 5:19-21). What these diverse expressions of the flesh have in common is that they represent a life choice oriented toward the realm of appearances and closed to the reality of the divine. One may therefore attribute to the flesh a singular φρόνημα (Rom 8:6-7): a perspective, an outlook, a worldview, or—in Bultmann's favored term—a self-understanding.

In John the κόσμος is characterized by its darkness (John 1:5). When Christ came into the world as its true light, "the world knew him not" (1:9, 10).[31] Yet this same world was not alien to him. It is his own, created through him and finding its life in him (1:3-4, 10-11). In its original created state, the world is a place of light—in the first instance, the daylight in which human beings can safely "work" and "walk" (cf. 9:4; 11:9-10), in which they orient themselves to their objects and their environment. In enabling human *self*-orientation and *self*-understanding, the daylight is an apt image of the true light that enlightens human existence (cf. 1:4, 9)—that is, a possible perception of oneself as a creature wholly dependent on its creator. Darkness is simply the absence of this light. The Johannine "darkness" is not some mythological or metaphysical entity but humanity's inexplicable preference for an illusory self-determination over the proffered truth of creature-hood. The Johannine "world" is creation corrupted by this original decision for darkness rather than light, falsehood rather than truth (cf. 378–85; ET, 2.26–32). The Johannine narrative tells how this decision is re-enacted as religious traditions are perversely used to provide criteria for rejecting the light of revelation (cf. 7:27; 9:16). The gospel narrative recounts "how the human quest for security [*Sicherungswille*] distorts the knowledge of God, how it makes God's demand and promise a possession and so closes itself against God" (380; ET, 2.27).

Salvation-Event

Using their own distinctive terminology and within different literary genres, Paul and John both offer accounts of the human situation as a seamless whole, relativizing all the binary oppositions that structure normal perceptions of human society: male and female, Jew and Gentile, Greek and barbarian, young and old, slave and free, ruler and ruled, educated and uneducated, and so on. These visible distinctions are of only secondary significance in the light of the primary reality of a world closed to the knowledge of God, yet opened up to a true understanding of God and self by the Christ-event and its proclamation. For Bultmann, it is the ability to abstract from the particular and conceptualize the universal that makes Paul and John theologians.

Into the closed world of unredeemed humanity break the righteousness and grace of God, establishing the new possibility of redeemed human existence that is summed up in the term "faith."[32] In Bultmann's reading of Paul, the sequential unfolding of Jesus' life from preexistence to exaltation (cf. Phil 2:6-11) is compressed into a singular "event" (*Ereignis, Geschehen*), which is at the same time an "act of God."[33] This event takes the form of a vertical incursion into the horizontal plane of human existence, and it always retains that vertical character and is not simply absorbed into the horizontal, in the form perhaps of doctrinal statements transmitted from one generation to another. The event is an act of God's grace and can therefore be characterized as the salvation-event (*Heilsereignis, Heilsgeschehen*). Originating in God, its goal is human well-being. The crucial question is how an occurrence at a particular point in space and time can benefit those located at a distance from that point. According to Paul, the Son of God "loved me and gave himself for me" (Gal 2:20), and the question of "my" involvement in Jesus' self-giving act remains an urgent one for Bultmann. An answer is found in Paul's reinterpretation of conventional eschatological themes. In traditional Jewish and Christian eschatology, a definitive divine judgment is pronounced on all human beings and their "works," and the judgment is thus the end or goal not just of the historical sequence as a whole but of every individual moment within it. In contrast, Paul views the coming of Christ as the eschatological event: "When the fullness of time had come, God sent forth his Son, born of woman, born under the law, to redeem those under the law, so that we might receive the adoption" (Gal 4:4-5). If a future event can be definitive in relation to every moment of the past, then a past event can be definitive in relation to every subsequent present: "Behold, *now* is the acceptable time, *now* is the day of salvation!" (2 Cor 6:2). Although Paul retains vestiges of traditional eschatological language, it is more characteristic of him to reinterpret the concept of the eschaton so as to ascribe finality and ultimacy to the Christ-event itself (271–80; ET, 1.270–79). If this event is final, ultimate, and definitive, then it is so "now" and "for me."

The same temporal shift occurs in John, although Bultmann sees in the Johannine account of the sending of the Son not the day of salvation but the world's judgment.[34] "For judgment I came into this world," says the Johannine Jesus, and this judgment brings both light and darkness: "so that those who do not see may see, and those who see may become blind" (John 9:39). Jesus is the Revealer in the form of the Word become flesh, and the presence of both the divine and the human creates a double possibility, of "revelation" as his "glory" is manifested in his signs, his words, and his death, and of "offense" (σκάνδαλον) as his human existence makes his claim to come from God seem incredible.[35] The humanity of the Revealer entails his paradoxical hiddenness (*Verborgenheit*), and the paradox is presented in its most extreme form when the final revelation of his "glory" is found not in his miracles or resurrection but in his cross (cf. John 12:23-33). The glorified and exalted Lord is none other than the earthly Jesus,[36] and the converse is also true: "Jesus' earthly life does not become an item of the historical past but remains constantly present" (402; ET, 2.49). Thus he is and remains "the Revealer," the bearer of the revelation that amounts simply to his own claim to reveal:

> Jesus as the Revealer of God reveals nothing else than that he is the Revealer, which also means that he is the One for whom the world is waiting and who brings in his own person the goal of all human longing [*das . . . , worauf alle Sehnsucht des Menschen geht*]: Life and Truth as the reality from which humanity can exist, Light as that total transparency of existence in which questions and problems come to an end. (418; ET, 2.66)

As light, truth, and life, Jesus calls for and enables a decision to exit the closed "world" of religious self-sufficiency, where humanity fabricates illusory answers to its own fundamental questions, and to reenter the world created and illuminated by God in the beginning.

Faith

According to Bultmann, New Testament theology is essentially the theology of Paul and John, and this theology is soteriology. As such it has a threefold structure, for the event of salvation must be preceded by a negative state in which salvation is required and followed by a positive state in which salvation has been attained. The two New Testament theologians offer complementary accounts of the salvation-event that enable the transformation of the negative into the positive. The event belongs to both the past and the present: the past in that it is identified with the life, death, and resurrection of Jesus; the present in that this life, death, and resurrection is the divine Word addressed also to ourselves. The past dimension of the single saving event is underlined especially by John, the present by Paul; we might say that John is concerned with the past of the present event, Paul with the presence of the past event.

It remains to give an account of the positive state that the salvation-event brings about in the human being and the human life that is addressed by it. Of this new life Paul writes, "It is no longer I that live but Christ who lives in me, and the life I now live in the flesh, I live by faith in the Son of God who loved me and gave himself for me" (Gal 2:20).

There is for Paul a "no longer" (οὐκέτι) and a "now" (νῦν); the transition between past and present is enabled by the self-giving of the Son of God, and the reorientation of ongoing bodily life is summed up in the term "faith" (πίστις). Using the verb πιστεύειν rather than the noun, the Johannine evangelist gives a similar account of the transition and its outcome: "Amen, amen, I say to you, whoever hears my word and believes the one who sent me has eternal life and does not come into judgment but has passed from death to life" (John 5:24).

Unencumbered by the English-language disjunction between the noun "faith" and the verb "believe," Bultmann characterizes both the Pauline and the Johannine accounts of the reoriented life as the life of "faith."[37] In his own more abstract terminology, the faith that responds to the kerygma is defined as a new "self-understanding [*Selbstverständnis*]" (589; ET, 2.241). Human life is always accompanied by one self-understanding or another—a perspective on reality, articulate or otherwise, mediated by communal tradition and its individual appropriation. The kerygma is the call to adopt a self-understanding that corresponds to revealed divine reality and so to abandon a previous self-understanding now exposed as the illusory product of a world closed against the divine. Viewed from within, "faith" is the affirmative answer to the question posed to human existence by the kerygma, the divine word that speaks of the Son of God's entry into human life. Viewed from without, faith is a particular instance of the universal human project of making sense of self and world. For Bultmann's "self-understanding," we might risk substituting the more contemporary term "spirituality." Faith as Bultmann understands it is spirituality of a particular kind. In his analysis, its core characteristics are articulated both by Paul and by John.

Faith is renunciation, abandonment, loss. It is negation as well as affirmation, and the affirmation is inseparable from the negation. "Whatever was gain for me I count as loss for Christ's sake" (Phil 3:7). Where there is faith, all "boasting" is excluded (Rom 3:27).[38] Nicodemus must abandon his former certainties as a "teacher of Israel" if he is to find the answer to his uncomprehending question, "How can these things be?" (John 3:9-10). His Pharisaic colleagues must abandon the pretence that they possess criteria that will determine whether or not Jesus' claim is true (John 9:13-34).

Faith is oriented toward the kerygma. A self-generated decision to renounce boasting and embrace humility would not be faith, for it is the kerygma's preaching of Christ crucified that enables faith and disables boasting (cf. 1 Cor 1:18–2:5). Faith stems from what is heard, and what is heard is the word of God (Rom 10:17). Similarly, John "came for testimony, so as to testify about the light, so that all might believe through him" (John 1:7). If faith is self-understanding, it is an understanding of the self in its relation to Jesus as proclaimed in Christian preaching.[39]

Faith is subject to the dialectic of gift and demand.[40] Pauline indicatives state that in Christ we are reconciled to God, that we have died to sin in baptism, that we live by the Spirit; corresponding Pauline imperatives exhort us to *be* reconciled to God, to *regard* ourselves as dead to sin, to *keep in line with* the Spirit (2 Cor 5:18-20; Rom 6:1-11; Gal 5:25). Jesus' followers have been grafted into the true vine, yet they must take active steps to ensure that they remain there: "Abide in me, and I in you" (John 15:4). For both writers, faith receives the divine gift but is also active through love (cf. Gal 5:6; John 13:1-10, 34-35).

* * *

Bultmann's theology *of* the New Testament is at the same time a theological reflection *on* the New Testament. For some, lacking theological interest or competence, the theological orientation is already sufficient to call the whole work into question. For others, the problem lies not with theology but with Bultmann himself, notorious as the great demythologizer and archskeptic. Yet these are old, tired, and unfruitful responses to this figure, whose best work retains its potential to challenge and provoke.

NOTES

Editors' Preface

1   Ernst Käsemann, *New Testament Questions of Today* (trans. W. J. Montague; Philadelphia: Fortress, 1979), 15. Compare the estimate of another of Bultmann's students, Schubert M. Ogden, writing in 1966 ("The Significance of Rudolf Bultmann for Contemporary Theology," in *The Theology of Rudolf Bultmann* [ed. Charles W. Kegley; London: SCM Press, 1966], 104): "By common consent, Ruldolf Bultmann is one of the most significant figures on the contemporary theological scene. . . . By whatever criteria one judges such significance . . . , his contribution is unchallengeably among the most important of our time."

2   John Reumann, "The Relevant Gospel According to Rudolf Bultmann," *Lutheran Quarterly* 10 (August 1958): 226–47 (226).

3   Quoted in Walter Schmithals, *An Introduction to the Theology of Rudolf Bultmann* (trans. John Bowden; London: SCM–Canterbury Press, 1968), 21.

Chapter 1: Byrskog

1   Rudolf Bultmann, *Jesus* (Berlin: Deutsche Bibliothek, 1926); idem, *Theologie des Neuen Testaments* (Tübingen: Mohr Siebeck, 1953); ET: *Theology of the New Testament* (trans. Kendrick Grobel; 2 vols. repr. in 1; Baylor University Press, 2007). The book *Jesus* was first published by Wolf Wertheim in the series "Die Unsterblichen. Die geistigen Heroen der Menschheit in ihrem Leben und Wirken." The first and second German "Lieferungen" of the *Theologie* appeared in 1948 and 1951.

2   Rudolf Bultmann, *Die Geschichte der synoptischen Tradition* (2nd ed.; FRLANT 29; Göttingen: Vandenhoeck & Ruprecht, 1931).

3   "Es kann aber kaum zweifelhaft sein, daß Jesus wie andere Aufrührer als messi-
    anischer Prophet am Kreuze starb" (*Jesus*, 22).

4   William Wrede, *Das Messiasgeheimnis in den Evangelien. Zugleich ein Beitrag
    zum Verständnis des Markusevangeliums* (Göttingen: Vandenhoeck & Ruprecht,
    1901).

5   Scholars soon realized that Bultmann, in his discussion of Jesus' message,
    employed material that he in his analysis of the synoptic tradition did not trace
    back to Jesus. Cf. Julius Schniewind, "Zur Synoptiker-Exegese," *TRu* 2 (1930):
    129–89 (172–74). Schniewind calls this "Querschnittexegese."

6   I evaluated Bultmann's history of the synoptic tradition in *JBL* 122 (2003):
    549–55.

7   For further discussion, see Samuel Byrskog, "The Transmission of the Jesus
    Tradition: Old and New Insights," *Early Christianity* 3 (2010): 1–28.

8   There are exceptions to this trend, e.g., Robert Funk, John Dominic Crossan,
    Helmut Koester, and Marcus Borg.

9   I am thinking of studies by scholars such as Walter Grundmann and Hugo
    Odeberg. For an evaluation of Grundmann's life and work, see Roland Dei-
    nes, Volker Leppin, and Karl-Wilhelm Niebuhr, eds., *Walter Grundmann—ein
    Neutestamentler im Dritten Reich* (Leipzig: Evangelische Verlagsanstalt, 2007).
    For an assessment of Bultmann's view on Jews and Judaism, see Anders Gerd-
    mar, *Roots of Theological Anti-Semitism: German Biblical Interpretation and the
    Jews, from Herder and Semler to Kittel and Bultmann* (SJHC 20; Leiden: Brill,
    2009), 373–414.

10 E. P. Sanders, *Paul and Palestinian Judaism: A Comparison of Patterns of Reli-
    gion* (Philadelphia: Fortress, 1977); idem, *Jesus and Judaism* (London: SCM
    Press, 1985); idem, *Judaism: Practice and Belief, 63 BCE–66 CE* (London: SCM
    Press, 1992); idem, *The Historical Figure of Jesus* (2nd ed.; London: Penguin,
    1995). For the plurality of "Judaisms," see Alan F. Segal, *The Other Judaisms of
    Late Antiquity* (BJS 127; Atlanta: Scholars Press, 1987). For Galilee, see Mark
    Chancey, *The Myth of a Gentile Galilee* (SNTSMS 118; Cambridge: Cambridge
    University Press, 2002); idem, *Greco-Roman Culture and the Galilee of Jesus*
    (SNTSMS 134; Cambridge: Cambridge University Press, 2006) and the litera-
    ture referred to there.

11 Sanders, *Jesus and Judaism*, 108–13, 200–204, denies that Jesus called for
    repentance. This is a minority position.

12 Cf. the debate between Hershel Shanks, "Is the Title 'Rabbi' Anachronistic
    in the Gospels?," *JQR* 53 (1962/63): 337–45; idem, "Origins of the Title
    'Rabbi,'" *JQR* 59 (1968/69): 152–57; and Solomon Zeitlin, "A Reply," *JQR* 53
    (1962/63): 345–49; idem, "The Title Rabbi in the Gospels Is Anachronistic,"
    JQR 59 (1968/69): 158–60.

13 Cf. John P. Meier, *Law and Love* (vol. 4 of *A Marginal Jew: Rethinking the His-
    torical Jesus*; New Haven: Yale University Press, 2009).

14 Joachim Jeremias, *Abba. Studien zur neutestamentlichen Theologie und Zeitgeschichte* (Göttingen: Vandenhoeck & Ruprecht, 1966), 15–67. For a refinement of Jeremias' argument, see Marianne Meye Thompson, *The Promise of the Father: Jesus and God in the New Testament* (Louisville, Ky.: Westminster John Knox, 2000), 21–34.

15 See Nils Alstrup Dahl, *The Crucified Messiah and Other Essays* (Minneapolis: Augsburg, 1974), 10–36. Martin Hengel's "Jesus als messianischer Lehrer der Weisheit und die Anfänge der Christologie," in *Sagesse et religion. Colloque de Strasbourg* (Paris: Presses Universitaires de France, 1979), 148–88, has been influential for the recent debate.

16 Delbert Burkett, *The Son of Man Debate: A History and Evaluation* (SNTSMS 107; Cambridge: Cambridge University Press, 1999); Mogens Müller, *The Expression "Son of Man" and the Development of Christology: A History of Interpretation* (Copenhagen International Seminar; London: Equinox, 2007).

17 James D. G. Dunn, *Jesus Remembered* (Grand Rapids: Eerdmans, 2003), 759–61.

18 Sanders, *Jesus and Judaism*, 294–318, has been influential for pointing to the importance of the temple incident.

19 The groundbreaking study is Odil Hannes Steck, *Israel und das gewaltsame Geschick der Propheten. Untersuchungen zur Überlieferung des deuteronomistischen Geschichtsbildes im Alten Testament, Spätjudentum und Urchristentum* (WMANT 23; Neukirchen-Vluyn: Neukirchener Verlag, 1967). It is today commonly applied to Jesus. See, e.g., Gerd Theissen and Annette Merz, *Der historische Jesus. Ein Lehrbuch* (3rd ed.; Göttingen: Vandenhoeck & Ruprecht, 2001), 378–79.

20 The most influential sacrificial interpretation is Joachim Jeremias, *Die Abendmahlsworte Jesu* (3rd ed.; Göttingen: Vandenhoeck & Ruprecht, 1960).

21 Cf. Dunn, *Jesus Remembered*, 809–18. Dunn ends this section with, "Much of this is speculative" (818).

22 "Die Verkündigung Jesu gehört zu den Voraussetzungen der Theologie des NT und ist nicht ein Teil dieser selbst" (*Theologie*, 1).

23 Dunn, *Jesus Remembered*, 73–78, places his discussion of Bultmann under "The Flight from History."

24 For discussion of the *Historismus* in the 1920s, see Friedrich Wilhelm Graf, *Der heilige Zeitgeist. Studien zur Ideengeschichte der protestantischen Theologie in der Weimarer Republik* (Tübingen: Mohr Siebeck, 2011), 111–38.

25 Ernst Bernheim developed Ranke's comments into a methodology. See Bernheim, *Lehrbuch der historischen Methode und der Geschichtsphilosophie. Mit Nachweis der wichtigsten Quellen und Hilfsmittel zum Studium der Geschichte* (5th and 6th eds.; Leipzig: Dunder, 1908).

26 Johann Gustav Droysen, *Historik* (ed. Peter Leyh; Stuttgart: Friedrich Frommann Verlag Günther Holzboog, 1977), 148.

27 Adolf von Harnack, *Das Wesen des Christentums* (Leipzig: Hinrichs'sche Buchhandlung, 1900).

28 Martin Kähler, *Der sogenannte historische Jesus und der geschichtliche biblische Christus* (2nd ed.; Leipzig: Deichert'sche Verlagsbuchhandlung, 1896). The first edition appeared in 1892.

29 The article is included in Troeltsch's collected essays: "Ueber historische und dogmatische Methode in der Theologie," in *Gesammelte Schriften*, vol. 2, *Zur religiösen Lage, Religionsphilosophie und Ethik* (Tübingen: Mohr Siebeck, 1913), 729–53.

30 For an account of the circumstances behind Bultmann's book, see Konrad Hammann, *Rudolf Bultmann. Eine Biographie* (2nd ed.; Tübingen: Mohr Siebeck, 2009), 179–92. The 2012 edition of Hamman's biography was not available to me.

31 Johannes Weiss, *Die Predigt Jesu vom Reiche Gottes* (2nd ed.; Göttingen: Vandenhoeck & Ruprecht, 1900; repr. from 1st ed., 1892); idem, *Jesus von Nazareth. Mythus oder Geschichte? Eine Auseinandersetzung mit Kalthoff, Drews, Jensen* (Tübingen: Mohr Siebeck, 1910); Wrede, *Das Messiasgeheimnis*; Albert Schweitzer, *Eine Geschichte der Leben-Jesu-Forschung* (2nd ed.; Tübingen: Mohr Siebeck, 1913). This is a revised version of *Von Reimarus zu Wrede. Eine Geschichte der Leben-Jesu-Forschung* (1906).

32 Rudolf Bultmann, *Der Stil der paulinischen Predigt und die kynisch-stoische Diatribe* (FRLANT 13; Göttingen: Vandenhoeck & Ruprecht, 1910); idem, *Die Exegese des Theodor von Mopsuestia* (published by Helmut Feld and Karl Hermann Schelke; Stuttgart: Kohlhammer, 1984).

33 Hammann, *Rudolf Bultmann. Eine Biographie*, 102.

34 Hammann, *Rudolf Bultmann. Eine Biographie*, 102.

35 David Friedrich Strauss, *Das Leben Jesu: kritisch bearbeitet* (Tübingen: C. F. Osiander, 1835). Strauss' work appeared in several revised editions.

36 Cf. Samuel Byrskog, "A Century with the *Sitz im Leben*: From Form-Critical Setting to Gospel Community and Beyond," *ZNW* 98 (2007): 1–27.

37 Ernst Baasland, *Theologie und Methode. Eine historiographische Analyse der Frühschriften Rudolf Bultmanns* (Wuppertal: Brockhaus Verlag, 1992), 32–76.

38 Hammann, *Rudolf Bultmann. Eine Biographie*, 180–81. In the long run, Bultmann felt closer to the dialectical theology of Friedrich Gogarten, who became a supporter of the demythologizing program. Cf. Bultmann, "Autobiographical Reflections of Rudolf Bultmann," in *The Theology of Rudolf Bultmann* (ed. Charles W. Kegley; New York: Harper & Row, 1966), xix–xxv (xxiv–xxv).

39 The original German is as follows: "Einen 'historischen Jesus' habe ich beschrieben, freilich nicht (wenigstens der Absicht nach) im Sinne des Historismus, der Jesus als ein Phänomen der Vergangenheit nimmt, sondern so, wie er zu dem geschichtlichen Verständnis spricht, das sich durch die Geschichte anreden lassen will, das sich also nicht 'betrachtend' außerhalb der Geschichte befindet." Quoted from Hammann, *Rudolf Bultmann. Eine Biographie*, 184.

40 The original German is as follows: "Dieser Dialog ist aber deshalb nicht ein geistreiches Spiel der Subjektivität des Betrachters, sondern ein wirkliches Befragen der Geschichte, bei dem der Geschichtsschreiber gerade seine Subjektivität in Frage stellt und bereit ist, die Geschichte als Autorität zu hören. . . . Denn gerade hier soll ja das, was am Betrachter das Relative ist, nämlich all die Voraussetzungen, die er aus seiner Zeit und seiner Schulung und seiner individuellen Haltung in ihnen mitbringt, preisgegeben werden, und die Geschichte soll wirklich reden. Sie redet aber nicht, wenn man sich die Ohren zustopft, d. h. wenn man eine Neutralität ihr gegenüber beansprucht, sondern wenn man bewegt durch Fragen zu ihr kommt und aus ihr lernen will." Bultmann, *Jesus*, 7–8.

41 This is what Bultmann claimed in a letter to Hans Hübner, dated June 5, 1972, and in conversation with Günther Bornkamm in early 1976. See Hübner, "Bultmanns 'existentiale Interpretation'—Untersuchungen zu ihrer Herkunft," *ZTK* 100 (2003): 280–324; Bornkamm, "*In memoriam* Rudolf Bultmann. * 20.8.1884 † 30.7.1976," *NTS* 23 (1977): 235–42 (239).

42 Rudolf Bultmann, *History and Eschatology: The Gifford Lectures 1955* (Edinburgh: The University Press, 1957). The lectures were also published as *The Presence of Eternity: History and Eschatology. The Gifford Lectures 1955* (New York: Harper & Brothers, 1957).

43 Bultmann, *History and Eschatology*, 155.

44 Rudolf Bultmann, "Das Verhältnis der urchristlichen Christusbotschaft zum historischen Jesus," in *Sitzungsberichte der Heidelberger Akademie der Wissenschaften, Philosophisch-historische Klasse 1960* (Heidelberg: Universitätsverlag C. Winter, 1962), 5–27.

45 Ernst Käsemann, "Das Problem des historischen Jesus," *ZTK* 51 (1954): 125–53. In 1956 Günther Bornkamm published *Jesus von Nazareth* (Stuttgart: Kohlhammer, 1956), pointing to the theme of confrontation with God as evident in the ministry of Jesus and the kerygma.

46 The original German is as follows: "Die Geschichte ist für sie [the historical-critical approach] Anrede, und sie besteht sozusagen im *Hören*, nicht im distanzierten *Sehen*." Bultmann, "Das Verhältnis," 18.

47 Hans-Georg Gadamer, *Wahrheit und Methode. Grundzüge einer philosophischen Hermeneutik* (6th ed.; Gesammelte Werke I: Hermeneutik I; Tübingen: Mohr Siebeck, 1990).

48 For a survey of recent historiography used in Jesus research, see Robert L. Webb, "The Historical Enterprise and Historical Jesus Research," in *Key Events in the Life of the Historical Jesus* (ed. Darrell L. Bock and Robert L. Webb; WUNT 27; Tübingen: Mohr Siebeck, 2009), 9–93.

49 See Ben F. Meyer, *Critical Realism and the New Testament* (Princeton Theological Monographs 17; Allison Park, Pa.: Pickwick, 1989); idem, *Reality and Illusion in New Testament Scholarship: A Primer in Critical Realist Hermeneutics* (Collegeville, Minn.: Liturgical Press, 1994).

50   Maurice Halbwachs, *Les cadres sociaux de la mémoire* (new ed.; Paris: Presses Universitaires de France, 1952).

51   Maurice Halbwachs, *La mémoire collective* (Paris: Presses Universitaires de France, 1950).

52   Werner H. Kelber, *The Oral and the Written Gospel: The Hermeneutics of Speaking and Writing in the Synoptic Tradition, Mark, Paul, and Q* (Philadelphia: Fortress, 1983; repr., Voices in Performance and Text; Bloomington: Indiana University Press, 1997), discusses Bultmann's form-critical program (2–8), but not his notion of history.

53   Anthony Le Donne, *The Historiographical Jesus: Memory, Typology, and the Son of David* (Waco, Tex.: Baylor University Press, 2009). Le Donne is inspired by Dunn, *Jesus Remembered*. Cf. also Le Donne, *Historical Jesus: What Can We Know and How Can We Know It?* (Grand Rapids: Eerdmans, 2011).

54   Barbara A. Misztal, *Theories of Social Remembering* (Philadelphia: Open University Press, 2003), 67–74.

55   Misztal, *Theories*, 70.

56   Richard A. H. King, *Aristotle and Plotinus on Memory* (Berlin: De Gruyter, 2010). Despite differences, both Aristotle and Plotinus regard memory, according to King, as a faculty of the mind that provides an indirect way to past reality via representation.

57   James Fentress and Chris Wickham, *Social Memory* (Oxford: Blackwell, 1992), ix.

Chapter 2: Rowe

1   All citations of Bultmann's *Theology* refer to *Theology of the New Testament* (Baylor University Press, 2007).

2   For Bultmann this lack of originality also explains a potentially confusing fact of the New Testament, namely, why so little of Jesus' synoptic (or synoptic-like) language appears in Paul's letters or the Gospel of John. So, too, does Jesus' rootedness within Judaism explain why "modern liberal Judaism" can esteem him as a teacher (1.35).

3   Bultmann of course does not really think that the historical Jesus called twelve (1.37).

4   In this he is right, as I suggested in "New Testament Theology: The Revival of a Discipline," *JBL* 125 (2006): 393–410.

5   C. Kavin Rowe, *Early Narrative Christology: The Lord in the Gospel of Luke* (Berlin: De Gruyter, 2006; repr., Grand Rapids: Baker, 2009).

6   Bultmann was not much concerned with the literary surface area of the New Testament. Writing well after Wrede's *Messiasgeheimnis*, he knew the synoptics were theological portraits. My point is that even those who understand now that the sort of form criticism Bultmann practiced has been hermeneutically problematized will still have to deal with the question he posed.

7   Lest this further significance go unnoticed: it is not only historical inaccuracy that is at stake here but also certain philosophical judgments about human beings that are coordinated with a particular picture of history; with Bultmann's historical picture now gone, his philosophical judgments should follow—or find independent ground.

8   It is an essential corollary to his emphasis on the preaching of the Word as that which calls for an existential decision: it is the event, not the specific content, of preaching that brings one to decision.

9   The kerygma is "real only in the act of existing" (2.241, et passim). For the argument that certain kinds of abstractions make it impossible for us to know what we are really talking about anymore, see Alasdair MacIntyre, "Colors, Cultures, and Practices," in *Selected Essays*, vol. 1, *The Tasks of Philosophy* (Cambridge: Cambridge University Press, 2006), 24–51, esp. 38. MacIntyre's chief example that is directly applicable here is that of an imagined person whose language was entirely his own (Wittgenstein's "private language"). This figure, MacIntyre argues against those who try to reason from this imagined experience, is so abstract as to become philosophically meaningless: since all of our language is nonprivate, we literally have no conceptual possibilities for knowing how to speak well about such an imaginary figure.

10 Alasdair MacIntyre, *After Virtue* (3rd ed.; Notre Dame, Ind.: University of Notre Dame Press, 2009); and idem, "The Intelligibility of Action," in *Rationality, Relativism, and the Human Sciences* (ed. J. Margolis, M. Krausz, and R. M. Burian; Dordrecht: Reidel, 1986), 63–80.

11 When Bultmann says that even a simple sentence such as "Jesus is Lord" already contains interpretation (of Lord, e.g.), he is hot on the trail of this insight. But he loses it again when he subsequently uses this example as proof that we cannot take the already interpreted New Testament statements as the kerygma.

12 Bultmann himself might reply that if we could find it by exegesis we would have mastered it and it would no longer be address. There is a certain way in which this would be right, but more deeply such a view cuts out a significant part of the theological *telos* of exegesis, which is to test the faith against the biblical witness and clarify the content of whatever formulations we could ever dream up. It is true, of course, that Bultmann does use implicit/explicit language as a way to think about continuity. And this is good as far as it goes. The trouble is that it does not go far enough; we need more precision. What exactly is the implicit/explicit language meant to convey theologically?

13 Ecclesiology, to return to our earlier question, is thus communal Christology; or, in directly New Testament terms, the church is the body of Christ.

14 Another major problem with this section is Bultmann's treatment of the resurrection/empty tomb (esp. 1.44–45), but he states things more elaborately elsewhere, hence my decision not to thematize it here. On this problem in general, see Richard B. Hays, "Reading Scripture in Light of the Resurrection," in *The*

Art of Reading Scripture (ed. Ellen F. Davis and Richard B. Hays; Grand Rapids: Eerdmans, 2003), 216–38.

15 Of course Jewish *or* Hellenistic has now long been seen as a problematic dichotomy (Martin Hengel and legions after him). The point here, however, is not about whether these are the right terms as much as it is about the philosophical commitment to the kind of history that makes this way of talking inevitable.

16 F. C. Baur's legacy is not hard to discern here: behind awkward texts we have to find a real group of people with a controversial opinion (a "party"). This is yet another way we can move beyond Bultmann: it is simply unnecessary to posit actual groups for literary characters. Unless there are other reasons to assume the existence of various groups—such as the letters to the Corinthians or Galatians provide, for example—creating parties on the basis of literary characters is building castles in the air.

17 The discerning reader will note that I do not debate with Bultmann on the particulars here. The reason is that I reject the idea that serious debate is possible. Conducting a mock-debate over origins that we simply cannot see would reproduce the Bultmannian assumption that I am here criticizing (viz., that there is enough or the right kind of information for historians to have a meaningful debate in the first place). I would not deny in general, of course, that historical work requires great imagination, nor that the so-called final form of the text raises the kinds of questions that Bultmann pursues. There are seams, tensions, outright awkwardness, and so forth, not to mention what seem to be differing accounts of same events—all these matters require both imagination and restraint.

18 Bultmann's book on Jesus begins of course with the admission that we do not know much about Jesus (*Jesus and the Word* [New York: Scribner, 1958], 8; of course, he does then go on to tell us quite a bit about Jesus). Bultmann obviously knows how to say "information is lacking" and "about that we know nothing" (57). My points are that he should say it far more frequently than he does and that he engages in the same basic inventive task as he takes the New Testament itself to engage in (i.e., create legend-ish material about the church). By disciplined historian, I have in mind something like the reserve of the great Theodor Mommsen and those in Mommsen's tradition: one can think, e.g., of Mommsen's admonishment of Adolf Harnack when the latter suggested that the period of the Roman emperors should receive a more thorough teaching in the schools. Said Mommsen, "I too am in favour of this in general, but in specifics I believe that provisions and qualifications are called for. In general, the teaching of this field is in part impracticable and in part dangerous, since the tradition consists too much in court tittle-tattle or even worse things. In my view, teaching would specifically have to focus first on the Caesarian-Augustan period, which the Republican age leads into . . . and second on the age of Constantine. I regard what lies in between as unsuitable for fruitful treatment in schools." Mommsen continued, "If the question is put: what was the best period of the

age of the emperors as a whole, the ancient Romans themselves answer: the first ten years of Nero's rule. Now, try representing . . . that the first ten years of Nero's rule were the best period, and one of the most fortunate epochs in human history! Is this possible? Of course it would be, if every teacher could be equipped with the ability required to extract the kernel concealed inside the shell of sordid court gossip. I have been studying this period ever since I have been able to think. I have not succeeded in extracting this kernel, and if I were a teacher I would refuse the task of teaching the history of the emperors in general. Much as I regret having to water down Mr Harnack's wine, I have to say I cannot accept this." Cited in Theodor Mommsen, *A History of Rome under the Emperors* (New York: Routledge, 1996), 5–6.

19 These are three threads that—if unraveled—would cause the garment to become completely tattered.

20 Careful readers will discern that the structure of the *Theology* is thus simultaneously a great strength (it beautifully displays the theological judgments of the Bultmannian program) and a great weakness (it rebuilds the cul-de-sac out of which Bultmann was trying to move).

21 I grant that Bultmann would not think he is of two minds; I deny, however, that he would be right to think that about his book.

Chapter 3: Schnelle

1 Regarding Bultmann's *Theology of the New Testament*, cf. Walter Schmithals, *Die Theologie Rudolf Bultmanns* (2nd ed.; Tübingen: Mohr Siebeck, 1967); regarding Bultmann's life, cf. Hammann, *Rudolf Bultmann. Eine Biographie.*

2 This is also clear in the terminology: Bultmann speaks of the "preaching" of Jesus, of the "kerygma" of the primitive and Hellenistic churches, but of "theology" only in reference to Paul and John!

3 All citations of Bultmann's *Theology* refer to Bultmann, *Theology of the New Testament* (Baylor University Press, 2007).

4 Rudolf Bultmann, *Das Urchristentum im Rahmen der antiken Religionen* (4th ed.; Zurich: Artemis Verlag, 1976), is not a history of early Christianity but more a description of its environment. Here, too, Bultmann only sketches pre- and non-Pauline developments.

5 Here, Bultmann follows his teacher Wilhelm Heitmüller, "Zum Problem Paulus und Jesus," *ZNW* 13 (1912): 320–37.

6 For the evidence, cf. Martin Hengel, "Zwischen Jesus und Paulus: Die Hellenisten, die Sieben und Stephanus (Apg 6,1-15; 7,54-8, 3)," *ZThK* 72 (1975): 161ff; M. Zugmann, *"Hellenisten" in der Apostelgeschichte* (WUNT 2.264; Tübingen: Mohr Siebeck, 2009), 11–88.

7 Regarding Stephen, cf. A. Weiser, "Zur Gesetzes und Tempelkritik der 'Hellenisten,'" in *Das Gesetz im Neuen Testament* (ed. K. Kertelge; QD 108; Freiburg: Herder, 1986), 146–68; K. Löning, "Der Stephanuskreis und seine Mission," in *Die Anfänge des Christentums: Alte Welt und neue Hoffnung* (ed. J. Becker;

Stuttgart: Kohlhammer, 1987), 80–101; Heikki Räisänen, "Die 'Hellenisten' der Urgemeinde" in *ANRW 26.2* (ed. H. Temporini and W. Haase; Berlin: De Gruyter, 1995), 1468–1514; Zugmann,*"Hellenisten" in der Apostelgeschichte,* 312–57.

8 E. Rau emphasizes this in *Von Jesus zu Paulus* (Stuttgart: Kohlhammer, 1994), 15–77.

9 According to Acts 11:20, "some of them" went to Antioch in order to preach the Gospel to the Greeks, too.

10 Regarding Diaspora Judaism, cf. John M. G. Barclay, *Jews in the Mediterranean Diaspora: From Alexander to Trajan (323 BCE–117 CE)* (Edinburgh: T&T Clark, 1996).

11 W. Speyer sketches the cultural conditions surrounding the early Christian mission: the decline of classical Greco-Roman culture, the development toward monotheism, the concept of the divine origins of a special human being, and the importance of ethics. See Speyer, "Hellenistisch-römische Voraussetzungen der Verbreitung des Christentums," in *Der neue Mensch in Christus* (ed. J. Beutler; QD 190; Freiburg: Herder, 2001), 25–35.

12 Cf. Plutarch, "Über die eingegangenen Orakel," in *Über Gott und Vorsehung, Dämonen und Weissagung* (ed. K. Ziegler; Zurich: Artemis Verlag, 1952), 106–69; Pliny, *Ep* 10.96.9–10.

13 Bultmann began with the early missionary preaching and then primarily treated monotheism and judgment preaching (*Theology*, 1.65–92).

14 Cf., e.g., Cicero, *Nat. d.* 3.47.

15 Cf., e.g., Plutarch, *Is. Os.* 67.68 ("Thus, there is a Logos that orders the cosmos and a providence that guides it"); Dio Chrysostom, *Or.* 12; cf. Stephen Mitchell and Peter van Nuffelen, eds., *One God: Pagan Monotheism in the Roman Empire* (Cambridge: Cambridge University Press, 2010).

16 Regarding Simon, cf. the recent Gerd Theissen, "Simon Magus—die Entwicklung seines Bildes vom Charismatiker zum gnostischen Erlöser," in *Religionsgeschichte des Neuen Testaments* (FS K. Berger; ed. A. v. Dobbeler, K. Erlemann, and R. Heiligenthal; Basel: A. Francke Verlag, 2000), 407–32.

17 Cf. Hans-Josef Klauck, *Magie und Heidentum in der Apostelgeschichte des Lukas* (SBS 167; Stuttgart: Verlag Katholisches Bibelwerk, 1996).

18 Regarding the rationale, cf. Axel von Dobbeler, *Der Evangelist Philippus in der Geschichte des Urchristentums. Eine Prosopographische Skizze* (TANZ 30; Tübingen: Francke, 2000), 217–48; cf. further B. Kollmann, "Philippus der Evangelist und die Anfänge der Heidenmission," *Bib* 81 (2000): 551–65.

19 Regarding Peter as a missionary, cf. also Chr. Böttrich, *Petrus: Fischer, Fels und Funktionär* (Leipzig: Evangelische Verlagsanstalt, 2001), 161–82; Martin Hengel, *Der unterschätzte Petrus: Zwei Studien* (Tübingen: Mohr Siebeck, 2006), 145–48.

20 On this point, cf. Markus Öhler, *Barnabas: Der Mann der Mitte* (Biblische Gestalten 12; Leipzig: Evangelische Verlagsanstalt, 2005).

21 The observation in Acts 18:25d, 26 that Apollos knew only the baptism of John and had to receive theological instruction from Aquila and Prisca obviously traces back to Luke, who consciously minimizes the importance of Apollos; cf. M. Wolter, "Apollos und die ephesinischen Johannesjünger (Act 18,24–19,7)," *ZNW* 78 (1987): 49–73.

22 Cf. Stephan Witetschek, *Ephesische Enthüllungen I: frühe Christen in einer antiken Grossstadt zugleich ein Beitrag zur Frage nach den Kontexten der Johannesapokalypse* (BiTS 6; Leuven: Peeters, 2008), 350–58.

23 Cf. Robert Jewett, *Romans* (Hermeneia; Minneapolis: Fortress, 2007), 961–64.

24 For all questions concerning the history of the text and the social setting, cf. the extensive study by Eldon J. Epp, *Junia: The First Woman Apostle* (Minneapolis: Augsburg Fortress, 2005).

25 James D. G. Dunn, who virtually overlooks Galilee as the locus of Christian communities, adopts the picture in Acts entirely; see Dunn, *Beginning from Jerusalem* (Grand Rapids: Eerdmans, 2009), 27–28, 135–36 (already in the title of the book!).

26 The information in Josephus (*J.W.* 2.561; 7.368) that ten or eighteen thousand Jews, respectively, fell victim to a massacre in Damascus is hyperbole.

27 Regarding the city of Damascus, cf. H. Bietenhard, "Die Dekapolis von Pompejus bis Trajan," *ZDPV* 79 (1963): 24–58; on the history of the Christian church there, cf. Martin Hengel and A. M. Schwemer, *Paulus zwischen Damaskus und Antiochien* (WUNT 108; Tübingen: Mohr Siebeck, 1998), 60–101, 139–52.

28 Cf. Josephus, *J.W.* 3.29, according to which, after Rome and Alexandria, Antioch "indisputably assumes third place in the world ruled by the Romans because of its size and general well-being." Regarding Antioch, cf. recently F. Kolb, "Antiochia in der frühen Kaiserzeit," in *Geschichte–Tradition–Reflexion* II (FS M. Hengel; ed. H. Cancik, H. Lichtenberger, and P. Schäfer; Tübingen: Mohr Siebeck, 1996), 97–118.

29 Cf. F. W. Norris, "Antiochien I," *TRE 3.1* (ed. G. Krause and G. Müller; Berlin: De Gruyter, 1978), 99.

30 Cf. Josephus, *J.W.* 7.45; the Jews "regularly arrange for a crowd of Greeks to come to their worship services and make some of them, in a sense, their own"; regarding Antioch, cf. also Hengel and Schwemer, *Paulus zwischen Damaskus und Antiochien*, 274–99.

31 Cf. Adolf von Harnack, *Mission und Ausbreitung des Christentums I* (4th ed.; Leipzig: Hinrichs, 1923), 425–26.

32 Cf. F. Kolb, *Rom. Die Geschichte der Stadt in der Antike* (2nd ed.; Munich: C. H. Beck, 2002), 457.

33 Concerning Judaism in Rome, cf. W. Wiefel, "Die jüdische Gemeinschaft im antiken Rom und die Anfänge des römischen Christentums," *Jud* 26 (1970): 65–88; H. Lichtenberger, "Josephus und Paulus in Rom," in *Begegnungen zwischen Christentum und Judentum in Antike und Mittelalter* (FS H. Schreckenberg; ed. D.-A. Koch and H. Lichtenberger; Göttingen: Vandenhoeck &

Ruprecht, 1993), 245–61; Leonard V. Rutgers, *The Jews in Late Ancient Rome: Evidence of Cultural Interaction in the Roman Diaspora* (Leiden: Brill, 1995); Carsten Claussen, *Versammlung, Gemeinde, Synagoge: das hellenistisch-jüdische Umfeld der frühchristlichen Gemeinden* (StUNT 27; Göttingen: Vandenhoeck & Ruprecht, 2002), 103–11.

34 Regarding the conditions for the development of the church(es) in Rome, cf. recently Peter Lampe, who conjectures that freed Jewish slaves and slaves of pagan masters served as a beachhead in Rome "via which Jewish Christianity from the Syro-Palestinian East reached the world capital Rome in the forties of the first century C.E. (127). See Lampe, "Urchristliche Missionswege nach Rom: Haushalte paganer Herrschaft als jüdisch-christliche Keimzellen," *ZNW* 92 (2001): 123–27.

35 Cf. Peter Lampe, *Die stadtrömischen Christen in den ersten beiden Jahrhunderten* (2nd ed.; WUNT 2.18; Tübingen: Mohr Siebeck, 1989), 141–53.

36 Cf. Lampe, *Die stadtrömischen Christen*, 301ff.; the factionalization of the church(es) was very important; according to Lampe, "in the 50s of the first century, there existed at least seven distinct Christian islands in the capital of the world. Signs of a spatial center for the various Christian circles dispersed across the city cannot be found anywhere either in this period nor later in the first two centuries. Each circle may have held worship services separately in a dwelling so that it can be described as a house church" (*Urchristliche Missionswege*, 126).

37 Regarding Χριστός, cf. esp. Werner Kramer, *Christos Kyrios Gottessohn* (AThANT 44; Zurich: Zwingli-Verlag, 1963), 15–60, 131–48; Ferdinand Hahn, *Christologische Hoheitstitel Göttingen* (5th ed.; Göttingen: Vandenhoeck & Ruprecht, 1995), 133–225, 466–72; Geza Vermes, *Jesus der Jude: Ein Historiker liest die Evangelien* (Neukirchen: Neukirchener Verlag, 1993), 115–43; Martin Karrer, *Der Gesalbte: Die Grundlagen des Christustitels* (FRLANT 151; Göttingen: Vandenhoeck & Ruprecht, 1990); Dieter Zeller, "Messias/Christus," *NBL* 3, 782–86; M. de Jonge, "Christ," in *Dictionary of Deities and Demons in the Bible* (2nd ed.; ed. K. van der Toorn, B. Becking, and P. Willem van der Horst; Leiden: Brill, 1999), 192–200; Larry W. Hurtado, *Lord Jesus Christ: Devotion to Jesus in Earliest Christianity* (Grand Rapids: Eerdmans, 2003).

38 Karrer, *Der Gesalbte*, 211.

39 Cf. Kramer, *Christos Kyrios Gottessohn*, 61–103, 149–81; Hahn, *Christologische Hoheitstitel*, 67–132, 461–66; Joseph A. Fitzmyer, "κύριος," *EDNT* 2:328–31, *EWNT* 2:811–20; Vermes, *Jesus der Jude*, 89–114; David B. Capes, *Old Testament Yahweh Texts in Paul's Christology* (WUNT 2.47; Tübingen: Mohr Siebeck, 1992); M. Frenschkowski, "Kyrios," *RAC* 22:754–94.

40 Cf. Martin Hengel, "Psalm 110 und die Erhöhung des Auferstandenen zur Rechten Gottes," *Anfänge der Christologie* (FS F. Hahn; ed. C. Breytenbach and H. Paulsen; Göttingen: Vandenhoeck & Ruprecht, 1991), 43–74.

41 Cf. de Jonge, *Christologie im Kontext. Die Jesusrezeption des Urchristentums* (Neukirchen-Vluyn: Neukirchener Verlag, 1995), 177–78.

42 Cf. Joseph A. Fitzmyer, "Der semitische Hintergrund des neutestamentlichen Kyriostitels," in *Jesus Christus in Historie und Theologie* (FS H. Conzelmann; ed. G. Strecker; Tübingen: Mohr Siebeck, 1975), 267–98.

43 Cf. Dieter Zeller, "Der eine Gott und der eine Herr Jesus Christus," in *Der lebendige Gott* (FS W. Thüsing; ed. Th. Söding; NTA 31; Münster: Aschendorff, 1996), 34–49.

44 The relevant material is discussed in Martin Hengel, *Der Sohn Gottes* (2nd ed.; Tübingen: Mohr Siebeck, 1977), 35–39, 67–89; cf. further Larry W. Hurtado, "Son of God," *DPL* 900–906; A. Labahn and M. Labahn, "Jesus als Sohn Gottes bei Paulus," in *Paulinische Christologie* (ed. U. Schnelle, Th. Söding, and M. Labahn; Göttingen: Vandenhoeck & Ruprecht, 2000), 97–120. On Qumran (cf. in addition 4QFlor I 11–13; 1QSa II 11 esp. 4Q 246), cf. Joseph A. Fitzmyer, "The 'Son of God' Document from Qumran," *Bib* 74 (1993): 153–74; J. Zimmermann, *Messianische Texte aus Qumran* (WUNT 2.104, Tübingen: Mohr Siebeck, 1998), 128–70.

45 Cf. Adela Yarbro Collins, "Mark and His Readers: The Son of God among Jews," *HTR* 92 (1999): 393–408; idem, "The Son of God among Greeks and Romans," *HTR* 93 (2000): 85–100.

46 Cf. R. Weber, "Christologie und 'Messiasgeheimnis': Ihr Zusammenhang und Stellenwert in den Darstellungsintentionen des Markus," *EvT* 43 (1983): 108–25.

47 On baptism, cf. G. Delling, *Die Taufe im Neuen Testament* (Berlin: Evangelische Verlagsanstalt, 1963); Gerhard Barth, *Die Taufe in frühchristlicher Zeit* (BThSt 4; Neukirchen: Neukirchener Verlag, 1991); Lars Hartman, *Auf den Namen des Herrn Jesus. Die Taufe in den neutestamentlichen Schriften* (SBS 148; Stuttgart: Verlag Katholisches Bibelwerk, 1992); Udo Schnelle, "Taufe im NT," *TRE* 32:663–74; David Hellholm, Tor Vegge, and Christer Hellholm, eds., *Ablution, Initiation and Baptism: Late Antiquity, Early Judaism, and Early Christianity* (BZNW 176; Berlin: De Gruyter, 2011).

48 Cf. the diverse positions of Wilhelm Heitmüller, *"Im Namen Jesu": Eine sprach- und religionsgeschichtliche Untersuchung zum Neuen Testament, speziell zur altchristlichen Taufe* (FRLANT 2; Göttingen: Vandenhoeck & Ruprecht, 1903); Gerhard Delling, *Die Zueignung des Heils in der Taufe* (Berlin: Evangelische Verlagsanstalt, 1961). For the recent discussion, cf. Udo Schnelle, *Gerechtigkeit und Christusgegenwart. Vorpaulinische und paulinische Tauftheologie* (2nd ed.; GTA 24; Göttingen: Vandenhoeck & Ruprecht, 1986), 37–46, 178–83; Hartman, *Auf den Namen des Herrn Jesus*, 39–52.

49 Cf. Hans Lietzmann, *Messe und Herrenmahl: Eine Studie zur Geschichte der Liturgie* (AKG 8; Berlin: De Gruyter, 1926); Joachim Jeremias, *Die Abendmahlsworte Jesu* (4th ed.; Göttingen: Vandenhoeck & Ruprecht, 1967); Helmut Merklein, "Erwägungen zur Überlieferungsgeschichte der neutestamentlichen Abendmahlstraditionen," in *Studien zu Jesus und Paulus* (ed. H. Merklein; WUNT 43; Tübingen: Mohr Siebeck, 1987), 157–80; Bernd Kollmann, *Ursprung und Gestalten der frühchristlichen Mahlfeier* (GTA 43; Göttingen:

Vandenhoeck & Ruprecht, 1990); Jens Schröter, *Das Abendmahl: Frühchrist-liche Deutungen und Impulse für die Gegenwart* (SBS 210; Stuttgart: Katholi-sches Bibelwerk, 2006).

50 Cf. Bultmann, *Theology* 1.92–108.

51 G. H. van Kooten (" 'ἐκκλησία τοῦ θεοῦ': The 'Church of God' and the Civic Assemblies [ἐκκλησίαι] of the Greek Cities in the Roman Empire: A Response to Paul Trebilco and Richard A. Horsley," *NTS* 58 [2012]: 522–48) emphasizes this aspect.

52 Cf. Deut 23:2-4, Num 16:3, 20:4, Mic 2:5, and 1 Chr 28:8; for the various theories concerning the derivation of the term, cf. J. Roloff, "ἐκκλησία," *EDNT* 1:410–15, *EWNT* 1:999–1001; Paul Trebilco, *Self-Designations and Group Identity in the New Testament* (Cambridge: Cambridge University Press, 2012), 164–207.

53 Cf. Trebilco, *Self-Designations*, 16–46.

54 Cf. Udo Schnelle, *Apostle Paul* (Grand Rapids: Baker, 2012), 559–66.

55 Cf. Trebilco, *Self-Designations*, 247–71.

56 Cf. Ign. *Eph.* 11:2; *Magn.* 4; *Rom.* 3:2; *Pol.* 7:3.

57 Cf. F. Blass, A. Debrunner, and F. Rehkopf, *Grammatik des neutestamentlichen Griechisch* (16th ed.; Göttingen: Vandenhoeck & Ruprecht, 1984), §5.

58 Cf. A. Mehl, "Sprachen im Kontakt, Sprachen im Wandel. Griechisch/Latein und antike Geschichte," in *Zur Evolution von Kommunikation und Sprache—Ausdruck, Mittelung, Darstellung* (ed. M. Liedtke; Graz: Austria-Medien-Ser-vice, 1998), 198, who sees in the creation of the word a measure on the part of the authorities "initially for use among themselves."

59 On Phil 2:6-11 cf. Ernst Lohmeyer, *Kyrios Jesus: Eine Untersuchung zu Phil 2,5-11* (SHAW 4; Heidelberg: C. Winter, 1928); Otto Hofius, *Der Christushymnus Philipper 2,6-11* (WUNT 17; Tübingen: Mohr Siebeck, 1976); S. Vollenweider, "Der 'Raub' der Gottgleichheit: Ein religionsgeschichtlicher Vorschlag zu Phil 2,6(-11)," *NTS* 45 (1999): 413–33.

60 Cf. the appearances of the great Armenian king Tiridates before Emperor Nero in 66 C.E. (Dio Cassius 63).

61 Regarding the interpretation of this text, cf. Hans Conzelmann, "Zur Ana-lyse der Bekenntnisformel 1 Kor 15,3-5," in *Theologie als Schriftauslegung* (ed. H. Conzelmann; BEvT 65; Munich: Chr. Kaiser Verlag, 1974), 131–41; Chr. Wolff, *Der erste Brief des Paulus an die Korinther* (2nd ed.; THKNT 7; Leipzig: Evangelische Verlagsanstalt, 2000), 354–70; Wolfgang Schrage, *Der erste Brief an die Korinther* (EKKNT 7.4; Neukirchen: Benziger Verlag, 2001), 31–53; Helmut Merklein with M. Gielen, *Der erste Brief an die Korinther* (ÖTK 7.3; Gütersloh: Gütersloher Verlagshaus Gerd Mohn, 2005), 247–83.

62 Cf. the analysis in Claus Bussmann, *Themen der paulinischen Missionspredigt auf dem Hintergrund der spätjüdisch-hellenistischen Missionsliteratur* (EHS 23.3; Bern: Lang, 1971), 38–56.

63 Cf. Klaus Wengst, *Christologische Formeln und Lieder des Urchristentums* (2nd ed.; StNT 7; Gütersloh: Gütersloher Verlagshaus Gerd Mohn, 1973), 78–86.
64 Cf. Wiard Popkes, *Christus traditus: Eine Untersuchung zum Begriff der Dahingabe* (AThANT 49; Zurich: Zwingli-Verlag, 1967), 131ff.
65 Regarding the analysis, cf. Eduard Schweizer, "Röm 1,3f und der Gegensatz von Fleisch und Geist bei Paulus," in *Neotestamentica: Deutsche und Englische Aufsätze* (ed. E. Schweizer; Zurich: Zwingli-Verlag, 1963), 180–89.
66 For a demonstration of its pre-Pauline character and a determination of its many relationships to other religions, cf. Schrage, *Der erste Brief an die Korinther*, 216–25; further Zeller, "Der eine Gott und der eine Herr Jesus Christus," 34–49.
67 For the analysis of the text, cf. Schnelle, *Gerechtigkeit und Christusgegenwart*, 57–62; Christian Strecker, *Die liminale Theologie des Paulus: Zugange zur paulinischen Theologie aus kulturanthropologischer Perspektiv* (FRLANT 185; Göttingen: Vandenhoeck & Ruprecht, 1999), 351–59; Bruce Hansen, *"All of You Are One": The Social Vision of Gal 3:28; 1 Cor 12, 13 and Col 3:11* (LNTS 409; London: T&T Clark, 2010).
68 On the development of Sunday, cf. Willy Rordorf, *Der Sonntag: Geschichte des Ruhe- und Gottesdiensttages im ältesten Christentum* (AThANT 43; Zurich: Zwingli-Verlag, 1962).
69 Cf. Chr. Markschies, "Gnosis/Gnostizismus," *NBL* 1:868–71 (869): "There was probably no pre-Christian Gnosticism; no sources whatsoever have been preserved."
70 So following the history of religions school, Rudolf Bultmann, "Johannesevangelium," in *RGG*³ (3rd ed.; Tübingen: Mohr Siebeck, 1959): 840–50 (847), interprets the Fourth Gospel against the background of a fully formed gnostic redeemer myth and, in this regard, also refers to Mandaean scriptures "which, admittedly, were first redacted in the seventh century, but which contain a great deal of old material."
71 Cf. Hans Jonas, *Gnosis und spätantiker Geist* I (4th ed.; FRLANT 33; Göttingen: Vandenhoeck & Ruprecht, 1988), 12ff.
72 Other definitions of Gnosticism: Gerhard Sellin, *Der Streit um die Auferstehung der Toten* (FRLANT 138; Göttingen: Vandenhoeck & Ruprecht, 1986), 200. "The world (and human being as fleshly creatures) is the creation of a being (Demiurge) that has fallen from the world of light and, is, thus, the product of a power inimical to God." C. Colpe, "Gnosis II," *RAC* 11:559, offers another definition: "Gnosticism is the function of an organ of perception that is substance, that is divided dualistically into two hypostases, and will be reunified through Gnosticism." Markschies, "Gnosis/Gnostizismus," designates the following motifs characteristic of Gnosticism: (1) the knowledge of an entirely transcendent supreme God; (2) the introduction of additional divine figures; (3) the assessment of the world and matter as an evil creation; (4) the introduction of a lesser creator god; (5) an explanation of the current negative state through a mythological drama; (6) knowledge of this situation bestowed by a

transcendent Redeemer figure; (7) redemption through gnosis; (8) predestination of the classes of human beings; and (9) a developed dualism on all levels (870).

Chapter 4: Hays

1   R. Bultmann, *Theology of the New Testament* (trans. Kendrick Grobel; 2 vols.; New York: Scribner, 1951, 1955), 2.251. Subsequent citations of this work appear in the text and provide the volume and page numbers in parentheses.

2   Parenthetically, I wonder just a little about Grobel's English rendering of Bultmann's chapter title. The German is "Der Mensch vor der Offenbarung der πιστις." Bultmann's "vor" might be understand as having a sense that is not only temporal but also figuratively spatial: man (standing) before the revelation of faith. The ambiguity of the German would be better preserved if the English translation of the unit were given as "Man before the Revelation of Faith."

3   "Nearly all the wisdom we possess, that is to say, true and sound wisdom, consists of two parts: the knowledge of God and of ourselves" (J. Calvin, *Institutes of the Christian Religion* I.i.1 [ed. J. T. McNeill, trans. F. L. Battles; LCC 20; Philadelphia: Westminster, 1960], 35). It is telling, however, to note how Calvin finally decides to proceed: "Yet, however the knowledge of God and of ourselves may be mutually connected, the order of right teaching requires that we discuss the former first, then proceed afterward to treat the latter" (*Institutes* I.i.3, 37). Bultmann makes the opposite methodological choice.

4   German original: "In Wahrheit kommt darin nur ein bestimmtes Daseinsverständnis zum Ausdruck" (*Theologie des Neuen Testaments*, 4th ed. [Tübingen: Mohr Siebeck, 1961], 259). All subsequent citations of Bultmann's German text are taken from this edition.

5   In his watershed essay "The Righteousness of God in Paul," Käsemann sharply takes issue with Bultmann's translation of Rom 1:16 as "the possibility of salvation [*Die Möglichkeit zum Heil*] is the Gospel." Käsemann writes, "Characteristically, Bultmann chooses the translation which substitutes for the motif of the God who acts and creates and who prevails in the Gospel the quite different motif of an alleged anthropological 'given'" (Käsemann, *New Testament Questions of Today*, 173n4). This essay originally appeared as "Gottesgerechtigkeit bei Paulus," *Zeitschrift für Theologie und Kirche* 58 (1961): 367–78, and was included, with additional notes, in *Exegetische Versuche und Besinnungen*, vol. 2 (Göttingen: Vandenhoeck & Ruprecht, 1964), 181–93. Again, in a later vigorous polemic against Hans Conzelmann (another of Bultmann's students), Käsemann complains that "misunderstandings . . . arise when one starts from the alternative between theology and anthropology, reduces faith to self-understanding and ends up in a liberal-Protestant variant of Christ as the cultic deity who brings the true gnosis to his people" (E. Käsemann, *Perspectives on Paul* [Philadelphia: Fortress, 1971], 77n27; originally *Paulinische Perspektiven*

[Tübingen: Mohr Siebeck, 1969], 138n27). It is not hard to see that this barb is really aimed at the master, Bultmann himself.

6   As Bentley Layton notes, "[t]he earliest surviving reference" to an actual group called *gnōstikoi* appears in the writings of Irenaeus of Lyon, around 180 C.E. And none of the writings identified with "Gnosticism" (a notoriously difficult term to define) appeared before the second century C.E. (*The Gnostic Scriptures* [Garden City, N.Y.: Doubleday, 1987], 5–8).

7   On this point, see also Richard B. Hays, *Echoes of Scripture in the Letters of Paul* (New Haven: Yale University Press, 1989), 7–8.

8   Hays, *Echoes*, 75–77.

9   In this context Bultmann also imports into Rom 4:13-16 the idea that the Law's purpose was to lead humanity into sin. He achieves this interpretation by offering a "translation" into which he has interpolated his own parenthetical gloss asserting that the purpose of the Law was "to yield wrath" and "to cause transgression"—statements not to be found in Paul's text at Rom 4:13-16 (1.265–66).

10 Interestingly, while in my judgment Bultmann's presentation misconstrues the role of Law in Paul's thought, it does have the virtue of recognizing that Paul's "conversion was not the result of an inner moral collapse. . . . It was not rescue from the despair into which the cleavage between willing and doing had allegedly driven him. His was not a conversion of repentance" (1.188). At this point, Bultmann's interpretation anticipates a theme later highlighted by Krister Stendahl in his landmark essay "The Apostle Paul and the Introspective Conscience of the West," *HTR* 56 (1963): 62–77.

11 On this criticism of Bultmann, see R. B. Hays, *The Faith of Jesus Christ: The Narrative Substructure of Paul's Theology in Gal 3:1–4:11* (2nd ed.; Grand Rapids: Eerdmans, 2002), 47–52.

12 For the classic broadside against the Kittel methodology, see James Barr, *The Semantics of Biblical Language* (Oxford: Oxford University Press, 1961); see especially "Some Principles of Kittel's Theological Dictionary," 206–62. Bultmann was, of course, a major contributor to *TWNT*; over the course of his career, he composed twenty-six articles for that widely used reference work.

13 By way of contrast, see the methodology employed by the SBL Pauline Theology Group, which sought to explore Paul's theology through studying the contingent development of his "theologizing" in individual letters. The essays produced by this collaborative group were published in four volumes: Jouette Bassler, ed., *Pauline Theology*, vol. 1, *Thessalonians, Philippians, Galatians, Philemon* (Minneapolis: Fortress, 1991); D. Hay, ed., *Pauline Theology*, vol. 2, *1 and 2 Corinthians* (Minneapolis: Fortress, 1993); D. Hay and E. E. Johnson, eds., *Pauline Theology*, vol. 3, *Romans* (Minneapolis: Fortress, 1995); E. E. Johnson, ed., *Pauline Theology*, vol. 4, *Looking Back, Pressing On* (SBL Symposium Series 4; Atlanta: Scholars Press, 1997).

14 I note parenthetically that the index is not comprehensive; instead, it offers a list of "New Testament Passages Discussed (a selection of the more important)." [In the German original, *Stellenverzeichnis (in Auswahl)*.] In fact, in Bultmann's later discussion of "Christ's Death and Resurrection as Salvation-Occurrence," there are passing references to 1 Cor 15:1-4 (1.293) and Gal 4:4-5 (1.297). Still, the fact that these references can be excluded from the "more important" passages discussed speaks volumes about the lines of emphasis in Bultmann's treatment. Similarly, it is worth noticing that the index includes passages from the NT and the Apostolic Fathers, but not from the OT.

15 See particularly "New Testament and Mythology," in *Kerygma and Myth: A Theological Debate* (vol. 1; ed. Hans Werner Bartsch; trans. Reginald H. Fuller; London: SPCK, 1953), 1–44 (German original published in 1941).

16 See Beverly Roberts Gaventa, "The Cosmic Power of Sin in Paul's Letter to the Romans," in *Our Mother Saint Paul* (Louisville, Ky.: Westminster John Knox, 2007), 125–36. See now also R. E. Moses, "Powerful Practices: Paul's Principalities and Powers Revisited" (Th.D. diss., Duke University, 2012; Minneapolis: Fortress, forthcoming).

Chapter 5: Barclay

1 Rudolf Bultmann, *Theology of the New Testament* (trans. Kendrick Grobel; 2 vols.; London: SCM Press, 1952, 1955), 1.270. In what follows I employ this English translation; both volumes were reprinted by Baylor University Press in 2007); references here in the form 1.275 are to volume 1 of the English translation, page 275. The German original of volume 1 was published in 1948 (*Theologie des Neuen Testaments*) and is cited here (from the "two volumes in one" edition of 1953) as *Theologie*, followed by the page number (thus here, *Theologie*, 266).

2 Bultmann's doctoral thesis was on Paul's preaching style in comparison with the Cynic-Stoic "diatribe" (Göttingen, 1910), but his distinctive engagement with Pauline theology began in response to Karl Barth's *Römerbrief* (1919); see his review of the second edition in *Die Christliche Welt* (1922), 320–23, 330–34, translated in *The Beginnings of Dialectical Theology* (ed. J. M. Robinson; Richmond: John Knox Press, 1968), 100–120. Thereafter he applied dialectical theology to Pauline ethics in "Das Problem der Ethik bei Paulus," *ZNW* 23 (1924): 123–40, translated as "The Problem of Ethics in Paul," in *Understanding Paul's Ethics: Twentieth-Century Approaches* (ed. B. S. Rosner; Grand Rapids: Eerdmans, 1995), 195–216. A subsequent review of Pauline scholarship ("Zur Geschichte der Paulus-Forschung," *TRu* n.f. 1 [1929]: 26–59), and a major dictionary article ("Paulus" in *Religion in Geschichte und Gegenwart* [vol. 4, Tübingen: Mohr Siebeck, 1930]: 1019–46, translated as "Paul" in *Existence and Faith: Shorter Writings of Rudolf Bultmann* [ed. and trans. Schubert M. Ogden; London: Hodder and Stoughton, 1961], 111–46) laid the foundations

for the treatment of Paul in the *Theology of the New Testament* (the *RGG* article uses the same headings and anticipates much of the later, fuller treatment). Another significant essay from the 1930s was "Römer 7 und die Anthropologie des Paulus," in *Imago Dei* (Giessen: A. Töpelmann, 1932), 53–62, translated in *Existence and Faith*, 147–57. Several articles in Kittel's *Theologisches Wörterbuch zum Neuen Testament* during the 1930s (e.g., on γινώσκω, πιστεύω, and καυχάομαι) provide the basis or model for the word studies that constitute a notable feature of the chapters on Paul.

3   Bultmann and his pupils established the current consensus that Colossians was deuteropauline. He also judged a number of passages in the authentic letters to be glosses to the original text (e.g., at Rom 2:16; 6:17; 7:25b; and the whole of 2 Cor 6:14–7:1).

4   See, e.g., 1.80–82, 118, 125, 145–46.

5   E.g., 1.62, 92, 106–8, 115–21, 144, 151–52, 163–65, 181–83. Paul (and John) also provide the criteria for assessment of developments in subsequent Christian texts (e.g., 2.158).

6   Thus part 2 opens, "Standing within the frame of Hellenistic Christianity [Paul] raised the theological motifs that were at work in the proclamation of the Hellenistic church to the clarity of theological thinking; he called to attention the problems latent in the Hellenistic proclamation and brought them to a decision" (1.187). Bultmann's leading questions and his references to "danger" (e.g., 1.117, 163) show how fully history and theology are integrated in his work.

7   "The meaning and importance of Paul's teaching on the Law can be recognized and appreciated only after a survey of all the possibilities has been made" (1.109).

8   Paul sees and resolves "problems" (1.111, 162, 187); he "clarifies" (1.187, 190), "develops" (1.153), "leads beyond" (1.246), "rises above" (*erheben*; 1.114), and "outgrows" (*entwächsen*; 1.91, 92) what he inherits.

9   "Since theological understanding has its origin in faith . . . man prior to the revelation of faith is so depicted by Paul as he is retrospectively seen from the standpoint of faith" (1.191; cf. 1.270; "Paul" [*Existence and Faith*], 128). E. P. Sanders voices a persistent misreading when he identifies as Bultmann's "principal fault" that "he proceeded from plight to solution and supposed that Paul proceeded in the same way" (*Paul and Palestinian Judaism*, 474).

10 The German titles of these chapters use "der Mensch," which is not gender-specific; the English translation dates from a time (1952) preceding sensitivities on the use of the English term "man." "Der Mensch" is also generic, but the singular form lends itself to the discussion of faith and salvation in individualistic terms, which is characteristic of Bultmann. Bultmann does not, to my knowledge, explain the use of the phrase "under faith" (*unter der* πίστις) in the title of our chapter; it does not mirror a Pauline locution (though cf. "under grace," Rom 6:14-15).

11 E.g., 1.264 (*Theologie*, 260): sin is "man's self-powered striving [*das eigen-mächtige Streben*] to undergird [*begründen*] his own existence [*Sein*] in forget-fulness of his creaturely existence, to procure his salvation by his own strength [*aus eigener Kraft sein Heil zu beschaffen*]."

12 Unlike Greek science, Paul does not take the phenomena of the world and "build them into a system, a distantly perceived *kosmos*" (ihn selbst . . . zum System eines in der Distanz wahrgenommenen κόσμος objektiviert, 1.190; *Theologie*, 187); the verb *objektivieren* ("objectify") is common in Bultmann's definition of everything that Paul's (and his own) theology is not.

13 Thus Bultmann prefaces the statement about God cited above with "Pauline theology is not a speculative system" (*kein spekulatives System*, 1.190; *Theologie*, 187). The adjective *spekulativ* is also frequently deployed by Bultmann, with negative connotations.

14 Bultmann elsewhere cites Melanchthon's saying, *Christum cognoscere hoc est; beneficia eius cognoscere* (to know Christ is this: to know his benefits), "Grace and Freedom," in *Essays Philosophical and Theological* (trans. James C. G. Greig; Library of Philosophy and Theology; London: SCM Press, 1955), 168–81 (173).

15 For a full biography, see Konrad Hammann, *Rudolf Bultmann: A Biography* (trans. P. E. Devenish; Salem, Ore.: Polebridge, 2013). For the philosophical underpinning of Bultmann's work, see John Macquarrie, *An Existentialist Theology: A Comparison of Heidegger and Bultmann* (London: SCM Press, 1955); Gareth Jones, *Bultmann: Towards a Critical Theology* (Cambridge: Polity, 1991); David Fergusson, *Bultmann* (London: Geoffrey Chapman, 1992).

16 See his essay "Is Exegesis without Presuppositions Possible?," in *New Testament and Mythology and Other Basic Writings* (trans. and ed. Schubert M. Ogden; London: SCM Press, 1985), 145–54.

17 In summary form, see the "Epilogue," 2.237–41 (with polemic against "objecti-fying" or "speculative" theology). Bultmann's hermeneutical goals are summa-rized in his famous essay "New Testament and Mythology," in *New Testament and Mythology*, 1–43.

18 Käsemann was one of many who asked whether Bultmann gave due weight to the "and vice versa" in the statements cited at the start of this section; see Ernst Käsemann, "On Paul's Anthropology," in *Perspectives on Paul* (trans. M. Kohl; Philadelphia: Fortress, 1971), 1–31 (12).

19 Bultmann took Romans to be a more or less complete summary of Paul's "basic theological position" (1.190). Elements of Rom 12–15 are discussed under "Freedom," but Bultmann did not find here much that was distinctively Pau-line. On the minimal discussion of Rom 9–11, see below.

20 Thus Paul's discussion of sin in Rom 5:12-21 is judged partly self-contradictory (1.250–53), but Bultmann searches for the "real theme" (*das eigentliche Thema*, 1.252; *Theologie*, 247).

21 Bultmann later issued a robust defense of this reading (against Käsemann and others) in "*Dikaiosunē Theou*," *JBL* 83 (1964): 12–16.

22 Emphasis added; in the translation, as in the German, the whole of this passage is emphasized.

23 Bultmann assumes a Lutheran understanding of "work," which entails an interpretation of one's deeds as accomplishments necessary for salvation. Recent New Testament discussion of agency has often misunderstood this point.

24 Moreover, since the possibility of faith is an "eschatological occurrence" and "since the believer experiences the possibility of the faith-decision as grace, it is only as a gift of grace that he can understand his decision—his own decision!" (1.329). However, Paul's statements about predestination are not to be taken literally: they are intended to express only that God's grace is prior, 1.329–30. Cf. "Grace and Freedom," 177–78.

25 For the notion of a condition that is not a human accomplishment, see 1.20–21.

26 Love is thus an all-encompassing term for Christian ethics, an "eschatological phenomenon" inasmuch as it is made possible by the freedom granted by grace: "Love, as sheer existence for one's neighbour, is possible only to him who is free from himself" (1.344).

27 Bultmann himself appeals to Luther in this regard (2.238, where *Sachkritik* is obscurely translated "content-criticism").

28 Cf. the contrast between the individual and the people (*Volk*) of Israel in relation to the message of Jesus (1.13, 34). The catchphrase "salvation-history" evokes the history of humankind as a whole, rather than of Israel in particular (e.g., 1.175, 269), but faith is not a "worldview" (*Weltanschauung*), nor can God be identified with world history: that would offer faith a false security (1.25–26). Bultmann's understanding of the relation between eschatology and history and of the address of God that occurs within history but transcends empirical history in its normal sense is indebted to dialectical theology and is everywhere taken for granted (e.g., 1.25–26, 53–54, 117–18, 182–83).

29 Cf. the leading questions posed at 1.92: "To what extent will eschatological faith outgrow mythological imagination? Will it confine itself to simply waiting for a coming event, or will it understand the present in the light of an already happened eschatological occurrence?"

30 1.295; cf. 1.305. Cf. Bultmann's 1926 essay on Barth's published lectures on 1 Corinthians (*Die Auferstehung der Toten*), translated as "Karl Barth, *The Resurrection of the Dead*," in *Faith and Understanding*, vol. 1 (ed. Robert W. Funk; trans. Louise Pettibone Smith; London: SCM Press, 1969), 66–94; for Bultmann, in 1 Cor 15:1-11, "Paul is betrayed by his apologetic into contradicting himself" (83).

31 "New Testament and Mythology," 7; see esp. 36–41. Since this way of thinking is now impossible for us, it is of no service to faith or to the preaching of the transformative gospel to keep repeating it: "we cannot understand a miraculous natural event such as the resuscitation of a dead man—quite apart from its being generally incredible—as an act of God that is in this sense of concern for us" (7).

32 One may speak here with K. Barth of an "articulated" unity, "in which Christology is prior to soteriology without being separated from it, and in which soteriology, while it is part and parcel of Christology, is nevertheless secondary to it and derivative from it" ("Rudolf Bultmann—An Attempt to Understand Him," in *Kerygma and Myth: A Theological Debate* [vol. 2; ed. Hans Werner Bartsch; trans. Reginald H. Fuller; London: SPCK, 1962], 83–132 [96]).

33 On interpretation and understanding, in dialogue with Barth, see Bultmann, "The Problem of Hermeneutics," in *New Testament and Mythology*, 69–93.

34 For instance, *pace* Bultmann, some Qumran texts appear to emphasize the presence of salvation and the incongruity of grace to the same degree as Paul.

35 See D. V. Way, *The Lordship of Christ: Ernst Käsemann's Interpretation of Paul's Theology* (Oxford: Clarendon, 1991).

36 This emerges more in his RGG article on "Paul" than in the *Theology* itself, where historical reconstructions are taken for granted (e.g., 1.192, 295).

37 See, e.g., in contrast to Bultmann's, the letter-by-letter discussion of Pauline anthropology in Robert Jewett, *Paul's Anthropological Terms: A Study of Their Use in Conflict Situations* (Leiden: Brill, 1971); cf. the SBL project on Pauline theology, which determined to tackle its subject letter by letter and rarely developed even a limited synthesis of results.

38 Dahl, *Crucified Messiah*, 90–128. In Dahl's eyes, "Bultmann detaches the fundamental meaning of Paul's theology from its historical situation. This is also clear in his whole treatment of the law" (115). The work of Stendahl, Sanders, Dunn, and Wright is indebted to Dahl's insistence on this point, developed here and in other essays on Paul during the 1960s and 1970s.

39 Cf. Bultmann's description of Judaism in *Primitive Christianity in Its Contemporary Setting* (London: SCM Press, 1960).

40 Sanders, *Paul and Palestinian Judaism*.

41 For a valuable survey of the intense and complex debates, see Stephen Westerholm, *Perspectives Old and New on Paul: The "Lutheran" Paul and His Critics* (Grand Rapids: Eerdmans, 2004).

42 I develop this hypothesis in *Paul and the Gift* (Grand Rapids: Eerdmans, forthcoming).

43 Käsemann, "On Paul's Anthropology."

44 Sanders famously declared participation in Christ to be the center of Pauline soteriology but confessed he could not understand it (*Paul and Palestinian Judaism*, 522–23); those who agree with his judgment on its centrality offer diverse accounts (using the categories of narrative, social identity, and deification, among others). Of modern interpreters, Troels Engberg-Pedersen is rare in repeating the Bultmannian challenge that our task is not just to repeat what Paul has said but to interpret it in terms that make some sense to us: see, e.g., his *Paul and the Stoics* (Edinburgh: T&T Clark, 2000).

45 See, e.g., David H. Kelsey, *Eccentric Existence: A Theological Anthropology* (2 vols.; Louisville, Ky.: Westminster John Knox, 2009).

46   For the relation between faith and work, see 1.283–84 (in dialogue with Mundle) and 1.315–16. For an exposition of the Lutheran interpretation of faith, against persistent misunderstandings in recent scholarship, see Jonathan Linebaugh, "The Christo-Centrism of Faith in Christ: Martin Luther's Reading of Galatians," *NTS* 59 (2013): 535–44.

47   "It is self-evident . . . that the New Testament's thought about the state and society are [*sic*] incomplete because the possibilities and the problems of forms of the state and society which history has introduced in the meantime could not be present to the minds of the New Testament authors" (2.238).

48   See J. M. G. Barclay, *Pauline Churches and Diaspora Jews* (Tübingen: Mohr Siebeck, 2011), 363–87. Bultmann rejected Deissmann's reading of Pauline terms as derived from, but opposed to, the emperor cult (1.87).

49   For an analysis of his work as New Testament *theology*, see R. Morgan's introduction to the 2007 Baylor University Press edition (xi–xxxvii); cf. idem, "Rudolf Bultmann," in *The Modern Theologians* (ed. D. Ford; Oxford: Blackwell, 1989), 109–33.

Chapter 6: Frey

1   Bultmann, *Theologie des Neuen Testaments* (Mohr Siebeck, 1953); hereafter *Theologie*. All English language citations of Bultmann's *Theology* refer to *Theology of the New Testament* (Baylor University Press, 2007).

2   For an introduction to Bultmann's theology, see the presentation by Schmithals, *Die Theologie Rudolf Bultmanns*. Regarding its development, see esp. Baasland, *Theologie und Methode*; Martin Evang, *Rudolf Bultmann in seiner Frühzeit* (BHTh 74; Tübingen: Mohr Siebeck, 1988); and Wolfgang Stegemann, *Der Denkweg Rudolf Bultmanns* (Stuttgart: Kohlhammer, 1978); for a recent biography, see Hammann, *Rudolf Bultmann. Eine Biographie*.

3   Regarding the structure of the work, see also Jörg Frey, "Zum Problem der Aufgabe und Durchführung einer Theologie des Neuen Testaments," in *Aufgabe und Durchführung einer Theologie des Neuen Testaments* (ed. C. Breytenbach and J. Frey; WUNT 205; Tübingen: Mohr Siebeck, 2007), 3–53 (29–32).

4   Bultmann, *Theologie*, 2.

5   See only the brief comments in Bultmann, *Theologie*, 357–58.

6   Bultmann, *Theologie*, 278.

7   Bultmann himself formulated his concerns as "striving for the unity of theology and exegesis, indeed, in such a way that exegesis receives primacy" (so Bultmann, "Vorwort des Verfassers," in *Exegetica: Aufsätze zur Erforschung des Neuen Testaments* [ed. Erich Dinkler; Tübingen: Mohr Siebeck, 1967], vii). Karl Barth objected "that there can hardly be one text whose treatment will not immediately reveal certain axioms of his thought as so dominant that virtually everything will be decided by the question of their validity" (*Kirchliche Dogmatik* III/2 [Zurich: Theologischer Verlag, 1980], 534).

8   Bultmann, *Das Evangelium des Johannes* (KEK 2; Göttingen: Vandenhoeck & Ruprecht, 1941; 21st ed., Göttingen: Vandenhoeck & Ruprecht, 1984).

9   Already most of his students disagreed with his rearrangements of the text and with the core of his source theory, the "Revelation Discourses Source." Recent research has also called into question other components of his reconstruction, the Semeia source, and the demarcation of the redaction.

10   On Bultmann's interpretation of John and its problems, see Jörg Frey, *Die johanneische Eschatologie I: Ihre Probleme im Spiegel der Forschung seit Reimarus* (WUNT 96; Tübingen: Mohr Siebeck, 1997), 85–157.

11   It is no accident that one of the first and most important of Bultmann's essays on the interpretation of John was "Die Eschatologie des Johannesevangeliums," in idem, *Glauben und Verstehen* I (Tübingen: Mohr Siebeck, 1933), 134–52 (hereafter *GuV*). Here he lays out the essence of the later interpretation in his *Theology*. Only Bultmann's student Ernst Käsemann then reversed this relationship: "For John . . . eschatology is no longer the context of Christology, but, conversely, Christology is the context of eschatology" (Käsemann, *Jesu letzter Wille nach Johannes 17* [Tübingen: Mohr Siebeck, 1967], 42).

12   Johannes Körner, *Eschatologie und Geschichte. Eine Untersuchung des Begriffs des Eschatologischen in der Theologie Rudolf Bultmanns* (ThF 13; Hamburg: Herbert Reich Evangelischer Verlag, 1957), 13–14.

13   Early in his career, as an adherent of the history of religions school, Bultmann saw the eschatology of primitive Christianity as only New Testament religion in time-bound clothing (so in Bultmann, "Die Bedeutung der Eschatologie für die Religion des Neuen Testaments," *ZThK* 27 [1917]: 76–87). With the turn to dialectical theology, this view changed. In his book on Jesus, he characterized the kingdom of God in Jesus' preaching as "eschatological" and "an entirely other-worldly entity," "assuming that the idea of the eschatological is truly conceived radically" (Bultmann, *Jesus* [Deutsche Bibliothek, 1926], 28).

14   They appreciated the eschatology of Jesus and his followers but concluded that Jesus' ethic, for example, cannot be transferred to contemporary theology, but was only intended for an "interim" before the imminent *parousia*. Ultimately, "consistent eschatology" systematically and consistently adopted eschatology.

15   Karl Barth, *Römerbrief* (2nd ed.; Munich: Chr. Kaiser, 1921), 298: "Christianity that is not wholly and solely eschatology has wholly and solely nothing to do with Christ."

16   Regarding Kierkegaard's influence, see Cora Bartels, *Kierkegaard Receptus I. Die theologiegeschichtliche Bedeutung der Kierkegaard-Rezeption Rudolf Bultmanns* (Göttingen: Vandenhoeck & Ruprecht, 2008); on Herrmann's influence, see Christoph Herbst, *Freiheit aus Glauben. Studien zum Verständnis eines soteriologischen Leitmotivs bei Wilhelm Herrmann, Rudolf Bultmann und Eberhard Jüngel* (TBT 157; Berlin: De Gruyter, 2012).

17   Regarding the development of Bultmann's theology, see Baasland (*Theologie und Methode*, 18–92), who distinguishes an *early dialectic* phase (ca. 1923–1926)

from an *existentialist* phase (after 1927) in which Bultmann refers explicitly to Heidegger and the terminology from *Sein und Zeit*. On the structural significance of *Sein und Zeit* for Bultmann's John commentary, see Marcel Lill, *Zeitlichkeit und Offenbarung. Ein Vergleich von Martin Heideggers "Sein und Zeit" mit Rudolf Bultmanns "Das Evangelium des Johannes"* (Frankfurt: Peter Lang, 1987).

18 Cf. Körner, *Eschatologie und Geschichte*, 77.

19 Bultmann, "Zum Problem der Entmythologisierung," in *Kerygma und Mythos: Ein theologisches Gespräch* II (ed. Hans Werner Bartsch; Hamburg: Reich & Heidrich, 1952), 179–208 (192): "The 'correct' philosophy is quite simply that philosophical work that strives to develop an understanding of the existence given with human existence in an appropriate terminology. Thus, it does not ask the question of the meaning of existence as an existential question, but in an analysis of existence, asks what existence, itself, might mean and knows that the existential question can only be answered in existing itself."

20 Martin Heidegger, *Sein und Zeit* (15th ed.; Tübingen: Mohr Siebeck, 1979), 42–43; G. W. Ittel, "Der Einfluß der Philosophie M. Heideggers auf die Theologie R. Bultmanns," *KD* 2 (1956): 90–108 (93–94).

21 Heidegger, *Sein und Zeit*, 382.

22 Heidegger, *Sein und Zeit*, 394.

23 So Heidegger, *Sein und Zeit*, 388.

24 Bultmann, "Die Bedeutung der 'dialektischen Theologie' für die neutestamentliche Wissenschaft," in *GuV* I, 114–33 (118).

25 Cf. Bultmann, *Jesus* (repr.; Tübingen: Mohr Siebeck, 1983), 7–8; idem, "Zum Problem der Entmythologisierung," in *Kerygma und Mythos: Ein theologisches Gespräch* VI/1 (ed. Hans Werner Bartsch; Hamburg: Reich & Heidrich, 1963), 20–27 (22–23).

26 Heinrich Ott, *Geschichte und Heilsgeschichte in der Theologie Rudolf Bultmanns* (BHTh 19; Tübingen: Mohr Siebeck, 1955), 10. For a critique of this principle in Bultmann, cf. Ott, *Geschichte*, 50–57.

27 Bultmann, *Das Urchristentum im Rahmen der antiken Religionen* (Zurich: Artemis Verlag, 1949), 8.

28 Schmithals, *Theologie*, 306.

29 Bultmann, "Zum Problem der Entmythologisierung," in *GuV* IV (Tübingen: Mohr Siebeck, 1965), 128–37 (136).

30 According to the portrayal by Albert Schweitzer, *Eine Geschichte der Leben-Jesu-Forschung* (2nd ed.; Tübingen: Mohr Siebeck, 1913), the Orientalist Hermann Samuel Reimarus, who was influenced by deism, ignited this fire; see Frey, *Eschatologie I*, 10–11.

31 Bultmann, "Welchen Sinn hat es, von Gott zu reden?," in *GuV* I, 26–37 (26).

32 Bultmann, "Welchen Sinn hat es, von Gott zu reden?," 27.

33 W. Herrmann, *Die Wirklichkeit Gottes* (1914), 42, cited in Bultmann, "Welchen Sinn hat es, von Gott zu reden?," 36. This statement adapts the classical

phrase from Philipp Melanchthon's *Loci Communes* (1521): "Hoc est Christum cognoscere, beneficia eius cognoscere." Bultmann quotes Melanchthon in "Die Frage der 'dialektischen Theologie,'" *Zwischen den Zeiten* 4 (1926): 40–59 (54).

34 Gotthold E. Lessing, *Gesammelte Werke* (ed. Paul Rilla; 10 vols.; Berlin: Aufbau-Verlag, 1958), 8:12.

35 Thus, paradigmatically in Harnack, *Das Wesen des Christentums*. Regarding the early Bultmann's reception of the core/shell model, see Baasland, *Theologie und Methode*, 96–98.

36 The first edition was titled *Von Reimarus bis Wrede* (Tübingen: Mohr Siebeck, 1906).

37 Baasland, *Theologie und Methode*, 107.

38 See Baasland, *Theologie und Methode*, 72–73.

39 Bultmann, "Die Eschatologie des Johannesevangeliums," 148.

40 Cf. Bultmann, *Evangelium*, 115; see also Ott, *Heilsgeschichte*, 121–23.

41 Körner, *Eschatologie und Geschichte*, 78.

42 Cf. Ott, *Heilsgeschichte*, 116–17. The concept of the course of time would incorporate the now, either causally or finally, into a sequence of causation or development and determine its meaning based on this superimposed scheme but would thereby misperceive the actual meaning lying in the present (cf. Ott, *Heilsgeschichte*, 118–19).

43 Cf. Bultmann, "Das Problem einer theologischen Exegese des Neuen Testaments," *Zwischen den Zeiten* 3 (1925), 334–57 (340).

44 Bultmann, *Urchristentum*, 222–23.

45 Cf. Körner, *Eschatologie und Geschichte*, 23.

46 Bultmann, "Die Bedeutung des geschichtlichen Jesus für die Theologie des Paulus," in *GuV* I, 188–213 (201).

47 Cf. Körner, *Eschatologie und Geschichte*, 31.

48 Körner, *Eschatologie und Geschichte*, 46. In reaction, Bultmann emphasized as late as 1917 that the Gospel of John "affirmed realistic eschatology" ("Die Bedeutung der Eschatologie," 79).

49 Bultmann, *Evangelium*, 193; idem, *Theologie*, 391.

50 Bultmann, *Evangelium*, 436.

51 Here, Bultmann wants more than simply to incorporate the cross: "His departure or 'exaltation' (i.e. upon the cross) not only belongs to the whole as its culmination but is that which makes the whole what it is: both revelation and offense" (2.48; *Theologie*, 400).

52 Bultmann, *Evangelium*, 146–47. From the standpoint of the history of religions, the presupposition of this view of the saving event as a punctiliar unity represents the incorporation of the individual acts into the whole in the "Gnostic Redeemer Myth," which, according to Bultmann, was available to the evangelist.

53 Bultmann, *Evangelium*, 26.

54 Bultmann, *Evangelium*, 483.
55 Cf. Bultmann, *Evangelium*, 196; idem, *Theologie*, 391.
56 So Körner, *Eschatologie und Geschichte*, 46.
57 On the whole question, cf. D. Moody Smith, *The Composition and Order of the Fourth Gospel: Bultmann's Literary Theory* (New Haven: Yale University Press, 1965), and, on the genesis of these concepts, Baasland, *Theologie und Methode*, 306–17, 452–61.
58 Clumsy page transpositions do not explain the, sometimes minor, rearrangements of the text that Bultmann accepts. This issue is one of the biggest problems with his literary theory.
59 See Bultmann's own presentation in Bultmann, "Johannesevangelium," in *Die Religion in Geschichte und Gegenwart. Handwörterbuch für Theologie und Religionswissenschaft* III (ed. Kurt Galling; 3rd ed.; Tübingen: Mohr Siebeck, 1959), 840–50, and Smith, *Composition*.
60 Cf. Bultmann, *Evangelium*, 542–47.
61 Bultmann, *Evangelium*, 360.
62 Bultmann, "Der religionsgeschichtliche Hintergrund des Prologs zum Johannesevangelium," in *Exegetica*, 10–35. Here, Bultmann uncovered a glossed, hymnic original from a document belonging to a circle of gnosticizing baptists (34–35); idem, "Analyse des ersten Johannesbriefes," in *Exegetica*, 105–23.
63 Cf. Smith, *Composition*, 20–22. It remains unclear, however, how the relationship between the Discourse Source in the Gospel and the prototype in the letter should be defined.
64 He attempted to reconstruct the original arrangement of the text, which then defined the arrangement in the evangelist's work, through the bold rearrangements of the text he suspected.
65 Cf. Bultmann, "Die Bedeutung der neuerschlossenen mandäischen und manichäischen Quellen für das Verständnis des Johannesevangeliums," in *Exegetica*, 55–104.
66 Bultmann, *Evangelium*, 76.
67 See Bultmann's summary in *Theologie*, 166–86, 358–59.
68 See the brief narration in Bultmann, "Johannesevangelium," 847: "From the world of light, a divine figure is sent to the earth ruled by demonic powers in order to liberate rays of light that originate in the world of light and are banished to human bodies as the result of a fall in the primordial period. The Sent One takes on human form and does on earth the works the Father commissions him to do, while he is not 'cut off' from the Father. He reveals himself in his speeches . . . and thus performs the separation between the seeing and the blind, to whom he appears as a foreigner. His own hear him, and he awakens in them the memory of their home of light, teaches them to recognize themselves, and teaches them the way to return home, along which he, himself a redeemed Redeemer, ascends again."
69 Bultmann, "Johannesevangelium," 847–48.

70 According to the analysis by Wolfgang Nethöfel, structurally, Bultmann's John commentary itself is not only an interpretation but also a reproduction of the scholarly myth of the Gnostic Redeemer. Wolfgang Nethöfel, *Strukturen existentialer Interpretation: Bultmanns Johanneskommentar im Wechsel theologischer Paradigmen* (Göttingen: Vandenhoeck & Ruprecht, 1983), 239–40.

71 Bultmann, "Die Eschatologie des Johannesevangeliums."

72 Bultmann, *Theologie*, 385; cf. idem, *Eschatologie*, 139.

73 Bultmann presupposes that references to the judgment (John 12:48) or the resurrection (John 6:39, 40, 44) on the "last day" and the statement in John 5:28-29 that stand in tension with John 5:25 are additions by the "church redaction," which wanted to correct this eschatology in the sense of the church's artless belief.

74 Bultmann, *Evangelium*, 38–43.

75 Bultmann, *Theologie*, 393.

76 Bultmann, *Evangelium*, 40.

77 Bultmann, *Theologie*, 33.

78 This is the consequence when Ernst Käsemann later saw the starting point of Johannine thought, not in John 1:14a and the paradoxical identity of σάρξ and δόξα, but (with the focus on John 1:14b) in the majesty of preexistence, based on which the Sent One can only be a "God striding above the earth." See Frey, *Eschatologie I*, 160–70.

79 Bultmann, *Theologie*, 397.

80 Bultmann, *Theologie*, 403.

81 He considered John 20:9 a redactional gloss.

82 Bultmann, *Theologie*, 420.

83 Bultmann, *Theologie*, 430.

84 So the critique in Baasland, *Theologie und Methode*, 457–58.

85 See my presentation in Frey, *Eschatologie I*, passim.

86 See Ruben Zimmermann, *Christologie der Bilder im Johannesevangelium* (WUNT 171; Tübingen: Mohr Siebeck, 2004).

87 On the interpretation of the temporal statements, see Jörg Frey, *Die johanneische Eschatologie II: Das johannische Zeitverständnis* (WUNT 110; Tübingen: Mohr Siebeck, 1998); on ἐγώ εἰμι, pp. 86–89.

88 The only students to follow Bultmann here were Philipp Vielhauer and (modified) Helmut Koester (see Frey, *Eschatologie I*, 129).

89 See Frey, *Eschatologie I*, 133–40.

90 So Roland Bergmeier, *Glaube als Gabe nach Johannes* (BWANT 112; Stuttgart: Kohlhammer, 1980), 22.

Chapter 7: Bauckham

1 In *Theology of the New Testament* Bultmann treats Johannine theology as the theology of the Gospel and the Epistles of John considered as a coherent unity. However, because the weight of his interpretation rests on the Gospel and

because subsequently it has become much more usual to treat the theology of the Gospel independently of that of the Epistles, this chapter will focus especially on the Gospel, though with some reference to the Epistles.

2   Rudolf Bultmann, *The Gospel of John* (trans. G. R. Beasley-Murray; Oxford: Blackwell, 1971).

3   All citations of Bultmann's *Theology* refer to *Theology of the New Testament* (Baylor University Press, 2007).

4   Bultmann writes, "Is the devil a reality for John in the mythical sense? That is very doubtful, to say the least" (*Theology*, 2.17).

5   In gnostic cosmological dualism, there is a distinction of nature between the children of light and the children of darkness, arising from the primeval cosmic fall.

6   For a brief survey of views on the relationship of the Gospel of John to Gnosticism, see Raymond E. Brown, *An Introduction to the Gospel of John* (ed. Francis J. Moloney; New York: Doubleday, 2003), 116–26.

7   I do not mean to deny that there is an essential social dimension to Johannine theology, which Bultmann particularly neglected, but I doubt if speculative reconstructions of the Johannine community and the dynamics of its allegedly very particular situation are the way to access it.

8   It is invidious to suggest particular candidates for consideration, but among other books from the past two decades that one might commend for their ambition and theological seriousness are (in chronological order) Thomas L. Brodie, *The Gospel According to John: A Literary and Theological Commentary* (Oxford: Oxford University Press, 1993); Andrew T. Lincoln, *Truth on Trial: The Lawsuit Motif in the Fourth Gospel* (Peabody, Mass.: Hendrickson, 2000); Dorothy Lee, *Flesh and Glory: Symbolism, Gender and Theology in the Gospel of John* (New York: Crossroad, 2002). See also a collection of essays whose aim was to be programmatic for the enterprise of theological interpretation of John: Richard Bauckham and Carl Mosser, eds., *The Gospel of John and Christian Theology* (Grand Rapids: Eerdmans, 2008).

9   See, for example, Fernando F. Segovia, "Inclusion and Exclusion in John 17: An Intercultural Reading," in *"What Is John?"* vol. 2 of *Literary and Social Readings of the Fourth Gospel* (ed. Fernando F. Segovia; SBLSymS 7; Atlanta: Scholars Press, 1998), 183–209. A very different obstacle for some is the longstanding problem of the relationship between the Johannine Jesus and the historical Jesus. See, for example, Maurice Casey, *Is John's Gospel True?* (London: Routledge, 1996).

10 See especially the essays collected in James H. Charlesworth, ed., *John and Qumran* (London: Geoffrey Chapman, 1972) and Mary L. Coloe and Tom Thatcher, eds., *John, Qumran, and the Dead Sea Scrolls* (SBLEJL 32; Atlanta: SBL Press, 2011).

11 Raymond E. Brown, "John, Gospel and Letters of," in *Encyclopedia of the Dead Sea Scrolls* (Oxford: Oxford University Press, 2000), 1:414–17 (415).

12 Raymond E. Brown, "The Qumran Scrolls and the Johannine Gospel and Epistles," *CBQ* 17 (1955): 403–19, 559–74; James H. Charlesworth, "A Critical Comparison of the Dualism in 1QS 3:13–4:26 and the 'Dualism' Contained in the Gospel of John," in *John and Qumran* (ed. James H. Charlesworth; London: Geoffrey Chapman, 1972), 76–106; Brown, "John, Gospel"; Joseph A. Fitzmyer, "Qumran Literature and the Johannine Writings," in *Life in Abundance: Studies in Tribute to Raymond E. Brown* (ed. John R. Donahue; Collegeville, Minn.: Liturgical Press, 2005), 117–33; James H. Charlesworth, "The Fourth Evangelist and the Dead Sea Scrolls: Assessing Trends over Nearly Sixty Years," in *John, Qumran, and the Dead Sea Scrolls* (ed. Coloe and Thatcher), 161–82, esp. 165–72.

13 Howard M. Teeple, "Qumran and the Origin of the Fourth Gospel," *NovT* 4 (1960–1961): 6–25; reprinted in *The Composition of John's Gospel* (ed. David E. Orton; Leiden: Brill, 1999), 1–20; David E. Aune, "Dualism in the Fourth Gospel and the Dead Sea Scrolls: A Reassessment of the Problem," in *Neotestamentica et Philonica: Studies in Honor of Peder Borgen* (ed. David E. Aune, Torrey Seland, and Jarl Henning Ulrichsen; NovTSup 106; Leiden: Brill, 2003), 281–303; Jörg Frey, "Licht aus den Höhlen? Der 'johanneische Dualismus' und die Texte von Qumran," in *Kontexte des Johannesevangelium* (ed. Jörg Frey and Udo Schnelle; WUNT 175; Tübingen: Mohr Siebeck, 2004), 117–203. See also Frey's "Recent Perspectives on Johannine Dualism and Its Background," in *Text, Thought, and Practice in Qumran and Early Christianity: Proceedings of the Ninth International Symposium of the Orion Center for the Study of the Dead Sea Scrolls and Associated Literature* (ed. Ruth A. Clements and Daniel R. Schwartz; STDJ 84; Leiden: Brill, 2009), 127–60, a book not accessible to me.

14 Richard Bauckham, "The Qumran Community and the Gospel of John," in Richard Bauckham, *The Testimony of the Beloved Disciple: Narrative, History, and Theology in the Gospel of John* (Grand Rapids: Baker, 2007), 125–36. This essay was published previously in two somewhat differing forms: "Qumran and the Gospel of John: Is There a Connexion?," in *The Scrolls and the Scriptures: Qumran Fifty Years After* (ed. Stanley E. Porter and Craig E. Evans; JSPSup 26; Sheffield: Sheffield Academic Press, 1997), 267–79; "The Qumran Community and the Gospel of John," in *The Dead Sea Scrolls: Fifty Years after Their Discovery* (ed. Lawrence H. Schiffman, Emmanuel Tov, and James C. VanderKam; Jerusalem: Israel Exploration Society, 2000), 105–15.

15 Frey, "Licht aus den Höhlen?"

16 Jörg Frey, "Different Patterns of Dualistic Thought in the Qumran Library: Reflections on Their Background and History," in *Legal Texts and Legal Issues: Proceedings of the Second Meeting of the International Organization for Qumran Studies, Cambridge 1995* (FS Joseph M. Baumgarten; ed. Moshe Bernstein, Florentino García Martínez, and John Kampen; STDJ 23; Leiden: Brill, 1997), 275–335; Klaus Koch, "History as a Battlefield of Two Antagonistic Powers in the Apocalypse of Weeks and in the Rule of the Community," in *Enoch and*

Qumran Origins: New Light on a Forgotten Connexion (ed. Gabriele Boccac-cini; Grand Rapids: Eerdmans, 2005), 185–99; Géza G. Xeravits, ed., *Dualism in Qumran* (LSTS 76; London: T&T Clark, 2010); Loren T. Stuckenbruck, "The Interiorization of Dualism within the Human Being in Second Temple Judaism: The Treatise of the Two Spirits (1QS III:13–IV:26) in Its Tradition-Historical Context," in *Light against Darkness: Dualism in Ancient Mediterra-nean Religion and the Contemporary World* (ed. Armin Lange, Eric M. Meyers, Bennie H. Reynolds, and Randall Styers; JAJSup 2; Göttingen: Vandenhoeck & Ruprecht, 2011), 145–68.

17   Charlesworth, "Fourth Evangelist," 171.

18   Fitzmyer, "Qumran Literature," 123.

19   Bauckham, "Qumran Community," 132–35.

20   Eric M. Meyers, "From Myth to Apocalyptic: Dualism in the Hebrew Bible," in *Light against Darkness*, 92–106 (94).

21   John G. Gammie, "Spatial and Ethical Dualism in Jewish Wisdom and Apoca-lyptic Literature," *JBL* 93 (1974): 356–85 (356–59).

22   Comparable material in 1 John is listed for comparison. It falls into a much simpler pattern of usage.

23   Lee, *Flesh and Glory*, chap. 2, is the best recent discussion of this topic.

24   Charles Kingsley Barrett, *Essays on John* (London: SPCK, 1982), 106.

25   Bauckham, "Qumran Community," 132–35. The "Treatise of the Two Spirits" (1QS 3:13–4:26) also has scriptural sources, perhaps including Gen 1:1-3, but, if so, its reading of Genesis is controlled by Isa 47:5 and thus very different from the Gospel's. While both texts draw to some extent on the dualism of the sapi-ential literature, only 1QS portrays the destiny of the righteous and the wicked as light and darkness, perhaps in dependence on Prov 4:17-18. Messianic light has no place in 1QS.

26   This is a hyperbolic picture that should not be read literally to mean that there was no light in the world before Jesus (cf. 5:35), but the hyperbole functions to highlight the new situation into which Jesus puts humanity.

27   See now especially Lee, *Flesh and Glory*.

28   Even André Feuillet, "Participation in the Life of God According to the Fourth Gospel," in André Feuillet, *Johannine Studies* (trans. Thomas E. Crane; New York: Alba House, 1964), 169–80, an essay written to reassert the "mystical" character of the Gospel against Bultmann, disappointingly neglects the dimen-sion of interpersonal communion.

Chapter 8: Johnson

1   Bultmann, *Theology of the New Testament* (Scribner, 1951, 1955; Baylor Univer-sity Press, 2007).

2   Peter Berger, *The Sacred Canopy: Elements in a Sociological Theory of Religion* (New York: Doubleday Anchor, 1969).

3   The distinction between a "true" biblical theology as distinct from a "pure" biblical theology derives from the lecture of Johann Philipp Gabler's Inaugural Lecture in 1787; for full discussion, see Hendrikus Boers, *What Is New Testament Theology? The Rise of Criticism and the Problem of a Theology of the New Testament* (GBS; Philadelphia: Fortress, 1979).

4   That this style is not peculiar to Bultmann among German scholars is shown by the recent study of the theology of Hans Urs von Balthasar by Karen Kilby, *Balthasar: A (Very) Critical Introduction* (Grand Rapids: Eerdmans, 2012).

5   Before this chapter, see the discussions in vol. 1, chap. 2, sec. 6; vol. 1, chap. 2, sec. 8; vol. 1, chap. 3, sec. 10; vol. 1, chap. 3, sec. 11; and vol. 1, chap. 5, sec. 34; as well as his concluding comments in vol. 2, chap. 8, sec. 61.

6   Rudolf Bultmann, *The History of the Synoptic Tradition* (trans. J. Marsh; rev. ed.; New York: Harper & Row, 1968), 5.

7   Bultmann, *History of the Synoptic Tradition*, 5.

8   Bultmann, *History of the Synoptic Tradition*, 337–67.

9   See Wilhelm Heitmüller, "Zum Problem Paulus und Jesus," *ZNW* 13 (1912): 320–37; and Wilhelm Bousset, *Kyrios Christos: A History of the Belief in Christ from the Beginnings of Christianity to Irenaeus* (trans. John E. Steely; Nashville: Abingdon, 1970; repr. from Göttingen: Vandenhoeck & Ruprecht, 1913).

10   See Philip Harland, *Associations, Synagogues and Congregations: Claiming a Place in Ancient Mediterranean Society* (Minneapolis: Fortress, 2003); it would be more accurate to say that Bultmann is *aware* of these parallels but does not systematically work out their implications (see *Theology*, 2.101–2).

11   See the challenges to the history of religions understanding, ranging from Edwin M. Yamauchi, *Pre-Christian Gnosticism: A Survey of the Proposed Evidence* (Grand Rapids: Eerdmans, 1973) to Michael Williams, *Rethinking "Gnosticism": An Argument for Dismantling a Dubious Category* (Princeton: Princeton University Press, 1996).

12   See, for example, Bruce M. Metzger, "Considerations of Methodology in the Study of the Mystery Religions and Early Christianity," *HTR* 48 (1955): 1–20; Walter Burkert, *Ancient Mystery Cults* (Cambridge, Mass.: Harvard University Press, 1987).

13   Following the pioneering work of Gershom G. Scholem, *Jewish Gnosticism, Merkabah Mysticism and Talmudic Tradition* (New York: Jewish Theological Seminary of America, 1960), research in this area has proliferated; see, for example, Martha Himmelfarb, *Ascent to Heaven in Jewish and Christian Apocalypses* (New York: Oxford University Press, 1993).

14   Sanders, *Paul and Palestinian Judaism*.

15   See Peter W. Flint and James C. VanderKam, eds., *The Dead Sea Scrolls after Fifty Years* (2 vols.; Leiden: Brill, 1998).

16   See Luke T. Johnson, *Among the Gentiles: Greco-Roman Religion and Christianity* (New Haven: Yale University Press, 2009), 26–31, 111–29.

17 Nils A. Dahl, "Rudolf Bultmann's *Theology of the New Testament*," in *Jesus the Christ: The Historical Origins of Christological Doctrine* (ed. Donald H. Juel; Minneapolis: Fortress, 1991), 187–216.

18 It is striking that Bultmann omits the name of Peter from his quick allusion to Matt 16:18-19 or any consideration of what the entailments might be for "building the church" on Peter.

19 Bultmann's reliance on Acts 2:42-47 for his description is clear from his discussion of baptism and common meals (1.39–41); this makes the omission of the leadership role of the apostles more glaring.

20 This is an important phrase, for the endgame of the "eschatological congregation" will be when Christianity conceives of itself as a "new religion" (2.116–18).

21 He supports this assertion by reference to 2 Cor 5:18-19.

22 Thus, Bultmann works hard in his depiction of the "eschatological congregation" to minimize any actual administrative acts or structures, as when he insists that tradition "need not be mediated by an institution or sacraments" (1.60).

23 Not only does this assertion fly in the face of the evidence—the usage in Paul, apart from Ephesians, moves in the opposite direction—the example of the collection cited by Bultmann (1.94–95) seems to support the position that the sense of a larger "church" actually arose through such efforts.

24 In the bibliography for this chapter, available in the 1951 Scribner original English edition (2.255), Bultmann refers to Rudolf Sohm, *Kirchenrecht* I (1892) and *Wesen und Ursprung des Katholizismus* (2nd ed., 1909), as well as to Adolf Harnack, *Entstehung und Entwicklung der Kirchenverfassung und des Kirchenrechts in den ersten drei Jahrhunderten* (1910).

25 For the history of scholarship, see Luke T. Johnson, *The First and Second Letters to Timothy: A New Translation with Introduction and Commentary* (AB 35A; New York: Doubleday, 2001), 20–54.

26 For example, Johnson, *First and Second Letters to Timothy*; and Philip H. Towner, *The Letters to Timothy and Titus* (NICNT; Grand Rapids: Eerdmans, 2006).

27 Compare Hans von Campenhausen, *Ecclesiastical Authority and Spiritual Power in the First Three Centuries* (trans. J. A. Baker; Stanford: Stanford University Press, 1969).

28 See Johnson, *Among the Gentiles*, 130–71.

29 See Luke T. Johnson, "*Koinonia*: Diversity and Unity in Early Christianity," *TD* 46 (1999): 303–13; and "The Material Expression of Friendship in the New Testament," *Int* 58 (2004): 158–71.

30 A sketch of my own position is found in Luke T. Johnson, *Scripture and Discernment: Decision-Making in the Church* (Nashville: Abingdon, 1996).

31 See Luke T. Johnson, *Prophetic Jesus, Prophetic Church: The Challenge of Luke-Acts to Contemporary Christians* (Grand Rapids: Eerdmans, 2011).

Chapter 9: Dunn

1   All citations of Bultmann's *Theology* refer to *Theology of the New Testament* (Baylor University Press, 2007).

2   William Wrede, "The Task and Methods of 'New Testament Theology,' " in *The Nature of New Testament Theology* (ed. Robert Morgan; London: SCM Press, 1973), 68–116.

3   For Bultmann, it should be recalled, the still future notes of John 5:28-29 were the result of subsequent redaction—"added by the editor, in an attempt to reconcile the dangerous statements in vv. 24-25 with traditional eschatology" (*The Gospel of John*, 261).

4   Hans Jonas, *The Gnostic Religion: The Message of the Alien God and the Beginning of Christianity* (Boston: Beacon, 1958).

5   See, e.g., Margaret E. Thrall, *The Second Epistle to the Corinthians* (ICC; 2 vols.; Edinburgh: T&T Clark, 1994, 2000), 1.412–14.

6   Richard A. Burridge, *What Are the Gospels? A Comparison with Graeco-Roman Biography* (SNTSMS 70; Cambridge: Cambridge University Press, 1992).

7   I echo Bultmann's usage here, although the usage is too casual (referring to the Jesus who missioned in Galilee), since the phrase properly denotes the Jesus as reconstructed by historical method so far as that is possible.

8   See, e.g., my *Jesus, Paul, and the Gospels* (Grand Rapids: Eerdmans, 2011), chap. 4.

9   C. H. Dodd, *According to the Scriptures: The Substructure of New Testament Theology* (Welwyn: Nisbet, 1952).

10   Sir 24.23; Bar 4.1-2.

11   1 Cor 1:30; 8:6; Col 1:15-16; Heb 1:3; John 1:1-11.

12   See further my *The Epistles to the Colossians and to Philemon* (NIGTC; Grand Rapids: Eerdmans, 1996).

13   Walter Bauer, *Orthodoxy and Heresy in Earliest Christianity* (trans. team from Philadelphia Seminar on Christian Origins; ed. Robert A. Kraft and Gerhard Krodel; Philadelphia: Fortress, 1971).

14   Acts 5:17; 15:5; 24:5, 14; 26:5; cf. also 1 Cor 11:19.

15   I have in mind particularly Daniel Boyarin, *Border Lines: The Partition of Judaeo-Christianity* (Philadelphia: University of Pennsylvania Press, 2004).

Chapter 10: Hurtado

1   All citations of Bultmann's *Theology* refer to *Theology of the New Testament* (Baylor University Press, 2007).

2   As to be expected for someone of Bultmann's scholarly stature and influence, there are many discussions and critiques of his theological views and his hermeneutical program. I can claim acquaintance with only some of these, among which I find the following accessible and helpful: Robert C. Roberts, *Rudolf Bultmann's Theology: A Critical Interpretation* (Grand Rapids: Eerdmans,

1976); Fergusson, *Bultmann*; and the memorable discussion of Bultmann in Stephen Neill and Tom Wright, *The Interpretation of the New Testament, 1861–1986* (2nd ed.; Oxford: Oxford University Press, 1988), 237–51.

3   Rudolf Bultmann, "Man between the Times According to the New Testament," in *Existence and Faith: Shorter Writings of Rudolf Bultmann* (ed. and trans. Schubert M. Ogden; Living Age Books; New York: Meridian Books, 1960), 248–49. This essay is a particularly clear discussion by Bultmann of the view of Christian existence that he advocated and found "most clearly expressed by Paul and John" (255).

4   For his classic discussion of what he regarded as myth and his "demythologizing" program, see Rudolf Bultmann, *Jesus Christ and Mythology* (New York: Scribner, 1958).

5   E.g., "Can the faithful understand their present as an 'interim' when this 'interim' is constantly extended, until finally it will soon be two thousand years?" ("Man between the Times," 249).

6   "Man between the Times," 251.

7   "Henceforth, the imperative is based on the indicative. To be crucified and risen with Christ does not mean the acquirement of a mysterious power of immortality, but rather the freedom of a life lived in the service of God" ("Man between the Times," 256).

8   See John Barclay's contribution in the present volume, chapter 5.

9   As will be apparent below, I have the same complaint about Bultmann's handling of the early Christian texts that he discusses in the chapter that I focus on here.

10   It is interesting to compare the amount of space given to various matters in Bultmann's *Theology of the New Testament*: some 30 pages to "The Earliest Church," 120 pages to "The Hellenistic Church," 165 pages to Paul, 90 pages to Johannine literature, and 141 pages to "The Development toward the Ancient Church."

11   On the formation of the New Testament canon, see the numerous contributions in the multiauthor volume edited by Lee Martin McDonald and James A. Sanders, *The Canon Debate* (Peabody, Mass.: Hendrickson, 2002), among which I cite particularly Harry Y. Gamble's essay, "The New Testament Canon: Recent Research and the *Status Quaestionis*," 267–95.

12   For my own fuller discussion, see Larry W. Hurtado, *Lord Jesus Christ: Devotion to Jesus in Earliest Christianity* (Grand Rapids: Eerdmans, 2003). In pp. 487–518 and 563–653, I engage many of the texts surveyed by Bultmann and the developments reflected in them.

13   For almost any question about Hebrews, an essential resource is Harold W. Attridge, *The Epistle to the Hebrews* (Hermeneia; Philadelphia: Fortress, 1989), on "The Aim and Message of Hebrews," 21–28.

14   See, e.g., Attridge, *Hebrews*, 13–21.

15   Attridge, *Hebrews*, 23.

16 Hurtado, *Lord Jesus Christ*, 498. I discuss Hebrews on pp. 497–504.

17 Attridge, *Hebrews*, 27. See pp. 25–27 for Attridge's summary of main christo-logical emphases.

18 Hurtado, *Lord Jesus Christ*, 499–500.

19 Identifiable quotations of Ps 110 include 1 Cor 15:25, Mark 12:36, Matt 22:44, Luke 20:42, and Acts 2:34; and it is commonly thought that all other numerous New Testament references to Jesus as exalted to the "right hand" of God derive from Ps 110:1. See esp. David M. Hay, *Glory at the Right Hand: Psalm 110 in Early Christianity* (SBLMS 18; Nashville: Abingdon, 1973).

20 I briefly discuss Jewish interest in Melchizedek (with references to other studies) in *Lord Jesus Christ*, 501.

21 Attridge, *Hebrews*, 392, notes "a liturgical style" and possible use of "a tradi-tional acclamation."

22 I do not have space here to treat Bultmann's frequent (and regrettable) ref-erences to Judaism, "the synagogue-tradition" (e.g., 2.163, 168), which seem always to carry a certain pejorative tone.

23 It is not necessary here to engage questions about the actual situation of churches/Christians, e.g., the level of Roman persecution at the time. Instead, I focus on how the author depicts the situation and predicts how things will develop. For a balanced discussion of the likely situation of the intended read-ers, see G. K. Beale, *The Book of Revelation* (NIGTC; Grand Rapids: Eerdmans, 1999), 28–33.

24 Hurtado, *Lord Jesus Christ*, 590 (590–94).

25 Larry W. Hurtado, "Revelation 4–5 in the Light of Jewish Apocalyptic Analo-gies," *JSNT* 25 (1985): 105–24.

26 Richard J. Bauckham, "The Worship of Jesus in Apocalyptic Christianity," *NTS* 27 (1981): 322–41. An expanded version of this essay appeared as "The Wor-ship of Jesus," in Bauckham's *The Climax of Prophecy: Studies on the Book of Rev-elation* (Edinburgh: T&T Clark, 1993), 118–49. This volume includes several other valuable studies of themes and features of Revelation. See also Richard J. Bauckham, *The Theology of the Book of Revelation* (Cambridge: Cambridge University Press, 1993). Loren T. Stuckenbruck, *Angel Veneration and Chris-tology* (WUNT 2/70; Tübingen: Mohr Siebeck, 1995), is an extended study prompted by Bauckham's seminal article.

27 The singular form of the participle γεγραμμένον ("written") in 14:1 might mean that the name of the Lamb and the Father's name are seen by the author of Revelation as one. But cf. 3:12, where Jesus promises to write on believers God's name, the name of the city of God, and "my new name," and 22:4, wherein the new Jerusalem believers see God's face and have God's name on their foreheads.

Chapter 11: Meeks

1 All citations of Bultmann's *Theology* refer to *Theology of the New Testament* (Bay-lor University Press, 2007).

2   Martin Buber, *The Prophetic Faith* (trans. C. Witton-Davies; New York: Harper & Row, 1960; repr. from New York: Macmillan, 1949).

3   Rudolf Karl Bultmann, "Forms of Human Community," in *Essays Philosophical and Theological*, 291–304; repr. from *Glauben und Verstehen* II (Tübingen: Mohr Siebeck, 1952), 262–73.

4   Bultmann, "Forms of Human Community," 291.

5   Rudolf Bultmann, *Glauben und Verstehen* II, 264, my translation; cf. Greig's translation in *Essays Philosophical and Theological*, 293.

6   Bultmann, *Essays Philosophical and Theological*, 300, emphasis in original.

7   Bultmann, *Essays Philosophical and Theological*, 303.

8   Heinz-Horst Schrey, "The Consequences of Bultmann's Theology for Ethics," in *The Theology of Rudolf Bultmann* (ed. Charles W. Kegley; New York: Harper & Row, 1966), 184.

9   Rudolf Bultmann, "Der Arier-Paragraph im Raume der Kirche," *TBl* 12, no. 12 (1933): cols. 359–70.

10 Schrey, "Consequences of Bultmann's Theology," 196, 198–99.

11 See Bultmann's "Autobiographical Reflections," in *Existence and Faith* (Meridian Books, 1960), 284.

12 Weiss, *Predigt Jesu* (1892), 5–6.

13 Weiss, *Predigt Jesu*, xi (from his foreword to the 2nd edition of 1900).

14 In Bultmann's introduction to the 1964 reprint of Weiss' *Predigt Jesu*, v.

15 Significantly, the words about the importance of Christianity's translocal sense of community in its eventual success echo a well-known thesis by Adolf von Harnack, on which see further below.

16 Max Weber, *The Theory of Social and Economic Organization* (trans. and ed. A. M. Henderson and Talcott Parsons; New York: Free Press, 1964), 328–92.

17 Franz Neumann, "The Social Sciences," in *The Cultural Migration: The European Scholar in America* (Philadelphia: University of Pennsylvania Press, 1953), 38, quoted by Peter Gay, *Weimar Culture: The Outsider as Insider* (New York: Harper & Row, 1970), 22.

18 Dahl, "Rudolf Bultmann's *Theology of the New Testament*," 191–93.

19 Bultmann made the "indicative and imperative" paradox the framework for discussing Paul's ethics already in his "Das Problem der Ethik bei Paulus," in *Exegetica*, 36–54; repr. from *ZNW* 23 (1924): 123–40. It has been a central issue in most subsequent discussions of Bultmann's ethics; see now Friedrich Wilhelm Horn and Ruben Zimmermann, *Jenseits von Indikativ und Imperativ* (Kontexte und Normen Neutestamentlicher Ethik = Contexts and Norms of New Testament Ethics, vol. 1; WUNT 238; Tübingen: Mohr Siebeck, 2009).

20 On the importance of placing atonement into the larger context implied by *redemption*, cf. David H. Kelsey, *Imagining Redemption* (Louisville, Ky.: Westminster John Knox, 2005), especially chap. 4, on the public and social dimensions of "redemption."

21 Karl Barth, *Rudolf Bultmann; ein Versuch, ihn zu verstehen* (Zollikon: Evangelischer Verlag, 1953), 18.

22 Barth, *Bultmann*, 34.

23 I have called attention to this trend, and its implications for describing early Christian morality, in Wayne A. Meeks, *The Origins of Christian Morality: The First Two Centuries* (New Haven: Yale University Press, 1993), chap. 1; and for historical inquiries about Jesus, in Wayne A. Meeks, *Christ Is the Question* (Louisville, Ky.: Westminster John Knox, 2006), 21, with further bibliography entries there. I have borrowed from these earlier publications much of the language in this paragraph.

24 David G. Horrell, *Solidarity and Difference: A Contemporary Reading of Paul's Ethics* (Edinburgh: T&T Clark, 2005), 103.

25 Abraham J. Malherbe, "Ethics in Context: The Thessalonians and Their Neighbors," *HvTSt* 68, no. 1 (2012).

26 H. Richard Niebuhr, *The Responsible Self: An Essay in Christian Moral Philosophy* (San Francisco: Harper & Row, 1978), 126.

27 Wayne A. Meeks, "Christian Beginnings and Christian Ethics: The Hermeneutical Challenge," *Bulletin ET* 9, no. 2 (1998): 171–81.

28 Stefan Alkier, *Urchristentum: Zur Geschichte und Theologie einer exegetischen Disziplin* (Tübingen: Mohr Siebeck, 1993).

29 I draw here on remarks I delivered to the third Congress of the European Society of Catholic Theology in 1998. See Meeks, "Christian Beginnings."

30 Dale B. Martin, *Sex and the Single Savior: Gender and Sexuality in Biblical Interpretation* (Louisville, Ky.: Westminster John Knox, 2006), 1–16.

31 Wayne A. Meeks, "Why Study the New Testament?," *NTS* 51 (2005): 155–70.

Chapter 12: Standhartinger

1 Letter from R. Bultmann to F. Gogarten dated June 10, 1945, in Hermann Götz Göckeritz, ed., *Rudolf Bultmann—Friedrich Gogarten Briefwechsel 1921–1967* (Tübingen: Mohr Siebeck, 2002), 232–33.

2 John Gimbel, *A German Community under American Occupation: Marburg 1945–1952* (Stanford, Calif.: Stanford University Press, 1961), 15. The German phrase "wirklichkeitsferner Professor" is from John Gimbel, *Eine Deutsche Stadt unter amerikanischer Besatzung. Marburg 1945–1952* (Cologne: Kiepenheuer & Witsch, 1964), 14.

3 Regarding the publishing contract, cf. Hammann, *Rudolf Bultmann. Eine Biographie*, 297. The first volume of the series, the *Phänomenologie der Religion* by Gradus van der Leeuw, had already appeared in 1933.

4 Letter 57 from Rudolf Bultmann to Gerhard Krüger dated September 29, 1940, in Frank Lilie, ed., "Rudolf Bultmann und Gerhard Krüger. Briefwechsel 1925–1971 Teil 5," *Zeitschrift für neuere Theologiegeschichte* 6 (1998): 274–307 (278–79). Indeed, Bultmann already mentions work on the *New Testament Theology*, e.g., in the letter to Martin Heidegger dated December 11 and 14, 1932,

in Andreas Großmann and Christof Landmesser, eds., *Rudolf Bultmann/Martin Heidegger. Briefwechsel 1925–1975* (Frankfurt: Klostermann, 2009), 186.

5 Postcard from Bultmann to Krüger (59) dated December 11, 1940, in Lilie, "Rudolf Bultmann," 280.

6 See letter 107 from Bultmann to Gerhard Krüger dated January 28, 1953, in Lilie, "Rudolf Bultmann," 294.

7 Bultmann, "Paulus," in *Religion in Geschichte und Gegenwart* (vol. 4; Tübingen: Mohr Siebeck, 1930), 1019–46 = "Paul," in *Existence and Faith* (Meridian Books, 1960), 111–46. Matthias Dreher, *Rudolf Bultmann als Kritiker in seinen Rezensionen und Forschungsberichten* (Münster: Lit Verlag, 2005), 19; Ulrich H. J. Körtner and Rudolf Bultmann, "Theologie des Neuen Testaments," in *Kanon der Theologie. 45 Schlüsseltexte im Portrait* (ed. Christian Danz; 2 vols.; Darmstadt: Wissenschaftliche Buchgesellschaft, 2010), 289–96 (291); Cf. also Werner G. Kümmel, "Rudolf Bultmann als Paulusforscher," in *Rudolf Bultmanns Werk und Wirkung* (ed. B. Jaspers; Darmstadt: Wissenschaftliche Buchgessellschaft, 1984), 175–93.

8 Listed in Bernd Jaspert, *Sachgemässe Exegese. Die Protokolle aus Rudolf Bultmanns Neutestamentlichen Seminaren 1927–1951* (Marburger Theologische Studien 46; Marburg: Elwert, 1996), 210–21. In the summer semester of 1922 and 1924, he lectured on "The Religion of Early Christianity (New Testament Theology)," then, in the winter semesters of 1925/26, 1927/28, 1929/30, 1932/33, 1934/35, 1938/39, 1940, 1942/43, and in the summer semester of 1946 and 1948, on "New Testament Theology." Furthermore, he lectured on "The History of the Religion of Hellenism and of Judaism in the Hellenistic Era (Prolegomena to New Testament Theology)" in the winter semester of 1923/24 and on "Early Christian and the History of Religion" in the summer semester of 1931.

9 Bultmann, *Theologie des Neuen Testaments* (9th ed., revised and supplemented by Otto Merk; Tübingen: Mohr Siebeck, 1984), 1 = Bultmann, *Theology of the New Testament* (Baylor University Press, 2007), 3: "The message of Jesus is a presupposition for the theology of the New Testament rather than a part of that theology itself." Cf. Bultmann, "Paul," 125: "Consequently, while the person and history of Jesus do indeed constitute a presupposition of his theology, they do not do so from the standpoint of their historical or ideal content, but rather as the act of God, as the occurrence of the revelation of salvation."

10 Bultmann, "Wissenschaft und Existenz (1955)," in *Glauben und Verstehen* (*GuV*) III (Tübingen: Mohr Siebeck, 1965), 107–21 (115) = "Science and Existence (Wissenschaft und Existenz 1955)," in *New Testament and Mythology and Other Basic Writings* (ed. Schubert M. Ogden; Philadelphia: Fortress, 1984), 131–44 (138–39).

11 Cf. Bultmann, "Karl Barths 'Römerbrief' in zweiter Auflage (1922)," in *Anfänge der dialektischen Theologie* I (ed. Jürgen Moltmann; Munich: Kaiser, 1985), 119–42; Bultmann, "Liberal Theology and the Latest Theological

Movement (German original 1924)," in *Faith and Understanding*, vol. 1 (ed.
Robert W. Funk; trans. Louise Pettibone Smith; New York: Harper & Row,
1969), 28–52. Regarding the discussion, cf. Gunnar Sinn, *Christologie und
Existenz. Rudolf Bultmanns Interpretation des paulinischen Christuszeugnisses*
(TANZ 3; Tübingen: A. Francke, 1991), 120–21.

12 Jaspert, *Sachgemässe Exegese*, lists participants in the seminars.

13 Cf. John R. Willertz, "Marburg unter dem Nationalsozialismus (1933–1945),"
in *Marburger Geschichte. Rückblick auf die Stadtgeschichte in Einzelbeiträgen*
(ed. Erhart Dettmering and Rudolf Grenz; Marburg: Elwert, 1980), 593–653.

14 Jochen-Christoph Kaiser, Andreas Lippmann, and Martin Schindel, eds., *Marburger Theologie im Nationalsozialismus. Texte zur Geschichte der Evangelisch-theologischen Fakultät im Reich* (Neukirchen: Neukirchener Verlag, 1998), 2.

15 Cf. Kaiser, Lippmann, and Schindel, *Marburger Theologie*, 54–63, 81–82.

16 Bultmann's political stance was liberal; cf. Walter Rebell, "Glaube und politisches Handeln bei Rudolf Bultmann," *ZEE* 31 (1987): 162–82 (165).

17 Bultmann to Martin Heidegger on December 11 and 14, 1932, in Großmann
and Landmesser, *Rudolf Bultmann/Martin Heidegger. Briefwechsel*, 188.

18 Bultmann to Martin Heidegger on June 18, 1933, in Großmann and Landmesser, *Rudolf Bultmann/Martin Heidegger. Briefwechsel*, 195.

19 Already in 1943 Bultmann wrote to his conscripted student Jochen Niemöller,
the son of Martin Niemöller, that existential philosophy had indeed shaped his
terminology. "No knowledge of existentialism is necessary in order to understand it, however. For the decisive element is, namely, that the terms I adopt
(e.g. existence, self-awareness, decision) designate phenomena, facts of life
themselves, denoted by these terms—they do not designate constructions, the
results of philosophical theory" (*Feldpost: Zeugnis und Vermächtnis. Briefe und
Texte aus dem Kreis der evangelischen Studentengemeinde Marburg/lahn und
ihrer Lehrer [1939–1945]* [ed. Erika Dinkler-von Schubert; Göttingen: Vandenhoeck & Ruprecht, 1993], 154).

20 R. Bultmann, "Die Aufgabe der Theologie in der gegenwärtigen Situation," in
Kaiser, Lippmann, and Schindel, *Marburger Theologie*, 28–34 (28) (Erstdruck:
Theologische Blätter 12 [1933]: 161–66) = "The Task of Theology in the Present
Situation," in *Existence and Faith*, 158–65 (158).

21 Bultmann, "Die Aufgabe der Theologie," 30; ET, 160.

22 Quotation from the twelve theses "Wider den undeutschen Geist!" ("Against
the un-German spirit!"), which surfaced as a pamphlet from "The students of
Germany" in April 1933 in Berlin and were then read, among other occasions,
at the book burning on May 10, 1933, in Frankfurt am Main. The complete
thesis reads as follows: "6. We want to eradicate lies, we want to denounce
treason, we want institutions of discipline and political education for us the
students, not mindlessness." The other theses address the supposed influence of
the Jewish spirit on German thought. Thus, the fourth thesis states, "Our most

dangerous enemy is the Jew and those who are his slaves." http://en.wikipedia.org/wiki/Twelve_Theses (accessed December 11, 2012).

23 Bultmann, "Die Aufgabe der Theologie," 34; ET, 165.

24 Bultmann, "Die Aufgabe der Theologie," 34; ET, 165.

25 Cf. Bultmann, "Jesus und Paulus" (1936), in *Exegetica*, 210–29 (220, 227) = "Jesus and Paul (1936)," in *Existence and Faith*, 182–201 (193, 199); "Das Verständnis von Welt und Mensch im Neuen Testament und im Griechentum (1940)," *GuV* II, 59–78 (75) = "The Understanding of Man and the World in the New Testament and in the Greek World (1940)," in *Essays Philosophical and Theological (EPT)*, 67–89 (86); "Die Frage der natürlichen Offenbarung (1941)," *GuV* II, 79–104 (98) = "The Question of Natural Revelation (1941)," in *EPT*, 90–118 (112–13); "Adam, wo bist du (1945)?," *GuV* II, 115–16 (116) = "Adam, Where Art Thou?" in *EPT*, 119–32 (131); "Anknüpfung und Widerspruch (1946)," *GuV* II 117–32 = "Points of Contact and Conflict (1946)," *EPT*, 133–50 (150); "Gnade und Freiheit (1948)," *GuV* II 149–61 (161) = "Grace and Freedom," *EPT*, 168–81 (181); "Die Bedeutung der alttestamentlich-jüdichen Tradition für das christliche Abendland," *GuV* I, 236–45 (243) = "The Significance of Jewish Old Testament Tradition for the Christian West," *EPT*, 262–72 (270); and the sermons from July 1934; December 1939, etc.; cf. Bultmann, *Marburger Predigten* (2 vols.; Tübingen: Mohr Siebeck, 1956).

26 Regarding Bultmann's relationships with Jews and his scholarly treatment of Judaism, cf. Angela Standhartinger, "Rudolf Bultmann im interreligiösen Dialog," *Evangelische Theologie* 71 (2011): 16–34.

27 Cf. the report from the Hessian daily newspaper on April 21, 1932, in Kaiser, Lippmann, and Schindel, *Marburger Theologie*, 6–8 (8): "The enthusiasts believed that, with Hitler, they had experienced the most glorious moment of their lives. The critic not biased by delirium regards the matter more soberly. He certainly does not mistake the numerous strengths of the Hitler Movement. This inspiration of the masses and the cult of personality surrounding Adolf Hitler are, however, sources of danger for Germany's future!"

28 Rudolf Bultmann, "Gott ruft uns," *Neuwerk* 15 (1933): 70–81 (73). Cf. Bultmann, *Das verkündigte Wort. Predigten–Andachten–Ansprachen 1906–1941* (ed. Erich Gräßer; Tübingen: Mohr Siebeck, 1984), 247–60.

29 Cf. Bultmann, "Gutachten der Theologischen Fakultät der Universität Marburg zum Kirchengesetz über die Rechtsverhältnisse der Geistlichen und Kirchenbeamten," *TBl* 12, no. 10 (1933): 289–94; "Neues Testament und Rassenfrage," *TBl* 12, no. 10 (1933): 294–96; "Der Arier-Paragraph im Raume der Kirche," *TBl* 12, no. 12 (1933): 359–70; "Zur Antwort auf Herrn Professor D. Wobermins Artikel: Nochmals die Arierfrage in der Kirche," *Deutsches Pfarrerblatt* 38 (1934): 87–88. The texts are collected in Hans Liebing, ed., *Die Marburger Theologen und der Arierparagraph in der Kirche. Eine Sammlung von Texten aus den Jahren 1933 und 1934* (Marburg: Elwert, 1977).

30 With reference to Barth's 1933 "Theologische Existenz heute," Bultmann challenged students in 1937 to pursue theology, then of all times. He considered Barth's 1933 statement to still be valid: "Students must also be clear . . . that, with the word that they have learned, they must go out with strenuous effort into the struggles of the time." Dorothee Stovesandt to K. Barth on February 24, 1937, in Stefan Holtmann and P. Zocher, eds., *Als Laien die Führung der Bekenntnisgemeinde übernehmen. Briefe aus dem Kirchenkampf von Karl Barth und Karl und Dorothee Stoevesandt (1933–1938)* (Neukirchen: Neukirchener Verlag, 2007), 112.

31 Andreas Lippmann, *Marburger Theologie im Nationalsozialismus* (Academia Marburgensis 9; Munich: Sauer, 2003), 125–26. A 1935 Gestapo report speaks of the "significant role of the two confessing professors Bultmann and von Soden and of their ominous influence on theology students." Hammann, *Rudolf Bultmann. Eine Biographie*, 266.

32 Cf. the statement by Georg Wünsch on April 27, 1936, in Kaiser, Lippmann, and Schindel, *Marburger Theologie*, 87–88.

33 Lippmann, *Marburger Theologie*, 212, 260–61.

34 Bultmann to Karl Barth on December 3, 1934, in Bernd Jaspert, ed., *Karl Barth–Rudolf Bultmann. Briefwechsel 1911–1966* (2nd ed.; Zurich: Theologischer Verlag, 1994), 154–55.

35 Bultmann, "Der Sinn des christlichen Schöpfungsglaubens," *Zeitschrift für Missionskunde und Religionswissenschaft* 51 (1936): 1–20 (19) = "The Meaning of the Christian Faith in Creation," in *Existence and Faith*, 206–25 (224). Cf. also Hammann, *Rudolf Bultmann. Eine Biographie*, 271.

36 Cf. Alfred Rosenberg, *Der Mythos des 20. Jahrhunderts* (published in 1930 with many re-editions until 1945) = *The Myth of the Twentieth Century: An Evaluation of the Spiritual-Intellectual Confrontations of Our Age by Alfred Rosenberg* (Torrance, Calif.: Noontide Press, 1982).

37 Bultmann, "Jesus und Paulus," 229; ET, 201: "One cannot flee from Paul and return to Jesus. For what one encounters in Jesus is the same God who is encountered in Paul." Regarding Rosenberg, see 210 and 224n17 (ET, 181 and 310n17). On the debate surrounding Rosenberg in the Lutheran Church, cf. Harald Ibner, *Christlicher Glaube oder rassischer Mythus* (Frankfurt: Peter Lang, 1987).

38 Bultmann, "Polis und Hades in der Antigone des Sophokles," in *GuV* II, 20–31 = "Polis and Hades in Sophocles' Antigone," in *EPT*, 22–35 (25).

39 Bultmann, "Polis und Hades," in *GuV* II, 29; ET, 33.

40 Bultmann, "Polis und Hades," in *GuV* II, 31; ET, 34.

41 Bultmann is said to have sent students home the next morning with the explanation, "If the synagogues are burning, we cannot have a lecture." Hammann, *Rudolf Bultmann. Eine Biographie*, 288.

42 Bultmann, "Christus des Gesetzes Ende," in *GuV* II, 32–58 = "Christ the End of the Law," in *EPT*, 36–66. Bultmann also criticizes Rosenberg's overestimation

of Nordic mythology in relation to the Jewish hope for a kingdom of righteousness and love in a sermon delivered on December 11, 1938, one month after the so-called Night of Broken Glass in Marburg. Cf. Bultmann, *Marburger Predigten*, 89.

43 Bultmann, "Christus des Gesetzes Ende," 32; ET, 36.

44 Bultmann, "Christus des Gesetzes Ende," 41; ET, 46.

45 Bultmann, "Weissagung und Erfüllung," in *GuV* II, 162–86, 195 = "Prophecy and Fulfillment," in *EPT*, 182–208 (191). Cf. Harry Waßmann, Jakob Matthias Osthof, and Anna-Elisabeth Bruckhaus, *Rudolf Bultmann (1884–1976)* (Nachlaßverzeichnisse der Universitätsbibliothek Tübingen 2; Wiesbaden: Harrassowitz, 2001), 280 no. 3086.

46 "Weissagung und Erfüllung," in *GuV* II, 184; ET, 206, with slight editorial adjustment in this volume.

47 "Weissagung und Erfüllung," in *GuV* II, 184–86; ET, 207–8.

48 Bultmann, "Die Frage der natürlichen Offenbarung" in *GuV* II, 79–104 (80) = "Question of Natural Revelation," in *EPT*, 90–118 (92).

49 Bultmann, "Die Frage der natürlichen Offenbarung," in *GuV* II, 85–86 (87); ET, 98, 100.

50 Bultmann, "Die Frage der natürlichen Offenbarung," in *GuV* II, 91; ET, 104.

51 Bultmann, "Die Frage der natürlichen Offenbarung," in *GuV* II, 92–93; ET, 105–6.

52 Bultmann, *Neues Testament und Mythologie* (Munich: Kaiser, 1986) = "New Testament and Mythology." Cf. Bernd Jaspert, "Existenz–Mythos–Theologie. Fünfzig Jahre nach Rudolf Bultmanns Entmythologisierungsprogramm," *Neue Zeitschrift für systematische Theologie und Religionsphilosophie* 34 (1992): 128, 145–46; and Wichmann von Meding, "Rudolf Bultmanns Widerstand gegen die Mythologisierung der christlichen Verkündigung," *TZ* 53 (1997): 203–5. In 1952 Bultmann himself denied any relationship between his concept of myth and Rosenberg. Cf. Bultmann, "Der Sinn des Mythos und der Entmythologisierung," in *Kerygma und Mythos* II, 180n2 = "On the Problem of Demythologizing," in *New Testament and Mythology*, 124n4. This may also be classified with the attacks of the Erlangen theologian Walter Künneth, who adopted the folk race ideas of the National Socialists in 1932–1936, but whom they dismissed in 1936; he then joined the Confessing Church. From the beginning, he was one of Bultmann's opponents in the demythologization controversy, later founding the anti-Bultmann movement called "No Other Gospel" and accusing Bultmann that his theory stood in "fatal proximity to Rosenberg's claim" since, in effect, it involves "the same dispute of the saving facts of Christianity." Walter Künneth, *Lebensführungen. Der Wahrheit verpflichtet* (Wuppertal: Brockhaus, 1979), 234–35.

53 Erich Dinkler, "Die christliche Wahrheitsfrage und die Unabgeschlossenheit der Theologie als Wissenschaft," in *Gedenken an Rudolf Bultmann* (ed. Otto Kaiser; Tübingen: Mohr Siebeck, 1977), 28.

316 — Notes to pp. 243–246

54 Hammann, *Rudolf Bultmann. Eine Biographie*, 421–32.

55 Bultmann, "Grußwort im Marburger Rundbrief zu Jahresbeginn Januar 1941," in *Feldpost*, 142–45.

56 Bultmann, "Zur Frage der wissenschaftlichen Ausbildung der Theologen," in *Studienbetreuung der Kriegsteilnehmer der Martin Luther-Universität Halle-Wittenberg* (ed. D. Fascher; Theologische Fakultät Halle in Verbindung mit den Theol. Fakultäten Marburg u. Tübingen; Halle: Klinz, 1944), 34–40.

57 Hammann, *Rudolf Bultmann. Eine Biographie*, 351–63, 357. Presumably, Hartshorne himself was the point of contact that resulted in this estimation of Bultmann. He was one of the initiators of the paper competition "My Life in Germany before and after January 30, 1933" held by Harvard University, which Karl Löwith, among others, entered telling of Bultmann's invitation the evening before he departed Germany (cf. Karl Löwith, *Mein Leben in Deutschland vor und nach 1933* [Stuttgart: J.B. Metzlersche Verlagsbuchhandlung, 1986], 81). Cf. Uta Gerhardt, "Nachwort: Nazi Madness. Der Soziloge Edward Y. Hartshorne und das Harvard-Projekt," in *Nie mehr zurück in dieses Land. Augenzeugen berichten über die Novemberpogrome 1938* (ed. Uta Gerhardt and Thomas Karlauf; Berlin: List, 2011), 319–54.

58 Bultmann, Georg Wünsch, "Evangelische Ethik des Politischen," *VF* 3 (1947): 253–66. Cf. Lippmann, *Marburger Theologie*, 427–35.

59 Bultmann, "Das Verhältnis der Universität zur Antike und Christentum," in *Berichte des Planungs-Ausschusses der Philipps-Universität Marburg zur Neugestaltung der deutschen Hochschulen* (Marburg: Marburger Presse, 1946), 22.

60 Bultmann, "Das Verhältnis der Universität," 24.

61 Bultmann, "Hochschule, Antike und Christentum," in *Marburger Hochschulgespräche. 12.–15. Juni 1946. Referate und Diskussionen* (Frankfurt: Vittorio Klostermann, 1947), 137. Cf. also "Humanismus und Christentum," in *GuV* II, 133–48 = "Humanism and Christianity," in *EPT*, 151–67.

62 Bultmann, "Adam, wo bist du?," in *GuV* II, 105–16; ET, 119–32.

63 Bultmann, "Adam, wo bist du?," in *GuV* II, 115; ET, 131.

64 Bultmann, *GuV* II, 111, 113; ET, 126, 128.

65 First published in Knud C. Knudsen, ed., *Welt ohne Hass. Führende Wissenschaftler nehmen Stellung zu brennenden deutschen Problemen* (Berlin: Christian-Verlag, 1950), 43–54. This volume also contains five contributions by Jewish scholars.

66 Bultmann, "The Significance of Jewish Old Testament Tradition for the Christian West," in *EPT*, 270—"Die Bedeutung der alttestamentlich-jüdischen Tradition für das christliche Abendland (1950)," in *GuV* II, 236–45 (243).

67 Cf. the report on the conference with extensive records of the presentations in *Europäische Zukunft* 1, no. 2 (1949): 88–89. It was published as Bultmann, "Formen menschlicher Gemeinschaft," in *GuV* II, 262–73 = "Forms of Human Community," in *EPT*, 291–304.

68 Bultmann, "Formen menschlicher Gemeinschaft," in *GuV* II, 262, 272; ET, 291, 303. The positive image of nihilism in this essay is noteworthy. It contrasts with the equation of nihilism, Russian communism, and atheist faith in the natural sciences in the contribution by Bultmann's colleague and former German Christian Ernst Benz in the first issue of the journal. Cf. Ernst Benz, "Europa zwischen westlichem und östlichem Nihilismus," *Europäische Zukunft* 1, no. 1 (1949): 16–21.

69 Bultmann, "Für die christliche Freiheit," in *Die Wandlung* 4 (1949): 417–22.

70 Bultmann, "Die Bedeutung des Gedankens der Freiheit für die abendländische Kultur," in *GuV* II, 274–93 = "The Significance of the Idea of Freedom for Western Civilization," in *EPT*, 305–25.

71 The epilogue originally appeared under the heading "Das Problem des Verhältnisses von Theologie und Verkündigung im Neuen Testament," in *Aux sources de la tradition chrétien. Mélanges offerts à Maurice Goguel à l' occasion de son soixante-dixème aniversaire* (Neuchatel: Delachaux & Niestlé, 1950), 32–42.

72 Cf. also the "Introductory Word" to Bousset, *Kyrios Christos* (Abingdon, 1970), 7–9.

73 *Theology* I, sec. 12 and secs. 5–18.

74 *Theology* I, sec. 13.

75 Cf. Wilhelm Wrede, *Über die Aufgabe und Methode der sogenannten neutestamentlichen Theologie* (Göttingen: Vandenhoeck & Ruprecht, 1897), 38–41. Regarding Ignatius, especially Bultmann, *Theologie*, 541–47; ET, 2.191–99.

76 Wrede, *Aufgabe*, 35, wrote, "Ultimately, we want to know, in any case, what was believed, thought, taught, hoped, required, and sought after in the earliest days of Christianity."

77 "That theological teachings were understood as an expression of faith and not as the object of faith" (*Theology*, 2.246; *Theologie*, 594).

78 Cf. *Theologie*, 598–99; ET, 2.248–50. Adolf Schlatter, *Die Theologie des Neuen Testaments und die Dogmatik* (Gütersloh: Bertelsmann, 1909), 251: "[T]he proclamation practiced in the New Testament admits no separation of the act of thinking from the other functions which, taken together, produce our standard of living. This is not because, in its low level of culture, it has not yet attained the heights of the scientific objective, but because it is an awareness of God that can only remain an awareness, substantiates nothing other than an act of thanksgiving, and rejects and judges as aberrant. It sees in God's relationship to us the whole act that motivates us and, in addition therefore, gives us God's assurance so that we believe in him, serve him, and live through him and for him." On Bultmann's initially very critical relationship with his Tübingen professor Schlatter, cf. Hammann, *Rudolf Bultmann. Eine Biographie*, 19.

79 It is interesting to note that a series of Bultmann's students wrote doctoral dissertations on extracanonical themes, e.g., Günther Bornkamm, "Mythos und Legende in den Thomasakten"; Ernst Fuchs, "Das Verhältnis des Glaubens zur Tat im Hermasbuch"; Hartwig Thyen, "Der Stil der jüdisch-hellenistischen

Homilie"; Helmut Koester, "Die synoptische Überlieferung bei den Apostolischen Vätern."

80 Walter Bauer, *Rechtgläubigkeit und Ketzerei im ältesten Christentum* (Tübingen: Mohr Siebeck, 1934) = *Orthodoxy and Heresy in Earliest Christianity* (Philadelphia: Fortress, 1971). Cf. Bultmann, *Theologie*, 489–90; ET, 2.137–38. Paragraphs 51–61, however, are infused more markedly with a concept of decline than with a concept of discourse. Cf. also Dieter Georgi, "Rudolf Bultmann's Theology of the New Testament Revisited," in *Bultmann, Retrospect and Prospect* (ed. Edward C. Hobbs; HTS 35; Philadelphia: Fortress, 1985), 81.

81 Cf. Georgi, "Rudolf Bultmann's," 80.

82 Bultmann, *Theologie*, 67; ET, 1.62. Five years later, in part 3 of his *Theology*, he stated, "How far the Christian Church was from thinking of remolding the world, of adopting an economic or political program, is indicated by its attitude toward property, slavery and the state. As for the matter of property, the picture of the original Church's 'love-communism' sketched in Acts 2:45, 4:32-35 stands isolated in the tradition and is representative only insofar as it is a pattern for the love which is prepared to bring about the 'equality' of which Paul speaks in II Cor. 8:13f: the surplus of one man is to supply the need of another" (*Theology*, 2.229–30; *Theologie*, 576–77).

83 Bultmann, *Jesus and the Word* (Scribner, 1958), 78 = *Jesus* (Tübingen: Mohr Siebeck, 1988 [1926]), 73.

84 Quoted with slight editorial adjustment in this volume.

85 "Almost everywhere else Christian faith sank back into legalism. . . . But Ignatius learned from Paul to understand Christian faith as a truly existential matter" (*Theology*, 2.198; *Theologie*, 547).

86 "John I, and II John, and Ignatius, too—demonstrate the relative appropriateness and the intent of Gnostic teaching; in opposition to a historizing of the eschatological occurrence, it expresses a legitimate interest of faith" (*Theology*, 2.127; *Theologie*, 479).

87 "For that reason one must not regard the attitude of Revelation as contradictory to the general Christian acknowledgment of the civil order. This order is simply not questioned, but it belongs, of course, to the transitory orders of this world. Consequently, no obligation is felt to take over responsibility for it or for the just administration of it—a situation for which one of the causes, of course, is the fact that the Christians still belonged primarily to those social classes for which such responsibility was out of the question" (*Theology*, 2.231; *Theologie*, 578). In an opinion rendered April 28, 1945, after the liberation of Marburg but before Germany's surrender on May 8, the Marburg theology faculty released the pastorate from the duty to obey the oath to the Führer. Cf. Kaiser, Lippmann, and Schindel, *Marburger Theologie*, 108–12; Lippmann, *Marburger Theologie*, 409–11.

88 Cf., e.g., Franz Peelinck, "Rudolf Bultmann und die Politik," in *Weiter aktuell. Die Theologie Rudolf Bultmann als Vermächtnis* (Evangelische Zeitstimmen 59/60; Hamburg: Reich, 1971), 42–49.

89 Quoted with slight editorial adjustment in this volume.

90 Bultmann, *Jesus* (Mohr Siebeck, 1988), 57. Two quotes from *'Abot* I.8 and I.2 follow; the latter is quoted again in *Theology* 1.14 but explained, "In demanding unconditional obedience Jesus and the rabbi agree. That the ideal of obedience is taken radically by Jesus follows from the whole context of his ethical utterances."

91 Cf. *Theologie*, 10, 26; ET, 1.11, 25. Cf. "Das Verständnis von Welt," *GuV* II, 59–78 (75) = "Understanding of Man and the World," 86: "the taking of man out of the world."

92 In "Paulus," *RGG2* (1930), 1032, the passage appears in relation to the theme of self-care and self-security.

93 Cf. "Paulus," *RGG2* (1930), 1024–25, 1029–31. Cf. also the positive reference to Bauer, *Rechtgläubigkeit und Ketzerei*, sec. 55.4 (*Theologie*, 487–91; ET, 2.135–38).

94 For criticism of Bultmann's image of Judaism, cf. also Shawn Kelly, *Racializing Jesus: Race, Ideology and the Formation of Modern Biblical Scholarship* (London: Routledge, 2002), 129–64.

95 Bultmann, "Paulus," 1031–38; 1038–43 = "Paul" in *EPT*, 128–37; "Man Prior to the Revelation of Faith," 137–46; "Man under Faith."

96 Bultmann, "Paulus," 1024–25; ET, 121–22.

97 Georgi, "Rudolf Bultmann's," 80.

98 Dorothee Sölle, *Politische Theologie. Auseinandersetzung mit Rudolf Bultmann* (Stuttgart: Kreuz-Verlag, 1971). The lecture was published under the title "Hoffnung verändert die Welt. Kritische Auseinandersetzung mit Rodolf Bultmann," *Evangelische Kommentare* 4, no. 1 (1971): 15–20.

99 Sölle, "Hoffnung verändert die Welt," 15. Cf. Yorick Spiegel, "Die Praxisrelevanz der Theologie," in *Theologie und gesellschaftliche Praxis* (ed. Yorick Spiegel and Ulrich Teichler; Der Pfarrer in der Großstadt 1; Munich: Chr. Kaiser, 1974), 125–26: "The existential theologians [pastors influenced by Bultmann and his students] hold the ideal of a democratic church that far exceeds the usual aspirations of their age group in this respect. . . . Their objective for the church is maturity and responsibility for the world. . . . [They] deal with more than just socio-political topics in their preaching, nurture the formation of political opinion, and are, by far, the best-informed regarding social legislation. Existential theologians convey the impression of broad-mindedness and openness to pressing ecclesial and social problems."

100 This letter from Bultmann to Dorothee Sölle is dated August 1971. The quotation is from p. 1, from Bultmann's papers in the library of the University of Tübingen (with thanks for cordially making them available), Ms 2-2386. The pages cited in the letter (pp. 79, 105) refer to Sölle, *Politische Theologie*, 79n111, 105. The letter is often interpreted as a critical rejection of Sölle's position (cf., e.g., Hammann, *Rudolf Bultmann. Eine Biographie*, 468–70; Walter Schmithals, "Zu Rudolf Bultmanns 100. Geburtstag," *TRu* 31 [1986]: 90), in my opinion totally without justification.

Chapter 13: Watson

1   Karl Barth, "Rudolf Bultmann: Ein Versuch ihn zu Verstehen" (1952), in *Rudolf Bultmann, Christus und Adam: Zwei theologische Studien* (Zurich: Evangelischer Verlag, 1964), 10–11; ET: *Kerygma and Myth*, vol. 2, 83–132 (84–85).

2   Bultmann, *Die Geschichte der Synoptischen Tradition*; ET: *History of the Synoptic Tradition* (Oxford: Blackwell, 1963); *Jesus* (Deutsche Bibliothek, 1926); ET: *Jesus and the Word* (Scribner, 1934); *Das Evangelium des Johannes* (Vandenhoeck & Ruprecht, 1941); ET: *The Gospel of John*; *Theologie des Neuen Testaments* (Mohr Siebeck, 1953); ET: *Theology of the New Testament* (SCM Press, 1952, 1955). In this chapter I shall cite the 5th German edition of the New Testament theology (1965), adding equivalent page numbers in the English translation. Translations (provided in the main text) are my own.

3   See especially the fifteen essays collected under the title *Glauben und Verstehen* I (*GuV* I); ET: *Faith and Understanding*, vol. 1 (ed. Robert W. Funk; trans. Louise Pettibone Smith; Philadelphia: Fortress, 1969). The English translation of *GuV* I postdated by fourteen years the translation of *GuV* II as *Essays Philosophical and Theological* (SCM Press, 1955).

4   Rudolf Bultmann, "Neues Testament und Mythologie: Das Problem der Entmythologisierung der neutestamentlichen Verkündigung," initially delivered as a lecture in April 1941 and published along with a study of "Die Frage der natürlichen Offenbarung" under the title *Offenbarung und Heilsgeschehen* (Munich: A. Lempp, 1941). The demythologizing essay was reprinted in *Kerygma und Mythos: Ein theologisches Gespräch* I (ed. Hans Werner Bartsch; Hamburg: Reich & Heidrich, 1948), 15–53; ET: *Kerygma and Myth*, vol. 1, 1–44; Bultmann, *New Testament and Mythology*, 1–43. For the circumstances of original composition and subsequent German controversy, see Hammann, *Rudolf Bultmann. Eine Biographie*, 307–19, 421–32. References to Bultmann's demythologizing essay are to the *Kerygma und Mythos* edition (*Kerygma und Mythos* I), along with the SPCK English translation.

5   Bultmann, *Kerygma und Mythos* I, 28, 30, 33; ET, 17, 19, 22.

6   Barth, "Rudolf Bultmann," 44–48; ET, 113–17.

7   Bultmann, *Kerygma und Mythos* I, 35; ET, 25.

8   The association of Bultmann's name with demythologizing is illustrated by titles such as the following: S. G. F. Brandon, "'De-mythologizing' the Gospel: The Significance of Dr Bultmann's Undertaking," *Modern Churchman* 43 (1953): 86–98; Sherman E. Johnson, "Bultmann and the Mythology of the New Testament," *AThR* 36 (1954): 29–47; Schubert M. Ogden, "Bultmann's Project of Demythologization and the Problem of Theology and Philosophy," *JR* 37 (1957): 156–73; John Macquarrie, *The Scope of Demythologizing: Bultmann and His Critics* (London: SCM Press, 1961); Roger A. Johnson, *The Origins of Demythologizing: Philosophy and Historiography in the Theology of Rudolf*

Bultmann (Leiden: Brill, 1974). Titles linking Bultmann to New Testament theology are notably absent.

9 Wilhelm Kamlah, *Christentum und Selbstbehauptung: Historische und philosophische Untersuchungen des Christentums und zu Augustins "Bürgerschaft Gottes"* (Frankfurt: Klostermann, 1940).

10 "Geschichtliches Sein ist . . . ein miteinander sich Behaupten gegen die unheimlichen Mächte der Fremde und der Vernichtung als ein miteinander Teilhaben an dem heimisch Vertrauten, an Wohnstatt und Nährland, an Kult und Recht, Sitte, Sprache, und so fort" (Kamlah, *Christentum und Selbstbehauptung*, 9). In his Foreword, significantly dated to New Year's Day 1940, the author remarks that his book "ist noch im Frieden geschrieben worden," although the self-assertion that is its theme is "offenbar ein Anliegen gerade des Krieges" (xi).

11 "Wer die Hingabe eigenmächtig verweigert, der sucht sich selbst als Einzelnen zu behaupten. In der Hingabe an das Vaterland aber ist die Selbstbehauptung des Einzelnen in geschichtliche Selbstbehauptung eingefügt und empfängt so ihre wahre Möglichkeit" (Kamlah, *Christentum und Selbstbehauptung*, 322).

12 Kamlah, *Christentum und Selbstbehauptung*, 333.

13 Kamlah, *Christentum und Selbstbehauptung*, 449.

14 Bultmann, in *Kerygma und Mythos* I, 35–40; ET, 25–28.

15 Significant elements of political critique are, however, found in "Die Frage der natürlichen Offenbarung," which preceded "Neues Testament und Mythologie" in the original 1941 publication (*Offenbarung und Heilsgeschehen*, 3–26 [esp. 11, 14–16] = *GuV* II, 79–104 [87–88, 91–93]; ET in *Essays*, 90–118 [100, 104–6]).

16 There are nine references to "das mythische Weltbild" in the first three pages of the article (*Kerygma und Mythos* I, 15–17; ET, 1–3).

17 Kamlah, *Christentum und Selbstbehauptung*, 3–4.

18 In the initial wartime debate Bultmann takes a certain pride in his relationship with Kamlah (a former student of his), asking one of his critics "warum diskutiert Kamlah mit mir und nicht mit Ihnen . . . ?" ("Zu J. Schniewinds Thesen, das Problem der Entmythologisierung betreffend," in *Kerygma und Mythos* I, 135–53 (153); ET, 102–23 (123). This is in response to Schniewind's trenchant dismissal of Kamlah as "der allzu rasch, allzu freudig die Hingabe an den All-Einen Bejahende," whose deity is "das X hinter unserer Hingabe an die Gemeinschaft, an das Vaterland" (*Kerygma und Mythos* I, 133; ET, 100).

19 Bultmann's published contributions to the demythologizing debate include the following: (1) The initial article and the response cited in note 18 above, together with "Zur Frage der Entmythologisierung des Neuen Testaments," *Deutsches Pfarrerblatt* 47 (1943): 3–4. (2) Four items written during 1951–1954: (i) *Jesus Christ and Mythology* (1951) (New York: Scribner, 1958); German: "Jesus Christus und Mythologie," *GuV* IV (Tübingen: Mohr Siebeck, 1965), 141–89; (ii) "Zum Problem der Entmythologisierung," in *Kerygma und Mythos* II, 179–208; partial ET in "Bultmann Replies to His Critics" (1953), in *Kerygma and Myth*, vol. 2, 191–211; full ET in *New Testament and Mythology*, 95–130;

(iii) "Zur Frage der Entmythologisierung: Antwort an Karl Jaspers," in *Kerygma und Mythos* III (ed. Hans Werner Bartsch; Hamburg: Reich & Heidrich, 1954), 47–59; (iv) "Die christliche Hoffnung und das Problem der Entmythologisierung" (1954), *GuV* III (Tübingen: Mohr Siebeck, 1961), 81–90. (3) A single article dating from 1963: "Zum Problem der Entmythologisierung," *GuV* IV, 128–37.

20   See Hammann, *Rudolf Bultmann. Eine Biographie*, 397–98.

21   For this criticism of Bultmann, see Heikki Räisänen, *Beyond New Testament Theology: A Story and a Programme* (London: SCM Press, 1990), 36–42. According to Räisänen, Bultmann constantly alternates between the roles of the historically minded "critic" and the "edifying theologian and preacher" (37). In the end it is the theological or homiletical role that predominates: Bultmann sees his task not in "the reconstruction of past thoughts and situations" but in "translating the message of the texts into modern language" (38). He "distinguishes between what is said and what is meant" (39), so that "historical understanding is overwhelmed by actualizing interpretation" (42).

22   ET: "Presuppositions and Motifs of New Testament Theology" (vii).

23   "Aus dem Verkündiger ist der Verkündigte geworden" (*Theologie*, 35; ET, 1.33).

24   Bultmann's formulation of this point presupposes his claim, derived from Wrede, that Jesus did not understand or present himself as Messiah (*Theologie*, 26–34; ET, 1.26–32; for the Wrede connection, cf. Bultmann, *Exegetica*, 2–4).

25   "Alles Frühere erscheint in einem neuen Licht—und zwar seit dem Osterglauben an die Auferstehung Jesu und auf Grund dieses Glaubens" (*Theologie*, 45; ET, 1.42–43).

26   Implicit within the earliest Christian community was "ein Verständnis der Person und Geschichte Jesu als des eschatologischen Geschehens" (*Theologie*, 39; ET, 1.37). In preaching "Jesus als den Christus, als das eschatologische Ereignis," the kerygma claims "dass in ihm Christus präsent ist. . . . An den im Kerygma präsenten Christus glauben, ist der Sinn des Osterglaubens" (*Exegetica*, 468–69).

27   "So wenig wir vom Leben und der Persönlichkeit [Jesu] wissen—von seiner Verkündigung wissen wir so viel, dass wir uns ein zusammenhängendes Bild machen können" (*Jesus*, 15; ET: *Jesus and the Word* [Scribner, 1934], 12). Yet we should bear in mind that "[w]as uns die Quellen bieten, ist ja zunächst die Verkündigung der Gemeinde, die sie freilich zum grössten Teil auf Jesus zurückführt" (*Jesus*, 15; ET, 12). Critical analysis of the synoptic tradition identifies a stratum deriving from the original post-Easter community, and "der Komplex von Gedanken, der in jener ältesten Schicht der Überlieferung vorliegt, ist der Gegenstand unserer Darstellung" (*Jesus*, 17; ET, 14).

28   See *GuV* I, 93–107, 245–52 (ET: *Faith*, 124–38, 262–69), where Bultmann engages in theological critiques of Hirsch, Herrmann, and Weiss that complement the historical consequences he elsewhere draws from his form-critical project (see *GuV* IV, 1–41; *Existence and Faith* [Meridian Books, 1960], 39–62).

29   The Synoptic Gospels feature in *Theology* as sources for the proclamation of

Jesus and the earliest community and as a way of highlighting the distinctiveness of John (2, 34, 355–57; ET, 1.3–4, 33; 2.3–5). Appeal is made to Mark's Messianic Secret in order to characterize the life of Jesus as unmessianic (33–34; ET, 32). Brief discussions of Hebrews occur in the context of developments also attested in the Apostolic Fathers (113–14, 517–19; ET, 1.111–12; 2.166–68). The groundbreaking redaction-critical work of the 1950s is associated not with Bultmann's Marburg but with Heidelberg (Conzelmann on Luke-Acts; Bornkamm, Barth, and Held on Matthew), Kiel (Marxsen on Mark), and Münster (Haenchen on Acts). Reviewing Haenchen's Acts commentary in 1959, Bultmann found too great an emphasis on compositional unity and advocated a return to source criticism (*Exegetica*, 412–25).

30　For Bultmann, "world" and "flesh" are the key terms for John and Paul, respectively. His analysis of "Johannine dualism" includes sections on "Welt und Mensch" and "Die Verkehrung der Schöpfung zur 'Welt'" (secs. 42, 44; 367–73, 378–85; ET, 2.15–21, 26–32). This is followed by an account of the Christ-event entitled "Die κρίσις der Welt" (secs. 45–48; 385–422; ET, 2.33–69). In the Pauline section, the initial account of neutral anthropological terms such as σῶμα, ψυχή, and καρδία (193–226; ET, 1.191–227) is preparatory for the analysis of "Fleisch, Sünde und Welt" as the context for the revelation of the kerygma and of faith (226–70; ET, 1.227–69).

31　Here and in the following sentences I paraphrase *Theologie*, 267–73; ET, 2.15–21.

32　Bultmann's account of Pauline theology is divided into two main sections, "A. Der Mensch vor der Offenbarung der πίστις" and "B. Der Mensch unter der πίστις." The first two of the four sections of the latter are devoted to the righteousness of God and to grace.

33　Event-language is prominent in Bultmann's section headings here: "§32, Die χάρις als Geschehen," "§32.2 Die χάρις als Tat Gottes und Ereignis," "§33, Tod und Auferstehung Christi als Heilsgeschehen," "§33.6a, Das Kreuz als Heilsereignis," "§34.2, Die Präsenz des Heilsgeschehens im Wort" (xii). The English translation lacks the detailed table of contents of the German original.

34　In Bultmann's account of Johannine theology, secs. 42–44 deal with the problematic human relationship with God and world, under the heading, "Der johanneische Dualismus" (367–85; ET, 2.15–32), while the christologically oriented secs. 45–48 are headed "Die κρίσις der Welt" (385–422; ET, 2.33–69).

35　"Offenbarung wie Anstoss ist sein Wirken als Ganzes" (400: ET, 2.48). Thus successive sections are entitled "Der Anstoss der ὁ λόγος σὰρξ ἐγένετο" and "Die Offenbarung der δόξα" (secs. 46, 47; 392–412; ET, 2.40–59).

36　"Der δοξασθείς ist immer der σὰρξ γενόμενος" (402; ET, 2.49).

37　The fundamental role of faith is evident in the construction of Bultmann's reading of Pauline and Johannine theology. Paul's theology is presented under the main headings, "A. Der Mensch vor der Offenbarung der πίστις" and "B. Der Mensch unter der πίστις." Under the latter heading, sections on "Die δικαιοσύνη θεοῦ" (secs. 28–31) and "Die χάρις" (secs. 32–34) are concerned with the divine or initiating side of the saving event, sections on "Die πίστις" (secs. 35–37) and "Die ἐλευθερία" (secs. 38–40) with the human or receptive side. The tripartite structure of salvation is especially clear in the presentation of Johannine theology: "A. Der johanneische Dualismus" (secs. 42–44), "B. Die κρίσις der Welt" (secs. 45–48), and "C. Der Glaube" (secs. 49–50).

38 Bultmann rightly assumes that the exclusion of boasting in Rom 3:27 is comprehensive and does not refer merely to Jewish covenant privileges (242–43; ET, 1.242–43; cf. 1 Cor 1:29, 31; 4:7). He does, however, move too freely and directly from Paul's critique of Jewish identification of righteousness with law observance to a universalizing interpretation of this theme. On these points see my *Paul, Judaism, and the Gentiles: Beyond the New Perspective* (rev. ed.; Grand Rapids: Eerdmans, 2007), 31–36, 245–52, 346–49, 351–52.

39 The relationship of faith and word is discussed in *Theologie*, 318–20 (Paul), 422–26 (John); ET, 1.317–19; 2.70–74.

40 *Theologie*, 332–35 (Paul), 430–35 (John); ET, 1.330–33; 2.78–82.

BIBLIOGRAPHY

Alkier, Stefan. *Urchristentum: Zur Geschichte und Theologie einer exegetischen Disziplin.* Tübingen: Mohr Siebeck, 1993.

Attridge, Harold W. *The Epistle to the Hebrews.* Hermeneia. Philadelphia: Fortress, 1989.

Aune, David E. "Dualism in the Fourth Gospel and the Dead Sea Scrolls: A Reassessment of the Problem." Pages 281–303 in *Neotestamentica et Philonica: Studies in Honor of Peder Borgen.* Edited by David E. Aune, Torrey Seland, and Jarl Henning Ulrichsen. Novum Testamentum Supplements 106. Leiden: Brill, 2003.

Baasland, Ernst. *Theologie und Methode. Eine historiographische Analyse der Frühschriften Rudolf Bultmanns.* Wuppertal: Brockhaus Verlag, 1992.

Balz, H., and G. Schneider, eds. *Exegetical Dictionary of the New Testament* [*EDNT*]. 3 vols. Grand Rapids: Eerdmans, 1990–1993. Translation of *Exegetisches Wörterbuch zum Neuen Testament* [*EWNT*]. Edited by H. Balz and G. Schneider. Stuttgart: Kohlhammer, 1980–1983.

Barclay, John M. G. *Jews in the Mediterranean Diaspora: From Alexander to Trajan (323 BCE–117 CE).* Edinburgh: T&T Clark, 1996.

———. *Paul and the Gift.* Grand Rapids: Eerdmans, forthcoming.

———. *Pauline Churches and Diaspora Jews.* Tübingen: Mohr Siebeck, 2011.

Barr, James. *The Semantics of Biblical Language.* Oxford: Oxford University Press, 1961.

Barrett, Charles Kingsley. *Essays on John.* London: SPCK, 1982.

Bartels, Cora. *Kierkegaard Receptus I. Die theologiegeschichtliche Bedeutung der Kierkegaard-Rezeption Rudolf Bultmanns.* Göttingen: Vandenhoeck & Ruprecht, 2008.

Barth, Gerhard. *Die Taufe in frühchristlicher Zeit.* Biblisch-Theologische Studien 4. Neukirchen: Neukirchener Verlag, 1991.

Barth, Karl. *Kirchliche Dogmatik* III/2. Zurich: Theologischer Verlag, 1980.

———. *Römerbrief.* 2nd ed. Munich: Chr. Kaiser, 1921.

———. *Rudolf Bultmann; ein Versuch, ihn zu verstehen.* Zollikon: Evangelischer Verlag, 1953.

———. "Rudolf Bultmann: Ein Versuch ihn zu Verstehen" (1952). Pages 9–65 in *Rudolf Bultmann, Christus und Adam: Zwei theologische Studien.* Zurich: Evangelischer Verlag, 1964. English translation in "Rudolf Bultmann—An Attempt to Understand Him." Pages 83–132 in *Kerygma and Myth: A Theological Debate.* Vol. 2 (SPCK, 1962).

Bassler, Jouette, ed. *Pauline Theology.* Vol. 1. *Thessalonians, Philippians, Galatians, Philemon.* Minneapolis: Fortress, 1991.

Bauckham, Richard J. *The Climax of Prophecy: Studies on the Book of Revelation.* Edinburgh: T&T Clark, 1993.

———. "The Qumran Community and the Gospel of John." Pages 105–15 in *The Dead Sea Scrolls: Fifty Years after Their Discovery.* Edited by Lawrence H. Schiffman, Emmanuel Tov, and James C. VanderKam. Jerusalem: Israel Exploration Society, 2000. Reprinted as pages 125–36 in *The Testimony of the Beloved Disciple: Narrative, History, and Theology in the Gospel of John.* Edited by Richard Bauckham. Grand Rapids: Baker, 2007.

———. "Qumran and the Gospel of John: Is There a Connexion?" Pages 267–79 in *The Scrolls and the Scriptures: Qumran Fifty Years After.* Edited by Stanley E. Porter and Craig E. Evans. Journal for the Study of the Pseudepigrapha: Supplement Series 26. Sheffield: Sheffield Academic Press, 1997.

———. *The Theology of the Book of Revelation.* Cambridge: Cambridge University Press, 1993.

———. "The Worship of Jesus in Apocalyptic Christianity." *New Testament Studies* 27 (1981): 322–41.

Bauckham, Richard J., and Carl Mosser, eds. *The Gospel of John and Christian Theology.* Grand Rapids: Eerdmans, 2008.

Bauer, Walter. *Orthodoxy and Heresy in Earliest Christianity.* Translated by a team from the Philadelphia Seminar on Christian Origins. Edited by Robert A. Kraft and Gerhard Krodel. Philadelphia: Fortress, 1971. Translated from *Rechtgläubigkeit und Ketzerei im ältesten Christentum.* Tübingen: Mohr Siebeck, 1934.

Beale, G. K. *The Book of Revelation.* New International Greek Testament Commentary. Grand Rapids: Eerdmans, 1999.

Benz, Ernst. "Europa zwischen westlichem und östlichem Nihilismus." *Europäische Zukunft* 1, no. 1 (1949): 16–21.

Berger, Peter. *The Sacred Canopy: Elements in a Sociological Theory of Religion.* New York: Doubleday Anchor, 1969.

Bergmeier, Roland. *Glaube als Gabe nach Johannes.* Beiträge zur Wissenschaft vom Alten und Neuen Testament 112. Stuttgart: Kohlhammer, 1980.

Bernheim, Ernst. *Lehrbuch der historischen Methode und der Geschichtsphilosophie. Mit Nachweis der wichtigsten Quellen und Hilfsmittel zum Studium der Geschichte.* 5th and 6th eds. Leipzig: Dunder, 1908.

Bietenhard, H. "Die Dekapolis von Pompejus bis Trajan." *Zeitschrift des deutschen Palästina-Vereins* 79 (1963): 24–58.

Blass, F., A. Debrunner, and F. Rehkopf. *Grammatik des neutestamentlichen Griechisch.* 16th ed. Göttingen: Vandenhoeck & Ruprecht, 1984.

Boers, Hendrikus. *What Is New Testament Theology? The Rise of Criticism and the Problem of a Theology of the New Testament.* Guides to Biblical Scholarship. Philadelphia: Fortress, 1979.

Bornkamm, Günther. "*In memoriam* Rudolf Bultmann. * 20.8.1884 † 30.7.1976." *New Testament Studies* 23 (1977): 235–42.

———. *Jesus von Nazareth.* Stuttgart: Kohlhammer, 1956.

Böttrich, Chr. *Petrus: Fischer, Fels und Funktionär.* Leipzig: Evangelische Verlagsanstalt, 2001.

Bousset, Wilhelm. *Kyrios Christos: A History of the Belief in Christ from the Beginnings of Christianity to Irenaeus.* Translated by John E. Steely. 5th ed. Nashville: Abingdon, 1970. Reprinted from Göttingen: Vandenhoeck & Ruprecht, 1913.

Boyarin, Daniel. *Border Lines: The Partition of Judaeo-Christianity.* Philadelphia: University of Pennsylvania Press, 2004.

Brandon, S. G. F. "'De-mythologizing' the Gospel: The Significance of Dr Bultmann's Undertaking." *Modern Churchman* 43 (1953): 86–98.

Brodie, Thomas L. *The Gospel According to John: A Literary and Theological Commentary.* Oxford: Oxford University Press, 1993.

Brown, Raymond E. *An Introduction to the Gospel of John.* Edited by Francis J. Moloney. New York: Doubleday, 2003.

———. "John, Gospel and Letters of." Pages 414–17 in *Encyclopedia of the Dead Sea Scrolls.* Vol. 1. Oxford: Oxford University Press, 2000.

———. "The Qumran Scrolls and the Johannine Gospel and Epistles." *Catholic Biblical Quarterly* 17 (1955): 403–19, 559–74.

Buber, Martin. *The Prophetic Faith.* Translated by Carlyle Witton-Davies. New York: Harper & Row, 1960. Reprinted from New York: Macmillan, 1949.

Bultmann, Rudolf. "Adam, Where Art Thou? Pages 119–32 in *Essays Philosophical and Theological* (SCM Press, 1955).

———. "Adam, wo bist du (1945)?" Pages 105–16 in *Glauben und Verstehen* II (Mohr Siebeck, 1952). English translation in "Adam, Where Art Thou?"

————. "Anknüpfung und Widerspruch (1946)." Pages 117–32 in *Glauben und Verstehen* II (Mohr Siebeck, 1952). English translation in "Points of Contact and Conflict (1946)." Pages 133–50 in *Essays Philosophical and Theological* (SCM Press, 1955).

————. "Der Arier-Paragraph im Raume der Kirche." *Theologische Blätter* 12, no. 12 (1933): cols. 359–70.

————. "Die Aufgabe der Theologie in der gegenwärtigen Situation." Pages 28–34 in *Marburger Theologie im Nationalsozialismus. Texte zur Geschichte der Evangelisch-theologischen Fakultät im Reich.* Edited by Jochen-Christoph Kaiser, Andreas Lippmann, and Martin Schindel. Neukirchen: Neukirchener Verlag, 1998. English translation in "The Task of Theology in the Present Situation." Pages 158–65 in *Existence and Faith* (Meridian Books, 1960).

————. "Autobiographical Reflections." In *Existence and Faith* (Meridian Books, 1960).

————. "Autobiographical Reflections of Rudolf Bultmann." Pages xix–xxv in Kegley, *The Theology of Rudolf Bultmann* (Harper & Row, 1966).

————. "Die Bedeutung der alttestamentlich-jüdichen Tradition für das christliche Abendland." Pages 236–45 in *Glauben und Verstehen* I (Mohr Siebeck, 1933). English translation in "The Significance of Jewish Old Testament Tradition for the Christian West." Pages 262–72 in *Essays Philosophical and Theological* (SCM Press, 1955).

————. "Die Bedeutung der 'dialektischen Theologie' für die neutestamentliche Wissenschaft." Pages 114–33 in *Glauben und Verstehen* I (Mohr Siebeck, 1933).

————. "Die Bedeutung der Eschatologie für die Religion des Neuen Testaments." *Zeitschrift fur Theologie und Kirche* 27 (1917): 76–87.

————. "Die Bedeutung des Gedankens der Freiheit für die abendländische Kultur." Pages 274–93 in *Glauben und Verstehen* II (Mohr Siebeck, 1952). English translation in "The Significance of the Idea of Freedom for Western Civilization." Pages 305–25 in *Essays Philosophical and Theological* (SCM Press, 1955).

————. "Die Bedeutung des geschichtlichen Jesus für die Theologie des Paulus." Pages 188–213 in *Glauben und Verstehen* I (Mohr Siebeck, 1933).

————. "Die Bedeutung der neuerschlossenen mandäischen und manichäischen Quellen für das Verständnis des Johannesevangeliums." Pages 55–104 in *Exegetica* (Mohr Siebeck, 1967).

————. "Die christliche Hoffnung und das Problem der Entmythologisierung" (1954). Pages 81–90 in *Glauben und Verstehen* III (Mohr Siebeck, 1961).

————. "Christus des Gesetzes Ende." Pages 32–58 in *Glauben und Verstehen* II (Mohr Siebeck, 1952). English translation in "Christ the End of the Law." Pages 36–66 in *Essays Philosophical and Theological* (SCM Press, 1955).

―――. *"Dikaiosunē Theou."* *Journal of Biblical Literature* 83 (1964): 12–16.

―――. "Die Eschatologie des Johannesevangeliums." Pages 134–52 in *Glauben und Verstehen* I (Mohr Siebeck, 1933).

―――. *Essays Philosophical and Theological.* Translated by James C. G. Greig. Library of Philosophy and Theology. London: SCM Press, 1955.

―――. *Das Evangelium des Johannes.* Kritisch-exegetischer Kommentar über das Neue Testament (Meyer-Kommentar). Göttingen: Vandenhoeck & Ruprecht, 1941. 21st ed., 1984. English translation in *The Gospel of John* (Blackwell, 1971).

―――. *Die Exegese des Theodor von Mopsuestia.* Published by Helmut Feld and Karl Hermann Schelke. Stuttgart: Kohlhammer, 1984.

―――. *Exegetica. Aufsätze zur Erforschung des Neuen Testaments.* Edited by Erich Dinkler. Tübingen: Mohr Siebeck, 1967.

―――. *Existence and Faith: Shorter Writings of Rudolf Bultmann.* Edited and translated by Schubert M. Ogden. Living Age Books. New York: Meridian Books, 1960. London: Hodder & Stoughton, 1961.

―――. *Faith and Understanding.* Edited by Robert W. Funk. Translated by Louise Pettibone Smith. Vol. 1. London: SCM Press, 1969. New York: Harper & Row, 1969. Philadelphia: Fortress, 1969.

―――. *Feldpost: Zeugnis und Vermächtnis. Briefe und Texte aus dem Kreis der evangelischen Studentengemeinde Marburg/lahn und ihrer Lehrer (1939–1945).* Edited by Erika Dinkler-von Schubert. Göttingen: Vandenhoeck & Ruprecht, 1993.

―――. "Formen menschlicher Gemeinschaft." Pages 262–73 in *Glauben und Verstehen* II (Mohr Siebeck, 1952). English translation in "Forms of Human Community." Pages 291–304 in *Essays Philosophical and Theological* (SCM Press, 1955).

―――. "Forms of Human Community." Pages 291–304 in *Essays Philosophical and Theological* (SCM Press, 1955). Translated from "Formen menschlicher Gemeinschaft." Pages 262–73 in *Glauben und Verstehen* II (Mohr Siebeck, 1952).

―――. "Die Frage der 'dialektischen Theologie.'" *Zwischen den Zeiten* 4 (1926): 40–59.

―――. "Die Frage der natürlichen Offenbarung (1941)." Pages 79–104 in *Glauben und Verstehen* II (Mohr Siebeck, 1952). English translation in "The Question of Natural Revelation (1941)." Pages 90–118 in *Essays Philosophical and Theological* (SCM Press, 1955).

―――. "Für die christliche Freiheit." *Die Wandlung* 4 (1949): 417–22.

―――. *Die Geschichte der Synoptischen Tradition.* Forschungen zur Religion und Literatur des Alten und Neuen Testaments 29. Göttingen:

Vandenhoeck & Ruprecht, 1921. 2nd ed., 1931. English translation in *The History of the Synoptic Tradition* (Blackwell, 1963).

———. *Glauben und Verstehen* I. Tübingen: Mohr Siebeck, 1933. English translation in *Faith and Understanding* (Fortress, 1969).

———. *Glauben und Verstehen* II. Tübingen: Mohr Siebeck, 1952. English translation in *Essays Philosophical and Theological* (SCM Press, 1955).

———. *Glauben und Verstehen* III. Tübingen: Mohr Siebeck, 1961, 1965.

———. *Glauben und Verstehen* IV. Tübingen: Mohr Siebeck, 1965.

———. "Gnade und Freiheit (1948)." Pages 149–61 in *Glauben und Verstehen* II (Mohr Siebeck, 1952). English translation in "Grace and Freedom." Pages 168–81 in *Essays Philosophical and Theological* (SCM Press, 1955).

———. *The Gospel of John*. Translated by G. R. Beasley-Murray. Oxford: Blackwell, 1971. Translated from *Das Evangelium des Johannes*.

———. "Gott ruft uns." *Neuwerk* 15 (1933): 70–81.

———. "Grace and Freedom." Pages 168–81 in *Essays Philosophical and Theological* (SCM Press, 1955).

———. "Gutachten der Theologischen Fakultät der Universität Marburg zum Kirchengesetz über die Rechtsverhältnisse der Geistlichen und Kirchenbeamten." *Theologische Blätter* 12, no. 10 (1933): 289–94.

———. *History and Eschatology: The Gifford Lectures 1955*. Edinburgh: The University Press, 1957. Also published as *The Presence of Eternity: History and Eschatology. The Gifford Lectures 1955*. New York: Harper & Brothers, 1957.

———. *The History of the Synoptic Tradition*. Translated by J. Marsh. 1963. Rev. ed. New York: Harper & Row, 1968. Translated from *Die Geschichte der Synoptischen Tradition*.

———. "Hochschule, Antike und Christentum." Pages 137–43 in *Marburger Hochschulgespräche. 12.–15. Juni 1946. Referate und Diskussionen*. Frankfurt: Vittorio Klostermann, 1947.

———. "Hoffnung verändert die Welt. Kritische Auseinandersetzung mit Rodolf Bultmann." *Evangelische Kommentare* 4, no. 1 (1971): 15–20.

———. "Humanismus und Christentum." Pages 133–48 in *Glauben und Verstehen* II (Mohr Siebeck, 1952). English translation in "Humanism and Christianity." Pages 151–67 in *Essays Philosophical and Theological* (SCM Press, 1955).

———. "Introductory Word." Pages 7–9 in Bousset, *Kyrios Christos* (Abingdon, 1970).

———. "Is Exegesis without Presuppositions Possible?" Pages 145–54 in *New Testament and Mythology and Other Basic Writings* (SCM Press, 1985).

———. *Jesus*. 5 vols. Berlin: Deutsche Bibliothek, 1926. Repr., Tübingen: Mohr Siebeck, 1983, 1988. English translation in *Jesus and the Word*. New York: Scribner, 1934, 1958.

————. *Jesus Christ and Mythology*. New York: Scribner, 1958. Translation of "Jesus Christus und Mythologie." Pages 141–89 in *Glauben und Verstehen* IV (Mohr Siebeck, 1965).

————. "Jesus und Paulus" (1936). Pages 210–29 in *Exegetica* (Mohr Siebeck, 1967). English translation in "Jesus and Paul (1936)." Pages 182–201 in *Existence and Faith* (Meridian Books, 1960).

————. "Johannesevangelium." Pages 840–50 in *Die Religion in Geschichte und Gegenwart. Handwörterbuch für Theologie und Religionswissenschaft* III. Edited by Kurt Galling. 3rd ed. Tübingen: Mohr Siebeck, 1959.

————. "Karl Barth, *The Resurrection of the Dead.*" Pages 66–94 in *Faith and Understanding.* Vol. 1 (SCM Press, 1969).

————. "Karl Barth, *Römerbrief.*" *Die Christliche Welt* (1922): 320–23, 330–34. English translation: pages 100–120 in *The Beginnings of Dialectical Theology.* Edited by J. M. Robinson. Richmond: John Knox Press, 1968.

————. "Karl Barths 'Römerbrief' in zweiter Auflage (1922)." Pages 119–42 in *Anfänge der dialektischen Theologie* I. Edited by Jürgen Moltmann. Munich: Kaiser, 1985.

————. *Kerygma and Myth: A Theological Debate.* Edited by Hans Werner Bartsch. Translated by Reginald H. Fuller. Vol. 1. London: SPCK, 1953. Vol. 2. London: SPCK, 1962.

————. *Kerygma und Mythos: Ein theologisches Gespräch* I. Hamburg: Reich & Heidrich, 1948. English translation in *Kerygma and Myth: A Theological Debate.* Vol. 1. Edited by Hans Werner Bartsch. Translated by Reginald H. Fuller. London: SPCK, 1953.

————. *Kerygma und Mythos: Ein theologisches Gespräch* II. Hamburg: Reich & Heidrich, 1952. English translation in *Kerygma and Myth: A Theological Debate.* Vol. 2. Edited by Hans Werner Bartsch. Translated by Reginald H. Fuller. London: SPCK, 1962.

————. *Kerygma und Mythos: Ein theologisches Gespräch* III. Hamburg: Reich & Heidrich, 1954.

————. *Kerygma und Mythos: Ein theologisches Gespräch* VI/1. Hamburg: Reich & Heidrich, 1963.

————. "Liberal Theology and the Latest Theological Movement (German original 1924)." Pages 28–52 in *Faith and Understanding.* Vol. 1 (Harper & Row, 1969).

————. "Man between the Times According to the New Testament." Pages 248–66 in *Existence and Faith* (Meridian Books, 1960).

————. *Marburger Predigten.* 2 vols. Tübingen: Mohr Siebeck, 1956.

————. *Neues Testament und Mythologie.* Munich: Kaiser, 1986. English translation in "New Testament and Mythology."

————. "Neues Testament und Mythologie: Das Problem der Entmythologisierung der neutestamentlichen Verkündigung." Lecture, April 1941. Published in *Offenbarung und Heilsgeschehen*. Munich: A. Lempp, 1941. Reprinted as pages 15–53 in *Kerygma und Mythos: Ein theologisches Gespräch* I (Reich & Heidrich, 1948). English translation as pages 1–44 in *Kerygma and Myth: A Theological Debate*. Vol. 1 (SPCK, 1953).

————. "Neues Testament und Rassenfrage." *Theologische Blätter* 12, no. 10 (1933): 294–96.

————. *New Testament and Mythology and Other Basic Writings*. Translated and edited by Schubert M. Ogden. Philadelphia: Fortress, 1984. London: SCM Press, 1985.

————. "New Testament and Mythology: The Problem of Demythologising the New Testament Proclamation." Pages 1–44 in *Kerygma and Myth: A Theological Debate*. Vol. 1 (SPCK, 1953). Pages 1–43 in *New Testament and Mythology and Other Basic Writings* (Fortress, 1984; SCM Press, 1985).

————. "Paul." Pages 111–46 in *Existence and Faith* (Meridian Books, 1960).

————. "Paulus." Pages 1019–46 in *Religion in Geschichte und Gegenwart*. Vol. 4. Tübingen: Mohr Siebeck, 1930. English translation in "Paul." Pages 111–46 in *Existence and Faith* (Hodder & Stoughton, 1961).

————. "Polis und Hades in der Antigone des Sophokles." Pages 20–31 in *Glauben und Verstehen* II (Mohr Siebeck, 1952). English translation in "Polis and Hades in Sophocles' Antigone." Pages 22–35 in *Essays Philosophical and Theological* (SCM Press, 1955).

————. *Primitive Christianity in Its Contemporary Setting*. London: SCM Press, 1960.

————. "Das Problem einer theologischen Exegese des Neuen Testaments." *Zwischen den Zeiten* 3 (1925): 334–57.

————. "Das Problem der Ethik bei Paulus." Pages 36–54 in *Exegetica* (Mohr Siebeck, 1967). Reprinted from *Zeitschrift für die neutestamentliche Wissenschaft und die Kunde der älteren Kirche* 23 (1924): 123–40. English translation in "The Problem of Ethics in Paul." Pages 195–216 in *Understanding Paul's Ethics: Twentieth-Century Approaches*. Edited by B. S. Rosner. Grand Rapids: Eerdmans, 1995.

————. "Das Problem des Verhältnisses von Theologie und Verkündigung im Neuen Testament." Pages 32–42 in *Aux sources de la tradition chrétien. Mélanges offerts à Maurice Goguel à l' occasion de son soixantedixème aniversaire*. Neuchatel: Delachaux & Niestlé, 1950.

————. "The Problem of Hermeneutics." Pages 69–93 in *New Testament and Mythology and Other Basic Writings* (Fortress, 1984).

————. "Der religionsgeschichtliche Hintergrund des Prologs zum Johannesevangelium." Pages 10–35 in *Exegetica* (Mohr Siebeck, 1967).

————. "Römer 7 und die Anthropologie des Paulus." Pages 53–62 in *Imago Dei*. Giessen: A. Töpelmann, 1932. English translation: pages 147–57 in *Existence and Faith* (Meridian Books, 1960).

————. "Der Sinn des christlichen Schöpfungsglaubens." *Zeitschrift für Missionskunde und Religionswissenschaft* 51 (1936): 1–20. English translation in "The Meaning of the Christian Faith in Creation." Pages 206–25 in *Existence and Faith* (Meridian Books, 1960).

————. "Der Sinn des Mythos und der Entmythologisierung." Pages 179–208 in *Kerygma und Mythos: Ein theologisches Gespräch* II (Reich & Heidrich, 1952). English translation in "On the Problem of Demythologizing." Pages 95–130 in *New Testament and Mythology and Other Basic Writings* (Fortress, 1984).

————. *Der Stil der paulinischen Predigt und die kynisch-stoische Diatribe.* Forschungen zur Religion und Literatur des Alten und Neuen Testaments 13. Göttingen: Vandenhoeck & Ruprecht, 1910.

————. *Theologie des Neuen Testaments.* Tübingen: Mohr Siebeck, 1953. 4th ed., 1961. Tübingen: Mohr Siebeck, 1961. 9th ed., revised and supplemented by Otto Merk, 1984. English translation in *Theology of the New Testament.* Translated by Kendrick Grobel. With a new introduction by Robert Morgan. 2 volumes reprinted in 1. Waco, Tex.: Baylor University Press, 2007. Reprinted from New York: Scribner, 1951, 1955. London: SCM Press, 1952, 1955.

————. *Theology of the New Testament.* Translated by Kendrick Grobel. With a new introduction by Robert Morgan. 2 volumes reprinted in 1. Waco, Tex.: Baylor University Press, 2007. Reprinted from New York: Scribner, 1951, 1955. London: SCM Press, 1952, 1955. Translated from *Theologie des Neuen Testaments.* Tübingen: Mohr Siebeck, 1953.

————. *Das Urchristentum im Rahmen der antiken Religionen.* Zurich: Artemis Verlag, 1949. 4th ed., 1976.

————. "Das Verhältnis der Universität zur Antike und Christentum." Pages 20–27 in *Berichte des Planungs-Ausschusses der Philipps-Universität Marburg zur Neugestaltung der deutschen Hochschulen.* Marburg: Marburger Presse, 1946.

————. "Das Verhältnis der urchristlichen Christusbotschaft zum historischen Jesus." Pages 5–27 in *Sitzungsberichte der Heidelberger Akademie der Wissenschaften, Philosophisch-historische Klasse 1960.* Heidelberg: Universitätsverlag C. Winter, 1962. English translation in "The Understanding of Man and the World in the New Testament and in the Greek World (1940)." Pages 67–89 in *Essays Philosophical and Theological* (SCM Press, 1955).

————. *Das verkündigte Wort. Predigten–Andachten–Ansprachen 1906–1941.* Edited by Erich Gräßer. Tübingen: Mohr Siebeck, 1984.

―――. "Das Verständnis von Welt und Mensch im Neuen Testament und im Griechentum (1940)." Pages 59–78 in *Glauben und Verstehen* II (Mohr Siebeck, 1952). English translation in "The Understanding of Man and the World in the New Testament and in the Greek World." Pages 67–89 in *Essays Philosophical and Theological* (SCM Press, 1955).

―――. "Vorwort des Verfassers." Page vii in *Exegetica* (Mohr Siebeck, 1967).

―――. "Weissagung und Erfüllung." Pages 162–86, 195 in *Glauben und Verstehen* II (Mohr Siebeck, 1952). English translation in "Prophecy and Fulfillment." Pages 182–208 in *Essays Philosophical and Theological* (SCM Press, 1955).

―――. "Welchen Sinn hat es, von Gott zu reden?" Pages 26–37 in *Glauben und Verstehen* I (Mohr Siebeck, 1933).

―――. "Wissenschaft und Existenz (1955)." Pages 107–21 in *Glauben und Verstehen* III (Mohr Siebeck, 1965). English translation in "Science and Existence (Wissenschaft und Existenz 1955)." Pages 131–44 in *New Testament and Mythology and Other Basic Writings* (Fortress, 1984).

―――. "Zu J. Schniewinds Thesen, das Problem der Entmythologisierung betreffend." Pages 135–53 in *Kerygma und Mythos: Ein theologisches Gespräch* I (Reich & Heidrich, 1948).

―――. "Zum Problem der Entmythologisierung." Pages 179–208 in *Kerygma und Mythos: Ein theologisches Gespräch* II (Reich & Heidrich, 1952). Also pages 20–27 in *Kerygma und Mythos* VI/1 (Reich & Heidrich, 1963). Also pages 128–37 in *Glauben und Verstehen* IV (Mohr Siebeck, 1965). English translation: pages 95–130 in *New Testament and Mythology and Other Basic Writings* (Fortress, 1984).

―――. "Zur Antwort auf Herrn Professor D. Wobermins Artikel: Nochmals die Arierfrage in der Kirche." *Deutsches Pfarrerblatt* 38 (1934): 87–88.

―――. "Zur Frage der Entmythologisierung: Antwort an Karl Jaspers." Pages 47–59 in *Kerygma und Mythos: Ein theologisches Gespräch* III (Reich & Heidrich, 1954).

―――. "Zur Frage der Entmythologisierung des Neuen Testaments." *Deutsches Pfarrerblatt* 47 (1943): 3–4.

―――. "Zur Frage der wissenschaftlichen Ausbildung der Theologen." Pages 34–40 in *Studienbetreuung der Kriegsteilnehmer der Martin Luther-Universität Halle-Wittenberg.* Edited by D. Fascher. Theologische Fakultät Halle in Verbindung mit den Theol. Fakultäten Marburg u. Tübingen. Halle: Klinz, 1944.

―――. "Zur Geschichte der Paulus-Forschung." *Theologische Rundschau* n.f. 1 (1929): 26–59.

Bultmann, Rudolf, and Georg Wünsch. "Evangelische Ethik des Politischen." *Verkündigung und Forschung* 3 (1947): 253–66.

Burkett, Delbert. *The Son of Man Debate: A History and Evaluation*. Society for New Testament Studies Monograph Series 107. Cambridge: Cambridge University Press, 1999.

Burkert, Walter. *Ancient Mystery Cults*. Cambridge, Mass.: Harvard University Press, 1987.

Burridge, Richard A. *What Are the Gospels? A Comparison with Graeco-Roman Biography*. Society for New Testament Studies Monograph Series 70. Cambridge: Cambridge University Press, 1992.

Bussmann, Claus. *Themen der paulinischen Missionspredigt auf dem Hintergrund der spätjüdisch-hellenistischen Missionsliteratur*. Europäische Hochschulschriften 23.3. Bern: Lang, 1971.

Byrskog, Samuel. "A Century with the *Sitz im Leben*: From Form-Critical Setting to Gospel Community and Beyond." *Zeitschrift für die neutestamentliche Wissenschaft und die Kunde der älteren Kirche* 98 (2007): 1–27.

———. "The Transmission of the Jesus Tradition: Old and New Insights." *Early Christianity* 3 (2010): 1–28.

Calvin, John. *Institutes of the Christian Religion* I.i.1. Edited by J. T. McNeill, translated by F. L. Battles. LCC 20. Philadelphia: Westminster, 1960.

Campenhausen, Hans von. *Ecclesiastical Authority and Spiritual Power in the First Three Centuries*. Translated by J. A. Baker. Stanford, Calif.: Stanford University Press, 1969.

Capes, David B. *Old Testament Yahweh Texts in Paul's Christology*. Wissenschaftliche Untersuchungen zum Neuen Testament 2.47. Tübingen: Mohr Siebeck, 1992.

Casey, Maurice. *Is John's Gospel True?* London: Routledge, 1996.

Chancey, Mark. *Greco-Roman Culture and the Galilee of Jesus*. Society for New Testament Studies Monograph Series 134. Cambridge: Cambridge University Press, 2006.

———. *The Myth of a Gentile Galilee*. Society for New Testament Studies Monograph Series 118. Cambridge: Cambridge University Press, 2002.

Charlesworth, James H. "A Critical Comparison of the Dualism in 1QS 3:13–4:26 and the 'Dualism' Contained in the Gospel of John." Pages 76–106 in Charlesworth, *John and Qumran* (Geoffrey Chapman, 1972).

———. "The Fourth Evangelist and the Dead Sea Scrolls: Assessing Trends over Nearly Sixty Years." Pages 161–82 in *John, Qumran, and the Dead Sea Scrolls*. Edited by Mary L. Coloe and Tom Thatcher. Society of Biblical Literature Early Judaism and Its Literature 32. Atlanta: SBL Press, 2011.

———, ed. *John and Qumran*. London: Geoffrey Chapman, 1972.

Claussen, Carsten. *Versammlung, Gemeinde, Synagoge: das hellenistisch-jüdische Umfeld der frühchristlichen Gemeinden*. Studien zum Umwelt des Neuen Testaments 27. Göttingen: Vandenhoeck & Ruprecht, 2002.

Collins, Adela Yarbro. "Mark and His Readers: The Son of God among Jews." *Harvard Theological Review* 92 (1999): 393–408.

———. "The Son of God among Greeks and Romans." *Harvard Theological Review* 93 (2000): 85–100.

Coloe, Mary L., and Tom Thatcher, eds. *John, Qumran, and the Dead Sea Scrolls.* Society of Biblical Literature Early Judaism and Its Literature 32. Atlanta: SBL Press, 2011.

Conzelmann, Hans. "Zur Analyse der Bekenntnisformel 1 Kor 15,3-5." Pages 131–41 in *Theologie als Schriftauslegung.* Edited by H. Conzelmann. Beiträge zur evangelischen Theologie 65. Munich: Chr. Kaiser Verlag, 1974.

Dahl, Nils Alstrup. *The Crucified Messiah and Other Essays.* Minneapolis: Augsburg, 1974.

———. "Rudolf Bultmann's *Theology of the New Testament.*" Pages 187–216 in *Jesus the Christ: The Historical Origins of Christological Doctrine.* Edited by Donald H. Juel. Minneapolis: Fortress, 1991. Reprinted from *Theologische Rundschau* 22 (1954): 21–49.

de Jonge, M. "Christ." Pages 192–200 in *Dictionary of Deities and Demons in the Bible.* 2nd ed. Edited by K. van der Toorn, B. Becking, and P. Willem van der Horst. Leiden: Brill, 1999.

———. *Christologie im Kontext. Die Jesusrezeption des Urchristentums.* Neukirchen-Vluyn: Neukirchener Verlag, 1995.

Deines, Roland, Volker Leppin, and Karl-Wilhelm Niebuhr, eds. *Walter Grundmann—ein Neutestamentler im Dritten Reich.* Leipzig: Evangelische Verlagsanstalt, 2007.

Delling, G. *Die Taufe im Neuen Testament.* Berlin: Evangelische Verlagsanstalt, 1963.

———. *Die Zueignung des Heils in der Taufe.* Berlin: Evangelische Verlagsanstalt, 1961.

Dinkler, Erich. "Die christliche Wahrheitsfrage und die Unabgeschlossenheit der Theologie als Wissenschaft." Pages 15–40 in *Gedenken an Rudolf Bultmann.* Edited by Otto Kaiser. Tübingen: Mohr Siebeck, 1977.

Dobbeler, Axel von. *Der Evangelist Philippus in der Geschichte des Urchristentums. Eine Prosopographische Skizze.* Texte und Arbeiten zum neutestamentlichen Zeitalter 30. Tübingen: Francke, 2000.

Dodd, C. H. *According to the Scriptures: The Substructure of New Testament Theology.* Welwyn: Nisbet, 1952.

Dreher, Matthias. *Rudolf Bultmann als Kritiker in seinen Rezensionen und Forschungsberichten.* Münster: Lit Verlag, 2005.

Droysen, Johann Gustav. *Historik.* Edited by Peter Leyh. Stuttgart: Friedrich Frommann Verlag Günther Holzboog, 1977.

Dunn, James D. G. *Beginning from Jerusalem.* Grand Rapids: Eerdmans, 2009.

————. *The Epistles to the Colossians and to Philemon*. New International Greek Testament Commentary. Grand Rapids: Eerdmans, 1996.

————. *Jesus, Paul, and the Gospels*. Grand Rapids: Eerdmans, 2011.

————. *Jesus Remembered*. Grand Rapids: Eerdmans, 2003.

Engberg-Pedersen, Troels. *Paul and the Stoics*. Edinburgh: T&T Clark, 2000.

Epp, Eldon J. *Junia: The First Woman Apostle*. Minneapolis: Augsburg Fortress, 2005.

Evang, Martin. *Rudolf Bultmann in seiner Frühzeit*. Beiträge zur Historischen Theologie 74. Tübingen: Mohr Siebeck, 1988.

Fentress, James, and Chris Wickham. *Social Memory*. Oxford: Blackwell, 1992.

Fergusson, David. *Bultmann*. London: Geoffrey Chapman, 1992.

Feuillet, André. "Participation in the Life of God According to the Fourth Gospel." Pages 169–80 in *Johannine Studies*. Edited by André Feuillet. Translated by Thomas E. Crane. New York: Alba House, 1964.

Fitzmyer, Joseph A. "Qumran Literature and the Johannine Writings." Pages 117–33 in *Life in Abundance: Studies in Tribute to Raymond E. Brown*. Edited by John R. Donahue. Collegeville, Minn.: Liturgical Press, 2005.

————. "Der semitische Hintergrund des neutestamentlichen Kyriostitels." Pages 267–98 in *Jesus Christus in Historie und Theologie*. Festschrift H. Conzelmann. Edited by G. Strecker. Tübingen: Mohr Siebeck, 1975.

————. "The 'Son of God' Document from Qumran." *Biblica* 74 (1993): 153–74.

Flint, Peter W., and James C. VanderKam, eds. *The Dead Sea Scrolls after Fifty Years*. 2 vols. Leiden: Brill, 1998.

Frey, Jörg. "Different Patterns of Dualistic Thought in the Qumran Library: Reflections on Their Background and History." Pages 275–335 in *Legal Texts and Legal Issues: Proceedings of the Second Meeting of the International Organization for Qumran Studies, Cambridge 1995*. Festschrift for Joseph M. Baumgarten. Edited by Moshe Bernstein, Florentino García Martínez, and John Kampen. Studies on the Texts of the Desert of Judah 23. Leiden: Brill, 1997.

————. *Die johanneische Eschatologie I: Ihre Probleme im Spiegel der Forschung seit Reimarus*. Wissenschaftliche Untersuchungen zum Neuen Testament 96. Tübingen: Mohr Siebeck, 1997.

————. *Die johanneische Eschatologie II: Das johannische Zeitverständnis*. Wissenschaftliche Untersuchungen zum Neuen Testament 110. Tübingen: Mohr Siebeck, 1998.

————. "Licht aus den Höhlen? Der 'johanneische Dualismus' und die Texte von Qumran." Pages 117–203 in *Kontexte des Johannesevangelium*. Edited by Jörg Frey and Udo Schnelle. Wissenschaftliche Untersuchungen zum Neuen Testament 175. Tübingen: Mohr Siebeck, 2004.

————. "Recent Perspectives on Johannine Dualism and Its Background." Pages 127–60 in *Text, Thought, and Practice in Qumran and Early Christianity: Proceedings of the Ninth International Symposium of the Orion Center for the Study of the Dead Sea Scrolls and Associated Literature*. Edited by Ruth A. Clements and Daniel R. Schwartz. Studies on the Texts of the Desert of Judah 84. Leiden: Brill, 2009.

————. "Zum Problem der Aufgabe und Durchführung einer Theologie des Neuen Testaments." Pages 3–53 in *Aufgabe und Durchführung einer Theologie des Neuen Testaments*. Edited by C. Breytenbach and J. Frey. Wissenschaftliche Untersuchungen zum Neuen Testament 205. Tübingen: Mohr Siebeck, 2007.

Gadamer, Hans-Georg. *Wahrheit und Methode. Grundzüge einer philosophischen Hermeneutik*. 6th ed. Gesammelte Werke I: Hermeneutik I. Tübingen: Mohr Siebeck, 1990.

Gamble, Harry Y. "The New Testament Canon: Recent Research and the *Status Quaestionis*." Pages 267–95 in *The Canon Debate*. Edited by Lee Martin McDonald and James A. Sanders. Peabody, Mass.: Hendrickson, 2002.

Gammie, John G. "Spatial and Ethical Dualism in Jewish Wisdom and Apocalyptic Literature." *Journal of Biblical Literature* 93 (1974): 356–85.

Gaventa, Beverly Roberts. "The Cosmic Power of Sin in Paul's Letter to the Romans." Pages 125–36 in *Our Mother Saint Paul*. Louisville, Ky.: Westminster John Knox, 2007.

Gay, Peter. *Weimar Culture: The Outsider as Insider*. New York: Harper & Row, 1970.

Georgi, Dieter. "Rudolf Bultmann's Theology of the New Testament Revisited." Pages 75–87 in *Bultmann, Retrospect and Prospect*. Edited by Edward C. Hobbs. Harvard Theological Studies 35. Philadelphia: Fortress, 1985.

Gerdmar, Anders. *Roots of Theological Anti-Semitism: German Biblical Interpretation and the Jews, from Herder and Semler to Kittel and Bultmann*. Studies in Jewish History and Culture 20. Leiden: Brill, 2009.

Gerhardt, Uta. "Nachwort: Nazi Madness. Der Soziloge Edward Y. Hartshorne und das Harvard-Projekt." Pages 319–54 in *Nie mehr zurück in dieses Land. Augenzeugen berichten über die Novemberpogrome 1938*. Edited by Uta Gerhardt and Thomas Karlauf. Berlin: List, 2011.

Gimbel, John. *Eine Deutsche Stadt unter amerikanischer Besatzung. Marburg 1945–1952*. Cologne: Kiepenheuer & Witsch, 1964.

————. *A German Community under American Occupation: Marburg 1945–1952*. Stanford, Calif.: Stanford University Press, 1961.

Göckeritz, Hermann Götz, ed. *Rudolf Bultmann—Friedrich Gogarten Briefwechsel 1921–1967*. Tübingen: Mohr Siebeck, 2002.

Graf, Friedrich Wilhelm. *Der heilige Zeitgeist. Studien zur Ideengeschichte der protestantischen Theologie in der Weimarer Republik.* Tübingen: Mohr Siebeck, 2011.

Großmann, Andreas, and Christof Landmesser, eds. *Rudolf Bultmann/Martin Heidegger. Briefwechsel 1925–1975.* Frankfurt: Klostermann, 2009.

Hahn, Ferdinand. *Christologische Hoheitstitel Göttingen.* 5th ed. Göttingen: Vandenhoeck & Ruprecht, 1995.

Halbwachs, Maurice. *Les cadres sociaux de la mémoire.* New ed. Paris: Presses Universitaires de France, 1952.

———. *La mémoire collective.* Paris: Presses Universitaires de France, 1950.

Hammann, Konrad. *Rudolf Bultmann. Eine Biographie.* 2nd ed. Tübingen: Mohr Siebeck, 2009. English translation by P. E. Devenish. Salem, Ore.: Polebridge, 2013.

Hansen, Bruce. *"All of You Are One": The Social Vision of Gal 3:28; 1 Cor 12, 13 and Col 3:11.* Library of New Testament Studies 409. London: T&T Clark, 2010.

Harland, Philip. *Associations, Synagogues and Congregations: Claiming a Place in Ancient Mediterranean Society.* Minneapolis: Fortress, 2003.

Harnack, Adolf von. *Mission und Ausbreitung des Christentums I.* 4th ed. Leipzig: Hinrichs, 1923.

———. *Das Wesen des Christentums.* Leipzig: Hinrichs'sche Buchhandlung, 1900.

Hartman, Lars. *Auf den Namen des Herrn Jesus. Die Taufe in den neutestamentlichen Schriften.* Stuttgarter Bibelstudien 148. Stuttgart: Verlag Katholisches Bibelwerk, 1992.

Hay, David M. *Glory at the Right Hand: Psalm 110 in Early Christianity.* Society of Biblical Literature Monograph Series 18. Nashville: Abingdon, 1973.

———, ed. *Pauline Theology.* Vol. 2, *1 and 2 Corinthians.* Minneapolis: Fortress, 1993.

Hay, David M., and E. E. Johnson, eds. *Pauline Theology.* Vol. 3, *Romans.* Minneapolis: Fortress, 1995.

Hays, Richard B. *Echoes of Scripture in the Letters of Paul.* New Haven: Yale University Press, 1989.

———. *The Faith of Jesus Christ: The Narrative Substructure of Paul's Theology in Gal 3:1–4:11.* 2nd ed. Grand Rapids: Eerdmans, 2002.

———. "Reading Scripture in Light of the Resurrection." Pages 216–38 in *The Art of Reading Scripture.* Edited by Ellen F. Davis and Richard B. Hays. Grand Rapids: Eerdmans, 2003.

Heidegger, Martin. *Sein und Zeit.* 15th ed. Tübingen: Mohr Siebeck, 1979.

Heitmüller, Wilhelm. *"Im Namen Jesu": Eine sprach- und religionsgeschichtliche Untersuchung zum Neuen Testament, speziell zur altchristlichen*

Taufe. Forschungen zur Religion und Literatur des Alten und Neuen Testaments 2. Göttingen: Vandenhoeck & Ruprecht, 1903.

———. "Zum Problem Paulus und Jesus." *Zeitschrift für die neutestamentliche Wissenschaft und die Kunde der älteren Kirche* 13 (1912): 320–37.

Hellholm, David, Tor Vegge, and Christer Hellholm, eds. *Ablution, Initiation and Baptism: Late Antiquity, Early Judaism, and Early Christianity*. Beihefte zur Zeitschrift für die neutestamentliche Wissenschaft 176. Berlin: De Gruyter, 2011.

Hengel, Martin. "Jesus als messianischer Lehrer der Weisheit und die Anfänge der Christologie." Pages 148–88 in *Sagesse et religion. Colloque de Strasbourg*. Paris: Presses Universitaires de France, 1979.

———. "Psalm 110 und die Erhöhung des Auferstandenen zur Rechten Gottes." Pages 43–74 in *Anfänge der Christologie*. Festschrift F. Hahn. Edited by C. Breytenbach and H. Paulsen. Göttingen: Vandenhoeck & Ruprecht, 1991.

———. *Der Sohn Gottes*. 2nd ed. Tübingen: Mohr Siebeck, 1977.

———. *Der unterschätzte Petrus: Zwei Studien*. Tübingen: Mohr Siebeck, 2006.

———. "Zwischen Jesus und Paulus: Die Hellenisten, Die Sieben und Stephanus (Apg 6,1-15; 7,54-8, 3)." *Zeitschrift für Theologie und Kirche* 72 (1975): 151–206.

Hengel, Martin, and A. M. Schwemer. *Paulus zwischen Damaskus und Antiochien*. Wissenschaftliche Untersuchungen zum Neuen Testament 108. Tübingen: Mohr Siebeck, 1998.

Herbst, Christoph. *Freiheit aus Glauben. Studien zum Verständnis eines soteriologischen Leitmotivs bei Wilhelm Herrmann, Rudolf Bultmann und Eberhard Jüngel*. Theologische Bibliothek Töpelmann 157. Berlin: De Gruyter, 2012.

Himmelfarb, Martha. *Ascent to Heaven in Jewish and Christian Apocalypses*. New York: Oxford University Press, 1993.

Hofius, Otto. *Der Christushymnus Philipper 2,6-11*. Wissenschaftliche Untersuchungen zum Neuen Testament 17. Tübingen: Mohr Siebeck, 1976.

Holtmann, Stefan, and P. Zocher, eds. *Als Laien die Führung der Bekenntnisgemeinde übernehmen. Briefe aus dem Kirchenkampf von Karl Barthund Karl und Dorothee Stoevesandt (1933–1938)*. Neukirchen: Neukirchener Verlag, 2007.

Horn, Friedrich Wilhelm, and Ruben Zimmermann. *Jenseits von Indikativ und Imperativ*. Kontexte und Normen Neutestamentlicher Ethik = *Contexts and Norms of New Testament Ethics*. Vol. 1. Wissenschaftliche Untersuchungen zum Neuen Testament 238. Tübingen: Mohr Siebeck, 2009.

Horrell, David G. *Solidarity and Difference: A Contemporary Reading of Paul's Ethics*. Edinburgh: T&T Clark, 2005.

Hübner, Hans. "Bultmanns 'existentiale Interpretation'—Untersuchungen zu ihrer Herkunft." *Zeitschrift für Theologie und Kirche* 100 (2003): 280–324.

Hurtado, Larry W. *Lord Jesus Christ: Devotion to Jesus in Earliest Christianity.* Grand Rapids: Eerdmans, 2003.

———. "Revelation 4–5 in the Light of Jewish Apocalyptic Analogies." *Journal for the Study of the New Testament* 25 (1985): 105–24.

———. "Son of God." Pages 900–906 in *Dictionary of Paul and His Letters.* Edited by G. F. Hawthorne and R. P. Martin. Downers Grove, Ill.: InterVarsity Press, 1993.

Ibner, Harald. *Christlicher Glaube oder rassischer Mythus.* Frankfurt: Peter Lang, 1987.

Ittel, G. W. "Der Einfluß der Philosophie M. Heideggers auf die Theologie R. Bultmanns." *Kerygma und Dogma* 2 (1956): 90–108.

Jaspert, Bernd. "Existenz–Mythos–Theologie. Fünfzig Jahre nach Rudolf Bultmanns Entmythologisierungsprogramm." *Neue Zeitschrift für systematische Theologie und Religionsphilosophie* 34 (1992): 128, 145–46.

———, ed. *Karl Barth–Rudolf Bultmann. Briefwechsel 1911–1966.* 2nd ed. Zurich: Theologischer Verlag, 1994.

———. *Sachgemässe Exegese. Die Protokolle aus Rudolf Bultmanns Neutestamentlichen Seminaren 1927–1951.* Marburger Theologische Studien 46. Marburg: Elwert, 1996.

Jeremias, Joachim. *Abba. Studien zur neutestamentlichen Theologie und Zeitgeschichte.* Göttingen: Vandenhoeck & Ruprecht, 1966.

———. *Die Abendmahlsworte Jesu.* 3rd ed. Göttingen: Vandenhoeck & Ruprecht, 1960. 4th ed., 1967.

Jewett, Robert. *Paul's Anthropological Terms: A Study of Their Use in Conflict Situations.* Leiden: Brill, 1971.

———. *Romans.* Hermeneia. Minneapolis: Fortress, 2007.

Johnson, Elizabeth E., ed. *Pauline Theology.* Vol. 4, *Looking Back, Pressing On.* SBL Symposium Series 4. Atlanta: Scholars Press, 1997.

Johnson, Luke T. *Among the Gentiles: Greco-Roman Religion and Christianity.* New Haven: Yale University Press, 2009.

———. *The First and Second Letters to Timothy: A New Translation with Introduction and Commentary.* Anchor Bible 35A. New York: Doubleday, 2001.

———. "*Koinonia*: Diversity and Unity in Early Christianity." *Theology Digest* 46 (1999): 303–13.

———. "The Material Expression of Friendship in the New Testament." *Interpretation* 58 (2004): 158–71.

———. *Prophetic Jesus, Prophetic Church: The Challenge of Luke-Acts to Contemporary Christians.* Grand Rapids: Eerdmans, 2011.

————. *Scripture and Discernment: Decision-Making in the Church.* Nashville: Abingdon, 1996.

Johnson, Roger A. *The Origins of Demythologizing: Philosophy and Historiography in the Theology of Rudolf Bultmann.* Leiden: Brill, 1974.

Johnson, Sherman E. "Bultmann and the Mythology of the New Testament." *Anglican Theological Review* 36 (1954): 29–47.

Jonas, Hans. *Gnosis und spätantiker Geist* I. 4th ed. Forschungen zur Religion und Literatur des Alten und Neuen Testaments 33. Göttingen: Vandenhoeck & Ruprecht, 1988.

————. *The Gnostic Religion: The Message of the Alien God and the Beginning of Christianity.* Boston: Beacon, 1958.

Jones, Gareth. *Bultmann: Towards a Critical Theology.* Cambridge: Polity, 1991.

Kähler, Martin. *Der sogenannte historische Jesus und der geschichtliche biblische Christus.* 2nd ed. Leipzig: Deichert'sche Verlagsbuchhandlung, 1896.

Kaiser, Jochen-Christoph, Andreas Lippmann, and Martin Schindel, eds. *Marburger Theologie im Nationalsozialismus. Texte zur Geschichte der Evangelisch-theologischen Fakultät im Reich.* Neukirchen: Neukirchener Verlag, 1998.

Kamlah, Wilhelm. *Christentum und Selbstbehauptung: Historische und philosophische Untersuchungen des Christentums und zu Augustins "Bürgerschaft Gottes."* Frankfurt: Klostermann, 1940.

Karrer, Martin. *Der Gesalbte: Die Grundlagen des Christustitels.* Forschungen zur Religion und Literatur des Alten und Neuen Testaments 151. Göttingen: Vandenhoeck & Ruprecht, 1990.

Käsemann, Ernst. *Exegetische Versuche und Besinnungen.* Vol. 2. Göttingen: Vandenhoeck & Ruprecht, 1964.

————. "Gottesgerechtigkeit bei Paulus." *Zeitschrift für Theologie und Kirche* 58 (1961): 367–78.

————. *Jesu letzter Wille nach Johannes 17.* Tübingen: Mohr Siebeck, 1967.

————. *New Testament Questions of Today.* Philadelphia: Fortress, 1969.

————. "On Paul's Anthropology." Pages 1–31 in *Perspectives on Paul.* Translated by M. Kohl. Philadelphia: Fortress, 1971. London: SCM Press, 1971.

————. *Perspectives on Paul.* Translated by M. Kohl. Philadelphia: Fortress, 1971. London: SCM Press, 1971. Originally *Paulinische Perspektiven.* Tübingen: Mohr Siebeck, 1969.

————. "Das Problem des historischen Jesus." *Zeitschrift für Theologie und Kirche* 51 (1954): 125–53.

Kegley, Charles W., ed. *The Theology of Rudolf Bultmann.* New York: Harper & Row, 1966. London: SCM Press, 1966.

Kelber, Werner H. *The Oral and the Written Gospel: The Hermeneutics of Speaking and Writing in the Synoptic Tradition, Mark, Paul, and Q.*

Voices in Performance and Text. Philadelphia: Fortress, 1983. Repr., Bloomington: Indiana University Press, 1997.

Kelly, Shawn. *Racializing Jesus: Race, Ideology and the Formation of Modern Biblical Scholarship*. London: Routledge, 2002.

Kelsey, David H. *Eccentric Existence: A Theological Anthropology*. 2 vols. Louisville, Ky.: Westminster John Knox, 2009.

———. *Imagining Redemption*. Louisville, Ky.: Westminster John Knox, 2005.

Kilby, Karen. *Balthasar: A (Very) Critical Introduction*. Grand Rapids: Eerdmans, 2012.

King, Richard A. H. *Aristotle and Plotinus on Memory*. Berlin: De Gruyter, 2010.

Klauck, Hans-Josef. *Magie und Heidentum in der Apostelgeschichte des Lukas*. Stuttgarter Bibelstudien 167. Stuttgart: Verlag Katholisches Bibelwerk, 1996.

Kluser, T., et al., eds. *Reallexikon für Antike und Christentum*. 25 vols. Stuttgart: Anton Hiersemann Verlag, 1950–2013.

Koch, Klaus. "History as a Battlefield of Two Antagonistic Powers in the Apocalypse of Weeks and in the Rule of the Community." Pages 185–99 in *Enoch and Qumran Origins: New Light on a Forgotten Connexion*. Edited by Gabriele Boccaccini. Grand Rapids: Eerdmans, 2005.

Kolb, F. "Antiochia in der frühen Kaiserzeit." Pages 97–118 in *Geschichte–Tradition–Reflexion* II. Festschrift M. Hengel. Edited by H. Cancik, H. Lichtenberger, and P. Schäfer. Tübingen: Mohr Siebeck, 1996.

———. *Rom. Die Geschichte der Stadt in der Antike*. 2nd ed. Munich: C. H. Beck, 2002.

Kollmann, Bernd. "Philippus der Evangelist und die Anfänge der Heidenmission." *Biblica* 81 (2000): 551–65.

———. *Ursprung und Gestalten der frühchristlichen Mahlfeier*. Göttinger theologischer Arbeiten 43. Göttingen: Vandenhoeck & Ruprecht, 1990.

Kooten, G. H. van. " 'ἐκκλησία τοῦ θεοῦ': The 'Church of God' and the Civic Assemblies [ἐκκλησίαι] of the Greek Cities in the Roman Empire: A Response to Paul Trebilco and Richard A. Horsley." *New Testament Studies* 58 (2012): 522–48.

Körner, Johannes. *Eschatologie und Geschichte. Eine Untersuchung des Begriffs des Eschatologischen in der Theologie Rudolf Bultmanns*. Theologische Forschung 13. Hamburg: Herbert Reich Evangelischer Verlag, 1957.

Körtner, Ulrich H. J., and Rudolf Bultmann. "Theologie des Neuen Testaments." Pages 289–96 in *Kanon der Theologie. 45 Schlüsseltexte im Portrait*. Edited by Christian Danz. 2 vols. Darmstadt: Wissenschaftliche Buchgesellschaft, 2010.

Knudsen, Knud C., ed. *Welt ohne Hass. Führende Wissenschaftler nehmen Stellung zu brennenden deutschen Problemen*. Berlin: Christian-Verlag, 1950.

Kramer, Werner. *Christos Kyrios Gottessohn.* Abhandlungen zur Theologie des Alten und Neuen Testaments 44. Zurich: Zwingli-Verlag, 1963.

Kümmel, Werner G. "Rudolf Bultmann als Paulusforscher." Pages 175–93 in *Rudolf Bultmanns Werk und Wirkung.* Edited by B. Jaspers. Darmstadt: Wissenschaftliche Buchgessellschaft, 1984.

Künneth, Walter. *Lebensführungen. Der Wahrheit verpflichtet.* Wuppertal: Brockhaus, 1979.

Labahn, A., and M. Labahn. "Jesus als Sohn Gottes bei Paulus." Pages 97–120 in *Paulinische Christologie.* Edited by U. Schnelle, Th. Söding, and M. Labahn. Göttingen: Vandenhoeck & Ruprecht, 2000.

Lampe, Peter. *Die stadtrömischen Christen in den ersten beiden Jahrhunderten.* 2nd ed. Wissenschaftliche Untersuchungen zum Neuen Testament 2.18. Tübingen: Mohr Siebeck, 1989.

———. "Urchristliche Missionswege nach Rom: Haushalte paganer Herrschaft als jüdisch-christliche Keimzellen." *Zeitschrift für die neutestamentliche Wissenschaft und die Kunde der älteren Kirche* 92 (2001): 123–27.

Lange, Armin, Eric M. Meyers, Bennie H. Reynolds, and Randall Styers, eds. *Light against Darkness: Dualism in Ancient Mediterranean Religion and the Contemporary World.* Journal of Ancient Judaism Supplements 2. Göttingen: Vandenhoeck & Ruprecht, 2011.

Layton, Bentley. *The Gnostic Scriptures.* Garden City, N.Y.: Doubleday, 1987.

Le Donne, Anthony. *Historical Jesus: What Can We Know and How Can We Know It?* Grand Rapids: Eerdmans, 2011.

———. *The Historiographical Jesus: Memory, Typology, and the Son of David.* Waco, Tex.: Baylor University Press, 2009.

Lee, Dorothy. *Flesh and Glory: Symbolism, Gender and Theology in the Gospel of John.* New York: Crossroad, 2002.

Lessing, Gotthold E. *Gesammelte Werke.* Edited by Paul Rilla. 10 vols. Berlin: Aufbau-Verlag, 1958.

Lichtenberger, H. "Josephus und Paulus in Rom." Pages 245–61 in *Begegnungen zwischen Christentum und Judentum in Antike und Mittelalter.* Festschrift H. Schreckenberg. Edited by D.-A. Koch and H. Lichtenberger. Göttingen: Vandenhoeck & Ruprecht, 1993.

Liebing, Hans, ed. *Die Marburger Theologen und der Arierparagraph in der Kirche. Eine Sammlung von Texten aus den Jahren 1933 und 1934.* Marburg: Elwert, 1977.

Lietzmann, Hans. *Messe und Herrenmahl: Eine Studie zur Geschichte der Liturgie.* Arbeiten zur Kirchengeschichte 8. Berlin: De Gruyter, 1926.

Lilie, Frank, ed. "Rudolf Bultmann und Gerhard Krüger. Briefwechsel 1925–1971 Teil 5." *Zeitschrift für neuere Theologiegeschichte* 6 (1998): 274–307.

Lill, Marcel. *Zeitlichkeit und Offenbarung. Ein Vergleich von Martin Heideggers "Sein und Zeit" mit Rudolf Bultmanns "Das Evangelium des Johannes."* Frankfurt: Peter Lang, 1987.

Lincoln, Andrew T. *Truth on Trial: The Lawsuit Motif in the Fourth Gospel.* Peabody, Mass.: Hendrickson, 2000.

Linebaugh, Jonathan. "The Christo-Centrism of Faith in Christ: Martin Luther's Reading of Galatians." *New Testament Studies* 59 (2013): 535–44.

Lippmann, Andreas. *Marburger Theologie im Nationalsozialismus.* Academia Marburgensis 9. Munich: Sauer, 2003.

Lohmeyer, Ernst. *Kyrios Jesus: Eine Untersuchung zu Phil 2,5-11.* Sitzungen der heidelberger Akademie der Wissenschaften 4. Heidelberg: C. Winter, 1928.

Löning, K. "Der Stephanuskreis und seine Mission." Pages 80–101 in *Die Anfänge des Christentums: Alte Welt und neue Hoffnung.* Edited by J. Becker. Stuttgart: Kohlhammer, 1987.

Löwith, Karl. *Mein Leben in Deutschland vor und nach 1933.* Stuttgart: J.B. Metzlersche Verlagsbuchhandlung, 1986.

MacIntyre, Alasdair. *After Virtue.* 3rd ed. Notre Dame, Ind.: University of Notre Dame Press, 2009.

———. "Colors, Cultures, and Practices." Pages 24–51 in *Selected Essays.* Vol. 1, *The Tasks of Philosophy.* Cambridge: Cambridge University Press, 2006.

———. "The Intelligibility of Action." Pages 63–80 in *Rationality, Relativism, and the Human Sciences.* Edited by J. Margolis, M. Krausz, and R. M. Burian. Dordrecht: Reidel, 1986.

Macquarrie, John. *An Existentialist Theology: A Comparison of Heidegger and Bultmann.* London: SCM Press, 1955.

———. *The Scope of Demythologizing: Bultmann and His Critics.* London: SCM Press, 1961.

Malherbe, Abraham J. "Ethics in Context: The Thessalonians and Their Neighbors." *Hervormde Teologiese Studies* 68, no. 1 (2012).

Markschies, Chr. "Gnosis/Gnostizismus." Pages 868–71 in *Neues Bibel-Lexikon.* Vol. 1. Edited by Manfred Görg and Bernhard Lang. Zurich: Benziger, 1991.

Martin, Dale B. *Sex and the Single Savior: Gender and Sexuality in Biblical Interpretation.* Louisville, Ky.: Westminster John Knox, 2006.

McDonald, Lee Martin, and James A. Sanders, eds. *The Canon Debate.* Peabody, Mass.: Hendrickson, 2002.

Meding, Wichmann von. "Rudolf Bultmanns Widerstand gegen die Mythologisierung der christlichen Verkündigung." *Theologische Zeitschrift* 53 (1997): 203–5.

Meeks, Wayne A. *Christ Is the Question*. Louisville, Ky.: Westminster John Knox, 2006.

———. "Christian Beginnings and Christian Ethics: The Hermeneutical Challenge." *Bulletin ET: Zeitschrift für Theologie in Europa* 9, no. 2 (1998): 171–81.

———. *The Origins of Christian Morality: The First Two Centuries*. New Haven: Yale University Press, 1993.

———. "Why Study the New Testament?" *New Testament Studies* 51 (2005): 155–70.

Mehl, A. "Sprachen im Kontakt, Sprachen im Wandel. Griechisch/Latein und antike Geschichte." Pages 191–230 in *Zur Evolution von Kommunikation und Sprache—Ausdruck, Mittelung, Darstellung*. Edited by M. Liedtke. Graz: Austria-Medien-Service, 1998.

Meier, John P. *Law and Love*. Vol. 4 of *A Marginal Jew: Rethinking the Historical Jesus*. New Haven: Yale University Press, 2009.

Merklein, Helmut, with M. Gielen. *Der erste Brief an die Korinther*. Ökumenischer Taschenbuch-Kommentar 7.3. Gütersloh: Gütersloher Verlagshaus Gerd Mohn, 2005.

———. "Erwägungen zur Überlieferungsgeschichte der neutestamentlichen Abendmahlstraditionen." Pages 157–80 in *Studien zu Jesus und Paulus*. Edited by H. Merklein. Wissenschaftliche Untersuchungen zum Neuen Testament 43. Tübingen: Mohr Siebeck, 1987.

Metzger, Bruce M. "Considerations of Methodology in the Study of the Mystery Religions and Early Christianity." *Harvard Theological Review* 48 (1955): 1–20.

Meyer, Ben F. *Critical Realism and the New Testament*. Princeton Theological Monographs 17. Allison Park, Pa.: Pickwick, 1989.

———. *Reality and Illusion in New Testament Scholarship: A Primer in Critical Realist Hermeneutics*. Collegeville, Minn.: Liturgical Press, 1994.

Meyers, Eric M. "From Myth to Apocalyptic: Dualism in the Hebrew Bible." Pages 92–106 in Lange et al., *Light against Darkness* (Vandenhoeck & Ruprecht, 2011).

Misztal, Barbara A. *Theories of Social Remembering*. Philadelphia: Open University Press, 2003.

Mitchell, Stephen, and Peter van Nuffelen, eds. *One God: Pagan Monotheism in the Roman Empire*. Cambridge: Cambridge University Press, 2010.

Mommsen, Theodor. *A History of Rome under the Emperors*. New York: Routledge, 1996.

Morgan, Robert. "Introduction." Pages xi–xxxvii in Bultmann, *Theology of the New Testament* (Baylor University Press, 2007).

———. "Rudolf Bultmann." Pages 109–33 in *The Modern Theologians*. Edited by D. Ford. Oxford: Blackwell, 1989.

Moses, R. E. "Powerful Practices: Paul's Principalities and Powers Revisited." Th.D. dissertation, Duke University, 2012; Minneapolis: Fortress, forthcoming.

Müller, Mogens. *The Expression "Son of Man" and the Development of Christology: A History of Interpretation.* Copenhagen International Seminar. London: Equinox, 2007.

Neill, Stephen, and Tom Wright. *The Interpretation of the New Testament, 1861–1986.* 2nd ed. Oxford: Oxford University Press, 1988.

Nethöfel, Wolfgang. *Strukturen existentialer Interpretation: Bultmanns Johanneskommentar im Wechsel theologischer Paradigmen.* Göttingen: Vandenhoeck & Ruprecht, 1983.

Neumann, Franz. "The Social Sciences." Page 38 in *The Cultural Migration: The European Scholar in America.* Philadelphia: University of Pennsylvania Press, 1953.

Niebuhr, H. Richard. *The Responsible Self: An Essay in Christian Moral Philosophy.* With an introduction by James M. Gustafson. San Francisco: Harper & Row, 1978.

Norris, F. W. "Antiochien I." Pages 99–103 in *Theologische Realenzyklopädie 3.1.* Edited by G. Krause and G. Müller. Berlin: De Gruyter, 1978.

Ogden, Schubert M. "Bultmann's Project of Demythologization and the Problem of Theology and Philosophy." *Journal of Religion* 37 (1957): 156–73.

———. "The Significance of Rudolf Bultmann for Contemporary Theology." Pages 104–26 in Kegley, *The Theology of Rudolf Bultmann* (SCM Press, 1966).

Öhler, Markus. *Barnabas: Der Mann der Mitte.* Biblische Gestalten 12. Leipzig: Evangelische Verlagsanstalt, 2005.

Ott, Heinrich. *Geschichte und Heilsgeschichte in der Theologie Rudolf Bultmanns.* Beiträge zur Historischen Theologie 19. Tübingen: Mohr Siebeck, 1955.

Peelinck, Franz. "Rudolf Bultmann und die Politik." Pages 42–49 in *Weiter aktuell. Die Theologie Rudolf Bultmann als Vermächtnis.* Evangelische Zeitstimmen 59/60. Hamburg: Reich, 1971.

Plutarch. "Über die eingegangenen Orakel." Pages 106–69 in *Über Gott und Vorsehung, Dämonen und Weissagung.* Edited by K. Ziegler. Zurich: Artemis Verlag, 1952.

Popkes, Wiard. *Christus traditus: Eine Untersuchung zum Begriff der Dahingabe.* Abhandlungen zur Theologie des Alten und Neuen Testaments 49. Zurich: Zwingli-Verlag, 1967.

Räisänen, Heikki. *Beyond New Testament Theology: A Story and a Programme.* London: SCM Press, 1990.

———. "Die 'Hellenisten' der Urgemeinde." Pages 1468–1514 in *Aufstieg und Niedergang der römischen Welt: Geschichte und Kultur Roms im Spiegel der neueren Forschung 26.2.* Edited by H. Temporini and W. Haase. Berlin: De Gruyter, 1995.

Rau, E. *Von Jesus zu Paulus.* Stuttgart: Kohlhammer, 1994.

Rebell, Walter. "Glaube und politisches Handeln bei Rudolf Bultmann." *Zeitschrift für evangelische Ethik* 31 (1987): 162–82.

Reumann, John. "The Relevant Gospel According to Rudolf Bultmann." *Lutheran Quarterly* 10 (August 1958): 226–47.

Roberts, Robert C. *Rudolf Bultmann's Theology: A Critical Interpretation.* Grand Rapids: Eerdmans, 1976.

Rordorf, Willy. *Der Sonntag: Geschichte des Ruhe- und Gottesdiensttages im ältesten Christentum.* Abhandlungen zur Theologic dcs Alten und Neuen Testaments 43. Zurich: Zwingli-Verlag, 1962.

Rosenberg, Alfred. *Der Mythos des 20. Jahrhunderts.* Published in 1930 with many reeditions until 1945. English translation in *The Myth of the Twentieth Century: An Evaluation of the Spiritual-Intellectual Confrontations of Our Age by Alfred Rosenberg.* Torrance, Calif.: Noontide Press, 1982.

Rowe, C. Kavin. *Early Narrative Christology: The Lord in the Gospel of Luke.* Berlin: De Gruyter, 2006. Repr., Grand Rapids: Baker, 2009.

———. "New Testament Theology: The Revival of a Discipline." *Journal of Biblical Literature* 125 (2006): 393–410.

Rutgers, Leonard V. *The Jews in Late Ancient Rome: Evidence of Cultural Interaction in the Roman Diaspora.* Leiden: Brill, 1995.

Sanders, E. P. *The Historical Figure of Jesus.* 2nd ed. London: Penguin, 1995.

———. *Jesus and Judaism.* London: SCM Press, 1985.

———. *Judaism: Practice and Belief, 63 BCE–66 CE.* London: SCM Press, 1992.

———. *Paul and Palestinian Judaism: A Comparison of Patterns of Religion.* Philadelphia: Fortress, 1977. London: SCM Press, 1977.

Schlatter, Adolf. *Die Theologie des Neuen Testaments und die Dogmatik.* Gütersloh: Bertelsmann, 1909.

Schmithals, Walter. *An Introduction to the Theology of Rudolf Bultmann.* Translated by John Bowden. London: SCM-Canterbury Press, 1968.

———. "Zu Rudolf Bultmanns 100. Geburtstag." *Theologische Rundschau* 31 (1986): 79–91.

———. *Die Theologie Rudolf Bultmanns.* 2nd ed. Tübingen: Mohr Siebeck, 1967.

Schnelle, Udo. *Apostle Paul.* Grand Rapids: Baker, 2012.

———. *Gerechtigkeit und Christusgegenwart. Vorpaulinische und paulinische Tauftheologie.* 2nd ed. Göttinger theologischer Arbeiten 24. Göttingen: Vandenhoeck & Ruprecht, 1986.

———. "Taufe im NT." Pages 663–74 in *Theologische Realenzyklopädie 32.* Edited by G. Krause and G. Müller. Berlin: de Gruyter, 2001.

Schniewind, Julius. "Zur Synoptiker-Exegese." *Theologische Rundschau* 2 (1930): 129–89.

Scholem, Gershom G. *Jewish Gnosticism, Merkabah Mysticism and Talmudic Tradition.* New York: Jewish Theological Seminary of America, 1960.

Schrage, Wolfgang. *Der erste Brief an die Korinther.* Evangelisch-katholischer Kommentar zum Neuen Testament 7.4. Neukirchen: Benziger Verlag, 2001.

Schrey, Heinz-Horst. "The Consequences of Bultmann's Theology for Ethics." Pages 183–200 in Kegley, *The Theology of Rudolf Bultmann* (Harper & Row, 1966).

Schröter, Jens. *Das Abendmahl: Frühchristliche Deutungen und Impulse für die Gegenwart.* Stuttgarter Bibelstudien 210. Stuttgart: Katholisches Bibelwerk, 2006.

Schweitzer, Albert. *Eine Geschichte der Leben-Jesu-Forschung.* 2nd ed. Tübingen: Mohr Siebeck, 1913.

Schweizer, Eduard. "Röm 1,3f und der Gegensatz von Fleisch und Geist bei Paulus." Pages 180–89 in *Neotestamentica: Deutsche und Englische Aufsätze.* Edited by E. Schweizer. Zurich: Zwingli-Verlag, 1963.

Segal, Alan F. *The Other Judaisms of Late Antiquity.* Brown Judaic Studies 127. Atlanta: Scholars Press, 1987.

Segovia, Fernando F. "Inclusion and Exclusion in John 17: An Intercultural Reading." Pages 183–209 in *"What Is John?"* Vol. 2 of *Literary and Social Readings of the Fourth Gospel.* Edited by Fernando F. Segovia. Society of Biblical Literature Symposium Series 7. Atlanta: Scholars Press, 1998.

Sellin, Gerhard. *Der Streit um die Auferstehung der Toten.* Forschungen zur Religion und Literatur des Alten und Neuen Testaments 138. Göttingen: Vandenhoeck & Ruprecht, 1986.

Shanks, Hershel. "Is the Title 'Rabbi' Anachronistic in the Gospels?" *Jewish Quarterly Review* 53 (1962/63): 337–45.

———. "Origins of the Title 'Rabbi.'" *Jewish Quarterly Review* 59 (1968/69): 152–57.

Sinn, Gunnar. *Christologie und Existenz. Rudolf Bultmanns Interpretation des paulinischen Christuszeugnisses.* Texte und Arbeiten zum neutestamentlichen Zeitalter 3. Tübingen: A. Francke, 1991.

Smith, D. Moody. *The Composition and Order of the Fourth Gospel: Bultmann's Literary Theory.* New Haven: Yale University Press, 1965.

Sölle, Dorothee. *Politische Theologie. Auseinandersetzung mit Rudolf Bultmann.* Stuttgart: Kreuz-Verlag, 1971.

Speyer, W. "Hellenistisch-römische Voraussetzungen der Verbreitung des Christentums." Pages 25–35 in *Der neue Mensch in Christus.* Edited by J. Beutler. Quaestiones disputatae 190. Freiburg: Herder, 2001.

Spiegel, Yorick. "Die Praxisrelevanz der Theologie." Pages 116–30 in *Theologie und gesellschaftliche Praxis*. Edited by Yorick Spiegel and Ulrich Teichler. *Der Pfarrer in der Großstadt* 1. Munich: Chr. Kaiser, 1974.

Standhartinger, Angela. "Rudolf Bultmann im interreligiösen Dialog." *Evangelische Theologie* 71 (2011): 16–34.

Steck, Odil Hannes. *Israel und das gewaltsame Geschick der Propheten. Untersuchungen zur Überlieferung des deuteronomistischen Geschichtsbildes im Alten Testament, Spätjudentum und Urchristentum*. Wissenschaftliche Monographien zum Alten und Neuen Testament 23. Neukirchen-Vluyn: Neukirchener Verlag, 1967.

Stegemann, Wolfgang. *Der Denkweg Rudolf Bultmanns*. Stuttgart: Kohlhammer, 1978.

Stendahl, Krister. "The Apostle Paul and the Introspective Conscience of the West." *Harvard Theological Review* 56 (1963): 62–77.

Strauss, David Friedrich. *Das Leben Jesu: kritisch bearbeitet*. Tübingen: C. F. Osiander, 1835.

Strecker, Christian. *Die liminale Theologie des Paulus: Zugange zur paulinischen Theologie aus kulturanthropologischer Perspektiv*. Forschungen zur Religion und Literatur des Alten und Neuen Testaments 185. Göttingen: Vandenhoeck & Ruprecht, 1999.

Stuckenbruck, Loren T. *Angel Veneration and Christology*. WUNT 2/70. Tübingen: Mohr Siebeck, 1995.

———. "The Interiorization of Dualism within the Human Being in Second Temple Judaism: The Treatise of the Two Spirits (1QS III:13–IV:26) in Its Tradition-Historical Context." Pages 145–68 in Lange et al., *Light against Darkness* (Vandenhoeck & Ruprecht, 2011).

Teeple, Howard M. "Qumran and the Origin of the Fourth Gospel." *Novum Testamentum* 4 (1960–1961): 6–25. Reprinted as pages 1–20 in *The Composition of John's Gospel*. Edited by David E. Orton. Leiden: Brill, 1999.

Theissen, Gerd. "Simon Magus—die Entwicklung seines Bildes vom Charismatiker zum gnostischen Erlöser." Pages 407–32 in *Religionsgeschichte des Neuen Testaments*. Festschrift K. Berger. Edited by A. v. Dobbeler, K. Erlemann, and R. Heiligenthal. Basel: A. Francke Verlag, 2000.

Theissen, Gerd, and Annette Merz. *Der historische Jesus. Ein Lehrbuch*. 3rd ed. Göttingen: Vandenhoeck & Ruprecht, 2001.

Thompson, Marianne Meye. *The Promise of the Father: Jesus and God in the New Testament*. Louisville, Ky.: Westminster John Knox, 2000.

Thrall, Margaret E. *The Second Epistle to the Corinthians*. International Critical Commentary. 2 vols. Edinburgh: T&T Clark, 1994, 2000.

Towner, Philip H. *The Letters to Timothy and Titus*. New International Commentary on the New Testament. Grand Rapids: Eerdmans, 2006.

Trebilco, Paul. *Self-Designations and Group Identity in the New Testament.* Cambridge: Cambridge University Press, 2012.

Troeltsch, Ernst. "Ueber historische und dogmatische Methode in der Theologie." Pages 729–53 in *Gesammelte Schriften*. Vol. 2, *Zur religiösen Lage, Religionsphilosophie und Ethik.* Tübingen: Mohr Siebeck, 1913.

Vermes, Geza. *Jesus der Jude: Ein Historiker liest die Evangelien.* Neukirchen: Neukirchener Verlag, 1993.

Vollenweider, S. "Der 'Raub' der Gottgleichheit: Ein religionsgeschichtlicher Vorschlag zu Phil 2,6(-11)." *New Testament Studies* 45 (1999): 413–33.

Waßmann, Harry, Jakob Matthias Osthof, and Anna-Elisabeth Bruckhaus. *Rudolf Bultmann (1884–1976).* Nachlaßverzeichnisse der Universitätsbibliothek Tübingen 2. Wiesbaden: Harrassowitz, 2001.

Watson, Francis. *Paul, Judaism, and the Gentiles: Beyond the New Perspective.* Rev. ed. Grand Rapids: Eerdmans, 2007.

Way, D. V. *The Lordship of Christ: Ernst Käsemann's Interpretation of Paul's Theology.* Oxford: Clarendon, 1991.

Webb, Robert L. "The Historical Enterprise and Historical Jesus Research." Pages 9–93 in *Key Events in the Life of the Historical Jesus.* Edited by Darrell L. Bock and Robert L. Webb. Wissenschaftliche Untersuchungen zum Neuen Testament 27. Tübingen: Mohr Siebeck, 2009.

Weber, Max. *The Theory of Social and Economic Organization.* Translated and edited by A. M. Henderson and Talcott Parsons. New York: Free Press, 1964.

Weber, R. "Christologie und 'Messiasgeheimnis': Ihr Zusammenhang und Stellenwert in den Darstellungsintentionen des Markus." *Evangelische Theologie* 43 (1983): 108–25.

Weiser, A. "Zur Gesetzes und Tempelkritik der 'Hellenisten.' " Pages 146–68 in *Das Gesetz im Neuen Testament.* Edited by K. Kertelge. Quaestiones disputatae 108. Freiburg: Herder, 1986.

Weiss, Johannes. *Jesus von Nazareth. Mythus oder Geschichte? Eine Auseinandersetzung mit Kalthoff, Drews, Jensen.* Tübingen: Mohr Siebeck, 1910.

———. *Die Predigt Jesu vom Reiche Gottes.* Göttingen: Vandenhoeck & Ruprecht, 1892. 2nd ed., 1900. 3rd ed., 1964.

Wengst, Klaus. *Christologische Formeln und Lieder des Urchristentums.* 2nd ed. Studien zum Neuen Testament 7. Gütersloh: Gütersloher Verlagshaus Gerd Mohn, 1973.

Westerholm, Stephen. *Perspectives Old and New on Paul: The "Lutheran" Paul and His Critics.* Grand Rapids: Eerdmans, 2004.

Wiefel, W. "Die jüdische Gemeinschaft im antiken Rom und die Anfänge des römischen Christentums." *Judaica* 26 (1970): 65–88.

Willertz, John R. "Marburg unter dem Nationalsozialismus (1933–1945)." Pages 593–653 in *Marburger Geschichte. Rückblick auf die Stadtgeschichte in Einzelbeiträgen*. Edited by Erhart Dettmering and Rudolf Grenz. Marburg: Elwert, 1980.

Williams, Michael. *Rethinking "Gnosticism": An Argument for Dismantling a Dubious Category*. Princeton: Princeton University Press, 1996.

Witetschek, Stephan. *Ephesische Enthüllungen I: frühe Christen in einer antiken Grossstadt zugleich ein Beitrag zur Frage nach den Kontexten der Johannesapokalypse*. Biblical Tools and Studies 6. Leuven: Peeters, 2008.

Wolff, Chr. *Der erste Brief des Paulus an die Korinther*. 2nd ed. Theologischer Handkommentar zum Neuen Testament 7. Leipzig: Evangelische Verlagsanstalt, 2000.

Wolter, M. "Apollos und die ephesinischen Johannesjünger (Act 18,24–19,7)." *Zeitschrift für die neutestamentliche Wissenschaft und die Kunde der älteren Kirche* 78 (1987): 49–73.

Wrede, William/Wilhelm. *Das Messiasgeheimnis in den Evangelien. Zugleich ein Beitrag zum Verständnis des Markusevangeliums*. Göttingen: Vandenhoeck & Ruprecht, 1901.

———. "The Task and Methods of 'New Testament Theology.'" Pages 68–116 in *The Nature of New Testament Theology*. Edited by Robert Morgan. London: SCM Press, 1973.

———. *Über die Aufgabe und Methode der sogenannten neutestamentlichen Theologie*. Göttingen: Vandenhoeck & Ruprecht, 1897.

Xeravits, Géza G., ed. *Dualism in Qumran*. Library of Second Temple Studies 76. London: T&T Clark, 2010.

Yamauchi, Edwin M. *Pre-Christian Gnosticism: A Survey of the Proposed Evidence*. Grand Rapids: Eerdmans, 1973.

Zeitlin, Solomon. "A Reply." *Jewish Quarterly Review* 53 (1962/63): 345–49.

———. "The Title Rabbi in the Gospels Is Anachronistic." *Jewish Quarterly Review* 59 (1968/69): 158–60.

Zeller, Dieter. "Der eine Gott und der eine Herr Jesus Christus." Pages 34–49 in *Der lebendige Gott*. Festschrift W. Thüsing. Edited by Th. Söding. *New Testament Abstracts* 31. Münster: Aschendorff, 1996.

———. "Messias/Christus." Pages 782–86 in *Neues Bibel-Lexikon*. Vol. 3. Edited by Manfred Görg and Bernhard Lang. Zurich: Benziger, 2001.

Zimmermann, J. *Messianische Texte aus Qumran*. Wissenschaftliche Untersuchungen zum Neuen Testament 2.104. Tübingen: Mohr Siebeck, 1998.

Zimmermann, Ruben. *Christologie der Bilder im Johannesevangelium*. Wissenschaftliche Untersuchungen zum Neuen Testament 171. Tübingen: Mohr Siebeck, 2004.

Zugmann, M. *"Hellenisten" in der Apostelgeschichte*. Wissenschaftliche Untersuchungen zum Neuen Testament 2.264. Tübingen: Mohr Siebeck, 2009.

CONTRIBUTORS

JOHN M. G. BARCLAY
Lightfoot Professor of Divinity, Department of Theology and Religion, Durham University, Durham, UK

RICHARD BAUCKHAM
Professor Emeritus of New Testament Studies, University of St Andrews, St Andrews, Scotland, and Senior Scholar, Ridley Hall, Cambridge

SAMUEL BYRSKOG
Centre for Theology and Religious Studies, Lund University, Sweden

JAMES D. G. DUNN
Emeritus Lightfoot Professor of Divinity, Department of Theology and Religion, Durham University, Durham, UK

JÖRG FREY
Lehrstuhl für Neues Testament mit Schwerpunkten Antikes Judentum und Hermeneutik, Theologische Fakultät, University of Zurich, Zurich, Switzerland

RICHARD B. HAYS
George Washington Ivey Professor of NT and Dean of the Divinity School, The Divinity School, Duke University, Durham, N.C.

LARRY W. HURTADO
Emeritus Professor of New Testament Language, Literature & Theology, New College (School of Divinity), University of Edinburgh, Edinburgh, UK

LUKE TIMOTHY JOHNSON
Robert W. Woodruff Professor of New Testament and Christian Origins, Candler School of Theology, Emory University, Atlanta, Ga.

BRUCE W. LONGENECKER
Professor of New Testament and W. W. Melton Chair of Religion, Department of Religion, Baylor University, Waco, Tex.

WAYNE A. MEEKS
Woolsey Professor Emeritus of Religious Studies, Yale University, New Haven, Conn.

MIKEAL C. PARSONS
Professor of New Testament and Kidd L. and Buna Hitchcock Macon Chair of Religion, Department of Religion, Baylor University, Waco, Tex.

C. KAVIN ROWE
The Divinity School, Duke University, Durham, N.C.

UDO SCHNELLE
Theologische Fakultät, Seminar für Neues Testament, Martin-Luther Universität Halle-Wittenberg, Halle, Germany

ANGELA STANDHARTINGER
Fachbereich Evangelische Theologie der Philipps-Universität Marburg, Marburg, Germany

FRANCIS WATSON
Chair of Biblical Interpretation, Durham University, Durham, UK

INDEX OF ANCIENT SOURCES

INDEX OF MODERN AUTHORS

SUBJECT INDEX

Adam, 57, 66, 89
Andronicus and Junia, 44
anthropology: New Testament theology
as, 266; Paul's theology as, 62, 63–65,
69, 71, 72, 76, 81, 82, 84, 93–94, 252
Antioch, church of, 40, 43, 45–46, 54
Apollos, 43–44
Apostles' Creed, 32
Apostolic Fathers, 174, 176, 178, 181

baptism, 27, 34, 45, 48, 50, 52, 55, 56,
59, 80, 85, 94, 95, 122, 160, 162, 176,
178, 180, 272; Bultmann's view of
origins of, 34; of Jesus, 50, 119; of John
the Baptist, 51; pre-Pauline traditions
of, 56; roots of Christian rite of, 50–51
Barnabas, 42, 43, 46
bishops , 165–67
body (σῶμα), 69–70, 72, 81, 93

Canon, New Testament, 36, 175–76, 182,
186, 187, 200–201
church: as ἐκκλεσία, 53; as eschatological
congregation, 26–28, 29, 30, 80, 159,
160, 161, 162, 163, 164, 168, 172,
217–18; as social community, 219; as
"The Way," 53–54
Confessing Church (of Germany), 238–39
Creator, God as, 4, 5, 6, 55, 58, 75, 135,
136, 137, 139, 142, 143, 149, 150, 216
critical realism, 18

Damascus, church of, 40, 45
dehistorization (desecularization), 6, 92,
116, 125, 246, 251–52, 253
demythologization, 11, 62, 90, 96, 109,
115, 116, 133, 134, 138, 139, 196, 234,
243, 250, 257, 259–60, 272; hermeneutics as, 62, 71, 72–74, 76; of the
kerygma, 221
dialectical theology, 14, 76, 104, 214,
215, 235

early Catholicism, 168, 170, 193, 219
eschatology, 16, 66, 112, 160, 168,
188, 214, 247, 269; apocalyptic, 215,
217; Bultmann's theology as, 103–5,
109–10, 175; and dualism, 142, 143;
as the end of history/the world, 166,
177, 219; futuristic, 103, 114, 138, 175;
Jesus' death as, 195; Johannine, 103,
111, 113, 116, 118, 128, 138; realized,
89, 117
eternal life, 66, 139, 145, 149, 153,
195–96, 271
existentialism: Heidegger and, 104, 116,
134, 137, 139, 258; as hermeneutic,
212–13; interpretation of eschatology
as, 109; interpretation of kerygma as,
33, 103, 134; Jesus' teaching as, 8, 22;
John's theology as, 131, 135, 174, 176;
NT theology as, 37, 62, 176, 178, 179,
190, 191, 194–95, 258; Paul's theology

as, 71, 73, 81, 83–84, 93, 174; and personal identity, 221–22; philosophy and, 11, 76, 116; response to kerygma as, 61, 75, 96, 108, 139, 182, 183, 195
faith, 4, 79, 81, 82, 83, 84, 85, 87, 89, 90, 96, 97, 102, 107, 112, 115, 116, 135, 136, 137, 139, 179, 180, 182, 194, 196, 263–64, 269; as authenticity, 260; Bultmann's understanding of, 270–72; as desecularization, 125–26; as endurance, 202–3; as eschatological existence, 102, 109, 112, 124, 126, 137; and history, 108; as isolating act, 215; as obedience, 86; orthodoxy contrasted to, 185; of Jesus, 95; Jesus as object of, 8, 120, 124, 203; and kerygma, 33; in kerygma, 32; relationship of world to, 237
Father, God as, 4, 5, 9, 11, 64, 123, 145, 146, 147, 148, 149
flesh (σάρξ), 74, 92, 95, 119, 145, 149, 177, 204, 266, 267
flesh and sin, as powers, 74, 95
form criticism, 11, 19, 29, 107, 159

Gnosticism, 39, 65, 143, 158, 161, 162, 167, 178, 180, 187, 189, 190, 191, 226, 250; existentialist character of, 186; as a presupposition to NT theology, 57–58; Redeemer myths of, 39, 57, 102, 110–11, 115, 116, 129, 130, 131, 134–35, 141, 173, 188; as a source for Paul's thought, 66–67, 76, 81, 85, 87, 89, 91, 162, 173, 175, 183, 184; as a source for John's thought, 102, 103, 113, 115, 117, 119, 123, 126, 129, 130–131, 133, 136, 137, 138, 141
grace, 25 (and law), 61, 75, 81, 83, 84, 85, 86, 93, 97, 98, 196, 197, 220–21, 241

historical criticism, 127
history: Bultmann's view of, 105; Christ as end of, 96; hermeneutics of, 18, 21; limitations of, 35; as medium of revelation, 242
human community: Bultmann's theory of, 213–14

Jerusalem, Church of, 40, 42–43, 44, 45, 52, 160

Jesus: bodily resurrection of (affirmed by Bultmann), 38, 60, 78, 100, 154, 192, 210, 230, 232, 256; historical Jesus, 3, 7, 11, 12, 14, 15, 16, 17, 18, 19, 21, 24, 25, 28, 29, 39, 115, 116, 120, 157, 177, 178, 180, 225, 262–63 (and the kerygma); as the Lamb, 189, 206–7; as Melchizedek, 204–5; message of, 25, 29, 32, 33, 34, 40, 101, 173, 175, 177, 180, 186, 211–12; as Messiah, 6, 9, 25, 26, 30, 40, 48, 119, 180, 262, 265; resurrection of, 51, 89, 90, 91, 121–22, 180, 186, 195, 196
Jewish apocalyptic, 5, 62, 66, 107, 110, 112, 162, 183, 187, 189, 190, 191, 216
Jewish legalism, 5, 7, 25, 98, 251; critique of Bultmann's view of, 30–31, 92
John the Baptist, 3, 50, 51, 115, 181
justification by faith, 94, 97, 111, 175, 198, 201, 216

kerygma, 11, 13, 14, 17, 24, 26, 31–32, 34, 35, 40, 70, 71, 76, 77, 97, 101, 108, 109, 110, 115, 121, 133, 137, 177, 178, 179, 182, 254, 255, 267; as avenue for grace, 221; Bultmann's reluctance to define, 221; Bultmann's understanding of, 262–65; as God's address to humanity/world, 32, 249; original purity of, 226; presence (or absence) in NT, 33
kingdom of God, 3, 4, 6, 8, 9, 10, 11, 17, 21, 22, 28, 51, 87, 110, 160 (of heaven), 175, 241, 249, 262; as eschatological, 216–17

law (Torah), 4, 5, 8, 25, 26, 30–31, 66–68, 70, 81, 85, 86, 87, 99, 160, 163, 183, 198–99, 201, 252, 264; critique of Bultmann's view of the, 67–68, 92–93
Lord, title of Jesus, 45, 48–49, 50, 52, 54, 80, 185, 204
Lord's Supper (Eucharist), 48, 49, 55, 59, 94, 95, 163, 176, 178; origins of, 51–52
love commandment, 4, 6, 8, 137, 223

memory, social or collective, 19, 20, 21; and time, 20
miracles, miraculous, 4–5, 26, 126, 181, 270